BASKETBALL DEFENSE
LESSONS FROM THE LEGENDS

Featuring Coaching Insights from 30 Naismith Hall of Fame Coaches

JERRY KRAUSE · RALPH PIM

© Copyright 2005 Coaches Choice. All rights reserved. Printed in the United States of America.

No part of this book may be reproduced, stored in a retrieval system, or transmitted in any form or by any means, electronic, mechanical, photocopying, recording, or otherwise, without the prior permission of Coaches Choice.

ISBN: 1-58518-892-1
Library of Congress Control Number: 2004104664

Book Design: Diana Michelotti, Artistic Enterprises, Cary, North Carolina
Diagrams, and Production: Nicole Blanchard and Rita Hewell, Artistic Enterprises, Cary, North Carolina
Cover Design: Bean Creek Studio

All logos contained herein, are the trademarks and copyrights of the school or organization represented.

Cover photos of Dean Smith and Morgan Wootten provided courtesy of photographer Hugh Morton. Cover photo of Pat Summitt: Otto Greule/Allsport. Photos of coaches John Chaney, Denny Crum, Don Haskins, Mike Krzyzewski, Joe Lapchick, John McLendon, James Naismith, Jack Ramsay, and Morgan Wootten courtesy of the Naismith Memorial Basketball Hall of Fame. All other photographs provided by the Sports Information Departments of the College or University of the particular coach in the image.

COACHES CHOICE
P.O. BOX 1828
Monterey, CA 93942

DEDICATION

The *Naismisth Lessons From The Legends* series is dedicated to:

The Zag players, coaches, and fans who have made
this part of my basketball life so very special.

— JERRY KRAUSE

My parents, Lorin and Alice Pim.
Thank you for instilling in me the
principles that I try to live by everyday.

My wife, Linda. You have brought peace and
happiness into my life. I love you with all my heart.

— RALPH PIM

ACKNOWLEDGMENTS

From start to finish, this book has been a team effort. Our deepest thanks go to:

Robin Jonathan Deutsch, Director of New Media & Library Services at the Naismith Basketball Hall of Fame, for his tremendous support of our project and his assistance in making the Hall of Fame library materials available to us.

John L. Doleva, President & Chief Executive Officer, Michael W. Brooslin, Curator, and Jim Mullins, Operations Manager, of the Naismith Hall of Fame for their warm hospitality on our many trips to Springfield, Massachusetts.

The following Naismith Basketball Hall-of-Famers who were kind enough to speak with us on selected subjects over the years: Leon Barmore, Larry Brown, John Bunn, Lou Carnesecca, Ben Carnevale, John Chaney, Clarence Gaines, Cliff Hagen, Marv Harshman, Bailey Howell, Bob Kurland, Earl Lloyd, Ed Macauley, Arad McCutchan, Ray Meyer, Ralph Miller, Pete Newell, C.M. Newton, Lute Olson, Arnie Risen, Bob Pettit, Adolph Rupp, Dolph Schayes, Bill Sharman, Dean Smith, Bob Wanzer, Stan Watts, John Wooden, Morgan Wootten, James Worthy, George Yardley, and Kay Yow.

Hank Raymonds, Les Robinson, Ellen Anderson, Tom Crean, and Jay Carter Biggs for providing valuable information that helped in our research.

Nicole Blanchard and Rita Hewell of Artistic Enterprises for their hard work and attention to detail creating the diagrams and laying out the book.
Penny Rose, our patient administrative assistant and word processor.

Finally, sincere appreciation goes to Diana Michelotti of Artistic Enterprises and Jim Peterson of Coaches Choice for their belief in and vision for the Legends series—to provide basketball fans and coaches with these valuable lessons of life and basketball.

FOREWORD

In my time in and around the game of basketball, I have been truly fortunate to have spent time with and learned from some of the true giants of the game. Mike Krzyzewski, Bob Knight, and Pete Newell are not only among the finest coaches in the game, but are among the greatest teachers and guardians of the game. From them, I have witnessed their respect and admiration for the coaches who were the innovators and strategists of their day. To be a truly great teacher of the game, one must have both an understanding of the evolution of the game and an appreciation for its history and those who advanced the game to where it is today. To best grasp where the game is and should be going, it is vital to understand where the game has been and how it got to this point.

The future of the game lies with its teachers, the bona-fide guardians of the game's history and its future. Two fine basketball minds and outstanding coaches, Jerry Krause and Ralph Pim, have provided us with a wonderful and comprehensive reference of lessons from these Hall of Fame coaches who are distinguished teachers. This book should serve as a useful guide and fascinating retrospective of the thoughts and ideas of the game's finest minds. Jerry and Ralph have done the game a fine service with this work; basketball coaches and fans alike will enjoy and benefit from the Legends series.

Jay Bilas
ESPN College Basketball Analyst

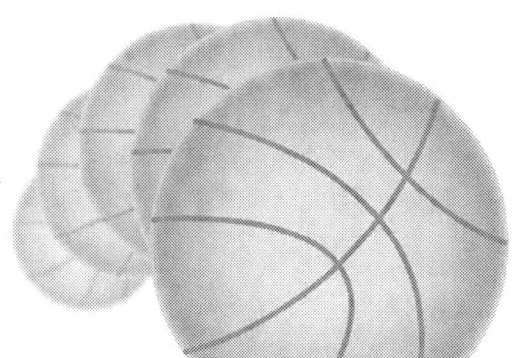

TABLE OF CONTENTS

Dedication .... *iii*

Acknowledgments .... *iv*

Foreword .... *v*

Preface .... *ix*

Diagram Legend 1

Allen, Dr. Forrest "Phog" 2
    The Stratified Transitional Man-to-Man Defense with Zone Principles 6

Barmore, Leon 8
    The Louisiana Tech "11" Defense (1-2-1-1 Zone) 12

Bee, Clair 18
    The History and Development of the Zone Defense 22
    The One-Three-One Zone Defense 25

Carnesecca, Lou 28
    Diagnostic Defensive Drills 32

Carnevale, Bernard "Ben" 40
    Pressing Defenses 44
    Preparing for an Opponent 47

Chaney, John 48
    Inside Defense Against the Stall 52
    The Temple of Zones 55

Crum, Denzil "Denny" 62
    Pressing Defenses 66

Gaines, Clarence "Big House" 70
    Combination Match-Up Defense 74

Gill, A.T. "Slats" 76
    Individual Defensive Play 80

Harshman, Marv 82
    Zone Defense 86

Haskins, Don "The Bear" 88
    Defensive Basketball Guidelines 92

Holzman, William "Red" 96
    Individual Defense 100

Iba, Henry "Hank" 104
    Oklahoma A&M's Man-to-Man Defense 108
    The Defensive Stance 111

Keogan, George **112**
    A Defense to Stop the Figure 8 Offense 116

Knight, Bob **118**
    Defensive Rules 122
    Five-on-Four Defensive Drill 125

Krzyzewski, Mike "Coach K" **126**
    Duke's Man-to-Man Defense 130

Lapchick, Joseph "Joe" **140**
    The Coach Philosophy 144
    Defensive Skills 146

Litwack, Harry **152**
    Zone Defenses 156
    The 3-2 Zone Defense 157

Lonborg, Arthur "Dutch" **162**
    Special Basketball Defenses 166

McLendon, John "Johnny Mac" **168**
    The Four Degrees of Defense Theory 172
    Relating Defense to the Fast Break Offense 174

Meyer, Raymond "Ray" **178**
    Principles of Man-to-Man Defense 182
    Offside Help and Recover Drill 187

Miller, Ralph "Cappy" **188**
    Philosophical Musings 192
    A Comprehensive Basketball Drill System for Pressure Offense and Defense 193

Olson, Robert "Lute" **200**
    Developing Defense Through Drills 204

Ramsay, Jack **212**
    The Role of Defense 216

Rupp, Adolph **218**
    The Seven Cardinal Rules of Defense 222

Smith, Dean **224**
    The Run-and-Jump Defense 228
    The North Carolina Four on Four Combination Drill 232

Summitt, Pat Head **236**
    Tennessee Lady Vols Man Defense Philosophy 240

Wooden, John **242**
    The 2-2-1 Zone Press 246

Woolpert, Phil **250**
    San Francisco's Three-Quarter Court Press 254

Wootten, Morgan **258**
    Blitz Defense 262

Lessons from the Legends Trivia Quiz **280**

About the Authors **282**

DR. JAMES NAISMITH, INVENTOR OF BASKETBALL

PREFACE

The information contained in this book is the authors' best attempt to preserve the legacy of the game's greatest coaches. We spent over three years researching the material that is included in the first edition of the Naismith Lessons from the Legends. We utilized many resources, including the archives at the Naismith Basketball Hall of Fame in Springfield, MA. We studied technical books written by Hall of Fame coaches, as well as articles that were published in professional journals. We read newspaper accounts describing their coaching exploits. In addition, we interviewed Hall of Fame coaches, players, assistant coaches, family members, and school administrators in order to capture the essence of each coach's personal and professional legacy.

Every attempt was made to sort through all the material and present the most accurate description of each coach. We may not have succeeded in every case, but we are confident that you will enjoy reading this one-of-a-kind-book, featuring the coaches who have made basketball the world's greatest game. We believe it truly is a close look at the "best from the best," the best ideas about basketball and life from the best people in this area—the Naismith Basketball Hall of Fame inductees.

Now it is your turn to help the authors improve and "make the next game" better in our second edition. If you have additional information, articles/clinics (technical basketball or just human interest), stories, or pictures that could be included in this book, we encourage you to contact the authors so we can share it with our readers in future editions. Please send materials or contact the authors/publisher at:

The Basketball Legends Series
Attn: Krause/Pim
Coaches Choice
P.O. Box 1828
Monterey, CA 93942
1-888-229-5745
www.coacheschoice.com

DIAGRAM LEGEND	
PLAYERS	① ② ③ ④ ⑤
MOVE DIRECTION	──────►
MOVE to SCREEN	─────┤
DRIBBLE	∿∿∿∿∿►
PASS DIRECTION	- - - - - - -►
PASS SEQUENCE	1st, 2nd, 3rd Pass
COACH	C
DEFENDER POSITION	X_1
DEFENSIVE PLAYERS	X_1, X_2, X_3, X_4, X_5

To create consistency throughout the book, the diagrams illustrating the Lessons from the Legends by the Hall of Fame Coaches have been redrawn using the diagram legend above.

LEGACY OF
Dr. Forrest "Phog" Allen

- Called the "Father of Basketball Coaches" by Dr. James Naismith.

- Co-founded the National Association of Basketball Coaches in 1927.

- Developed a defense during the 1920s and 1930s that combined man-to-man and zone defensive techniques called the "stratified transitional man-to-man defense with zone principles."

- Introduced a pressure man-to-man defense in 1952 that overplayed all passing lanes and made it difficult to complete even the simplest pass. John Wooden called it a defensive turning point in basketball.

- Became one of college sports' first entrepreneurs. Allen marketed items such as basketball shoes, basketballs, rulebooks, and medicine kits that all carried the "Phog" Allen name.

- Led Kansas to the Helms Athletic Foundation national championship in 1923 and 1924 and the NCAA title in 1952.

- Retired as the all-time winningest coach in collegiate basketball history.

DR. FORREST "PHOG" ALLEN

"Give to the world the best you've got, and the best will come back to you."
—Phog Allen

BIOGRAPHY

Born: November 18, 1885 in Jamesport, Missouri

Died: September 16, 1974

Inducted into the Naismith Basketball Hall of Fame in 1959

Forrest "Phog" Allen played basketball at the University of Kansas from 1905 to 1907 for the game's founder, Dr. James Naismith. Allen began his coaching career in 1908 and coached at Baker University, Haskell Institute, Warrensburg Teachers College, and the University of Kansas. His innovative tactics and coaching prowess earned him the title, "The Father of Basketball Coaching." Allen coached forty-eight seasons and compiled a 746-264 won-lost record. At the time of his retirement, Allen was the all-time winningest coach in collegiate basketball history. During thirty-nine years at the University of Kansas, his teams won or shared thirty championships in the Missouri Valley, Big Seven, and Big Eight Conferences. Allen's 1952 squad won the NCAA championship and his 1923 and 1924 teams were selected national champions by the Helms Athletic Foundation. He was instrumental in establishing basketball as an Olympic sport and was an assistant coach for the USA team that won the gold medal in the 1952 Olympics. Allen was so proud of his Olympic experience that he requested to be buried in his Olympic USA sweatshirt. Allen was co-founder of the National Association of Basketball Coaches (NABC) and its first president. In 1953, the University of Kansas named their new basketball facility the Forrest C. Allen Field House. Allen was enshrined in the Naismith Memorial Basketball Hall of Fame in 1959.

...SCOUTING REPORT.....SCOUTING REPORT.....

Dr. Forrest "Phog" Allen...

"Phog" Allen and James Naismith became basketball's first "odd couple." Even though Allen played for Naismith at the University of Kansas and they became lifelong friends, their views on basketball were as different as night and day. Naismith invented basketball as a leisure-time activity to promote healthy exercise and saw no need for someone to coach the game. Allen, on the other hand, envisioned universities competing against each other for national championships, large arenas built to accommodate masses of spectators, and coaches who were compensated for their coaching ability. Allen reputedly was hired as one of the first basketball coaches in the country at nearby Baker University (KS). He rushed back to Lawrence and excitedly told the news to his mentor, Naismith. Naismith was less than enthusiastic with his response, "You don't coach basketball, you just play basketball."

During the 1909 season, Allen accomplished a feat never replicated again in college basketball. He simultaneously coached three different teams to a combined 74-10 record. He directed Kansas to a 25-3 record; Baker University to a 22-2 mark; and the Haskell Institute Indian School to a 27-5 record.

To most everyone, Allen was known as "Phog." He acquired the nickname as a young man when he umpired baseball games and people thought his voice sounded like a foghorn. Allen's friends initially called him "Foghorn," and then a sportswriter shortened it to just "Phog." To keep his throat clear during basketball games, Allen kept quart bottles filled with water under his seat, and it wasn't uncommon for him to drink six quarts during the course of a contest. At practice or in the office, "Phog" devoured horehound candies which he bought in 60-pound boxes.

To his players, Allen was known as "Doc," as in doctor of osteopathy. He completed osteopathy school in 1912 and was often thought of as a "miracle man" for his ability to quickly rehabilitate athletes. The medical profession criticized Allen for treating just about anything less serious than a broken bone, but that did not keep well-known athletes such as Casey Stengel, Ralph Houk, George Halas, Johnny Mize, and Mickey Mantle from seeking his services. Allen spent hours pushing, pulling, rubbing, and cracking the bones of his athletes, and the players were convinced his medical attention helped them win games. Rubdown tables were kept in "Phog's" office, home, and were taken with the team on every road trip.

Allen was one of college sports' first entrepreneurs. He marketed items such as basketball shoes, basketballs, rulebooks, and medicine kits that all carried the "Phog" Allen name. In 1939, Allen invented a game similar to basketball that he called Goal-Hi. It was played with one goal that was positioned in the center of a circular playing court. Unlike basketball, the goal was not attached to a backboard. The height of the goal was adjusted, depending on the age of the participants (8 foot for elementary; 9 foot for junior high; and 10 foot for high school and college). A successful field goal was returned through a chute in one of three directions, and shots made from beyond 15 feet counted three points. Allen thought it was perfect for women's teams and elementary-aged children because it was less strenuous than basketball. Unfortunately for Allen, the manufacturer of Goal-Hi ceased production in 1942 due to World War II.

.....SCOUTING REPORT.....SCOUTING REPORT...

Allen's insights into the medical profession helped in the formation of his basketball philosophy. He believed natural body movements must be incorporated in the daily practice routine. Allen preached the importance of the "ape man" theory. "Look at any animal," explained Allen. "Whether attacking or defending, he assumes a semi-crouching position. How can you react otherwise? The knees are the only springs in the body. Bend them slightly, and you can make any move rapidly required in basketball." (Padwe, 1970, p. 65)

Allen believed defense was the key to success. During the 1920s and 1930s, Allen made famous a defense that he called the "stratified transitional man-to-man defense with zone principles." It was a fancy name for a defense that combined man-to-man and zone techniques. In the 1950s, Allen implemented a pressure man-to-man defense that cut off the passing lanes and made it difficult to complete even the simplest of passes. It carried his Kansas Jayhawks to the 1952 national championship and stands as Allen's tactical legacy in college basketball. Legendary coach John Wooden referred to Allen's pressure defense as a defensive turning point in the game of basketball. His 1953 Kansas team, using this pressure defense, returned to the Final Four after graduating a majority of players. During the summer of 1953, future Hall of Fame coach Phil Woolpert visited the University of Kansas to study Allen's pressure defense. Woolpert incorporated many of Allen's defensive concepts, and his San Francisco teams went on to win back-to-back national championships in 1955 and 1956.

One of Allen's greatest attributes was his motivational skill. He was charismatic and moved people to action through his inspirational speeches. After Kansas lost consecutive games during the 1951-52 season, Allen read to his team the story, Casey at the Bat. At the end of the story, Allen wept and implied that the Jayhawks, like Casey, had hit bottom. With his players listening to every word, the master psychologist picked up and read the lesser-known sequel to the story, called Casey's Revenge, written by Grantland Rice. Allen dramatically revealed how the washed-up Casey returned to the jeers of the fans to hit the game-winning home run. The poem ends, "He came through hell to scramble back—and prove a champ belongs." (Kerkoff, 1996, p. 171) Allen's speech made an impact on his players, because Kansas came charging back to win not only the Big Seven Conference, but also the NCAA championship.

Allen was sharp-tongued and opinionated. In his own words he stated, "I've never been accused of being a shrinking violet." (Kerkoff, 1996, p. xv) Unfortunately, his accomplishments were often overshadowed by his feisty and provocative comments. He battled with rival coaches, the AAU, the NCAA, and at times his own administration. Allen angrily declared that the letters AAU stood for "Asinine and Unfair" and the NCAA meant "Nationally Confused Athletic Absurdity." He further stated, "I like the AAU like a fellow likes garlic for dessert." (Kerkoff, 1996, p. 198)

In basketball's infancy, there probably was no more passionate a supporter than Forrest "Phog" Allen. In 1951, future Hall of Fame coach Hank Iba expressed his thoughts about Allen in these words, "Since 1908, no man has contributed as much to the game." (Kerkoff, 1996, p. 158)

Adolph Rupp, legendary Kentucky coach and Hall of Famer, proclaimed in 1974 that Allen was "the greatest basketball coach of all time." (Kerkoff, 1996, p. 204)

SOURCE

Allen, Forrest. Vertical Files, Archives. Naismith Memorial Basketball Hall of Fame. Springfield, MA.

Kerkhoff, Blair. (1996). *Phog Allen The Father of Basketball Coaching.* Indianapolis: Masters Press.

Padwe, Sandy. (1970). *Basketball's Hall of Fame.* Englewood Cliffs, N.J.: Prentice-Hall, Inc.

Smith, Dean. (2002). *A Coach's Life: My 40 Years in College Basketball.* New York: Random House, Inc.

LESSONS FROM THIS LEGEND...

THE STRATIFIED TRANSITIONAL MAN-TO-MAN DEFENSE WITH ZONE PRINCIPLES

By Forrest "Phog" Allen

When an outnumbered defense is confronted with the problem of defending the basket, the Stratified Transitional Man-to-Man Defense with Zone Principles should be utilized. Two situations which need this principle are: 1) when one defensive player is confronted with two offensive players; and 2) when two defensive players are confronted with three offensive players.

When the defense is outnumbered, it must become strong and prevent the lay-up shot. The defense must guard the player who has the ball and at the same time use the principle of the zone defense. Hence, a defense that is outnumbered will play a stratum of the man-for-man and a stratum of the zone. Therefore, we arrive at the complex title, Stratified Transitional Man-to-Man Defense with Zone Principles.

The common conception of teamwork is that it applies only to the offense, but, in reality, it operates at its best on the defense. This misconception can be attributed to the fact that, in the early development of the game, the players in possession of the ball were the centers of attraction, and the players not in possession drew very little attention.

TWO-ON-ONE

In this discussion, the situation of one defensive player confronted by two offensive forwards will be considered. The defensive player is stationed under the basket with the obligation of preventing either of the two offensive players from scoring.

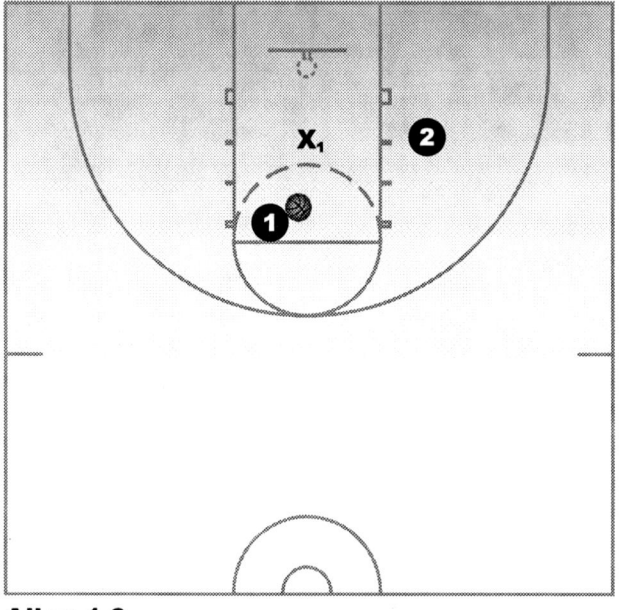

Allen 1.0

As shown in **Diagram 1.0**, the defender, X1, is a wary performer. Never will he let either of the two forwards get behind him, nor will he go out too deep and leave the basket undefended. As new situations arise, the defender will know just when to advance or to retreat. Should the offense attempt a shot from the outside, the defender will constantly project his physique and his personality into both the visual and the mental paths of the shooter. Neither will X1 ever turn his back to either O1 or O2. As an aid to efficient footwork, X1 will interchange between the first baseman's step and the boxer's stance.

THREE-ON-TWO

In this discussion, the situation of two defensive players being opposed by three offensive players will be dealt with according to the principles of the Stratified Transitional Man-to-Man Defense with Zone Principles.

As shown in **Diagram 1.1**, three offensive players are attacking X1 and X2. It is the

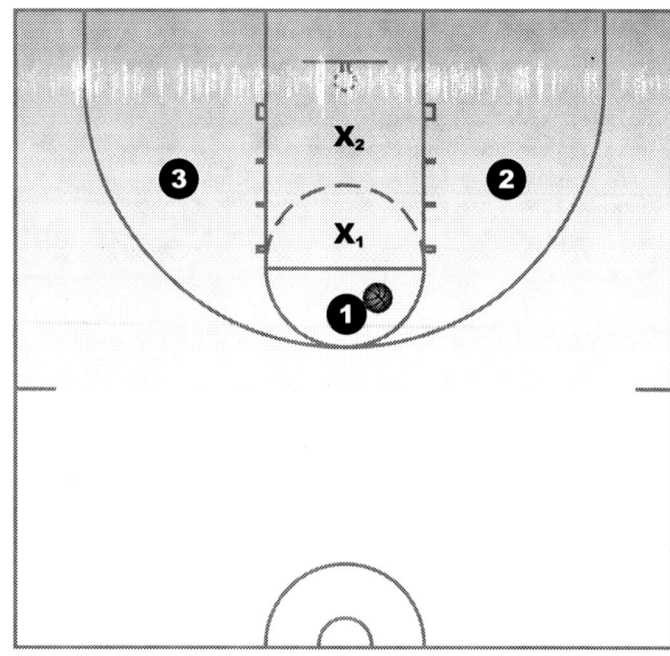

Allen 1.1

LESSONS FROM THIS LEGEND...

job of the two defenders to stop all scoring thrusts. This is a tandem defensive formation. The rear defender, X2, is not more than 3-to-5 ft. directly in front of the basket, and the front defender, X1, plays about 7 ft. in front of X2.

Whether the offense attempts a shot or a pass, the defensive players will always shift the spearhead of their defense in the direction of the ball. Furthermore, both of the defenders will be using every talent at their command to hurry and to confuse the offensive ballhandlers.

In **Diagram 1.2**, O1 passes to O3. The front defensive player, X1, has shifted back and over to thwart the shot attempt. X2 shifts his position and is now facing the ball in its new location. X2 is also keeping close watch upon O2. The two defenders are, at all times, making it their first concern to protect the basket, and, at the same time, to play the man who is in the most dangerous scoring position. Should O3 attempt a shot, X2 is in excellent defensive position to secure the rebound.

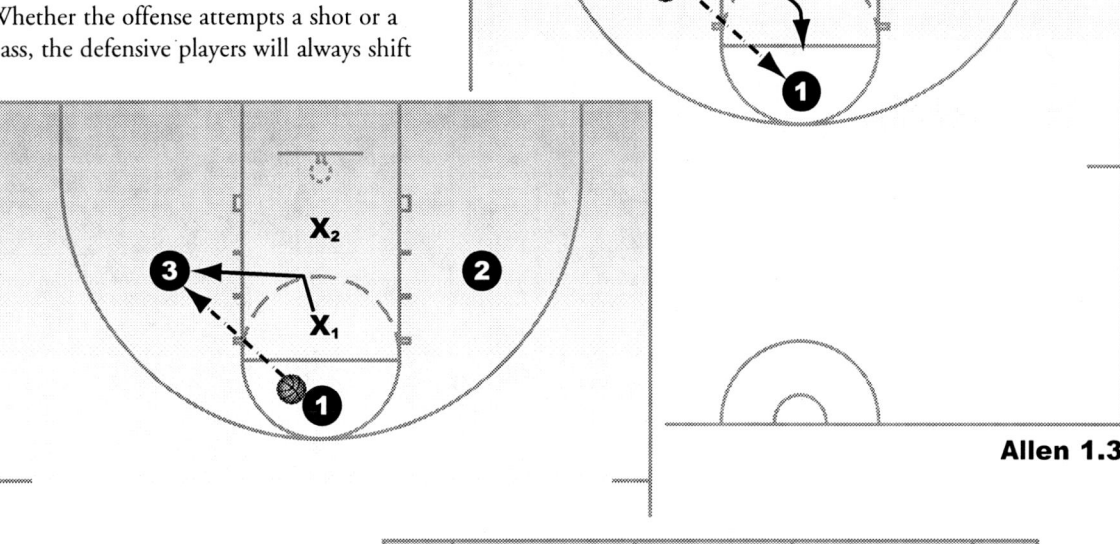

Allen 1.2

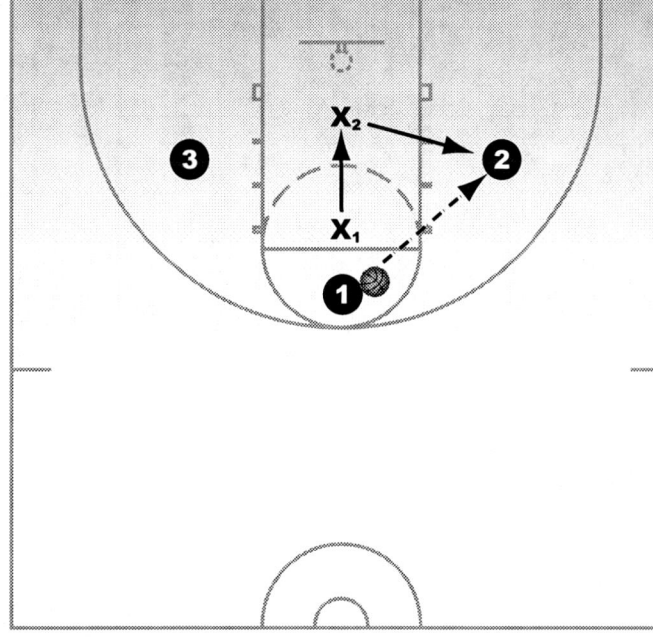

Allen 1.3

Allen 1.4

In **Diagram 1.3**, the ball has been passed back to O1 who is in a favorable position to pass to an open player in either direction. The rear defender, X2, must be very wily in handling these two corner offensive players. X2 must be in a well-poised stance ready to break to either corner to cover O2 or O3. X1 has shifted forward to prohibit O1 an open shot in front of the basket. The two defenders are again in their original positions. This situation is in accordance with the zone principle of eternal vigilance of the defensive area, while not on detail assignment with man-for-man defense. In this type of defense, the guards are constantly shifting their positions in their unyielding torment of the player who is about to receive the pass.

In **Diagram 1.4**, O1 passes the ball to O2. The rear defender, X2, shifts over to defend O2. X1 drops back to be near the basket in case a shot is attempted. But, the main reason that X1 is dropping back is to be in the ball's line of flight, if O2 attempts a pass across the court to O3. X1 is also in position to shift quickly forward should the ball be returned to O1. If O3 attempts a shot, X1 must secure a floor position on the other side of the basket for the rebound.

SOURCE

Allen, Forrest C. (1937) *Better Basketball*. New York: McGraw-Hill

LEGACY OF
Leon Barmore

- Recorded the best women's college winning percentage (.869) in history.

- Became the first women's coach to register 13 seasons of 30 or more victories.

- Compiled a conference record of 190-13, which included a conference winning streak of 77 games (third longest in the history of women's college basketball).

- Led his teams to 20 consecutive NCAA tournament appearances, nine Final Four berths, and five championship game appearances.

- Directed Louisiana Tech to 10 straight conference championships (in three different conferences).

- One of only three players in Louisiana Tech men's basketball history to have his jersey number retired.

LEON BARMORE

"You've got to put the players first. If you are in this business for any other reason, you are making a mistake."
—Leon Barmore

BIOGRAPHY

Born: June 3, 1944 in Ruston, Louisiana

Inducted into the Naismith Basketball Hall of Fame in 2003

Born in Ruston, Louisiana, Leon Barmore grew up there and never left. He has spent his entire personal life and professional career in the community of Ruston. Barmore graduated from Ruston High School in 1962, after playing on state championship teams his junior and senior years. After graduation from Louisiana Tech in 1966, he began his teaching and coaching career at Bastrop High School, where he spent four years. His final two teams were 31-7 and 28-4; as they became District Champions and advanced to the state tourney. His overall record was 84-41 (67.2%). In 1970, Barmore went on to unparalleled success at his high school alma mater, Ruston, where he spent six years and forged a record of 148-39 (75.1%), while advancing to the Louisiana state playoffs each year. Coach Barmore went to Louisiana Tech in 1977 and stayed there until his retirement on August 20, 2002. He was assistant coach for five years, co-head coach for three years, and head coach for 18 years until 2002, when he retired with a head coaching record of 576-87 (86.9%). His Tech years as assistant coach produced an even higher record of 163-18 (90.0%). This percentage of 86.9% is the all-time best in NCAA Division I college basketball (men's or women's). Barmore is the only coach in NCAA Division I collegiate basketball history (men's or women's) to post six consecutive seasons of 30-plus wins (1995-2001). He is also the fastest coach in history to 500-wins (500-76). His record in conference play was summed up as "complete and total domination."

...SCOUTING REPORT.....SCOUTING REPORT.....

Leon Barmore...

This was the story of a small-town coach who stayed at home his entire career and excelled in the world of big-time college basketball. He lifted Ruston and Louisiana Tech to the top and kept them there for his whole career.

Barmore's teams excelled throughout his career in all settings: high school, small college, and NCAA Division I. In the early days of women's college basketball, the Association of Intercollegiate Athletics (AIAW) organized and sponsored the first national tournament for women in 1972. Louisiana Tech won the AIAW championship in 1980-81 (34-0), after being semi-finalists the previous two years (40-5 and 34-4). In his last season (1981-82) as an assistant coach, the Techsters were the first NCAA I national champions at 35-1.

Louisiana Tech was among several smaller schools from small markets that excelled at the top levels of the AIAW. But, all of them dropped out of the picture after NCAA I competition began in 1981-82. All but one, that is...Louisiana Tech. They made every NCAA tournament since its inception (20 straight years). The difference was the drive, determination, competitiveness, and coaching excellence of Leon Barmore. Tech had been a "top-tier" team, seriously competing for the national championship for 21 straight years with a budget dwarfed by other national powers in women's basketball. Barmore was the fastest coach to reach 500 wins in NCAA I college basketball (500-76). Twenty-one straight NCAA tournament bids (ranks No. 2), 13-thirty win seasons (ranks No.1), nine Final Fours, five national championship game appearances and a NCAA I national championship in 1988 (32-2) are the hallmarks of excellence left by Barmore's teams. He never went four straight years without taking a team to the Final Four. Louisiana Tech and Tennessee are the only two schools to play in every NCAA Tournament in history.

Yet, as the power conferences began to dominate women's college basketball and the budget gap widened, Leon's record improved. In seven years, from 1995 on, his winning percentage was 89%, and his teams averaged 30 wins a year. Leon Barmore simply refused to lose. He is the only coach in NCAA I history to post six straight 30-win seasons.

When women's basketball started serious competition, the sleeved jersey was standard for women's uniforms. Under Barmore, Tech's teams continued to be the only team in the modern era to retain the unique and different sleeves—the Techsters were set apart by their sleeves and winning.

The teams coached by Sonja Hogg, his predecessor, and Barmore were noted for up-tempo basketball, rebounding, and tough "player-to-player" defense. The last Barmore team (2001-02) was the best ever defensively in the 28-year history of the program, allowing opponents only 53 points a game and a 33-percent field-goal percentage.

As a coach and teacher, Barmore became a unique oddity; tied closely to his small town roots, he reached the pinnacle of women's college basketball at a school with very modest resources. And in so doing, he mobilized an entire university. Lady Techster basketball was the biggest thing in town and on campus; bigger than men's basketball or football; not many women's basketball programs could make that claim. He had accomplished that while remaining the consummate teacher and coach—emphasizing education, modeling ethical behavior, and graduating over 90% of his student-athletes. Over fifteen former players or assistant coaches went on to coach at the college level.

Barmore was an all-state player at Ruston (LA) H.S. and earned All-Gulf States Conference honors at Louisiana Tech. He was known for his gutsy play, uncanny perimeter shooting, and defensive tenacity. Barmore is one of only three players in the history of Louisiana Tech basketball to have his jersey number retired. One of the others is two-time NBA Most Valuable Player, Karl Malone.

Barmore credits Scotty Robertson, his coach at Tech, with teaching him about practice planning, fast-break basketball, and the importance of defensive basketball. Besides Robertson, Barmore said that Dean Smith, Bob Knight, Hubie Brown, and John Wooden greatly influenced his coaching philosophy.

A little known fact about Barmore is that he won 232 games as a boys' coach at Ruston H.S. and Bastrop H.S., prior to moving into the college ranks as the women's assistant coach at Louisiana Tech. Barmore said that he carried the same competitive nature into the women's game, but that he learned to be more positive. "With women, if I said 10 things," said Barmore (2003), "I wanted nine of them to be positive. If I were to coach men again, I would be more positive. It may have just been the times and the fact that I was a beginning coach."

.....SCOUTING REPORT.....SCOUTING REPORT...

If there is one word to describe Leon, it would be competitive. Barmore's reputation has always been that of a stern taskmaster, impatient with the results and intent on getting the very best out of his players. The other side of his personality is that of a caring individual who truly cares about his players and assistant coaches.

"He's been a tremendous influence on my life," said Nell Fortner, former Louisiana Tech assistant and head coach of the U.S. Olympic women's team. "That goes for hundreds of other women who have either played or coached for him. He had a huge impact on me as a coach. What makes me proud to have known him, too, is that he's always had sound principles in whatever he has done." (Davis, 2002)

Angela Turner, a former Kodak All-American at Tech, said, "Coach Barmore will do anything for you. He may appear tough when he's coaching during a game or in a practice, but he's a good, gentle, kindhearted person." (Davis, 2003)

Barmore was a master at putting together winning teams. Barmore's formula for selecting players—he coached four Olympians, 12 Kodak All-Americans, and 37 first team All-Conference players—was hard to dispute. "Talent is first," said Barmore (2003). "They must have a high level of talent. Secondly, they must be hard working and put a lot of effort into their game. Thirdly, they must be really aggressive and possess a great desire to win." Barmore had the following expectations for his players:
1. Perform at the best of your ability.
2. Always be on time.
3. Be honest and never lie.
4. Place the team above yourself.
5. Play aggressive defense.
6. Go to class.

Barmore (2003) gave this advice to today's young coaches:
1) Study the game, become knowledgeable, and understand the X's and O's.
2) Put your players first. If you do that, they will lead you. If you care about them, they will take care of you. If you are in this business for any other reason, you are making a mistake.
3) Care for your assistants. Your assistant coaches help make you successful. Getting the right chemistry on your staff is essential. The common thread is that everyone must be highly competitive.

Barmore became the sixth person—and first male—enshrined in the Naismith Basketball Hall of Fame for coaching women. Reflecting on his career, Barmore said, "I started out getting my first basketball in 1956, and I wanted to be a good player. In 1957, I saw my first game on television and future Hall of Famer and Celtic star Bob Cousy became my idol. I wanted to handle the ball, dribble, and pass like Cousy. I then wanted to be a good coach, but I never dreamed that I would ever be in a position that I would be elected into the Basketball Hall of Fame. It took a lot of work to get here, and it took a lot of people helping me."

SOURCE

Barmore, Leon. Vertical Files, Archives. Naismith Memorial Basketball Hall of Fame. Springfield, MA.

Barmore, Leon. Interview by Ralph Pim, September 5, 2003.

Davis, O.K. (November 26, 2002). Barmore's Success Known Far and Wide. *The Ruston Daily Leader.*

Davis, O.K. (2003) Competitive seeds. *Naismith Memorial Hall of Fame Enshrinement Program.*

LESSONS FROM THIS LEGEND...
THE LOUISIANA TECH "11" DEFENSE (1-2-1-1 ZONE)
By Leon Barmore

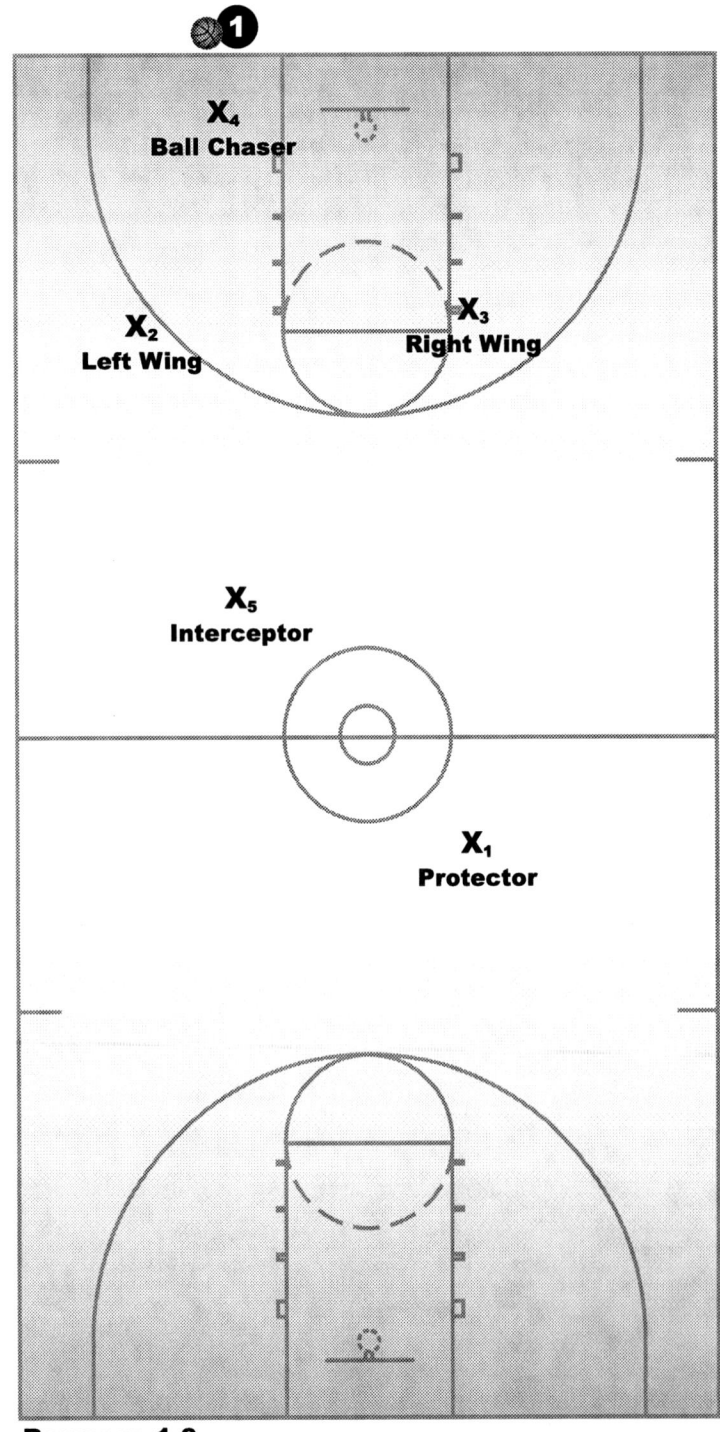

Barmore 1.0

THE 1-2-1-1 ZONE PRESS DEFENSE

1. PURPOSE
    a. To control the tempo of the game.
    b. To complement your man-to-man or run-and-jump defense.
    c. To build defensive pride in your players.
    d. To enable your team the opportunity to win, no matter what degree of talent they possess.
    e. To get the basketball!
    Note: You must convince yourself and your players of these purposes.
    f. Objectives:
        1. Press with all five defenders.
        2. Trap three times in a possession.
        3. Maintain the ball as the focal point of defense.
        4. Keep ball from middle of floor by pass or dribble.

2. PERSONNEL
    (See **Diagram 1.0**)
    a. Ball Chaser: (X4)
        1. Good speed
        2. Stamina
        3. Aggressive
        4. Determination
        5. Self-discipline
        6. Good size, if possible
    b. Right and Left Wings: (X2,X3)
        1. Good speed
        2. Good quickness
        3. Aggressive
        4. Determination
        5. Self-discipline
        6. Stamina
        7. Peripheral vision
        8. Good man-to-man fundamentals
        9. Ability to anticipate
        10. Good size, if possible

LESSONS FROM THIS LEGEND...

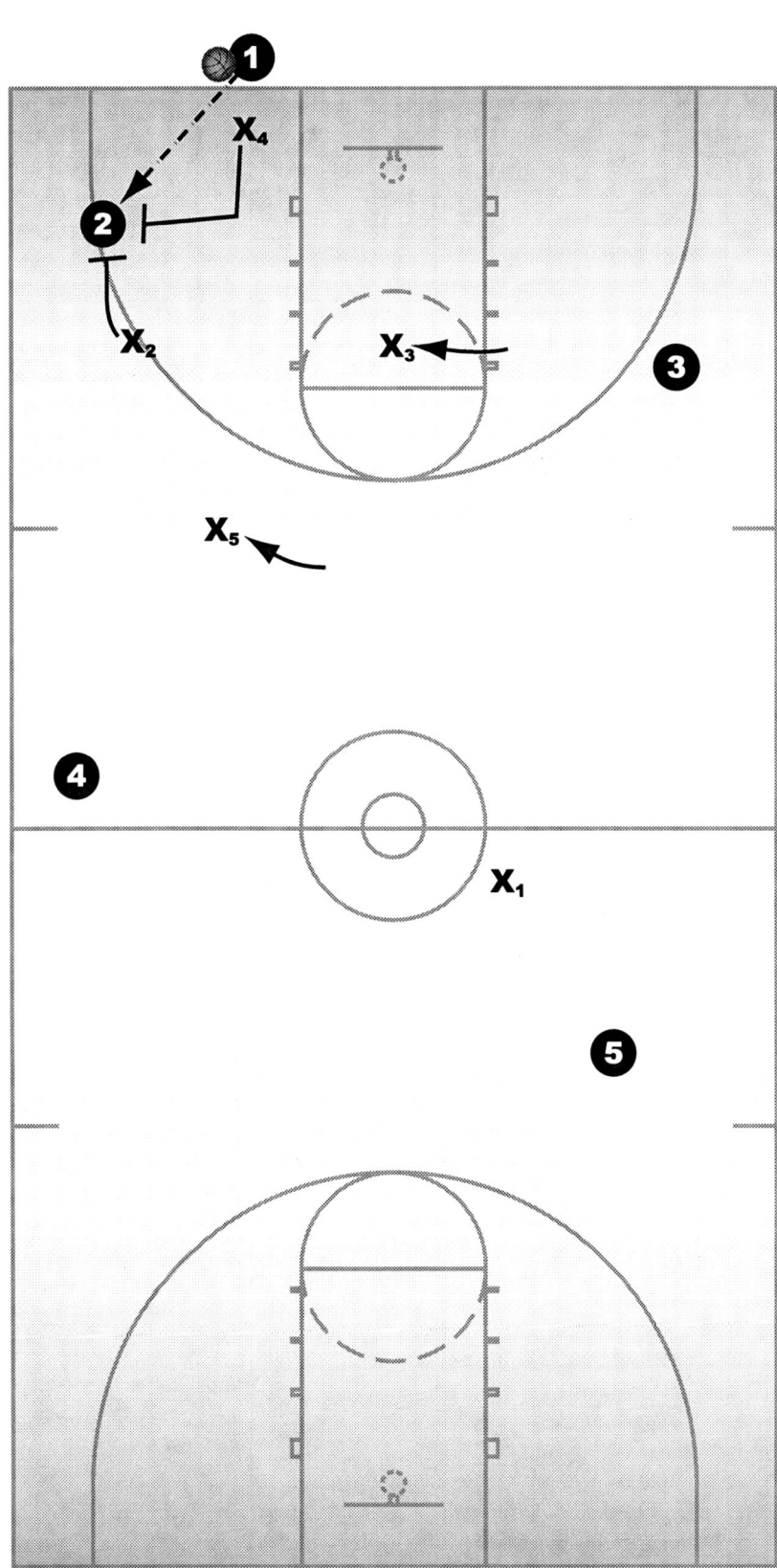

Barmore 1.1

    c. Interceptor: (X5)
        1. Good speed
        2. Good quickness
        3. Aggressive
        4. Peripheral vision
        5. Excellent ability to anticipate
        6. Good floor presence
        7. Good jumping ability
        8. Good judgment
        9. Good hands
    d. Protector: (X1)
        1. Excellent judgment
        2. Ability to anticipate
        3. Good floor presence
        4. Peripheral vision
        5. Good quickness
        6. Good speed
        7. Good hands
        8. Good jumping ability

3. ZONE PRESS TEACHING POINTS

    a. Ball line—line across the court, through the ball, and parallel to the endlines
    b. Mid-line—line between the baskets on the court
    c. Must work on man-to-man fundamentals
    d. Must learn to trap properly
    e. The ball is focal point of the defense
    f. To press, you must go all out and realize/accept that you are gambling and that mistakes will be made. But, hustle and desire will make up for 95% of the mistakes. Don't get upset if the opponents score lay-ups on occasion.

4. POINTS ON TRAPPING

(See **Diagram 1.1**)

    a. Two players toe-to-toe.
       Note: Angle at which they come toe-to-toe is important.
    b. Do not allow ball to split trap.
    c. Do not foul.
    d. Each player uses one hand to mirror the ball and the other hand to distract an area that needs protecting.

LESSONS FROM THIS LEGEND...

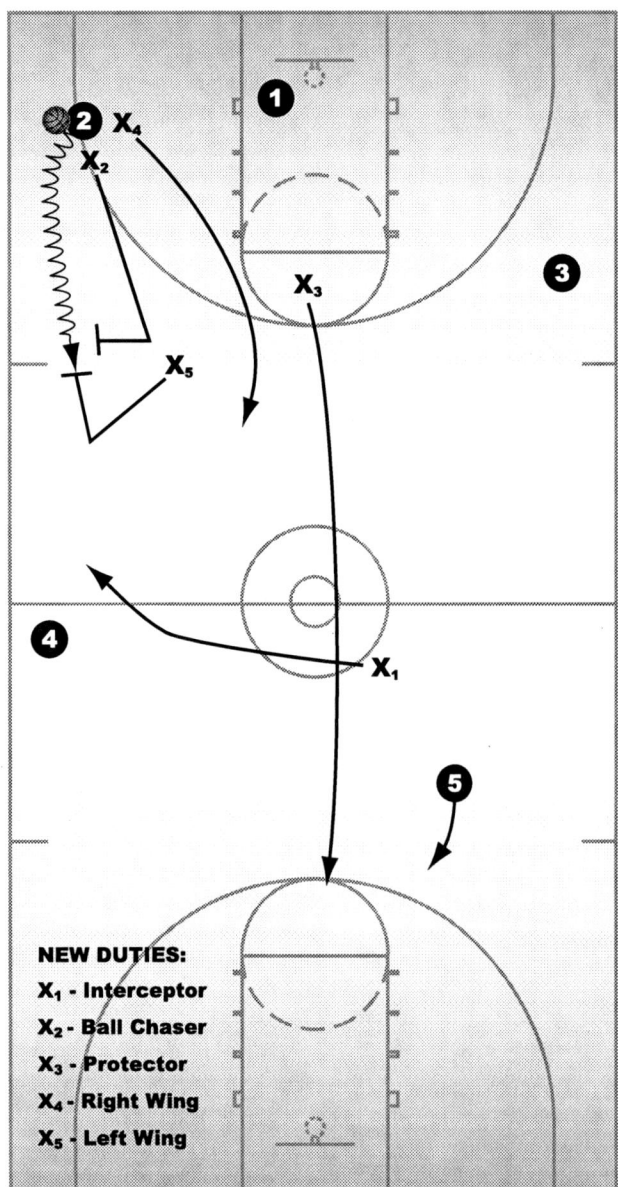

NEW DUTIES:
X_1 - Interceptor
X_2 - Ball Chaser
X_3 - Protector
X_4 - Right Wing
X_5 - Left Wing

Barmore 1.2

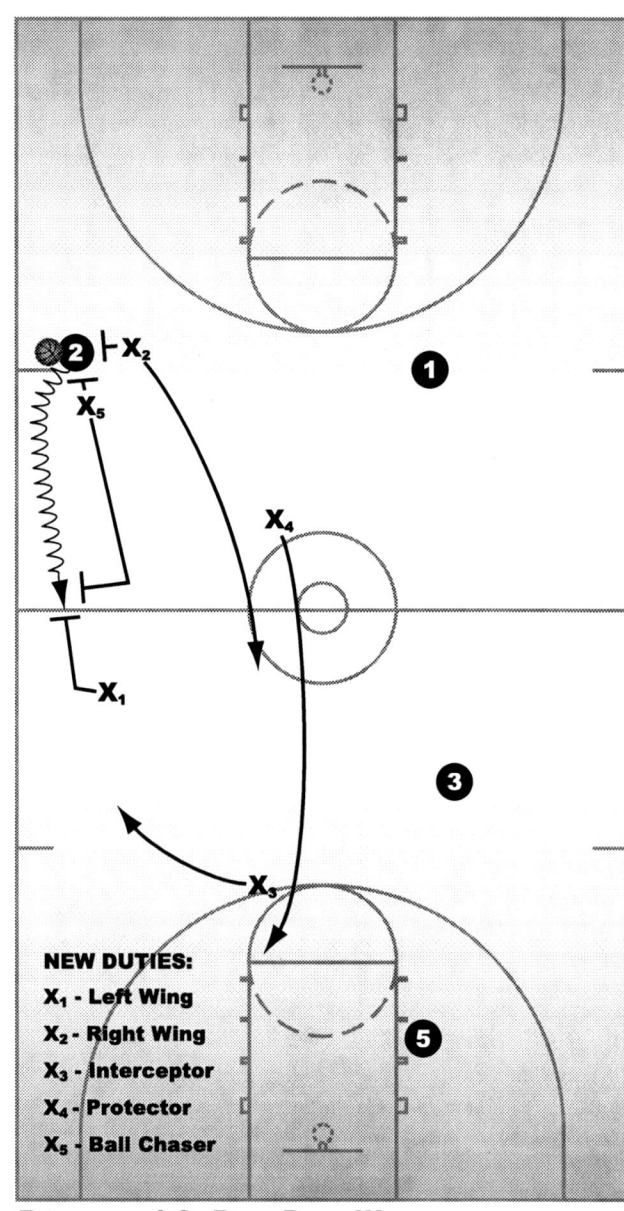

NEW DUTIES:
X_1 - Left Wing
X_2 - Right Wing
X_3 - Interceptor
X_4 - Protector
X_5 - Ball Chaser

Barmore 1.3 BALL POST WING

   e. Try to force the player with the ball to turn her back on the defenders.
   f. Allow only two types of passes:
      1. Bounce
      2. Lob
      Note: If you allow straight passes and dribbling, you had better get out of the press.
   g. Continue trapping ball on sidelines from baseline-to-baseline. (See **Diagram 1.2**)

5. INDIVIDUAL PLAYER RESPONSIBILITIES
   a. Ball Chaser: (X4)
      1. Be responsible for the ball.
      2. Totally harass the throw-in player.
      3. Force lob or bounce pass on throw-in.
      4. Dictate area of the floor where ball is thrown in.
      5. Chase ball as soon as it leaves the fingertips of the throw-in player.
      6. Trap with wing—don't allow the ball to split the trap or reverse the to backside.
      7. If the ball gets around the wing, get to the middle one step ahead of the ball. (See **Diagram 1.2**)
      8. If the ball gets around the interceptor, protect the goal.
   b. Right and Left Wings: (X2, X3)
      1. Be responsible for first player to ball on their side.

LESSONS FROM THIS LEGEND...

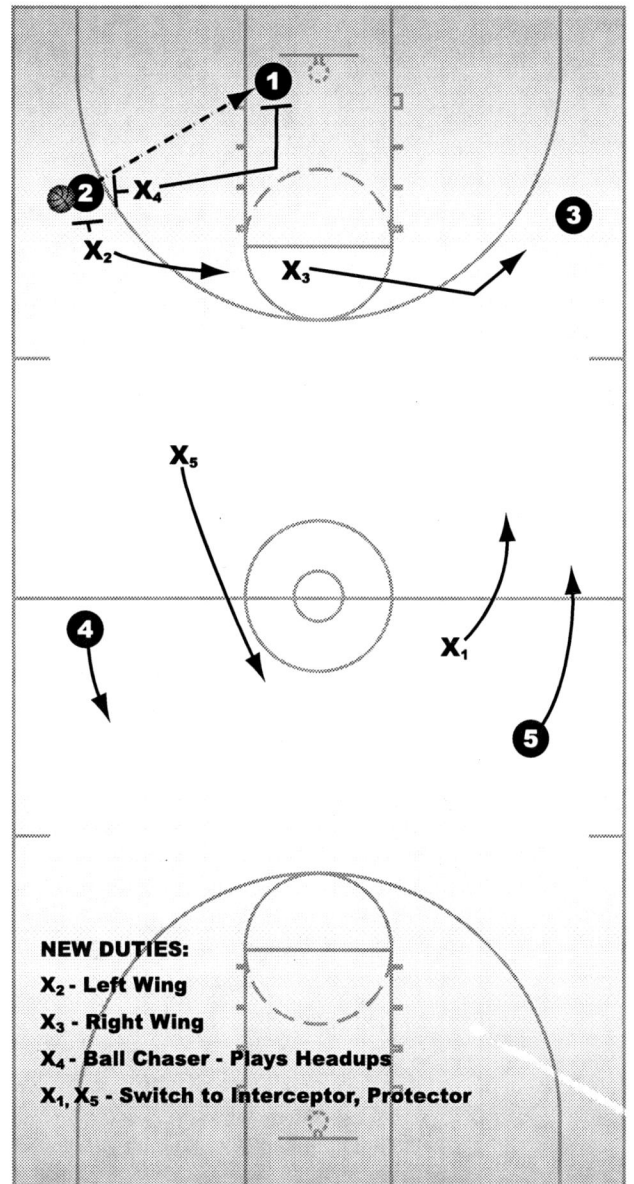

Barmore 1.4 BALL REVERSE TO MIDDLE

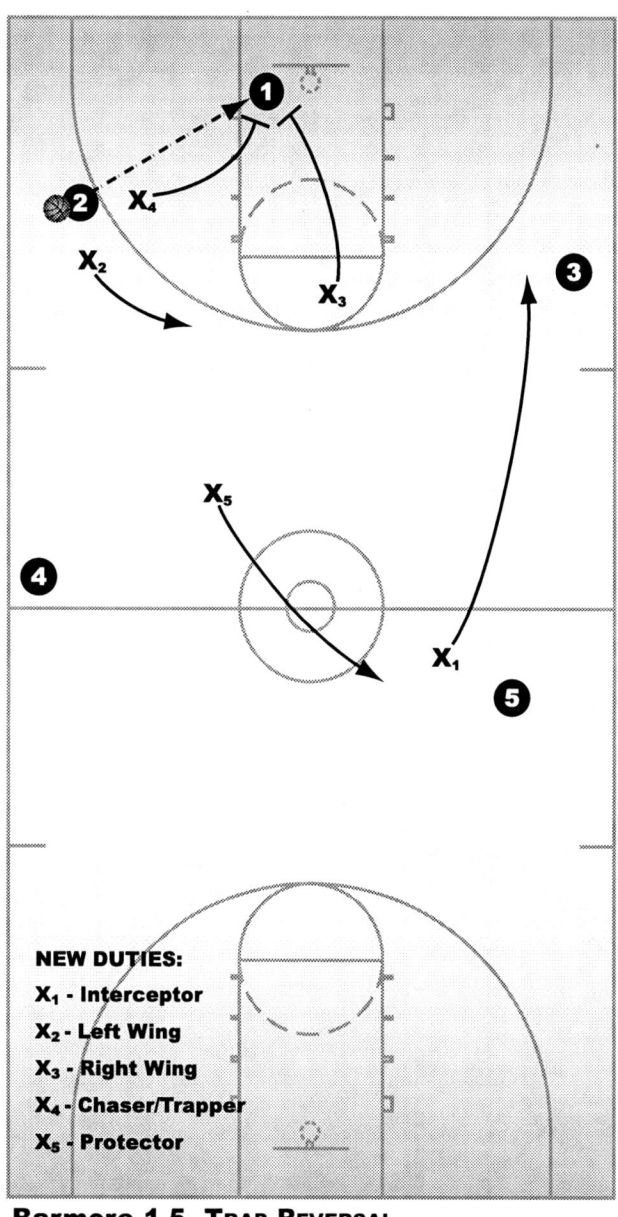

Barmore 1.5 TRAP REVERSAL

2. Deny the in-bounds pass. Play ball-me-man theory and force the offensive player to the corner.
3. Force the offensive player outside and turn the ball to the chaser for trap; keep the ball in front and trap with the chaser.
4. Get to mid-line and be one step ahead of the ball if the ball goes to opposite side.
5. Protect the goal if the ball gets around the opposite wing (become protector).
6. Become the interceptor if the protector comes up and stops the ball.
7. Attack the person receiving the throw back from the side

c. Interceptor: (X5)
   1. Be responsible for the second player up the floor on the ballside.
   2. Deny the long in-bounds pass.
   3. Be alert to any throw over the front line of defense; steal the pass down the side or to the middle.
   4. Stop and turn the ball to the wing if the ball gets around the wing.
   5. Chase the ball and trap with the protector if it gets around her.
   6. Become the protector if the ball is thrown in opposite (switch assignments).

d. Protector: (X1)
   1. Be responsible for the fifth player on the floor; prevent cross-court passes or the long pass up the floor to the fifth player.

LESSONS FROM THIS LEGEND...

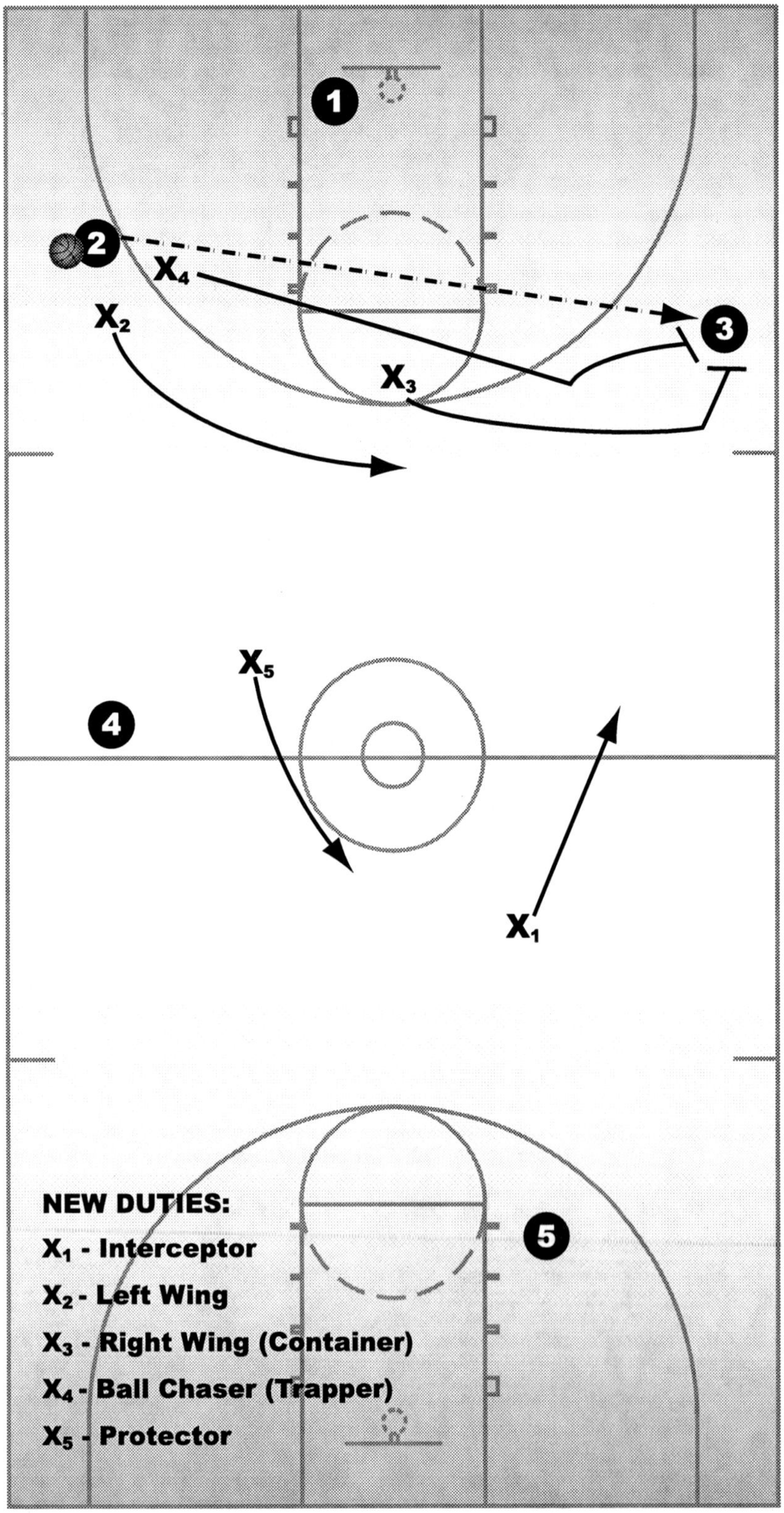

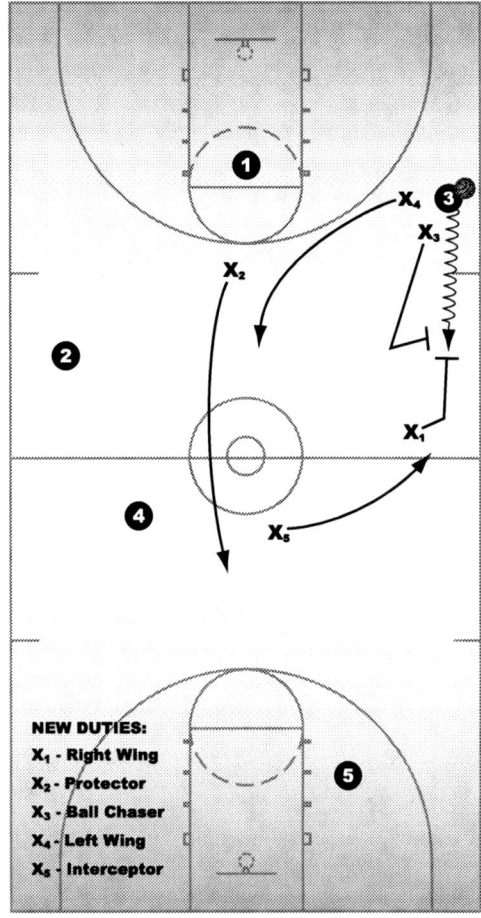

NEW DUTIES:
- X_1 - Interceptor
- X_2 - Left Wing
- X_3 - Right Wing (Container)
- X_4 - Ball Chaser (Trapper)
- X_5 - Protector

Barmore 1.6 SKIP PASS

NEW DUTIES:
- X_1 - Right Wing
- X_2 - Protector
- X_3 - Ball Chaser
- X_4 - Left Wing
- X_5 - Interceptor

Barmore 1.7 SKIP PASS & SIDE PENETRATION

2. Deny the long in-bounds pass.
3. Be alert of any throw over the front line of the defense.
4. Protect the goal and to anticipate long passes to weakside.
5. Come up and become the interceptor if the ball gets around the wing.
6. Turn the ball back to the interceptor and trap with her if the ball gets around her.
7. Become the interceptor if the ball is thrown in to her side.

SOURCE

Barmore, Leon. (2003) Clinic Notes. Ruston, LA.

LESSONS FROM THIS LEGEND...

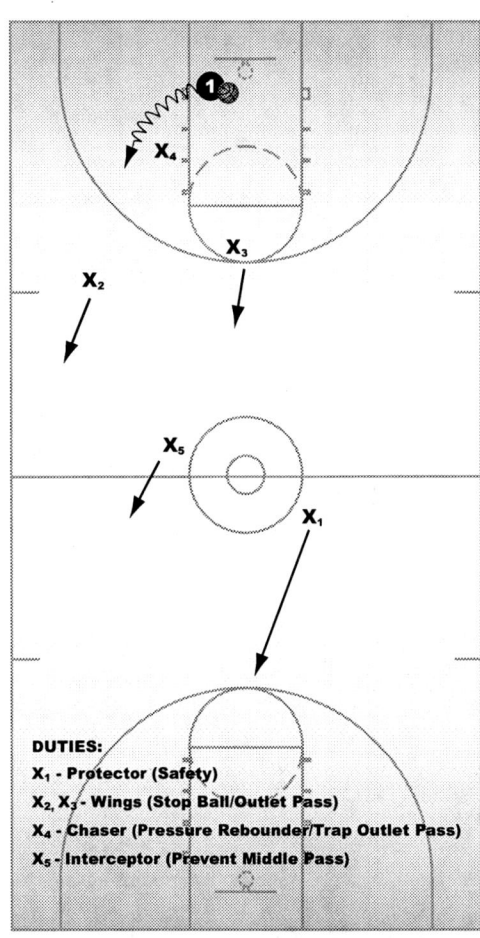

Barmore 1.8 Dribble Contain

DUTIES:
- X₁ - Protector (Safety)
- X₂, X₃ - Wings (Stop Ball/Outlet Pass)
- X₄ - Chaser (Pressure Rebounder/Trap Outlet Pass)
- X₅ - Interceptor (Prevent Middle Pass)

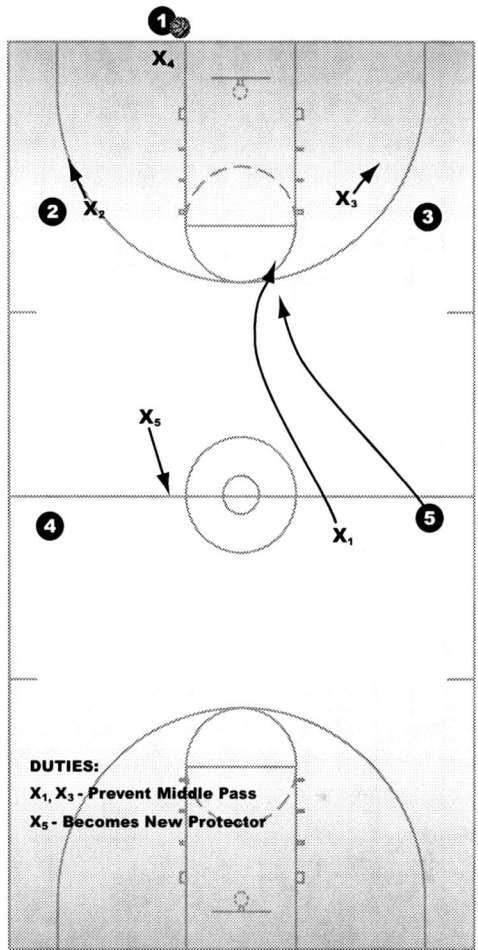

Barmore 1.9 Out-of-Bounds—Middle Cut

DUTIES:
- X₁, X₃ - Prevent Middle Pass
- X₅ - Becomes New Protector

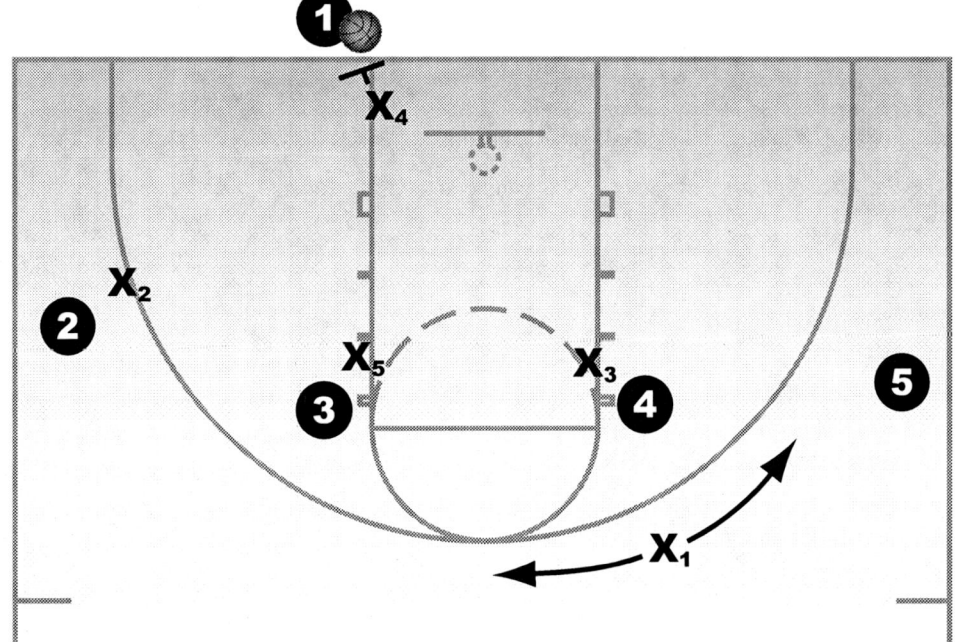

Barmore 1.10 Out-of-Bounds—Full Denial

LEGACY OF
Clair Bee

- Regarded as one of the game's greatest strategists and teachers.

- Designed and developed the 1-3-1 zone defense.

- Originated the recommendation for the 3-second rule.

- Known as an exceptional teacher of the game.

- Suffered through college basketball's first cheating scandal, which he stated was caused by the departure from educational sports concepts for business sports.

- Launched one of the first all-sports summer camps.

- Author of more than 50 books on basketball, including the popular Chip Hilton's Sport Stories for Young People series.

"In no other profession does the character and personality of a director play a more vital role in the development of young men than in the coaching of athletics."
—Clair Bee

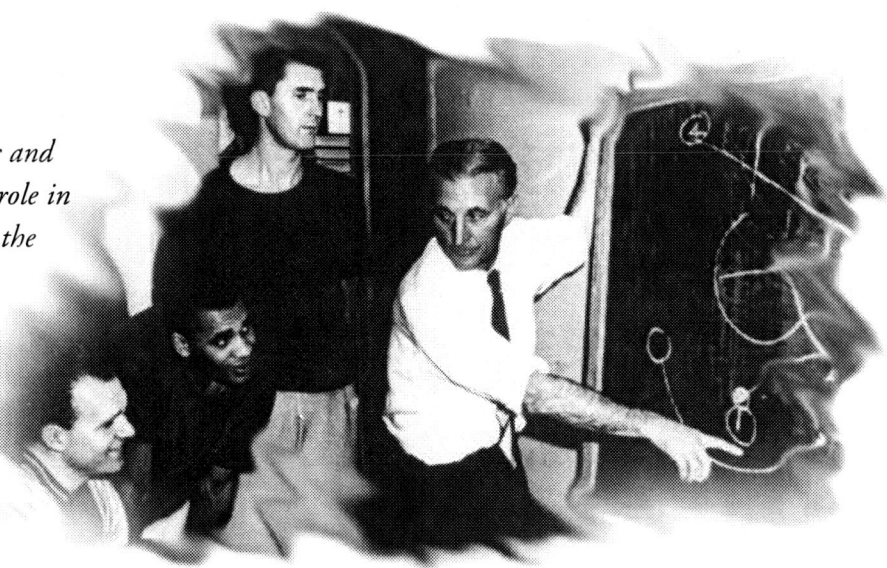

BIOGRAPHY

Born: March 2, 1896 in Grafton, West Virginia

Died: May 20, 1983

Inducted into the Naismith Basketball Hall of Fame in 1968

Clair Bee coached at Rider, Long Island, and in the NBA with the Baltimore Bullets. As a college coach, he won over 80 percent of his games, including two NIT titles. In the 1930's and 1940's, Bee's name was synonymous with the game of basketball. At LIU, he directed the Blackbirds into the national limelight. LIU appeared in the NIT seven times and recorded undefeated seasons in 1935-36 and 1938-39. His LIU teams won 139 straight home games. Bee developed the 1-3-1 zone defense and was instrumental in the adoption of the 3-second rule. He also was a proponent of the 24-second clock in the NBA. Bee authored more than fifty books on basketball including the Chip Hilton's Sport Stories for Young People series. Bee was the director of Kutsher's Sports Academy and Camps and served as athletic director at the New York Military Academy for thirteen years. Bee was enshrined in the Naismith Memorial Basketball Hall of Fame in 1968.

...SCOUTING REPORT.....SCOUTING REPORT.....

Clair Bee...

Clair Bee was one of the most respected basketball coaches in the history of the game. He earned fame during a time when college basketball grew from a sport played before a handful of spectators in school gymnasiums to the capacity crowds of more than 18,000 at Madison Square Garden.

Bee, a small, handsome man, was a scholarly coach who held five degrees and authored more than fifty books. In his writing, he created an ideal athlete, the fictional character Chip Hilton (a Norman Rockwell sports hero for young men) who demonstrated honesty, intelligence, industriousness, athleticism, and diligence.

Bee tried to instill those same qualities in the teams that he coached. He accepted his first collegiate job at Rider College in 1928. He directed his basketball teams to a record of 53-7 and his football teams to a record of 17-7-1. From there, Bee established a national power at Long Island University, where he became a New York icon. His basketball teams won over 80 percent of their games during his 18-year tenure and received seven NIT berths. LIU won the NIT in 1939 and 1941 and recorded undefeated seasons in 1935-36 and 1938-39. Stanford broke LIU's 43-game winning streak in 1936, in a game that saw Hank Luisetti introduce the one-handed shot in the East. Over a 13-year span, Bee's LIU teams compiled a 222-3 home record. In those years, his teams ran off winning streaks of: 43, 38, 28, 26, and 20, plus 139 straight home wins at LIU.

As a youngster growing up in Grafton, West Virginia, Bee suffered from tuberculosis, and his family physician urged him to spend as much time outside as possible. "That prescription," said Bee, "helped to push me into sports." (Padwe, 1970, p. 145)

To stay physically active, Bee went to the YMCA. "All they had for basketball was a cage-like area with chicken wire hoops at each end," said Bee. "There wasn't any net and few rules. It was almost like playing football." The games were crude and dictated by the confines of makeshift courts, but they laid the foundation for Bee's passion for basketball. "Even when I was a small kid, I always wanted be a teacher and coach," said Bee. (Griffith, 1977)

By the time Bee was ten years old, basketball had become an important part of his life. He and his friends used to sneak into a church gymnasium and practice for hours. "After a while, the priests caught on, but they turned their heads the other way and let us keep playing," remembered Bee.

Propelled by energy and intensity, Bee played football, basketball, and baseball at Grafton H.S. (WV) and even wrote a sports fiction story at the age of fourteen for the high-school annual. He quit high school to serve in World War I. When the war ended, Bee came home to finish his education.

Bee had an amazing capacity for long, intensive hours of physical or mental effort. He completed a full four-year liberal arts course at Waynesburg College (PA) in three years and, at the same time, participated in three sports. In his final year, Bee was the acting academic registrar and faculty athletic manager.

Bee has been called one of basketball's greatest strategist and teachers. Hall of Fame coach Frank McGuire praised Bee's contributions to the game. "He was one of the most brilliant basketball coaches ever, on a par with Nat Holman," said McGuire. "He was always going out of his way to help young coaches coming up." (Young, 1983)

Hall of Famer Bob Knight received one of his coaching cornerstones from Clair Bee. "It was the important role of teaching in basketball—teaching the game's fundamentals and philosophies, including all things involved in a team approach and a determination throughout the team, not just to play well, but to win." (Knight, 2002, p. 15)

"He pounded into me," continued Knight, "that the very first thing you had to be was a teacher, and you had to teach kids how to play basketball. You had to teach them the game. His .826 winning percentage did not just happen. The sustaining, significant thing with him was his determination to win." (Knight, 2002, p. 16)

Bee was a pioneer in equality and civil rights. Black athlete Dolly King played for Bee at LIU and was later the first black in the NBL. When LIU played Marshall at

.....SCOUTING REPORT.....SCOUTING REPORT...

Huntington, West Virginia, King was told he couldn't eat with the team in the hotel's dining room. Coach Bee immediately marched his entire team into the kitchen, sat everybody down, and said, "serve us." He would not tolerate unfair treatment due to race or religion.

As chairman of the NABC Rules Recommendation Committee, Bee originated the recommendation for the 3-second rule in basketball. To demonstrate the importance of his recommendation, Bee had his LIU team play a regular season game against St. John's using the 3-second rule.

Bee believed in a seven-man playing group, and he clearly defined roles for each of his players based on their strengths. He claimed that he found it easier to practice with a group this size. He continually exchanged players, until the seven knew each other's moves perfectly. "I believe teamwork is paramount." stated Bee. "You cannot get precision teamwork with a large number of men; it has to be achieved with the same men practicing and working together as much as possible." (Padwe, 1970, p. 148)

Bee's life took a drastic turn in 1951 when he learned that three of his LIU stars were involved in a point-shaving scandal. As an aftermath of the scandal, LIU canceled its future schedule, and Bee, cloaked in shame, assumed an administrative position. It was the darkest period of Bee's life. Addressing an audience in Newport News, Virginia that same year, Bee told the audience, many of whom were coaches, "We—you and I—have flunked. We have not done the job that was expected of us in training young people. I am not bitter. I am hurt, hurt desperately. When I was told that three of my boys had sold themselves, it was a deep bereavement. I am not ashamed to say that I wept. It was then that something died within me." (Goldaper, 1983)

Bee looked back at the scandal and the pressure of big-time sports and said, "I was so absorbed in the victory grail that I lost sight of the educational purposes of athletics. They say the loudest psalm singer is a reformed sinner... I still believe competitive sports have a high educational value when handled properly. I guess I was too concerned with my own doings. Each coach says it couldn't happen to him. I refused to believe it when it happened, because I never suspected a player. You know, in my opinion, a coach is like a father. He is the last to recognize the weaknesses of his son, and if he recognizes imperfections, he can't believe it, because his hopes for the youngster are so high." (Padwe, 1970, p. 150)

While Bee is best remembered for his coaching exploits, it must not be overlooked that he was an outstanding academician and administrator. Bee originated the idea of all-sports summer camps for boys and girls. The first operation was launched at Manhattan Beach in Brooklyn in 1934. The project was an instant success and had an enrollment of 1000 campers the first year. Bee also initiated the establishment of the legendary Kutsher's Sports Camp in upstate New York.

Bee coached the Baltimore Bullets in the NBA from 1952 to 1954 and was a proponent of the 24-second shot clock.

After retiring from the coaching ranks, Bee remained close to the game that he loved by conducting clinics, operating summer camps, writing basketball books, and assisting and mentoring young coaches. He mentored Bob Knight at Army while Bee was Athletic Director of nearby New York Military Academy. Knight later joined his mentor in the Naismith Memorial Basketball Hall of Fame.

Clair Bee, the man that gave his complete life to basketball, died in 1983.

SOURCE

Bee, Clair. Vertical Files, Archives. Naismith Memorial Basketball Hall of Fame. Springfield, MA.

Griffith, Gerrill (1977, May 25). He Gained Fame in Basketball, But Started in Baseball. *Clair Bee Testimonial Program.*

Goldaper, Sam (1983, May 21). Clair Bee, Ex-L.I.U. Coach, Dies; Gained Basketball Hall of Fame. *New York Times.*

Padwe, Sandy. (1970). *Basketball's Hall of Fame.* Englewood Cliffs, N.J.: Prentice-Hall.

Young, Dick. (1983, May 21). Clair Was Truly the King Bee. *New York Post.*

LESSONS FROM THIS LEGEND...

THE HISTORY AND DEVELOPMENT OF THE ZONE DEFENSE

By Clair Bee

"Stop! Look! Listen! If the discussion centers about the effects of the zone defense on basketball—beware! Statements you make will be misunderstood; discretion at such times may prove the better part of valor. For probably no other sport can boast or bemoan a game principle that has been debated so thoroughly and so long without losing its importance through rule changes or obsolescence. The zone reigns supreme as basketball's perennial point of issue.

During its popularity or unpopularity, whichever you wish, the zone defense has been the cause of "sit-down" strikes; booing and heckling on the part of spectators; feuds between towns; 1 to 0 scores, as well as impersonal and personal arguments between coaches, writers, and rule-makers.

Many coaches contend that the use of the zone defense will ruin spectator interest in basketball. Some believe that it violates all defensive principles, while others claim it is the only defense permitted by strict interpretation of the rules.

Basketball nomenclature is not at all uniform and has been "garbled" to such an extent that it is best to accompany debatable phrases by description. It is not uncommon to find two coaches at odds in an argument, because the terms and topic under discussion have not been clearly defined. Certain coaches believe only the "zone" can be called a "team defense." They base their argument upon the coordination required of zone defensive players through talking, shifting positions, expanding or contracting in unison, etc. Other coaches correctly feel man-to-man defense is a team defense. They also cite the necessity of talking, switching, and shifting in unison.

A man-to-man defense may be defined as one in which each defensive player is assigned or lines up opposite a particular opponent and, during the rest of the game, personally endeavors to keep this adversary from scoring. A temporary shift or switch of men may occur when the defensive player is blocked or screened. At the first opportunity, however, the original opponent is again played.

When a zone defense is in use, players are stationed in front of their defensive basket in certain territories. The players concentrate on the ball and shift to new positions depending upon its movement. No particular player is opposed unless he enters a scoring zone. Man-to-man tactics are then used to keep him from scoring or receiving the ball. Perhaps a little defensive history will clear up the background of this discussion.

Dr. James Naismith intended basketball to be an open game with a minimum of personal contact. Defense in the early days of the game was of the man-to-man type. Each player contacted his opponent as quickly as possible when his team lost possession of the ball.

Confusion arose because Dr. Naismith stressed the principle that players should "play the ball." This resulted in a school of thought that adopted that phrase as authority for exclusive use of the zone defense. Other popularized phrases referred to man-to-man tactics.

In an early publication, Dr. Naismith described the play of the game in these words; "When the opponents have the ball, stick to your man like glue. Cover him so effectively that the ball cannot by any manner or means be passed into his hands. Follow him anywhere and prevent him from getting the ball. When the ball is thrown, then try and get it yourself if it comes your way. If, instead of playing this way, you run off to block the man who has the ball, while you may make it harder for him to make a good throw, still you left your man uncovered, and the ball can and probably will be thrown to him."
(Naismith, 1894, p. 16)

The use of the term "your man" and the description of defensive play described by the inventor of the game provide substantiation for arguments by proponents of man-to-man defense.

Individualized man-to-man type of offense and defense continued until about 1910. Center and game plays were evident, but the offensive and defensive formations common today were unknown. When offensive teams began massing players under the basket, such concentration was countered by the massing of defensive players. This was called "five-man" defense. The writer likes to remember basketball of that particular period. One of the guards was known as the "standing guard," he stood; the other as the "running guard," he ran; the "center" jumped; the "feeding forward," fed; the "shooting forward," made all the baskets, shot all the fouls, was captain of the team, president of the class, married the banker's daughter, became governor, always believed he should have been President, and what was more tragic, got all the "write-ups." The above is a little exaggerated, but players of those days will recognize the description.

The "standing guard" was in full charge of the defense. He stood like a "Rock of

LESSONS FROM THIS LEGEND...

Gibraltar" under the basket and directed his teammates to their defensive positions. On the offense he was stationed in the rearcourt and served as a safety post to which the ball could be passed when other players were closely pressed.

Shortly before 1910, a new offense and defense formation made its appearance in the East. It was known as position style. It permitted players more time to rest—especially on the defense, since they were not compelled to follow an opponent unless he was in possession of the ball. Offensively and defensively, the team shifted back and forth as a whole. The center and the two forwards formed the front line, and the two guards, stationed near the basket, became the back line of defense. The court was divided into three vertical lanes. The two forwards and the guards played in the outside lanes, and the center took charge of the middle area. The center could move from one basket to the other and thus laid the groundwork for the basic zones—the 3-2, the 2-3, and the 2-1-2. The center often dropped back under the basket to assist the guards. This led to the development of the rebound triangle.

The writer's first experience with the zone defense was in 1914. School schedules did not begin until January, and high school players filled in on the YMCA team for preseason experience whenever possible. Around Christmas time, the Grafton "Y" had scheduled a game with the Bristol, West Virginia "town" team. Several members of the "high" squad, including the writer, were asked to go along.

A blizzard was in progress—the train was late,—and it was a two-mile walk through deep snow to the "town hall" where the game was to be played. A girl's game, scheduled as a preliminary, had been dragged out for two hours in an effort to keep the spectators (all fifty of them) from going home.

Green pine lumber had been use in the floor construction, and it was as slippery as glass. The game was hard played, and practically everything except a "full nelson" was used. The smart player in those days wore about all of his football uniform except the shoes. Officials were wise too—they tossed up the ball at center and then kept out of the way.

Both teams were using a man-to-man defense, but found it difficult to keep up with opponents because of the sap from the pine flooring. The players hit the floor with their backs more often than with their feet. When the second half started, the Bristol team did not use the man-to-man defense. The players stationed themselves in certain zones which they did not leave until a shot was taken. The new defense was crude, but so far as those who played that night were concerned, it presented a new development in basketball.

Cam Henderson, who was the coach of the Bristol team, said he got the idea between halves while discussing the slippery floor with his players. Incidentally, he has successfully used the zone defense ever since in his coaching at Davis-Elkins and Marshall College in West Virginia.

Midway between 1910 and 1920, the alternate rise and fall in popularity of each type of defense was initiated. Both had periods of success. In the early 1920's, the zone was about to be recognized as superior. Stalling tactics by the offense then countered this popularity, and the man-to-man regained and held first standing for some years. In 1932, the zone received a "blood transfusion" when the rule-makers eliminated stalling tactics by means of the ten-second rule. This legislative brilliance forced the team in possession to advance the ball across the middle of the court within ten seconds.

Before this new rule was adopted, teams using the zone defense and behind in the score were forced to abandon their defensive half of the court and play the ball. This weakened the effectiveness of the zone. After the ten-second rule was passed, teams could fall back under their basket secure in the knowledge that the ball must be advanced. Dr. Naismith was bitterly opposed to this rule.

The zone received further assistance in 1936. A three-second restriction was placed upon an offensive player in the free-throw area. The writer originated this rule after watching a "wrestling match" staged by Leroy Edwards of the University of Kentucky and "King-Kong" Klein of New York University in a game played in Madison Square Garden on January 5, 1936. Edwards was the high scorer for Kentucky and used the under-basket pivot to score his points. He outweighed Klein by fifty pounds, but they struggled forty minutes to a draw. NYU won by a score of 23-22. Much bitterness existed during and after the game, and the pivot problem "shook every backboard in the country."

The three-second provision was tested in the St. Johns-Long Island University game played January 25, 1936 in Madison Square Garden. Ben Kramer, captain of the undefeated "Blackbird" team of 1935-36, was the leading scorer of the East in the previous season using the pivot attack. He was not permitted in the lane for more than three seconds, with or without the ball, during this game. There was no holding and no complaints. The provision applying to the lane was recommended to the Rules Committee through the medium of the National Basketball Coaches Association. The rules committee incorporated not only the lane in the rule but also included the free-throw circle. This was, of course, more than had been "bargained for."

The offense lost one of its most potent attack weapons through this "no parking" ordinance, while the defense was given legal protection in a dangerous scoring area. These rule changes encouraged zone enthusiasts.

Fully as important as the rules was the development of block and screen plays. The man-to-man defense is peculiarly susceptible to those offensive tactics. A great many coaches met these attack methods with

LESSONS FROM THIS LEGEND...

some form of zone. Blocking and screening tactics may be used in attacking a zone, but they are more effectively used against the man-to-man defense.

The zone defense has weaknesses, but it also possesses strengths. A good zone will give most teams and coaches a "headache." Players and coaches who denounce the zone in basketball are usually unfamiliar with its use and methods of attacking it.

The cry that use of the zone defense would ruin basketball is more popular than ever, although a large percent of high schools and colleges throughout the country use some form of the zone defense.

The writer uses man-to-man as the basic defense. Nevertheless, zone formations are studied, practiced, and used many times by his teams during the season. During the 1941-42 season, the writer won twenty-five out of twenty-seven games using the 1-3-1 zone. Although the scores of zone games have not been as high as those in which the man-to-man defense was utilized, it would be unfair to say they were less interesting.

It is not difficult to have low-scoring games under the present rules. Stalling tactics can still be used in the front court. Fortunately, most teams are offense-minded and attack quickly and eagerly. Furthermore, many teams that now employ the zone use offensive tactics—endeavoring to intercept the ball and score quickly. This leads to an open zone—using the offense and taking chances—rather than use of the ancient formula of retreat and mass under the basket.

The man-to-man and the zone defenses, with their variations, belong in basketball. The intelligent coach recognizes the strength and weakness of each defense and impartially adapts either both, or a variation, to the material available.

As this opinion is being written, a disturbing recollection comes to mind. During a ten-year period, LIU lost but three games on their home court. All three defeats were at the hands of teams using the zone defense.

SOURCE

Bee, Clair. (1942). *Zone Defense and Attack*. New York: A.S. Barnes.

Naismith, James. (1894, January). *Basketball*. Spaulding's Library.

LESSONS FROM THIS LEGEND...

THE ONE-THREE-ONE ZONE DEFENSE

By Clair Bee

The 1-3-1 zone has been a favorite of the Long Island University teams since 1937. It was developed because of a defeat suffered in the National AAU tournament. LIU was fortunate in winning the Metropolitan AAU championship in 1937 with a team composed of freshmen and varsity reserves. The varsity had been a senior team and was not used in the tournament so players who would represent the school the following year could gain experience. In Denver, the "neophytes" won their way to the quarter-finals where they met the Denver Safeways, the eventual winners of the championship.

The center and pivot player of the Safeways was Bob "Ace" Gruening, 6'6" in height and well proportioned. LIU had no experienced player to cope with him, and in the first few minutes of the game, he scored 12 points. Between halves, it was decided to try a method just then becoming popular—playing in front of a dangerous pivot man. A second defensive man was used behind Gruening under the basket. A zone defense including these tactics was used during the second half and practically eliminated further under-the-basket scoring. The Safeways were far too good for the inexperienced Blackbirds and had no difficulty winning. Nevertheless, the defeat developed a type of zone defense which has been a standby ever since.

The 1-3-1 zone attempts to keep three defensive players between the ball and the basket. Should an opponent manage to elude a front-line chaser, a second defensive player will charge the ball and confront him. Behind this second man, will be a third player to protect the under-basket area. This three-in-line principle is applied at every opportunity.

The 1-3-1 zone is especially strong in the free-throw area and under the basket. This zone is not strong against long and corner shots. Since these are two of the most difficult shots in the game, their use should not be too effective, unless the opponents possess unusual shooting ability. If defensive players employ their slides consistently and move as a team, very few close shots will be available. Offensively, the set-up is such that the quick-break may be used immediately and efficiently. In practically every shift, one player is in position to become the leading quick-break player, with two teammates in position to form the second-line of the attack.

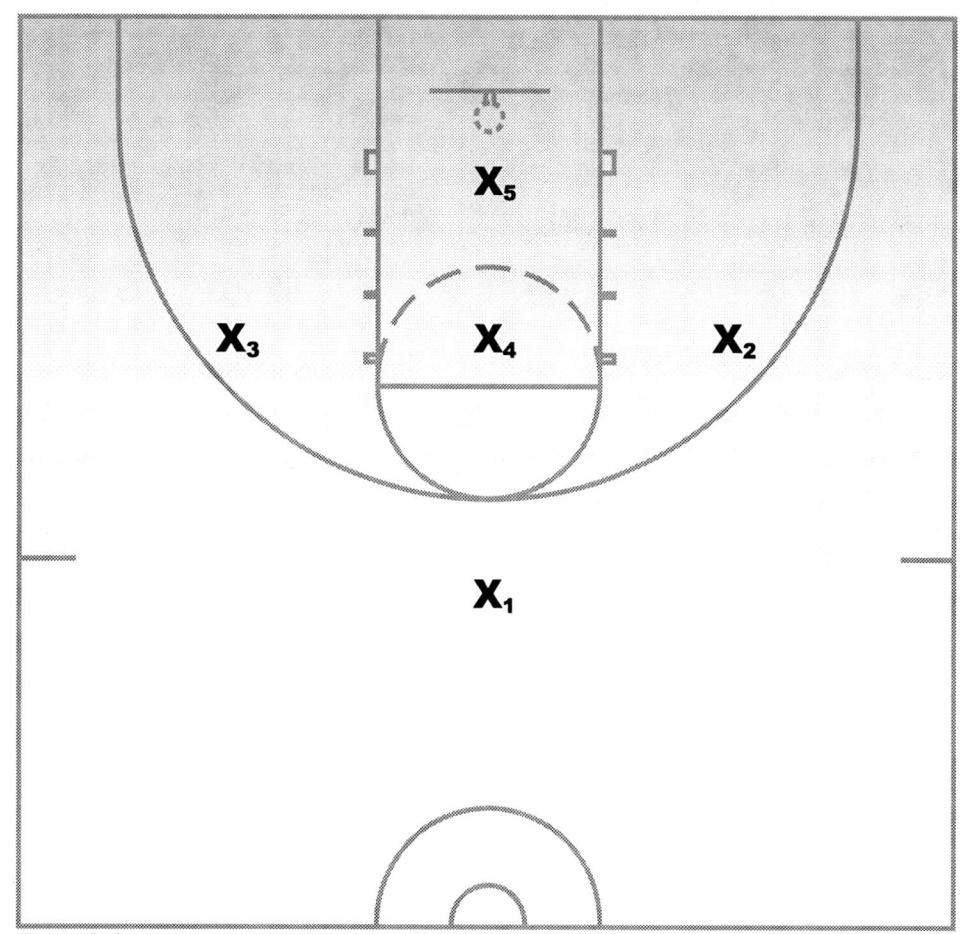

Bee 1.0 BASIC ALIGNMENT

LESSONS FROM THIS LEGEND...

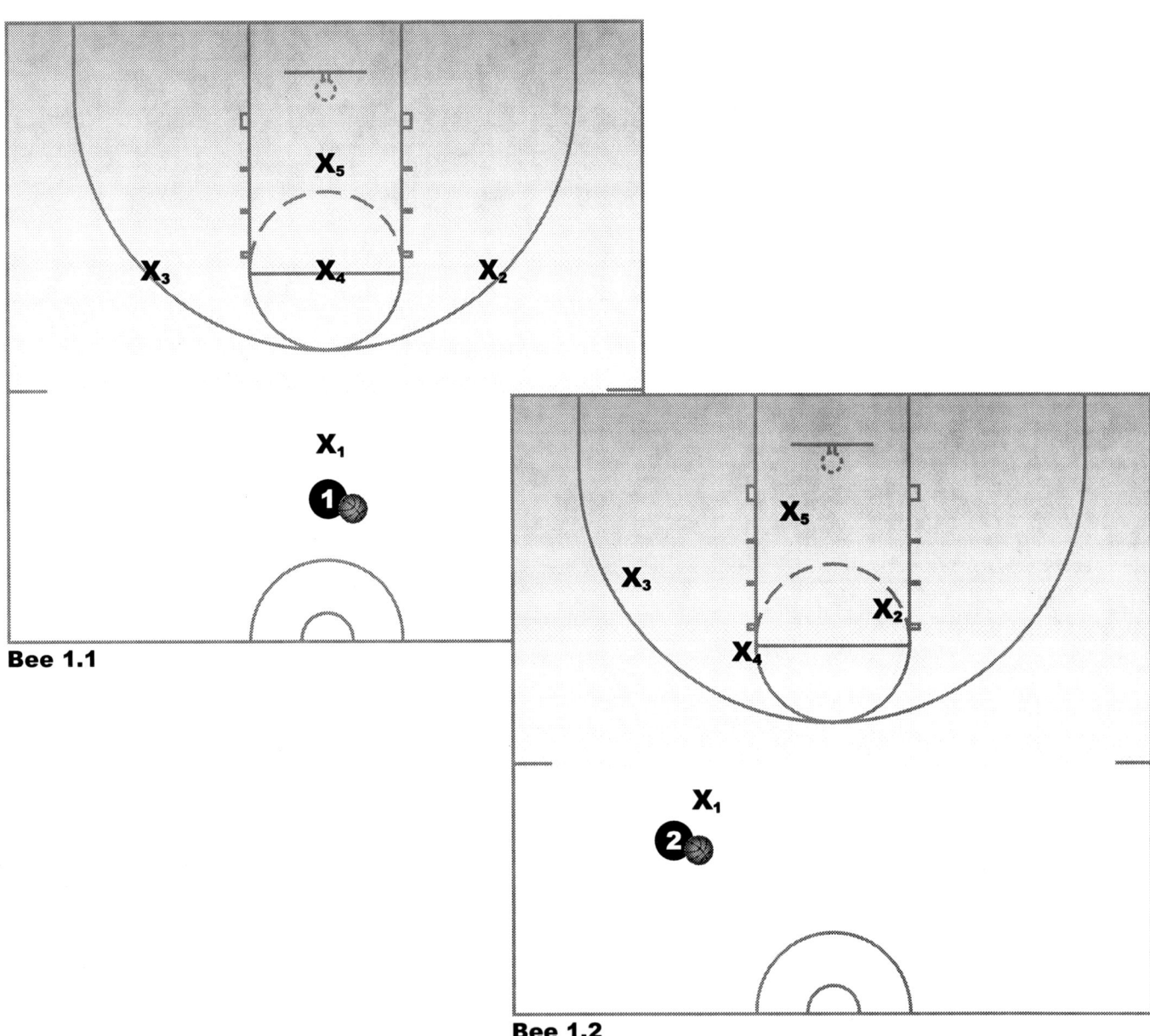

Bee 1.1

Bee 1.2

The 1-3-1 is a defensive zone. All players help out in the defense and think about the quick-break only when possession of the ball is assured. Regardless of the use of revolving or straight slides, the three-in-line principle must be observed. Players quickly grasp the theory that the ball must be guarded first, and there must be three players between the ball and the basket.

The initial alignment of the 1-3-1 zone is shown in **Diagram 1.0**. Player requirements are not unusual. Should a coach be fortunate in having two goaltenders, they should occupy positions X4 and X5. The under-basket position will be alternated when a right or left corner defense is required. These two players—X4 and X5—are the rebound guards. Slides often shift them away from the basket but not too far for rebound work. Defense chaser X1 must be rugged, aggressive, and conditioned to maintain a strong pace for the entire game. His territory and slides extend across the entire court, and tremendous leg power is necessary. Players X2 and X3 should possess the usual chaser and quick-break characteristics of wing players.

Passes to pivot men at the free-throw line or under the basket are practically impossible. Should the ball get through, two or three defensive men can surround the receiver. Pivot attacks are discouraged by the three-in-line principle. Consequently, the ball is usually passed around outside the zone until a long or corner shot can be obtained.

LESSONS FROM THIS LEGEND...

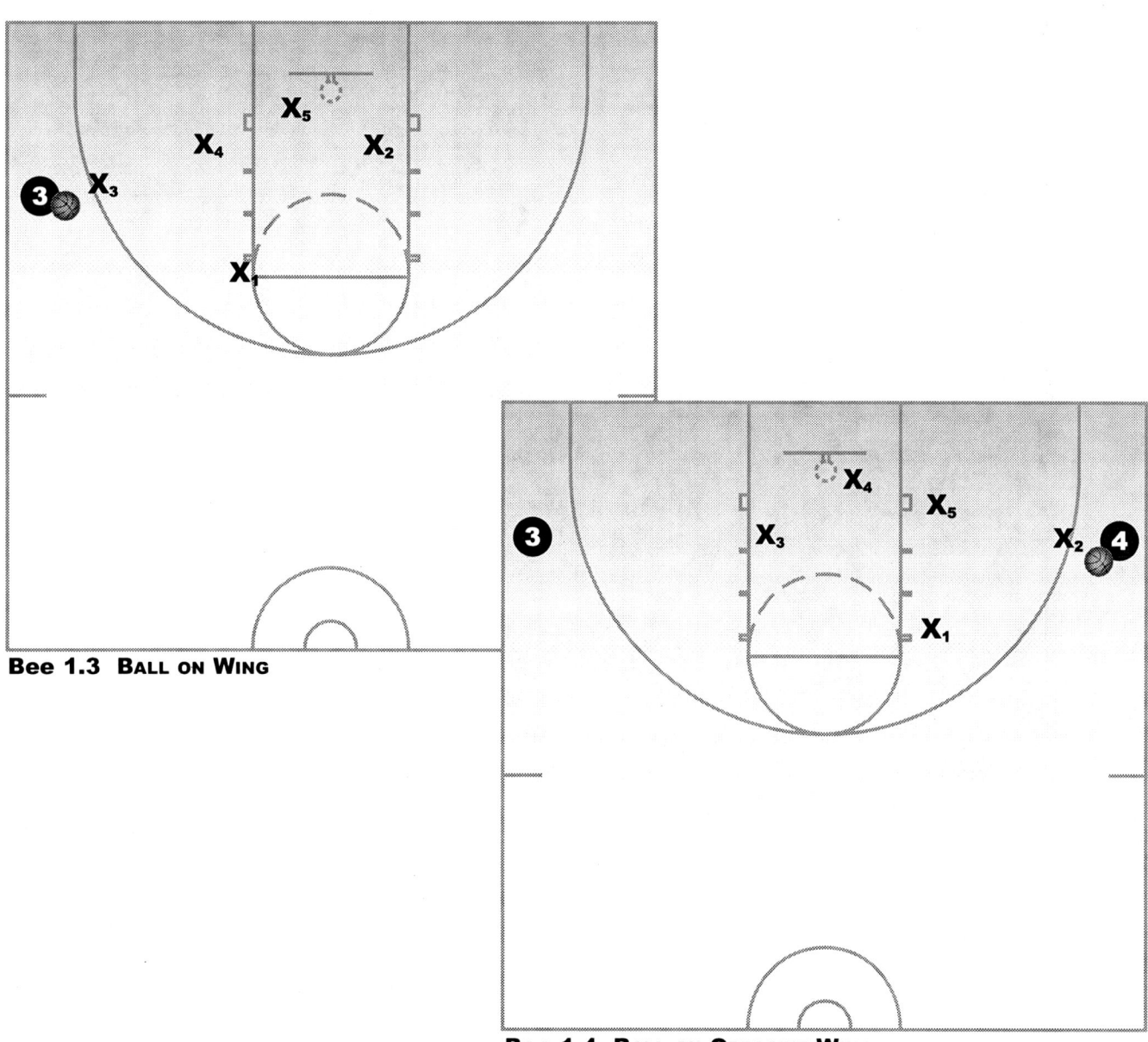

Bee 1.3 Ball on Wing

Bee 1.4 Ball on Opposite Wing

STRAIGHT SLIDES IN THE ONE-THREE-ONE ZONE

The straight slides necessary to maintain the three-in-line principle are illustrated in the following figures:

Diagram 1.1
O1 is in possession of the ball. Note the formation of the 1-3-1. (Three defensive players are between the ball and the basket.)

Diagram 1.2
O2 has the ball. X1 is the chaser and has followed the pass. X1, X4, and X5 form the three-in-line principle. X2 and X3 have adjusted according to the position of the ball.

Diagram 1.3
O3 has the ball. He was rushed by X3. Teammates X4 and X5 fell in line. Note the positions of X1 and X2 (defensive zone principles).

Diagram 1.4
O3 makes a difficult pass to O4, who was covered by X2. Defensive teammates X5 and X4 backed him up. Should O4 get around X2, he will be met by X5.

SOURCE
Bee, Clair. (1942). *Zone Defense and Attack*. New York: A.S. Barnes.

LEGACY OF
Lou Carnesecca

- Coached 24 years at St. John's and led everyone of his teams into postseason tournament play (18 NCAA tournaments and 6 NITs).

- Directed St. John's to the NIT championship in 1989.

- Demonstrated enthusiasm, passion, and respect for the basketball profession.

- Maximized the talents of gifted players within a team concept.

- Became the 30th coach in NCAA history to reach the 500-victory mark.

- Led the New York Nets to the 1972 ABA Finals.

LOU CARNESECCA

"The one thing I have always asked of any player is that he give me 100 percent."
—Lou Carnesecca

BIOGRAPHY

Born: January 5, 1925 in New York, New York

Inducted into the Naismith Basketball Hall of Fame in 1992

Lou Carnesecca was the head coach at St. John's University for 24 years and led every one of his teams to postseason play (18 NCAA tournaments and 6 NITs). He compiled a 526-200 record during his head coaching tenure at St. John's. Carnesecca was an assistant to future Hall of Fame coach Joe Lapchick for seven years, before becoming the head coach in 1965. He left the college game to coach the New York Nets from 1970 to 1973 and led New York to the ABA Finals in 1972. Carnesecca returned as head coach to St. John's in 1973 and stayed until he retired in 1992. The highly energetic Carnesecca directed St. John's to an NIT championship in 1989 and a Final Four appearance in 1985. He was selected National Coach of the Year by the NABC and USBWA in 1983 and 1985. He was named Big East Conference Coach of the Year on three occasions. Carnesecca served in the Coast Guard during World War II and then attended St. John's University. He played baseball for legendary coach Frank McGuire and led his team to the 1949 College World Series. After graduation, Carnesecca's first coaching position was on the high-school ranks at his alma mater, St. Ann's Academy. Carnesecca is a member of the New York City Sports Hall of Fame and was enshrined in the Naismith Memorial Basketball Hall of Fame in 1992.

...SCOUTING REPORT.....SCOUTING REPORT.....

Lou Carnesecca...

Lou Carnesecca was affectionately called "Looie" by sports fans everywhere. "Looie" developed a passion for sports at an early age and played whichever sport was in season, every available moment. Carnesecca did this against the wishes of his father who thought that sports were a waste of time. His parents came to New York City from Italy, and Italian was the only language spoken in the home. Carnesecca did not start speaking English until he was six years old.

Carnesecca attended St. Ann's Academy and knew even then that he wanted to become a basketball coach. He was highly influenced by future Hall of Fame official Dave Tobey. Tobey had an illustrious career, both as a coach and as an official, and authored one of the first books on basketball officiating. Carnesecca played both basketball and baseball at St. Ann's but admitted that he was not a very good athlete. "I was a lousy basketball player," stated Carnesecca. "It took me three years to make the junior varsity, and when I finally made it, I think it was because the coach, Brother James, realized I loved the game so much that he put me on the team. I didn't play very much. Instead, I learned the game from the seat of my pants, which, looking back, may have been a blessing in disguise." (Carnesecca, 1988, p. 25)

When Carnesecca graduated from St. Ann's in 1943, the United States was engaged in World War II. Carnesecca joined the Coast Guard and traveled to Okinawa, Guam, Yokohama, and Tokyo. He was discharged at the end of World War II and enrolled at St. John's University. Carnesecca was a second baseman on the baseball team and played in the 1949 College World Series. St. John's legendary basketball coach Frank McGuire also coached the baseball team. McGuire recognized Carnesecca's love for the game of basketball and put him to work refereeing scrimmages, scouting players, and scouting opponents. "It was Frank who gave me my chance," said Carnesecca. "I've never forgotten that. Thanks to him, I always saw the game from a coach's point of view." (Carnesecca, 1988, p. 34)

Carnesecca's first job was at his alma mater, St. Ann's Academy. He worked around the clock to become the best coach possible. "Once I had the job at St. Ann's, it was total immersion in basketball," stated Carnesecca. "It became a passion with me, a fixation, a mania. I don't think I spent one day, or part of a day, when I wasn't thinking about basketball. If there ever was a fanatic, I was it. Basketball was something I loved and couldn't get enough of." (Carnesecca, 1988, p. 40)

Carnesecca worked for Hall of Fame coach Joe Lapchick at St. John's for seven years before becoming the head coach in 1965. Carnesecca gave credit to St. John's coaches Lapchick, Buck Freeman, and Frank McGuire for establishing his coaching philosophy. They taught Carnesecca that talented players win games and that coaches should never think that they are geniuses. Freeman believed that 65-75 percent of a team's success was determined by the talent of its players, 15-20 percent was coaching, and the remaining 5-20 percent was luck. Lapchick was a low-key, humble man and despised the so-called geniuses of the game, the coaches who thought they were so smart and better than everybody else. Lapchick was a brilliant strategist and a master psychologist who got the maximum out of his players. Carnesecca called Lapchick, Freeman, and McGuire "three of basketball's greatest minds." (Carnesecca, 1988, p. 7)

Carnesecca always believed that players win, not the coach. He never criticized his players in the press because that destroyed confidence and team unity. Carnesecca was a master at building the confidence of his team members. "My way of trying to motivate my players is to tell them how good they can be; to build them up, instead of tearing them down," said Carnesecca. "Tearing them down can be counter-productive. I try to put myself in their place. Nobody likes to hear about his faults, especially in public. I can always do that in private. I'm a believer in the old adage that you can attract more bees with honey than you can with vinegar." (Carnesecca, 1988, p. 206)

The first quality that Carnesecca looked for in a recruit was talent. "There's no substitute for talent," stated Carnesecca. "After that, I'm interested in his attitude. Is he coachable? Will he get along with the other players on the team? Is he selfish or unselfish? I want to know what his work habits are. I want to know about his character,

.....SCOUTING REPORT......SCOUTING REPORT...

his family background, and what kind of person he is." (Carnesecca, 1988, p. 123)

On game night, the animated and energetic Carnesecca often wore brown pants, a blue button-down shirt, and a tie. Spectators could watch Carnesecca's tie and know how the game was going. Most of the time, he loosened the knot, and it was hanging around his chest. The tougher the game, the lower the knot. Later in his coaching career, Carnesecca's colorful sweaters became his trademark.

The biggest change in basketball during Carnesecca's career was the size, strength, and skill of the players. Carnesecca said, "When I first started in the game, the "big man" on a team was maybe 6 foot 7 inches or 6 foot 8 inches. Joe Lapchick was the big man of his day at 6 foot 5 inches." (Carnesecca, 1988, p. 207)

With so many more bigger, taller, and faster players, Carnesecca recommended increasing the size of the court. He was not in favor of raising the height of the basket, because no matter how high you raise it, the rules will always favor the taller player. Carnesecca campaigned for years for a red, white, and blue basketball, similar to the ball used in the American Basketball Association. He thought it would be so much easier for the fans in the cheap seats to see the ball, and it would make the game more interesting and appealing to the spectators.

Few coaches have ever been as happy in their jobs as Carnesecca was. He had a passion for the game and a deep respect for the coaching profession. Carnesecca was a man of great depth, compassion, and warmth.

SOURCE

Carnesecca, Lou. Vertical Files, Archives. Naismith Memorial Basketball Hall of Fame. Springfield, MA.

Carnesecca, Lou and Phil Pepe. (1988) *Louie In Season*. New York: McGraw-Hill.

LESSONS FROM THIS LEGEND...

DIAGNOSTIC DEFENSIVE DRILLS

By Lou Carnesecca

The purpose of these drills is to help you improve your man-to-man defense by incorporating three-and four-man drills into your daily workouts.

Rather than emphasizing basic individual fundamentals, like stance and foot position, these exercises deal with various defensive problems and assignments.

These drills will cover how to defend the one-on-one moves; how to overplay; how to handle screens; and finally, how to beat the player to the spot. We will also be able to key on boxing out and also react from offense to defense, and vice-versa.

In a short time, these drills will enable you, as a coach, to diagnose your players' defensive weaknesses and then make the necessary corrections.

Since you are working with three and four people per drill, you can easily identify the error and correct it immediately. The drills are flexible in that you don't need the whole team; you can work with three or four players or with part of the team. Alternate two of the four exercises into your daily workouts for about 10-12 minutes a day, and by doing this, you will be preparing your players both mentally and physically for most defensive maneuvers. You will also be able to check the quickness and aggressiveness of your players and those who are prone to commit costly fouls.

RULES OF OPERATION

1. In the 3-player drills (one-on-one from the side, one-on-one from the middle, and one-on-one overplay) the ball is kept alive until someone scores. Then, the next three players will begin the drill.

2. In the two-on-two drills, if the offensive team retrieves their own rebound, they continue playing until they score. Should the defensive team either steal the ball or stop the offense from scoring, the next group in line starts the drill.

3. The defensive players should be set before the offense begins to play.

4. The coach calls all fouls, and in the beginning dictates whether the offense should drive or take perimeter shots. This will zero in on the particular phase of defensive play that needs to be emphasized.

5. In the beginning, I would suggest that you don't call fouls, but after two weeks, when defensive players commit a costly foul, make them repeat the drill. This will help make them aware how costly fouls can be.

6. At the coach's discretion, any time the offense scores, the coach can make the defenders repeat the drill. This continues until the defense successfully stops the offense.

LESSONS FROM THIS LEGEND...

ONE-ON-ONE: SIDE

Basic Set-up: As shown in **Diagram 1.0**, the ballhandler, 1, is at the top of the circle. 2 and 3 take positions at the foul-line extended.

1 passes to 2 and goes behind 2 and takes an offensive position on the side of the court. As 1 is passing to 2, 3 fakes baseline and comes to the foul-line area to receive a pass from 2; after 2 passes to 3, he cuts around 3 and takes a helpside defensive position in the lane area.

With 2 in a helping position, 3 passes to 1 and goes to cover him defensively. 1 can either drive right or left, with 2 helping out should 1 get by 3. (See **Diagram 1.1**)
Remember: 1 should not start his offensive moves until 3 and 2 are in position and ready to play defense.

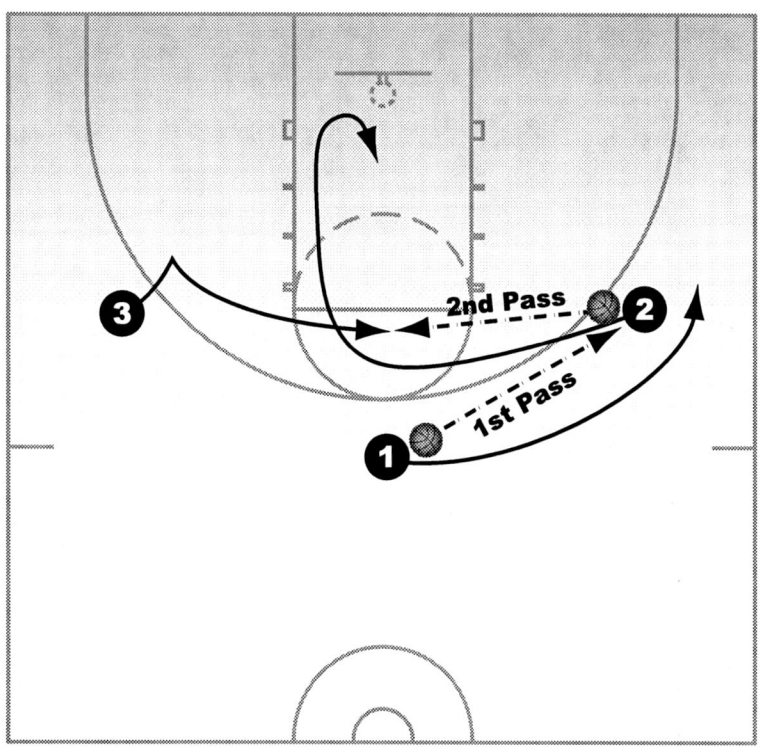

Carnesecca 1.0

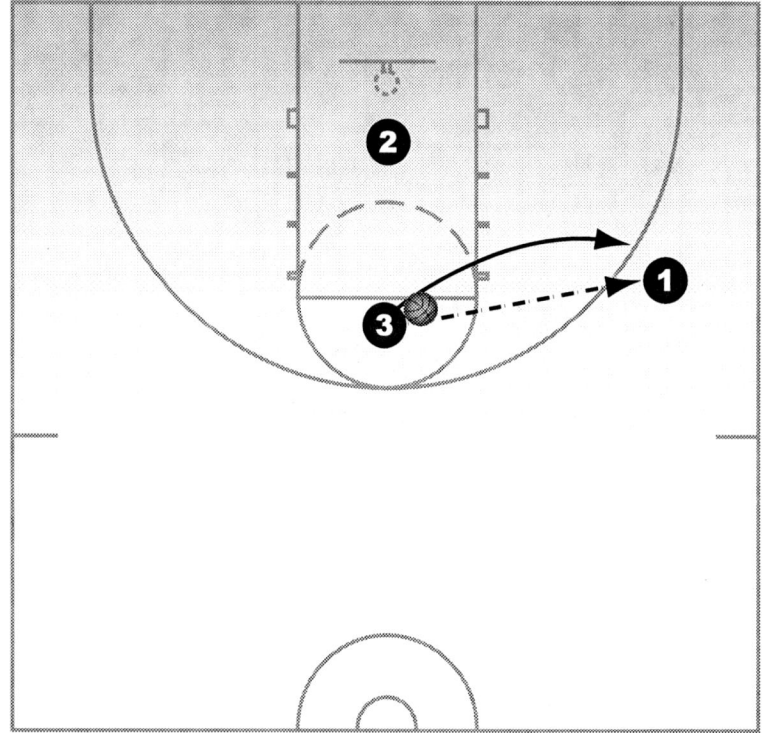

Carnesecca 1.1

LESSONS FROM THIS LEGEND...

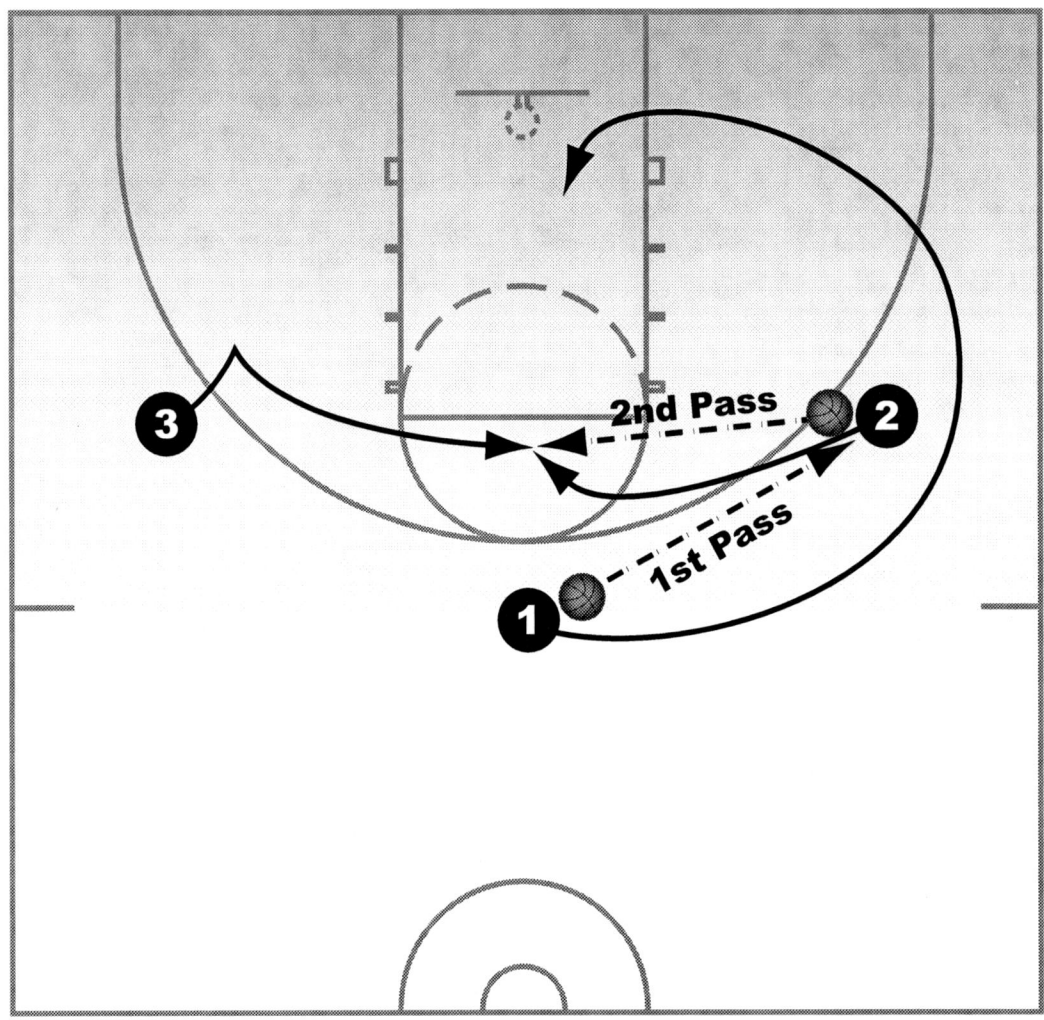

Carnesecca 1.2

ONE-ON-ONE: MIDDLE
(Same initial set-up as 1-on-1 from the side)

As shown in **Diagram 1.2**, 1 passes to 2 and goes around 2, taking a defensive position in the foul-lane area looking to help out. 2 passes to 3 breaking to the foul line. 2 goes behind 3 for a hand-off. 3 hands 2 the ball and is ready to play him defensively.

2 can either drive right or left, or take jump shots off the move. If 2 gets by 3, 1 is ready to help out.

LESSONS FROM THIS LEGEND...

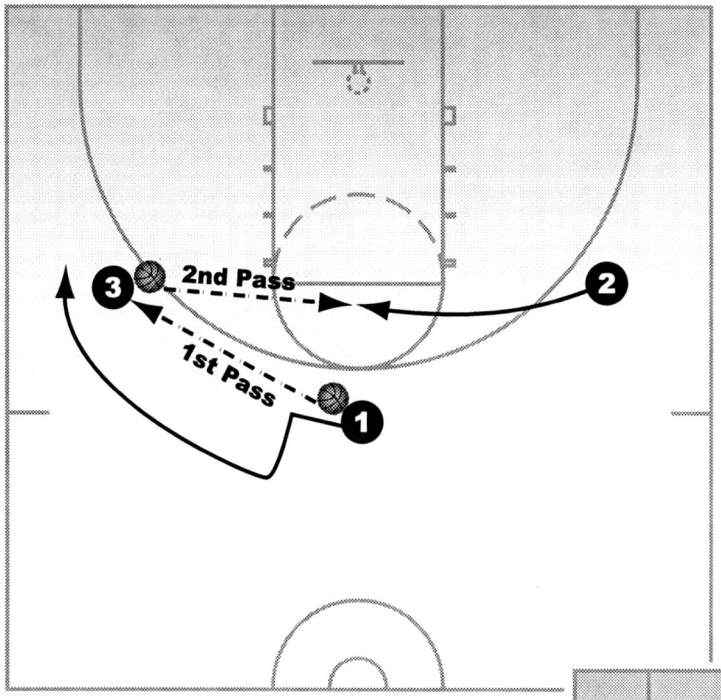

Carnesecca 1.3

OVERPLAY: ONE-ON-ONE

Basic Set-up: In all these set-ups, 1 can either start his play to the right or left.

As shown in **Diagram 1.3**, 1 passes to 3 and goes directly behind 3. 3, after passing to 2 coming to the foul-line area, turns around and takes a denial defensive position on 1.

As 2 starts to dribble toward 1, 3 denies the pass and, should 1 go back-door, 3 opens up looking to steal the pass from 2. (See **Diagram 1.4**)

Carnesecca 1.4

LESSONS FROM THIS LEGEND...

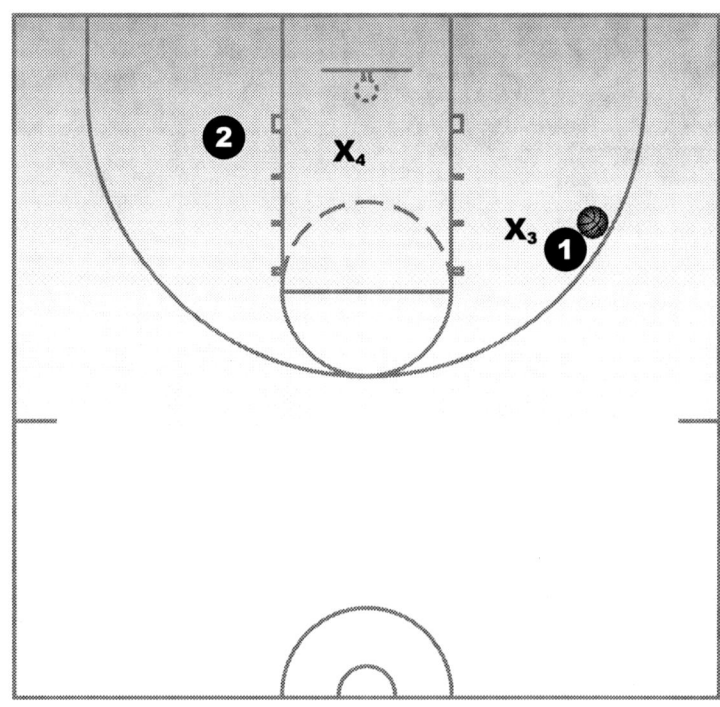

Carnesecca 1.5

Carnesecca 1.6

BEAT TO SPOT: TWO-ON-TWO DRILL

The basic set-up is the same, except we add a fourth player who initially stands out of bounds under the basket. When the first pass is made, 4 steps onto the court and always takes a position opposite from the 1st pass.

As shown in **Diagram 1.5**, the drill begins with 1 passing to 2 and going behind. 2 passes to 3 and takes an offensive position on the helpside. 4 steps onto the court and defends 2.

3 passes to 1 and follows his pass to defend 1. (See **Diagram 1.6**) We are emphasizing the importance of defending 2 coming across for an easy pass or establishing a strong pivot position. Again, 4 has dual responsibilities; he must defend 2 but must be ready to help should 1 get by 3 on the drive.

LESSONS FROM THIS LEGEND...

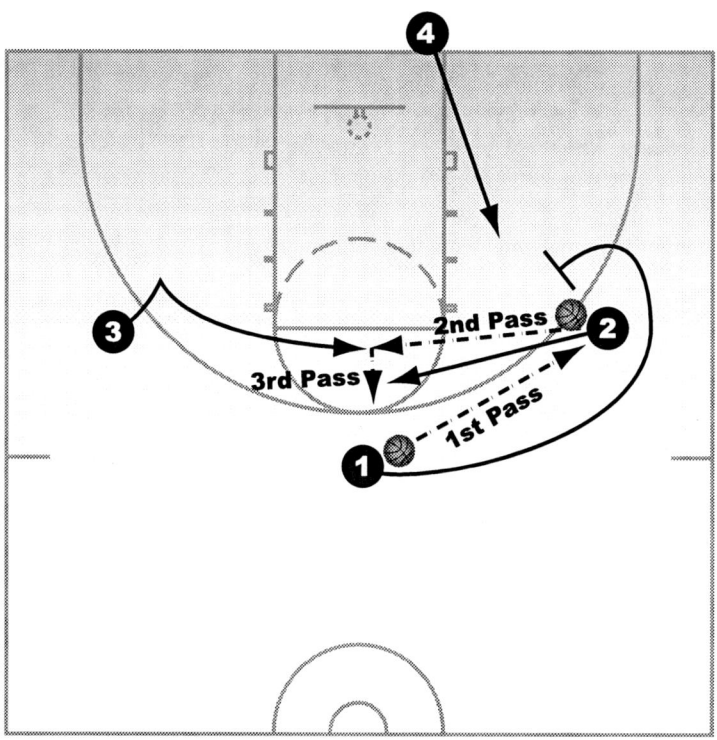

Carnesecca 1.7

SCREENS: TWO-ON-TWO

We use the same basic set-up as the Beat To Spot: Two-On-Two Drill.

As shown in **Diagram 1.7**, 1 passes to 2 and goes around 2 to set a screen at the foul-line extended. 2 passes to 3 and goes behind 3 to receive a hand-off. As this last action is occurring, 4 comes up and takes a defensive position on 1, shouting "pick left."

Carnesecca 1.8

In **Diagram 1.8**, we are now set to work assignments: 3 defends 2, and 4 defends 1 setting the pick. 4, being the back defender, calls all the defensive instructions, such as over-top, switch, etc.

LESSONS FROM THIS LEGEND...

Carnesecca 1.9

OVER THE TOP
3 playing 2 gets over the top of the screen set by 1. 4 helps in pushing 3 over the screen. (See **Diagram 1.9**) Getting over the top is especially important when playing a very good jump shooter close to the basket.

IN-BETWEEN
In this maneuver, 4 steps back and pushes 3 through. (See **Diagram 1.10**) We like to use this move whenever 2 is a poor outside shooter, or when 2 is outside his shooting range.

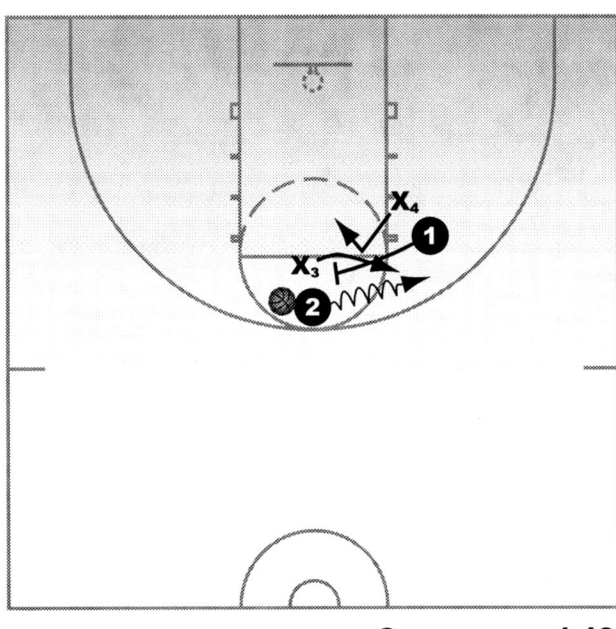

Carnesecca 1.10

Carnesecca 1.11

SWITCH
Whenever 3 is picked off by the offensive move, 4 should switch aggressively to 2. 4 must put as much pressure on 2 as possible to avoid an easy pass to 1 rolling to the basket. 3 should fight to get in front of 1 to avoid the mismatch. (See **Diagram 1.11**)

LESSONS FROM THIS LEGEND...

Carnesecca 1.12

HEDGE
Whenever 4 sees that 3 is late playing the dribbler, he jumps out in front of the dribbler to delay or stall until 3 catches up to 2. Again, we do this to avoid the mismatch. (See **Diagram 1.12**)

Carnesecca 1.13

REVERSE DRIBBLE TO SCREEN
In all of these screening maneuvers, if the defense has defended well, the offensive man 2 can reverse dribble and come off the screen set again by 1. (See **Diagram 1.13**)

SOURCE

Carnesecca, Lou. (1982). Diagnostic Defensive Drills. *Medalist Flashback Notebook.*

LEGACY OF
Bernard "Ben" Carnevale

- Was a master of taking teams with average ability and molding them into championship units.

- His teams were always well-disciplined and played aggressive defense.

- Considered a great teacher and classic clinician, a coach of coaches.

- One of the first college coaches to base game preparation on meticulous scouting of opponents.

- Served as chairman of the U.S. Olympic Basketball Committee from 1964 to 1968.

- Campaigned to adopt international basketball rules and predicted that the United States would be beaten in future Olympic games if they did not modify their rules.

BERNARD "BEN" CARNEVALE

"Basketball is like a game of chess. We try to predetermine our moves depending upon what the opposition is doing. As soon as they find the answer to our moves, we want to come back with something else."
—Ben Carnevale

BIOGRAPHY

Born: October 30, 1915 in Raritan, NJ

Inducted into Naismith Basketball Hall of Fame in 1970

Ben Carnevale entered the coaching ranks at Cranford H.S. (NJ) in 1940, and his teams reached the state tournament three successive years. From 1944 to 1946, Carnevale coached at the University of North Carolina and led the Tar Heels to two Southern Conference titles and a second-place finish in the 1946 NCAA tournament. As basketball coach at the United States Naval Academy from 1947 to 1966, Carnevale's teams made five NCAA and two NIT appearances. He compiled an impressive 257-160 record at Navy. Carnevale was named College Coach of the Year in 1947. He served as the NABC president in 1965-66 and was chairman of the U.S. Olympic Basketball Committee from 1964 to 1968. He served as the director of athletics at NYU and the College of William and Mary. Carnevale played college basketball at NYU for future Hall of Fame coach Howard Cann and participated in the first NIT in 1938. Carnevale was enshrined in the Naismith Memorial Basketball Hall of Fame in 1970.

...SCOUTING REPORT.....SCOUTING REPORT.....

Bernard "Ben" Carnevale...

The first basketball game that Ben Carnevale ever saw was in 1921 when he was six years old. (Muse, 1999) This was the beginning of a lifelong relationship with the game that he loved. Carnevale's father, who coached a team called the Trenton (NJ) Moose, also sparked his interest and encouraged his participation.

When Carnevale entered high school, he was cut from the basketball team. He vowed that this would never happen again. He immediately put up a basketball hoop at his home and practiced continually. Four years later, Carnevale was a standout for Sommerville High School (NJ) and earned All-County, All-Section, and Honorable Mention All-State honors.

Carnevale wanted to continue his basketball career and attended NYU as a walk-on. He eventually earned a basketball scholarship and went on to become a team captain for future Hall of Fame coach Howard Cann. After graduation from NYU in 1938, Carnevale played professionally with the Jersey City Reds for two years and was a member of their championship team in 1939.

In 1942, Carnevale entered the U.S. Navy and was sent to Annapolis to teach midshipmen physical fitness. "I arrived there one morning." Carnevale recalled, "and then somebody said that the Navy needed twenty men in a hurry to be gunnery officers on merchant ships. They took the first twenty men alphabetically, so I went quickly. Two weeks later, I was at sea."

In December, a German submarine off the coast of North Africa torpedoed Carnevale's ship. He spent one night in the water clinging to a raft. The next morning, Carnevale was picked up and crowded in a lifeboat along with twenty-six others. "We didn't know what we were doing or where we were going," said Carnevale. "It was going to be up to God. The winds and tides were in our favor. The boat drifted five and one-half days, and it drifted right to North Africa. We were able to beach just north of Dakar." Of the seventy-two men on the ship, only twenty-seven survived. (Janoff, 1966)

Carnevale was brought back to the U.S. and then sent to the Canal Zone, where he served as a gunnery officer and also coached the basketball team to the area championship.

Carnevale was reassigned in 1944 as director of athletics for the Navy V-12 program at the University of North Carolina. The North Carolina basketball team had lost most of its players from the year before, and the coach had quit. No one wanted the job, and Carnevale was asked if he would take it. He accepted with one condition: "I told them, I needed a two-week furlough to find players." North Carolina administrators agreed, and Carnevale went to Army and Navy bases and to New York City to assemble his team. This talented group of athletes won two Southern Conference titles and lost to Oklahoma A&M, 43-40, in the NCAA championship game in 1946.

In 1947, Carnevale accepted the coaching position at the United States Naval Academy. The only "big men" Carnevale saw during his twenty year tenure at Navy were on the opposition. Restricted by height regulations, his teams didn't have a single player over 6 foot 4 inches until the early 1960's, when the height limit was raised to 6 foot 6 inches. Despite the height handicap, Carnevale's Navy teams won 257 of 415 games and beat Army thirteen times in twenty games. When asked how he was able to accomplish this, Carnevale (2003) said, "It was simple. The players followed directions. They did what I told them to do. Another key was our preparation. We scouted our opponents, and our teams were always very well-prepared." Carnevale received accolades from Hall of Fame coach Joe Lapchick who stated "With the material he had at Navy, he was one of the toughest coaches in the country to beat." (White, 1966)

.....SCOUTING REPORT.....SCOUTING REPORT...

"It was all about defense—I studied it, analyzed it, spent time with it," Carnevale said. To compliment his defense, Carnevale designed game plans based upon detailed scouting reports. "I'd scout almost every night of the week. I was never home. I'd watch the team that we were going to play next and then devise a defense to take away their strength, their first option." (Muse, 1999)

Carnevale was a master at maintaining his poise. He weighed his words carefully, and his words carried a lot of weight.

Carnevale was admired for his ability to teach the game of basketball. "He's a classic clinician," stated Lapchick. "It's at clinics where you separate the men from the boys in coaching. Ben can impart knowledge to other coaches, always teaching them something new." (White, 1966) Hall of Fame coach Lou Carnesecca agreed and said, "Ben was a great teacher of basketball—maybe the best I ever met. Watching his practices was like watching a composer at a piano. He'd break the game down into pieces and analyze each one." (Muse, 1999)

Carnevale helped to expand basketball to all parts of the world. He served as chairman of the U.S. Olympic Committee from 1964 to 1968. In 1969, he recommended changing the U.S. college rules to conform to the international standards. Carnevale based his plea on the need to get players ready for the Olympic Games every four years. "Sooner or later we're going to have to come around to the international rules," said Carnevale. "We could be beaten in the Olympics if we don't conform to these rules, and we should never be beaten."

At the time of his retirement in 1966, Carnevale stated, "Coaching is a lot different now than when I started, and it's getting tougher every year. Recruiting, scouting—all that time involved. It gets so busy you have to forget about your family, and I don't like that." (Fischler, 1966)

In 1999, Carnevale offered this advice for young coaches. "Coaches have to develop their own philosophy. Study the game. The only way to succeed is to work. You can't take a success pill. Adjust your coaching for the personnel that you have. Teach your players to be physical and develop good footwork." (Muse, 1999)

SOURCE

Carnevale, Ben. Vertical Files, Archives. Naismith Memorial Basketball Hall of Fame. Springfield, MA.

Carnevale, Ben. Interview with Ralph Pim. September 5, 2003.

Fischler, Stan. (1966, February 3). Coaching Keeps Getting Tougher. *The Journal American.*

Horwitz, Jay (1970, January 30). Carnevale Selected for the Naismith Basketball Hall of Fame. *New York University News Bureau.*

Janoff, Murray. (1966, July 8). Real Estate Salesmen, Beware! *Long Island Press.*

Muse, Dan. (1999). Gentle Ben. *Naismith Memorial Hall of Fame Enshrinement Program.*

White, Gordon S. Jr. (1966, February 3). Basketball Round Table Sets a Place for Carnevale. *New York Times.*

LESSONS FROM THIS LEGEND...

PRESSING DEFENSES

By Ben Carnevale

Authors' Note: This article, written in the 1960s, shows the evolution/development of pressure defense.

One of the best defensive weapons a team can possess is the ability to apply a press effectively. I feel that pressing defenses are the coming thing in basketball, and I think that in a few years most teams will be using some sort of pressing defense.

Why Press?

There are many factors involved when considering whether or not to press, and the coach has to decide when to use it and when to call if off. The coach knows his team's capabilities and limitations better than anyone else. If a team doesn't have depth, the coach might decide not to press, since you are more foul prone while pressing.

If his team doesn't have speed or quick reactions, it would be foolish for him to press. On the other hand, maybe he can successfully press one team and be unsuccessful with the next team because they are quicker, better ballhandlers, or their particular attack overcomes his press. Consequently, I think he must analyze every team that he faces. The coach must decide whether his press will hurt that particular ball club or whether their attack is good enough to make his using the press foolish.

There are many conditions that warrant the use of a press. It could be as a surprise element against a slow team or a poor ballhandling team. You may want to press a team that has a good big man in the pivot to force them to commit their offense prior to their getting down in their offensive territory. You may decide to press a team with weak guards or a team whose outlet passers are poor ballhandlers. You may decide to press a young, inexperienced ball club, or you might decide to press the slow, deliberate team in order to speed up the game.

One big thing to consider is the fear aspect. Many coaches fear a press, and they subconsciously pass this fear on to their players. Such a team has two strikes against it before you even start your press against them.

Don't Try to Steal the Ball

My basic philosophy is that we are not trying to steal the ball. All we are trying to do is maintain good defensive balance, plug outlets, and force the other team into errors. I think the team that tries to steal the ball over-commits itself, fouls too often, and does not do a basically sound defensive job. Try to force the other team into awkward situations. This will force errors and obtain the same result as stealing the ball, without the hazards listed above.

Do a Selling Job

A coach has to do a tremendous selling job on the press to his players. A pressing defense is a team defense. You are not only overplaying your man, but you are also playing the ball. You have to talk on defense and switch a great deal. The responsibilities are so much greater, and you therefore have to act as a unit, helping each other out.

There is a lot of coaching involved as a result of the careful attention that must be paid to every minute detail. The offensive team knows where it is going and what it is trying to do. The defensive team cannot commit itself until the offense has made its move. Therefore, the pressing team has to learn to talk; it has to get its point of vision or angle on the ball and on the players. It has to decide whether it is going to force the ball outside or force the ball inside into a trap.

Scouting

A large amount of the success of a press depends upon scouting. You must have the knowledge of how the other team will react to the press. You must know what particular press will be most effective against that team.

Our pressing strategy against a team is definitely determined by scouting reports. We do a tremendous amount of scouting. We scout four or five nights a week. Because we are not satisfied with only one scouting report, we sometimes scout a team three, four, or five times. Also, to check ourselves, we will have an outside scout send us a report. We want to know exactly what the opposition will do in almost every situation. I truthfully feel that any success we have had in pressing is due to our scouting.

Many Types of Presses

In today's game there are many different types of presses. There are presses that attack you full-court. There are some that allow you to throw the ball in and then attack you at three-quarter court. There is another press that will attack you at mid-court. Also, there is the frontcourt press after you get into you offensive territory. There are combination presses, such as the top two men playing a man-to-man press and the back three are playing a zone. Just to say that a team will press doesn't actually tell much of the story. There are many variations.

LESSONS FROM THIS LEGEND...

BE FLEXIBLE
Don't become known just as a full-court pressing team or a zone pressing team or a half-court, man-to-man pressing team. We like to feel that our opponents never know exactly how we will press them.

Sometimes, we allow you to throw the ball in and then we attack you. The next time, maybe in the same game, we will try to stop the throw-in. My philosophy is always to keep the other team off balance and never let them know exactly what you are going to do next. We may force the dribbler outside and the next time force him inside. Sometimes you may get a full-court press, other times a half-court. It may be a zone press or a man-to-man.

We want to keep the other team off balance. We will sometimes press early in the game just to test the other team's reaction to a press. At half time in the dressing room, we then tell our players how best to overcome the attack of the opposition. We might even come out the second half using a different type press. We do this because we feel that the opposing coach has been instructing his players during the half on how to overcome our first half press. Often a completely different type of press in the second half so unnerves your opposition that it has a devastating effect. When you are getting ready to play my ball club, I don't want you to feel that I am going to play you any one way. I think this is the secret to the press.

Of course, you want to take advantage of the other team's weaknesses, and you want to neutralize their strengths. Their personnel and the particular game situation will help you determine what type of press to use. If a team has a great dribbler or a great passer throwing the ball in, we may concede the throw-in and cover that good ball-handler. Consequently, they will have a weak dribbler handling the ball coming down court. Another time, maybe a weaker ballhandler is throwing the ball in. In this case, we wouldn't concede the throw-in, rather, we would play him tight and try to force a bad pass.

Basically, I like the man-to-man press, but when pressing a dribbling team, I would use the zone press. If a team has several good sharp passers, however, a zone press would overcommit itself, and then you would really be in trouble. That situation calls for a man-to-man press. Your choice as to whether you use the full-court, three-quarter court, or the half-court press would depend upon the situation.

No matter what type press you choose, always remember to be sure you spend enough time in practice on good basic defense. If your players can't play good defense, they can't begin to press.

FULL-COURT MAN-TO-MAN PRESS
The first thing you will have to decide is whether or not to overplay the man throwing the ball in. Then, you want to decide whether to play receivers tight and prevent the throw-in or to allow the opponent to successfully throw the ball in and then attack the receivers with the ball. Many teams will attack the man throwing the ball in; others will play away from him and double-team the most logical receivers. Both methods can be very successful, depending upon the situation.

Next, you will have to determine how your opponents are attacking the full-court press. Do they attack with two players, three players, or do they use just one dribbler? Where do they place their other men? The answers to these questions determine how you are going to play your other men.

THREE-QUARTER COURT MAN-TO-MAN PRESS
The three-quarter court man-to-man press allows the throw-in. Then you must decide if you are going to force the ball to the sideline or if you are going to force the ball into a trap in the middle. We like to do it both ways, depending upon the situation and the personnel involved. Again, we want to know how the opposing players will be positioned. This determines the placing of our defensive players. What moves they make determines our reaction. Remember, we are not trying to steal the ball. We are trying to force an error or a jump-ball situation.

HALF-COURT MAN-TO-MAN PRESS
Some teams let you cross the mid-court line and press you at that point. We prefer to attack right at the line. We don't want you coming in too far, because with a hard dribble, you can penetrate us a little too much. We want you to start committing yourself almost before you get to the mid-court line. We feel we can force the dribbler in the desired direction a little better at this point. We force both to the sideline and to the middle for the trap. We want you to throw the wild pass. And, again, we want to capitalize on weaknesses that have been uncovered by our scouting reports.

ZONE PRESSES
Just like all the other phases of defense, the zone press has to be adjusted to the offensive maneuvers. I don't think you can simply play a 3-1-1, a 1-2-1-1, a 2-1-2, or a 2-2-1 zone press and be successful. It depends on the other team's attack as to how you should place your players. If your team becomes known for one particular type of zone press, it will lose a lot of its effectiveness. Your opposition can spend all of its time preparing for your one and only one press and do a good job of overcoming it.

When you play us, you might be facing a 2-2-1 zone press one time down the floor and a 1-2-1-1 the next time down. It all depends upon how you attack our zone press. We don't use any one set-up on a zone press. I feel the team that uses only one zone press is actually giving inches to his opposition, in a manner of speaking.

PHILOSOPHY OF THE PRESS
You have to know exactly what you are going to do when you go on the floor. I think you and your philosophy can force the other team out of its best moves. We always want to force the opposition into their secondary moves. My entire defensive philoso-

LESSONS FROM THIS LEGEND...

phy is to take away the opposition's best moves, thereby taking away their offense.

Of course, you can't stop everything they do; but by capitalizing on their weakness, you are much closer to adding a game to the win column.

Basketball is much like a game of chess. We try to predetermine our moves, depending upon what the opposition is doing. As soon as they find the answer to our moves, we want to come back with something else.

Seldom a day goes by that we don't spend some part of our practice on the presses. We have basic fundamental drills that help a player become a better defender. This, in turn, helps him to apply the press much more effectively. We have drills that use all five players and incorporate all the ideas on pressing that we have. Then, we actually practice our pressing defenses.

It all boils down to one important fact; you only get out of something what you put into it. It takes much hard work, both on the part of the coach and of the players, to have a team feared for its devastating press.

SOURCE

Carnevale, Ben. (1965). Pressing Defenses. In. Hardin McLane (ed.), *Championship Basketball by 12 Great Coaches.* Englewood Cliffs, NJ: Prentice-Hall.

LESSONS FROM THIS LEGEND...

PREPARING FOR AN OPPONENT

By Ben Carnevale

MAXIMIZE YOUR TEAM'S STRENGTHS

During my tenure, Navy earned five trips to the NCAA tournament and two NIT bids. I did not have the best athletes but my players were superbly conditioned and gifted academically. They used their intelligence to their advantage and did not beat themselves. Their military training also played a key role because they followed directions and exhibited outstanding drive and determination. They would not be outworked. They did what I wanted them to do. If I told them to run through a wall, they would run through a wall.

SCOUTING REPORTS

An important key to our success was our scouting of opponents. I wouldn't scout a team just once, but four or five times. I'd scout almost every night of the week. I was never home. I wanted to know exactly what an opponent would do in almost every situation. This enabled me to design game plans that maximized my team's strengths and at the same time exploited our opponent's weaknesses.

DEFENSE

With Navy's height restriction and academic requirements, the only way I was able to compete on the national level was with our defense. Our players were hard-nosed and tenacious defenders. They would not back down from a challenge. We used different types of defenses based on our scouting report. I would always press a slow team or a poor ballhandling team. I would also press a young, inexperienced team and force them into mistakes.

Another thing that helped my team was that we changed our defenses. We would vary the pick-up point of our defense and frequently change from a man-to-man to a zone defense. We would deny passes and put pressure on the ballhandler. We never let our opponent get comfortable. We used the element of surprise to always keep our opponent off balance.

PRACTICE PLANNING

Practice sessions are a coach's classroom. The same way that teachers make lesson plans, coaches must make practice plans. I planned every minute of every practice. I kept files of each practice plan so I could go back and make sure that we had worked on everything.

Everything was done for a reason. It was a time to improve individual skills as well as team fundamentals. Never underestimate the importance of good footwork. Practice footwork drills every day. It will help your players become quicker. With your drills, simulate game conditions. Make everything as game-like as possible. Practice defense and demand that your players play hard and rebound. Always get your team ready defensively to take away the opponent's first option in their offense.

Practices are also a time to build team unity. No matter how talented a team may be, if the players do not play together, they will not win. Reward players for unselfish play such as assists, rebounds, and strong defense. Your greatest satisfaction as a coach comes from developing teams that are unselfish, harmonious, and committed to doing their best.

Source

Carnevale, Ben. Interview with Ralph Pim. September 5, 2003.

Muse, Dan. (1999). Gentle Ben. *Naismith Memorial Hall of Fame Enshrinement Program.*

LEGACY OF
John Chaney

- Prepared players for success in life through his disciplined system and emphasis on character development and teamwork.

- Scheduled the toughest teams in the nation to prepare his players for conference play.

- Conducted daily practice sessions during the early morning hours to help instill discipline in his players.

- Became the all-time winningest coach at Temple University in 1999.

- Led Cheney State to the Division II national championship in 1978.

- Earned a reputation as one of the top defensive coaches in the nation because of his match-up zone defense.

JOHN CHANEY

"The only thing that can save a poor person's life is education."
—John Chaney

BIOGRAPHY

Born: January 21, 1932 in Jacksonville, FL

Inducted into the Naismith Basketball Hall of Fame in 2001

John Chaney began his collegiate coaching career at Cheney State University in 1972. In ten seasons at Cheney State, his teams compiled a 225-59 record, won the 1978 NCAA Division II national championship, finished third in the nation in 1979, and participated in eight NCAA tournaments. Chaney was named the Division II National Coach of the Year in 1978. He accepted the head-coaching position at Temple University in 1982 and led the Owls to 20 consecutive postseason tournaments. During a remarkable five-year stretch between 1983 and 1988, Temple won 25 or more games each season. The USBWA, AP, UPI, NABC, and CNN/USA named Chaney the National Coach of the Year in 1988. Chaney became Temple's all-time winningest basketball coach in 1999, surpassing the legendary Harry Litwack, also a Hall of Fame coach. Chaney was enshrined in the Naismith Memorial Basketball Hall of Fame in 2001.

...SCOUTING REPORT.....SCOUTING REPORT.....

John Chaney...

"Be...the Dream," was John Chaney's motto. He had it written on the walls in the lockerroom and coaches' offices. Chaney's players were walking examples of his philosophy. He taught young men how to be successful in life.

Chaney was a dedicated and strong-willed teacher who molded the character of his players with positive values of discipline, teamwork, and common decency. Chaney did not think of discipline as a form of punishment. "Discipline is an order, an orderly situation," stated Chaney. "It's a well-thought out plan to direct somebody. It's another form of higher intellect. When you get a team that wants to play together, combines their skills together, and they go out and play well together, that to me is one of the higher forms of intellect." (Cornfield, 2001)

According to many of his players, Chaney was the father figure that they never had. He taught players how to become better-rounded individuals and how to become successful members of society. "The winning or losing of basketball games should not be the thing that gives me access to having an influence on someone's life or to be viewed as a good coach or a good person," said Chaney. "The thing that should give me access is the fact that my major concern is to try and develop good character in the people I have under my wing. What is truly important is the growth of another human being and knowing you had something to do with it." (Wartenberg, 1991, p. 65)

It bothered Chaney that many people equated winning with being a successful coach. "The most bothersome and misunderstood aspect of this business, as I see it, is that people who win are looked at as people who are good coaches," said Chaney. "That disturbs me. I don't think you can measure a good coach based just on winning. A coach must be judged on some of the altruistic things that sports are all about: developing character, good sportsmanlike conduct, developing confidence, good will, good competitive spirit, the will to win, and the knowledge to know and distinguish that winning has nothing to do with the score. A coach with a lesser record or from a less prestigious program could have a greater impact on the lives of people." (Wartenberg, 1991, p. 144).

Chaney did not want his players focused on the opposition. His theme was "winning is within you." Chaney said, "The strength of a great team is they are effective in what they do and force the other team to surrender. You make the other team deal with who you are. If you move toward what the other team is about and worry about stopping what they do, you're moving toward their side of the court." (Wartenberg, 1991, p. 171)

Chaney believed in making the toughest non-conference schedule possible for his teams. He scheduled the nation's top opponents in the most hostile basketball environments knowing his teams might suffer some losses. Chaney believed this helped his players mature and learn how to handle adversity. He wanted his players to know that on the road to any goal worth striving for, there would always be obstacles. "We've always made the schedule so my teams can experience playing the best teams early. That's not going to be a successful adventure. You're going to go out, you're going to get beat, and you're going to get scraped. That's why they are great teams. But somewhere along the line, in the first part of January, latter part of January, or the beginning of February, a light comes on, and they begin to play well." (Cornfield, 2001)

Chaney's disciplined system required players to begin practice at 5:30 a.m. He began this routine when he was a substitute teacher and coach of the cadet team (one step below the junior varsity) at Overbrook High School (PA), and it was the only time that he could get the gymnasium. Chaney believed it helped create self-discipline and incorporated the early morning practice sessions at every school he coached. "I've always worked with youngsters who very often are from tough situations in the inner city," stated Chaney. "It's always been my contention that you have to start somewhere, by raising the bar for young people and making sure they understand that it's not an easy trip that they're on."

Chaney was a high school basketball legend at Benjamin Franklin HS in Philadelphia and earned the Public League's MVP honors in 1951. His specialty was dribbling and scoring, and he was one of the first high school players in Philadelphia to shoot a jump shot. Chaney was an All-American at Bethune-Cookman College and was named MVP of the 1953 NAIA championship. Chaney played professionally in the Eastern Basketball League for ten seasons and was the league's MVP in 1959 and 1960.

One of the tenets of Chaney's basketball philosophy was to protect the ball at all times. He detested turnovers and wanted his team to average less than ten turnovers per game. He preached that ball possession created scoring opportunities, while turnovers were nothing more than wasted opportunities. Chaney believed that nothing in life was worse than wasting an opportunity. "In basketball, you try to avoid as many mistakes as you can when you have possession," said Chaney. "A great team—every time they come down the floor something good happens. You cannot play basketball here if you're going to commit turnovers." (Wartenberg, 1991, p. 36)

Chaney was very superstitious and believed the clothes that he wore could affect the outcome of a game. If he felt a particular article of clothing was unlucky, he discarded it immediately. After one game, Chaney gave his assistant coach a pair of Italian leather shoes, because he felt they were cursed. Conversely, once an article of clothing proved itself to be a good luck charm, he wore it repeatedly. Other superstitions included a fear of black cats, no open umbrellas in the house, and no hats on the bed.

Chaney was a fighter who always believed in standing up for what was right. He battled the NCAA, because he thought that Proposition 48 and 42 were unfair to disadvantaged youngsters and poor inner-city children. "There should be more emphasis on helping children in the primary grades," said Chaney. "You have to spend more time with the kids from K through 12. The NCAA makes a lot of money. If they could give some of the money to the schools and communities where most of the players come from, that would make a big difference." (Hunt, 2003, p. 14)

John Chaney rose from poverty and overcame prejudice and lack of opportunity to become one of the most respected and successful coaches in the country. His mission in life was to help others become winners both on and off the court. He helped his players understand that success has a narrow door and only through hard work was someone able to step through. Chaney believed fear and anger were prerequisites to success. "Fear says I will not leave any stone unturned," explained Chaney. "I will remember all of the things that I have to remember. Fear opens your eyes to what you must overcome. Anger says I'm going to play the game tough and mean, so fear and anger work together."

"As a coach, I've had plenty of players go to the NBA, but that's not important to me. I'm just happy we were able to give them a chance to improve their lives. Now, they can go out and help others who didn't have the same opportunities they did." (Hunt, 2003, p. xiii)

SOURCE

Chaney, John. Vertical Files, Archives. Naismith Memorial Basketball Hall of Fame. Springfield, MA.

Cornfield, Josh. (2001). Interview with John Chaney. *The Temple News*.

Hunt, Donald. (2003) *Chaney: Playing for a Legend*. Chicago: Triumph Books.

Wartenberg, Steve. (1991). *Winning Is An Attitude*. New York: St. Martin's Press.

LESSONS FROM THIS LEGEND...

INSIDE DEFENSE AGAINST THE STALL

By John Chaney

One of the biggest challenges in coaching is how to defend the four-corner offense. I have found it to be a problem not only defending it, but also when I have used it as an offensive strategy. Ballhandling, passing, and decision-making are essential in my old fashioned mind, yet throughout all of basketball, a talented point guard that can direct the four-corner stall is hard to find.

The "Inside Defense" is another approach to stopping the four-corner stall. This new concept must be introduced and practiced at the beginning of the season so as to become a stratagem. All players, regardless of position, should learn the "Inside Defense." The defense can be employed from zone, man-to-man, or combination defenses. We have found that it is easier for us to employ the "Inside Defense" from zone defenses, such as the 2-3 zone or the 1-3-1 zone. However, our opponents have been more confused when we have played man-to-man and then went into our "Inside Defense" on a designated signal.

THE COURT IS DIVIDED INTO THREE LANES
(See **Diagram 1.0**)
- All players and coaches must have the same concept of the court layout.
- There are two outside lanes and a middle lane.
- The outside lanes are dribbling and passing lanes only.

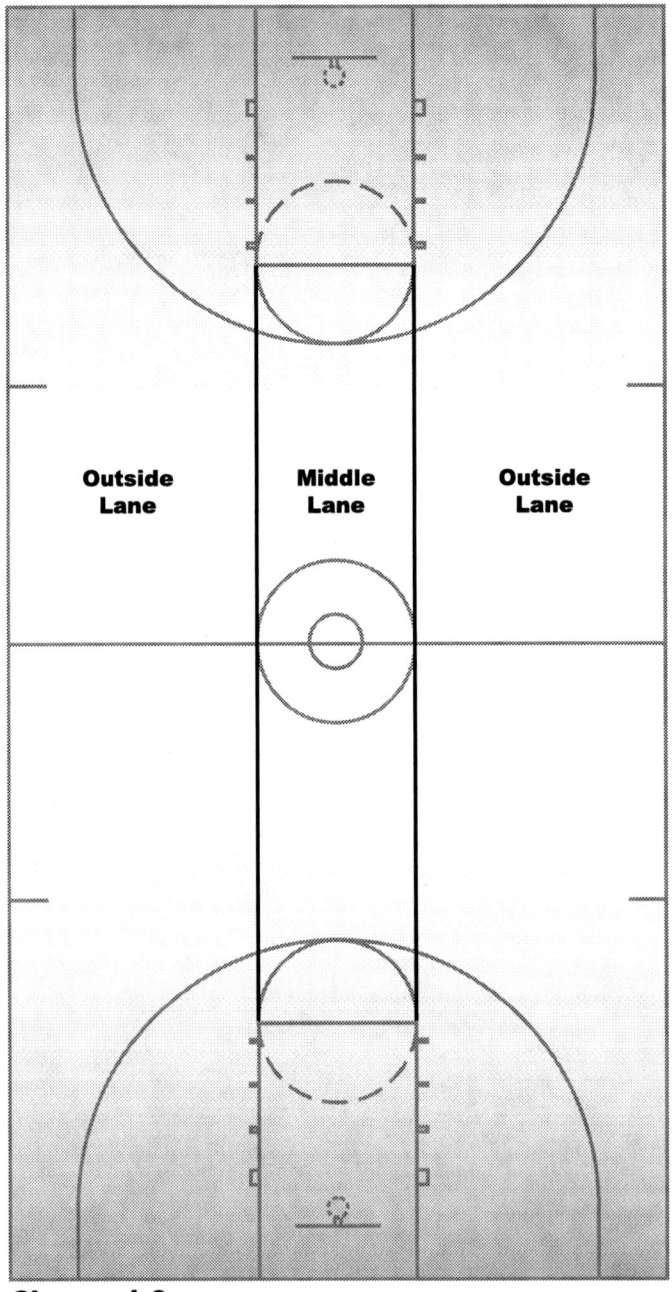

Chaney 1.0

LESSONS FROM THIS LEGEND...

DEFENDING A BALLHANDLER IN THE MIDDLE LANE
(See **Diagram 1.1**)
- Pressure the ball.
- Never allow penetration down the middle of the floor.
- Force the ballhandler to dribble or pass to either outside lane.

DEFENDING PLAYERS IN THE OUTSIDE LANE WHEN BALL IS IN THE MIDDLE
(See **Diagram 1.1**)
- Play ballside.
- Cut off the passing lanes.

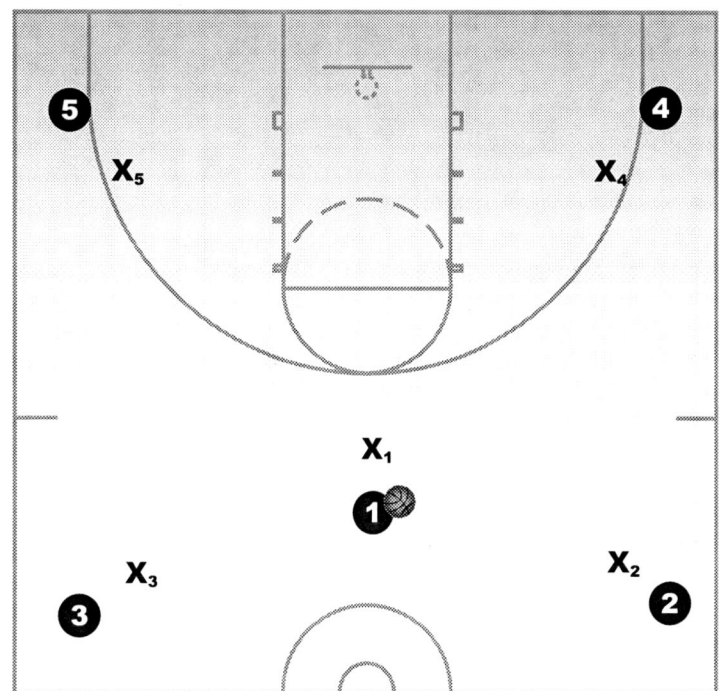

Chaney 1.1

DEFENDING A BALLHANDLER IN THE OUTSIDE LANE
(See **Diagram 1.2**)
- Pressure the ball.
- Do not allow the ball to be dribbled or passed back to the middle lane.

DEFENDING A PLAYER IN THE MIDDLE LANE WHEN BALL IS IN THE OUTSIDE LANE
(See **Diagram 1.2**)
- Cut off the passing lane,
- Deny entry back into the middle lane.

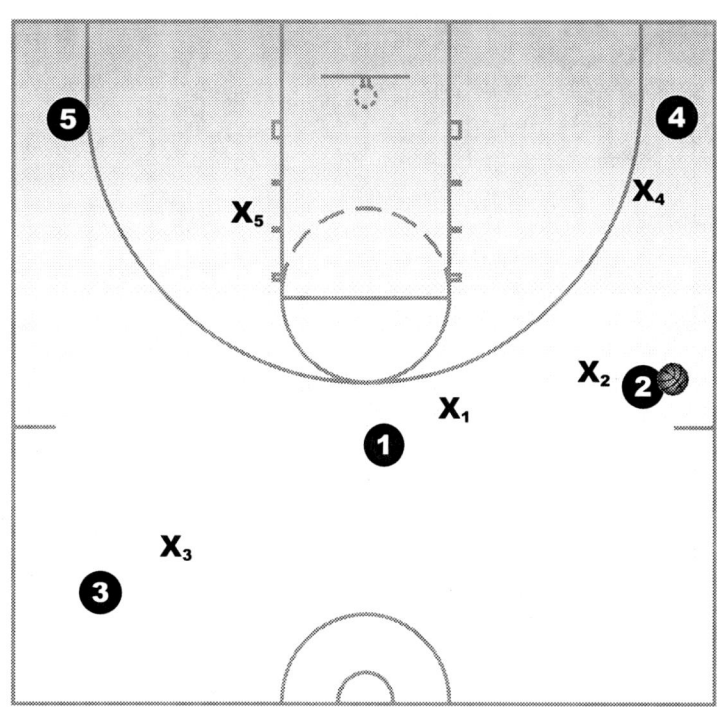

Chaney 1.2

LESSONS FROM THIS LEGEND...

THE "INSIDE DEFENSE" FROM A ZONE DEFENSE ALIGNMENT

You may change zone roles and defensive responsibility of the players to your particular situation. However, once you employ the "Inside Defense," you must stay within the basic concepts that were illustrated in **Diagrams 1.1** and **1.2**.

Diagram 1.3 shows the "Inside Defense" from a 2-3 zone initial alignment.

Diagram 1.4 shows the "Inside Defense" from a 1-3-1 zone initial alignment.

DOS AND DON'TS OF THE "INSIDE DEFENSE"

1. Introduce at the beginning of the season.
2. Spend time daily on the basic concepts.
3. Avoid trapping.
4. Force the dribbler to the outside lanes.
5. Deny entry back to the middle lane whenever the ball is on the outside.
6. Assign point guards to defend the best ballhandler, if possible.
7. All defenders in the outside lanes play their men toward ballside and cut off the passing lanes from the middle lane.
8. If there is a breakdown on defense, close the middle lane quickly and then resume the principles of the "Inside Defense."

SOURCE

Chaney, John. (1980). Inside Defense Against the Stall. *Pro-Keds Coaching Digest*.

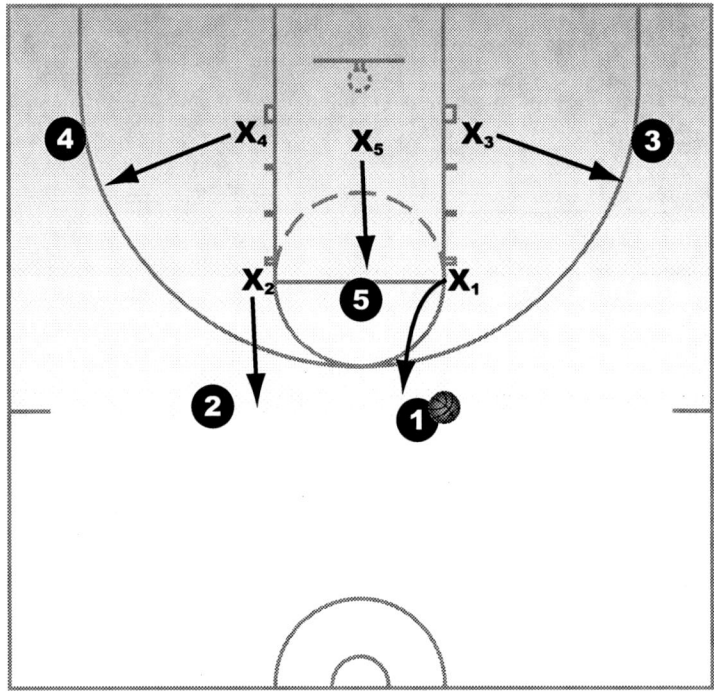

Chaney 1.3

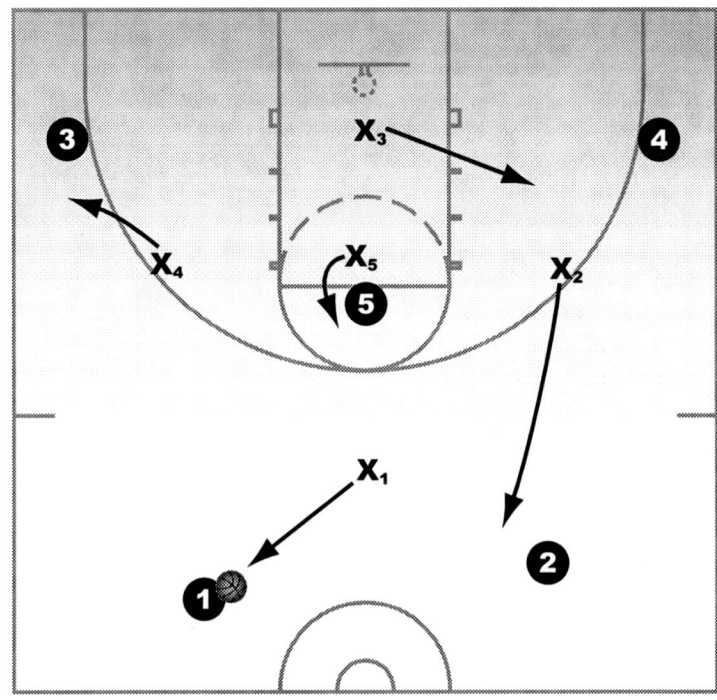

Chaney 1.4

LESSONS FROM THIS LEGEND...

THE TEMPLE OF ZONES

By Don Casey

Authors' Note: John Chaney earned a reputation as one of the top zone defensive coaches in the country. Don Casey, who also coached at Temple, presents many of Chaney's coaching principles in this article.

There is no reason why a team, no matter the level, cannot use zone defenses. It is not a cop-out defense. It is not a sign of weakness. You can't get scared playing a zone. Sometimes you are going to get burned, but you must be patient.

We are going to cover the 3-2 or 1-2-2 zone defense. We are seeing more of this now with the 3-point line. Let's show the zone in its entirety and then break it down.

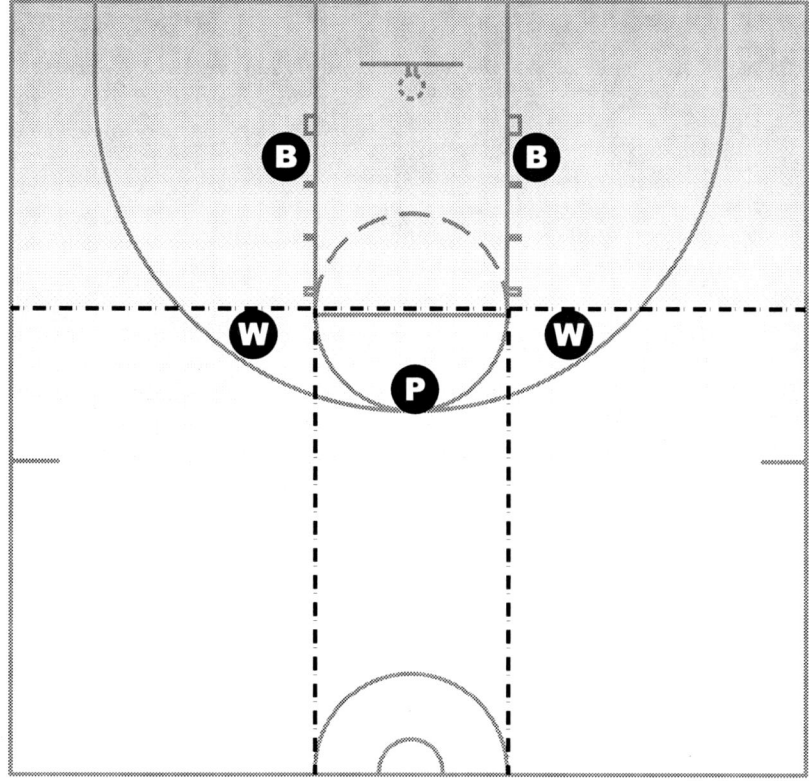

Chaney 2.0

INITIAL ALIGNMENT

We use a point, two wings, and two back men. We do not want our point man to come out past the circle. We want the inside foot of the wing touching the lane line, and we want the back man to straddle the lane line and come as high as the offense will allow. You want to try to keep the front and back lines as close together as possible. If we use the dotted lines, it shows the areas that the front three players must cover. (See **Diagram 2.0**)

LESSONS FROM THIS LEGEND...

POINT

We want the point man to stay tight, so as not to elongate the zone. The point man must cover the high post if there is someone there or not, because someone will usually flash to the high post. How low does the point man go? Low enough so that when the ball is passed back on top, he can get there. When the ball goes to the corner or short corner, he slides to the elbow. (See **Diagram 2.1**) If the ball goes to the high post over his head, he should go there and double team. (See **Diagram 2.2**)

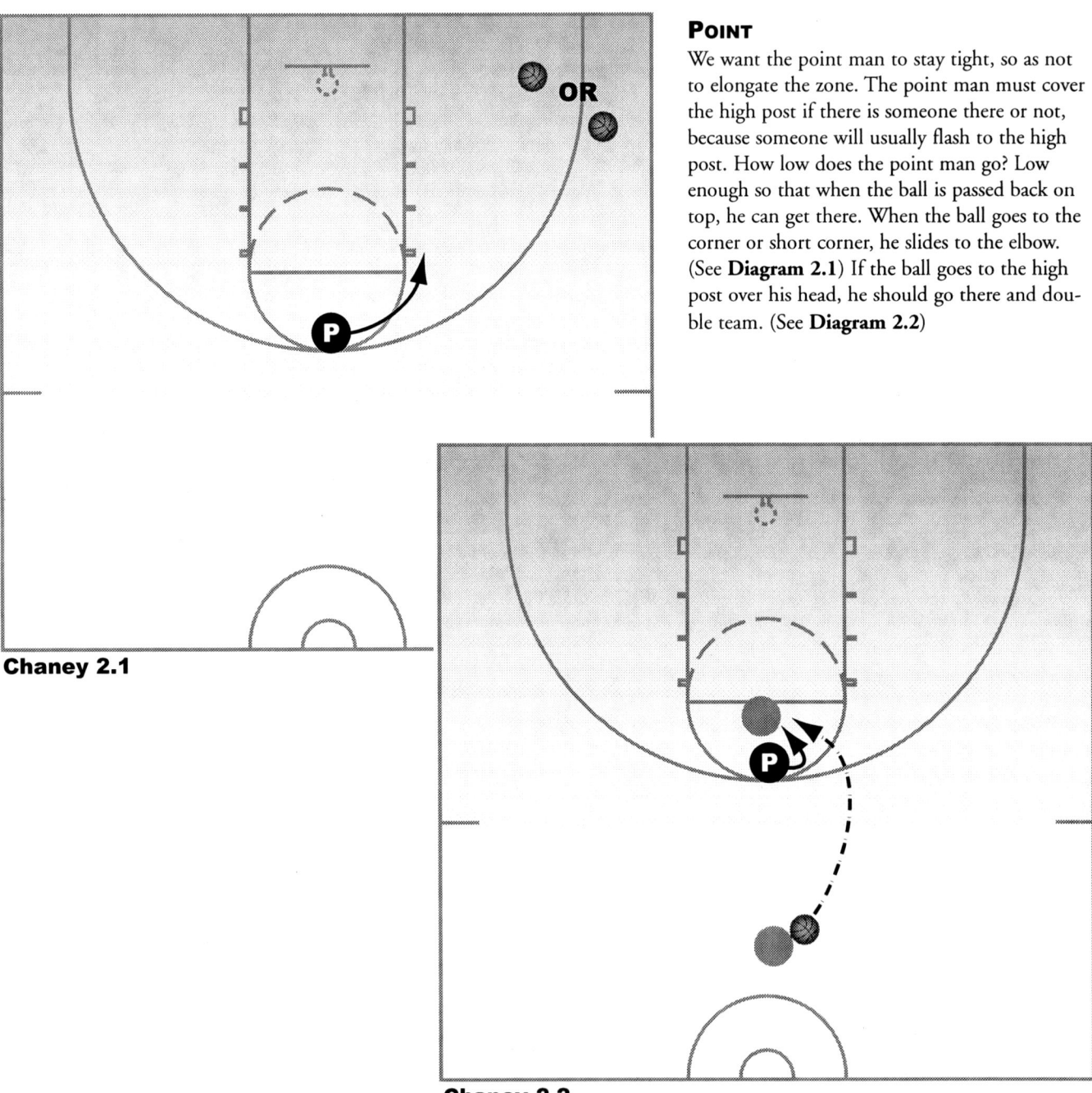

Chaney 2.1

Chaney 2.2

LESSONS FROM THIS LEGEND...

WING

The wing on the ballside plays the ball as it enters his alley—whether by dribble or pass. (See **Diagram 2.3**) The wingman should stay between the man with the ball in his area and the basket and don't let him dribble into the middle.

When the ball is passed to the corner, the wing can do several things. As shown in **Diagram 2.4**, he can face the ball in the corner and deny the pass back to the wing. The second thing he can do is plug the middle and help cover the low post. (See **Diagram 2.5**) The third thing that he can do is to follow the ball into the corner and trap the ballhandler with the back man. (See **Diagram 2.6**) If the man in the corner starts dribbling up, the wing should trap down, so as not to split the zone. (See **Diagram 2.7**)

If the ball is passed to the high-post area, the wings drop back and will cover the next pass out on their side. The high post will be covered by one of the back men who happen to be free. (See **Diagram 2.8**)

If the pass is made from the wing into the high-post area, the wing should step down and help plug the middle. (See **Diagram 2.9**) The offside wing has the next pass to his side, whether it is reversed or moved by a skip pass. He is going to be your offside rebounder also. (See **Diagram 2.10**) He has the next pass on his side and tries to get in line with the ball.

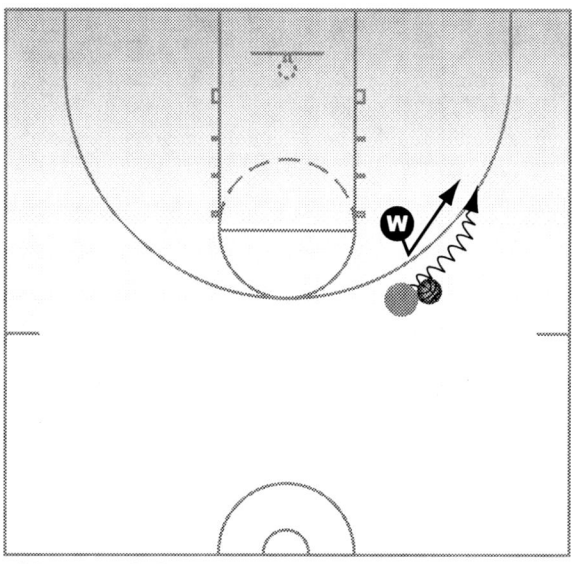
Chaney 2.3

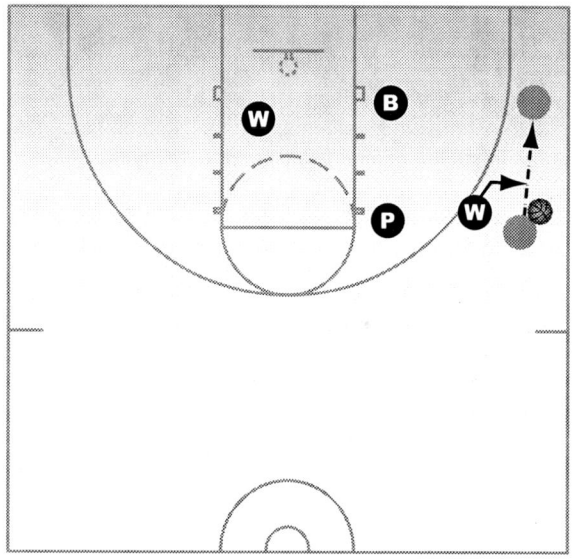
Chaney 2.4

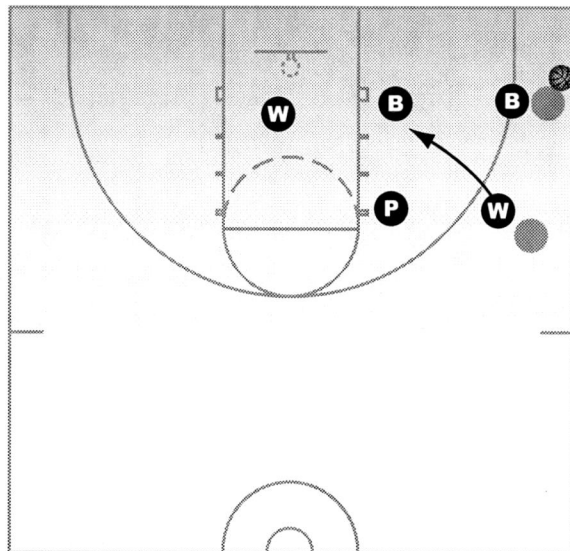
Chaney 2.5

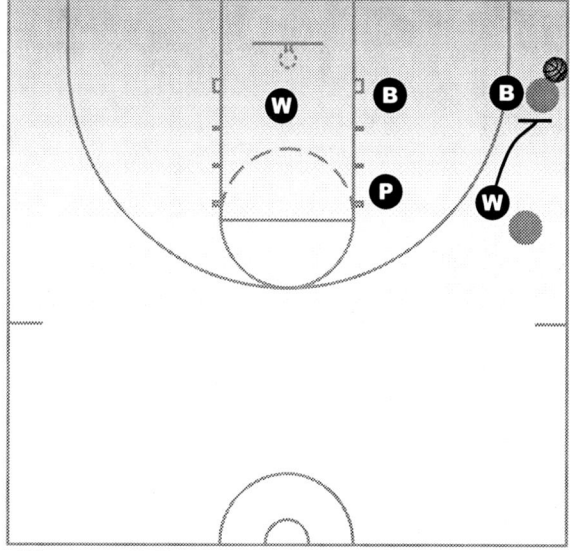
Chaney 2.6

LESSONS FROM THIS LEGEND...

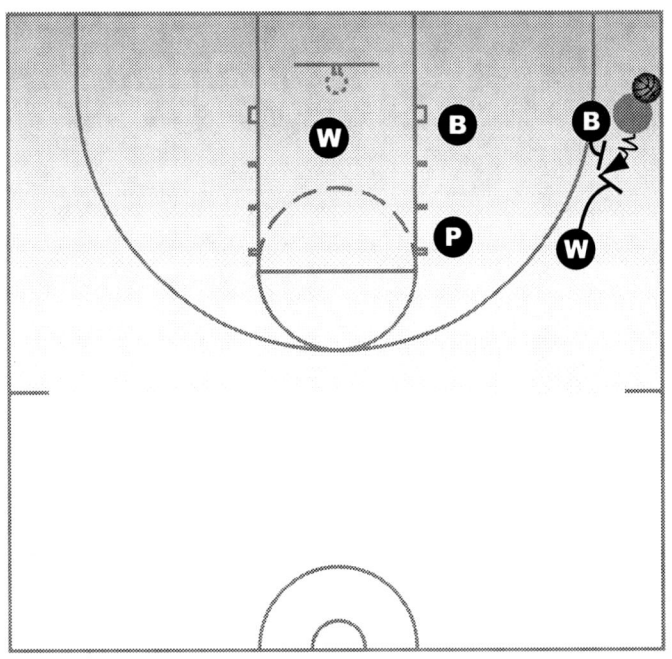

Chaney 2.7

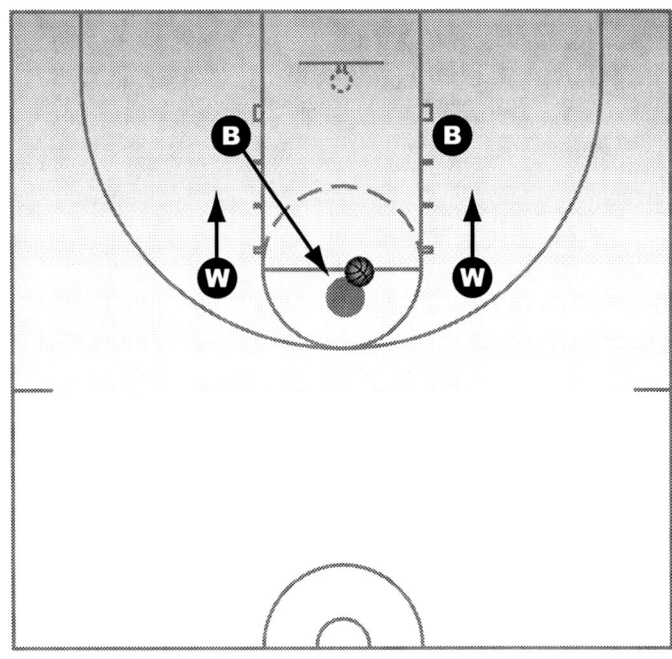

Chaney 2.8

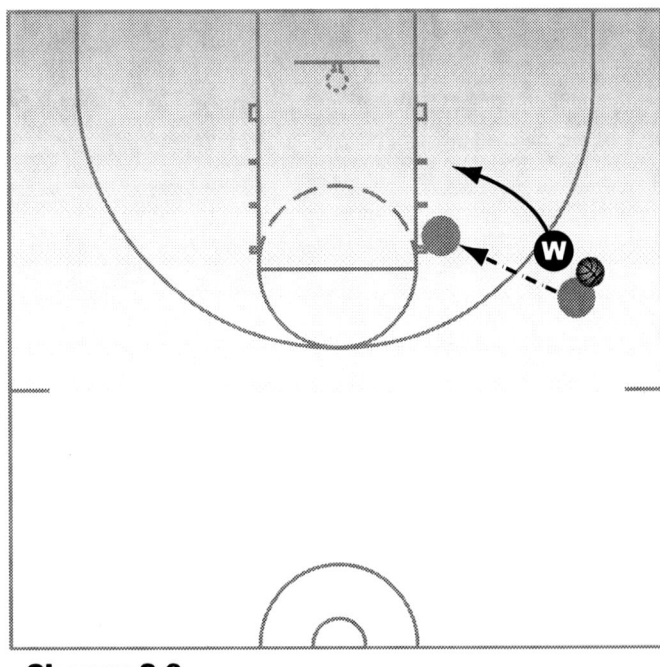

Chaney 2.9

Chaney 2.10

LESSONS FROM THIS LEGEND...

BACK LINE

We will front the low-post man if he is a decent player. Again, they should try to come as high as the offense will allow them. When the ball goes to the wing, the back men move to the cheat position, so that they can get to the next pass under control. (See **Diagram 2.11**)

When the ball goes to the corner position, the ballside back man plays the ball, and the weakside back man steps in front of the block. (See **Diagram 2.12**) If the offensive man catches the ball in front of the back man, we have done a good job because we have pushed him out. It's very important to try to get one step in front of the block.

As the ball is passed back to the wing, the back men must take a step toward the ball first and then slide back to the cheat position. (See **Diagram 2.13**) The reason for this is to prevent a gap in the zone.

When the ball goes into the post, the back men move into post position. As the ball goes into the post, the back man opposite the ball goes up. (See **Diagram 2.14**) If the ball is passed in from the top, the players must communicate, and the one who is free steps up. (See **Diagram 2.15**) The man who steps up plays the ball man-to-man until the offensive player gives the ball up. The other back man moves into the middle. They play like a tandem, protecting a fast break. If the high post man passes opposite, we rotate over. (See **Diagram 2.16**)

Chaney 2.11

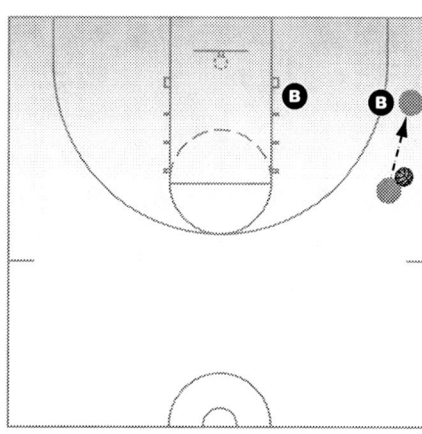
Chaney 2.12

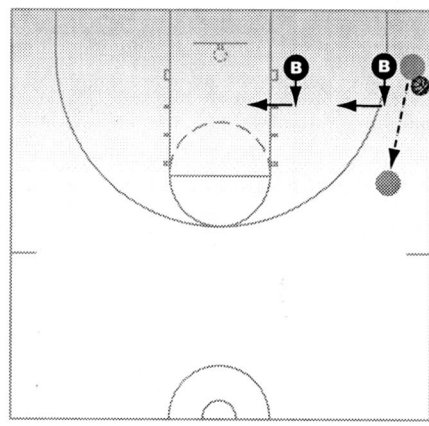
Chaney 2.13

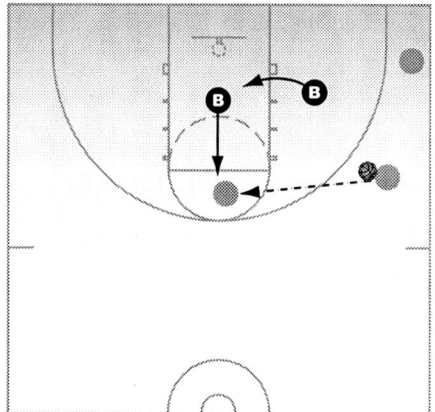
Chaney 2.14

Chaney 2.15

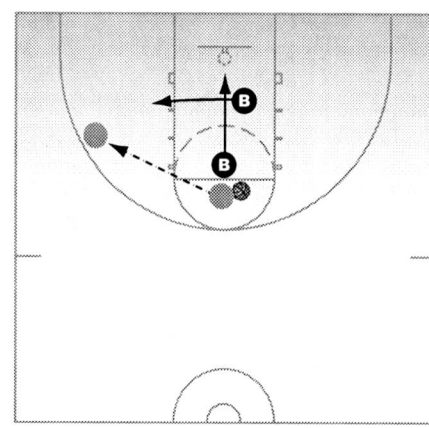
Chaney 2.16

LESSONS FROM THIS LEGEND...

DRILL WORK

To practice and put this into a whole, we work against five offensive players who pass the ball around but do not shoot. (See **Diagram 2.17**)

Now, we add a 6th, 7th, and 8th player to cover all offensive situations. They simply move the ball, and the defensive players work on their slides. (See **Diagram 2.18**)

We also break it down into halves. At one end of the court, we have our front three players working against six passers. At the other end of the court, we have our two back men working against six passers. Have each group work for about 30 seconds and then get another group in. How do you improve? You work on these fundamentals every day.

Your opponent will not always come down and line up in a 1-3-1 alignment. You have to make adjustments. If you face a two-guard front, you might have to adjust your initial position. (See **Diagram 2.19**)

Concerning rebounding in the zone defense, we treat a shot like a pass into the post. Our back man opposite the ball must step up into the middle. (See **Diagram 2.20**) The elbows and the blocks must be covered.

Remember that zones are an effective defense. Break the slides down and teach the proper coverage. To be a good zone defensive team, you must work on it every day.

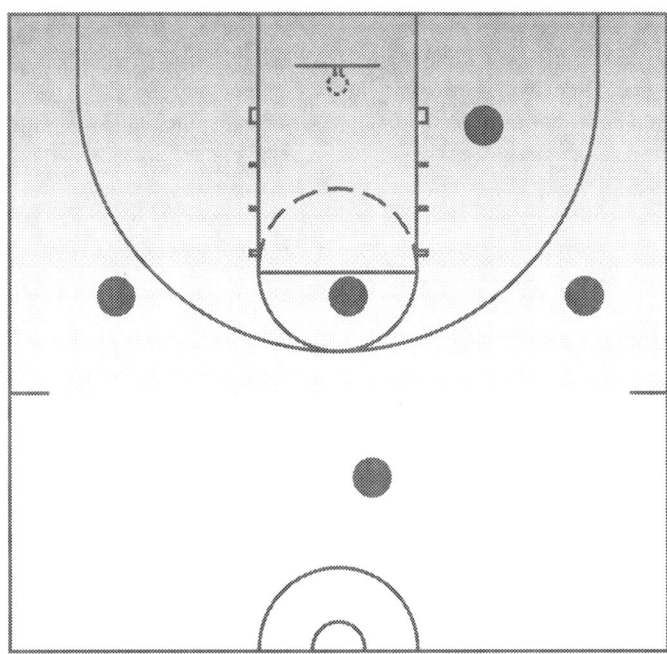

Chaney 2.17

Chaney 2.18

LESSONS FROM THIS LEGEND...

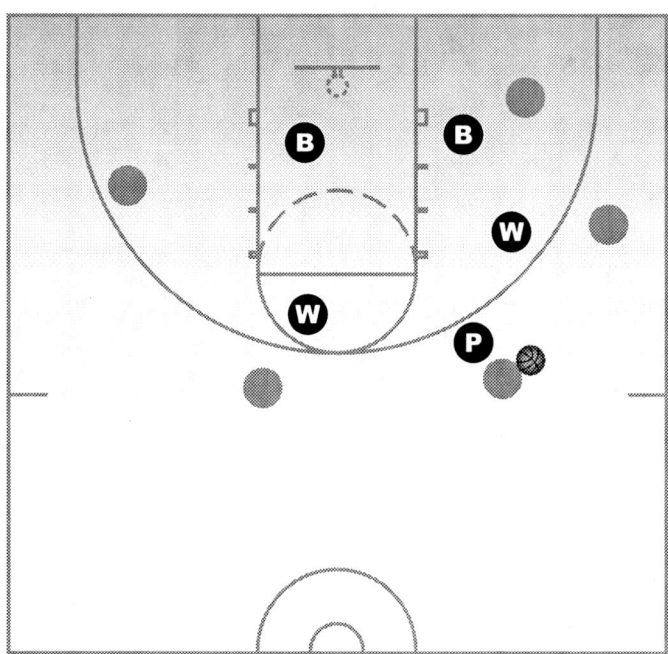

Chaney 2.19

Chaney 2.20

SOURCE

Casey, Don. (1987). *The Temple of Zones.*
MacGregor Flashback Notebook (Vol. 13).

LEGACY OF
Denzil "Denny" Crum

- Believed athleticism, rather than size, was crucial to a team's success. Louisville won championships without a dominating center.

- Built his teams around full-court pressure defenses and a half-court switching, man-to-man defense.

- Became the second fastest coach in NCAA men's basketball history to win 500 games.

- Directed Louisville to six Final Four appearances and two NCAA national championships.

- Recognized as an outstanding teacher who believed the most important thing was to prepare his players for the game of life.

DENZIL "DENNY" CRUM

"Pressure defense is the name of the game."
—Denny Crum

BIOGRAPHY

Born: March 5, 1937 in San Fernando, CA

Inducted into the Naismith Basketball Hall of Fame in 1994

Denny Crum coached at the University of Louisville from 1971 to 2001 and directed the 1980 and 1986 teams to the NCAA championship. Louisville participated in 23 NCAA tournaments and made six Final Four appearances under Crum. He was named National Coach of the Year three times (1980, 1983, and 1986). On the international level, Crum coached the 1977 USA World University team to a gold medal and the 1987 Pan American team to a silver medal. In 1993, Crum became the second fastest coach in history to win 500 games. Crum began his coaching career at Pierce College (CA) and compiled a 86-40 record over four years. He then served as an assistant at UCLA under Coach John Wooden, where the Bruins compiled an 86-4 record and won three NCAA championships (1969, 1970, 1971). Crum was enshrined in the Naismith Memorial Basketball Hall of Fame in 1994.

Denzil "Denny" Crum...

Denny Crum always appeared calm, cool, and collected and earned the nickname "Cool Hand Luke" because of his ability to keep his emotions in check. Crum seldom used pep talks to fire up his team. "He pretty much just mapped the game out for us, got us well prepared, and told us if we went out and executed, we'd win," said Louisville player Roger Burkman. "He was always right."

Louisville trailed Duke at halftime by three points in the 1986 NCAA championship game, and substitute Robbie Valentine thought Coach Crum would "take out a clipboard and start knocking heads." Instead, he stood quietly by the chalkboard and calmly explained the only way that Louisville was going to win the ballgame was to play better defense and proceeded to draw up the necessary strategy. Duke shot only 40 percent from the field, and Louisville won the national title, 72-69.

Crum knew at an early age that he wanted to coach. After his sophomore season at San Fernando H.S. (CA), the sixteen year-old Crum coached his teammates and played point guard in summer leagues. He convinced several car dealerships to sponsor the team, and then he designed the uniforms and drove his teammates to and from games in his father's pickup truck.

After graduating from high school, Crum earned a basketball scholarship to Pierce College in Los Angeles. He led the state's junior colleges in scoring at 27 points per game during his freshman year and signed a basketball scholarship at UCLA after his sophomore year. In a questionnaire filled out when he enrolled at UCLA, Crum wrote only one word after the entry, "Professional Objective," and that word was "Coach."

"Denny was a natural," Coach Wooden said. "He was the only player I ever had who I said was born to coach. He would come into my office after practice from time to time. He wanted to know exactly why we did things and why we didn't do others. He was the most inquisitive player I ever had, and in the proper way. Denny wanted the reasoning behind everything." (Crawford, 2001)

UCLA went 22-4 during Crum's junior season, and he received the Bruin Basketball Award as the most improved all-around player his senior year. Crum stayed at UCLA for one year as a student assistant to Wooden, before returning to Pierce College as an assistant coach in 1961. Crum took over the program for a four-year period when the head coach went on a Mormon mission and directed Pierce to an 86-40 record. In 1968, Crum became Coach Wooden's top assistant and chief recruiter at UCLA.

"Denny is the most competitive person I've ever known," said Len Miller, one of Crum's closest friends and former roommate at UCLA. "But at the same time, you'll never meet a better loser than Denny. I know how much he hurts inside, but he is gracious and poised in defeat." (Crawford, 2001)

After three national championships in three seasons at UCLA, Crum accepted the head coaching position at Louisville in 1971. "Denny was so good that I knew I wasn't going to keep him very long," Wooden said. "I was pleased when he got the job at Louisville. I had always hoped when I retired that he'd be the one to succeed me, but he left and proved to be just what I thought he was." (Crawford, 2001)

Crum's recruiting philosophy at Louisville was to recruit the best athletes regardless of size because his system relied mostly on quickness, jumping, conditioning, and desire. "Basketball is a game for good athletes," said Crum. "That doesn't mean that you don't recruit players with

.....SCOUTING REPORT.....SCOUTING REPORT...

certain skills to fill certain roles. But over the years, we've relied essentially on quickness, jumping, and anticipation. It has been difficult for us to get a big man, so we have compensated with players who can jump and really go to the boards." (Reed, 1986, p. 116)

Team rules were kept to a minimum under Crum's leadership. He required his players to be on time and put the team above individual goals. "If you treat players like adults, there's a better chance they'll act like adults," Crum said. "Part of an education is learning to make decisions and accepting the consequences. If I tried to restrict and control their every movement, I would be doing them a disservice." (Reed, 1986, p. 117)

Crum was an outstanding basketball strategist who always seemed to have the right players on the floor in every situation. "When we get down to the end of the game, I always feel we have an edge, because our players are in good condition, our schedule has given us the confidence to play against the best, the players have confidence in my ability to make the right decision, and they have been drilled enough to know what to do," stated Crum. (Reed, 1986, p. 119)

Crum believed that defense was the most important part of the game. His basketball philosophy was to pressure opponents for forty minutes. "Pressure is the name of the game as far as we're concerned," stated Crum. "We hope the other team will crack somewhere, and we'll get a little spurt, which is really all it takes. It's human to err—and pressure causes errors. In golf, for example, it's tougher to make a three-foot putt on No. 17 or No. 18 with all the money on the line than it is to make the same putt on No. 1. You can never relax when you play us because of our continuous pressure." (Reed, 1986, p. 118)

Crum stated the key to his half-court defense was switching on all screens both on and off the ball. He learned this concept from his days as an assistant for Hall of Fame coach John Wooden. "There's no question that it is the best defense," stated Wooden. "Many people forget that we won ten national championships playing the switching man-to-man defense." (Crum, 1981, p.55)

Crum listed the following advantages of a switching defense:
1. Combines the weakside help of a zone defense and the strongside pressure of a man-to-man defense.
2. Keeps your big men in excellent rebounding position.
3. Keeps your guards out front in position for a quick pass on a fast break.
4. Forces opponents to go to their third and fourth options in their offense for which they are less proficient.
5. You don't have to use practice time to prepare against all the different offenses you will face.

Denny Crum did more than just win games at Louisville. He was an excellent teacher who instilled confidence in his players and prepared them for life after their basketball days were over. Junior Bridgeman played for Louisville from 1972 to 1975 and described the impact that Crum had on his life in these words. "Coach made you grow up. He taught everybody who played for him that if you were going to be successful, it was going to come from within. He could teach you, work with you, and help you. But in the end, you knew that it was your job to get better and to push yourself in order to reach your goals. You came to realize that he was teaching you as much about life as about basketball. He let you know from the start that the most important thing was the game of life, not basketball. His impact on my life, and on many lives, has been tremendous." (Bridgeman, 2001)

SOURCE

Bridgeman, Junior. (2001). The Players Remember. *The Courier-Journal*.

Crawford, Eric. (2001). Wooden Knew a Great Coach When He Saw One Beside Him at UCLA. *The Courier-Journal*.

Crum, Denny. Vertical Files, Archives. Naismith Memorial Basketball Hall of Fame. Springfield, MA.

Reed, Billy. (1986). *Born To Coach*. The Courier-Journal & The Louisville Times.

LESSONS FROM THIS LEGEND...

PRESSING DEFENSES

By Denny Crum

The key to Louisville's success is our defense and the ability to control the tempo of the game, two factors that go hand-in-hand on the court. By using a full-court press and a switching man-to-man defense, we can speed up the game and put pressure on the opponent.

THOUGHTS ON PRESSING

No press can steal the ball every time. In fact, I don't think that you can steal the ball as much now from the press as you could five or ten years ago. The reason for this is very simple. Players see the press from a very early age, because you teach them the press. They grow up more accustomed to it. It used to be more of a psychological advantage than it is now.

BY-PRODUCTS OF THE PRESS

I learned from Coach Wooden that the by-products of the press are far more valuable than the press itself. The reason his teams pressed was not to steal the ball but rather to dictate the tempo of the game. Other byproducts of the press include the following:
- Players love to press and fans love to watch it.
- A press at the beginning of the game can cause a turnover, which relaxes your players and puts extra pressure on your opponents.
- Pressing requires your players to be in excellent physical condition.
- It allows a coach to use more players
- It teaches anticipation, which is carried over to other defensive plays.
- When you press, your players are prepared to attack a press, because they play against it every day.
- Most importantly, the press sets the tempo and edges your opponents out of their offensive strategies, forcing them to do things they don't normally do.

THE 2-2-1 PRESS

When I talk about the 2-2-1 press, I like to go back to the great 1964 UCLA team who ran it so well, and evaluate the type of player they had at each position. I think they typified the types of players you need to run this press. The initial alignment for the press is shown in **Diagram 1.0**. The player in the X1 spot was Gail Goodrich. He played this position for a reason. One reason was that he was the quickest player they had. The way they played this press was to let you have the inbounds pass. Ninety percent of the time, the ball is inbounded on the right side and because of this, they wanted their quickest player to be on the ball when it came in. If you allow the ball inbounds, you will be going against their best ballhandler from the #1 spot. Goodrich was left-handed, and Coach Wooden felt that it was not to UCLA's advantage to allow a good ballhandler to go up the sidelines. Gail, being left-handed, would be stronger to his left and could turn and control the ball better on that side than anyone else. I have seen teams run this press and try to trap the ball

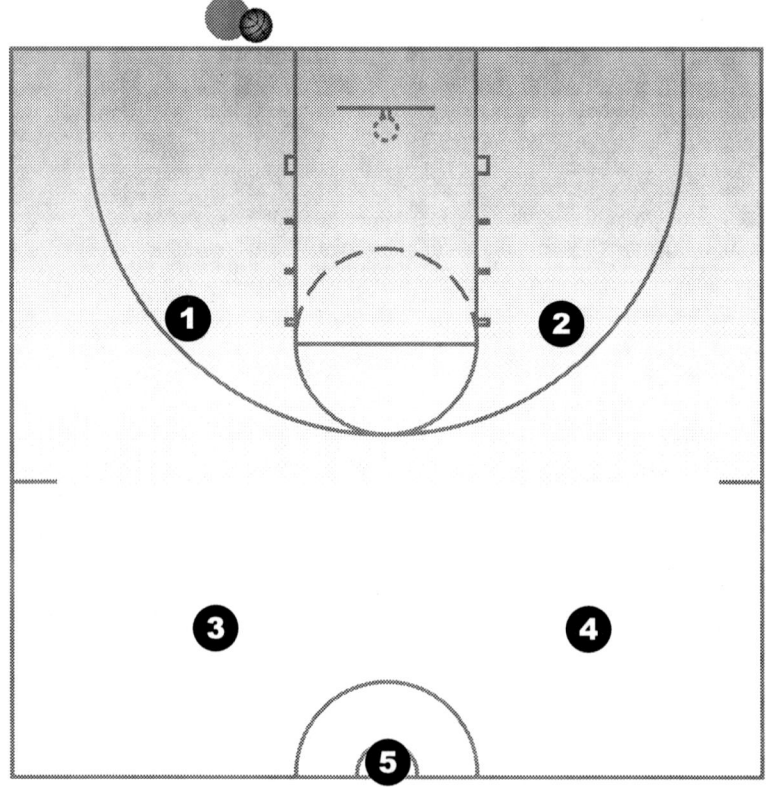

Crum 1.0

LESSONS FROM THIS LEGEND...

on the sidelines. You just can't trap good dribblers and good ballhandlers.

What UCLA wanted to do was to pressure the ball to the middle. He wanted the opponent to dribble the ball. When they put the ball on the floor, X1 and X2 would trap in the middle of the floor, not the sideline (See **Diagram 1.1**). The reason this trap is good is because it allows you to combat the passes the opponent can make to hurt you. If the offense throws the ball back, it doesn't hurt you.

The X2 spot was covered by a freshman by the name of Fred Slaughter. He was placed in this position because he was big and quick. His size improved the effectiveness of the trap and forced the ballhandler to make either a lob or bounce pass. These are slower types of passes and allow the defenders time to read just the press. Any quick, direct pass will beat the press, so a slower pass must be forced. Fred was also very strong when the ball was stolen.

In the X3 spot was Walt Hazzard (See **Diagram 1.0**). He played there because he was the worst defensive player they had. Coach Wooden felt that the weakest defensive player could handle the X3 position.

What most teams do against the press is to bring someone from the weakside into the middle. This is the responsibility of the X4 man (See **Diagram 1.2**). Coach Wooden put a player by the name of Hirsh in this position, and he was called the garbage man. He was 6-foot 3-inches and quick and left-handed. The advantage that a left-handed player would have here is that his dominant hand would be on the ballside. The cutter is also coming from your weak to your strong hand. It is human nature to reach with your best hand. You will steal more balls with it.

The players were placed in certain positions for a reason. Therefore, if you analyze the players by position for a reason, it tells you what kind of player you need at each spot.

Crum 1.1

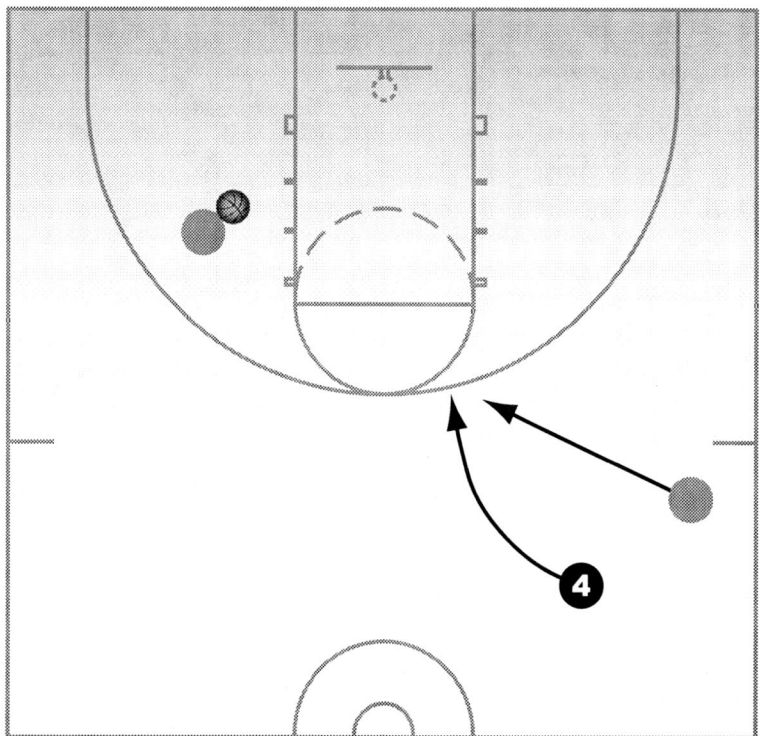

Crum 1.2

LESSONS FROM THIS LEGEND...

If you analyze a press in terms of what you are trying to get out of it, you have two or three different ways to play this press. UCLA played it by letting the ball get inbounds, and then double team and anticipate with the other three players. What else could be done with this press? We have all seen teams force you down the sidelines and trap with the X3 man; X5 rotates and covers the sideline. X2 drops back to the middle, and X4 rotates back to protect the basket. If you think you can trap a good ballhandler on the sideline, you might want to play the press like this.

UCLA found that most teams were becoming very deliberate in attacking this press, and it was slowing the tempo of the game rather than speeding it up. They decided to move X1 and X2 up and force the lob pass over the front-line players. Instead of letting the ball come inbounds, now you are denying the pass in. X3 and X4 must be moved up a little bit to play the lob. The best anticipators now should be X3 and X4. This forces the opponent to run and increases the tempo of the game.

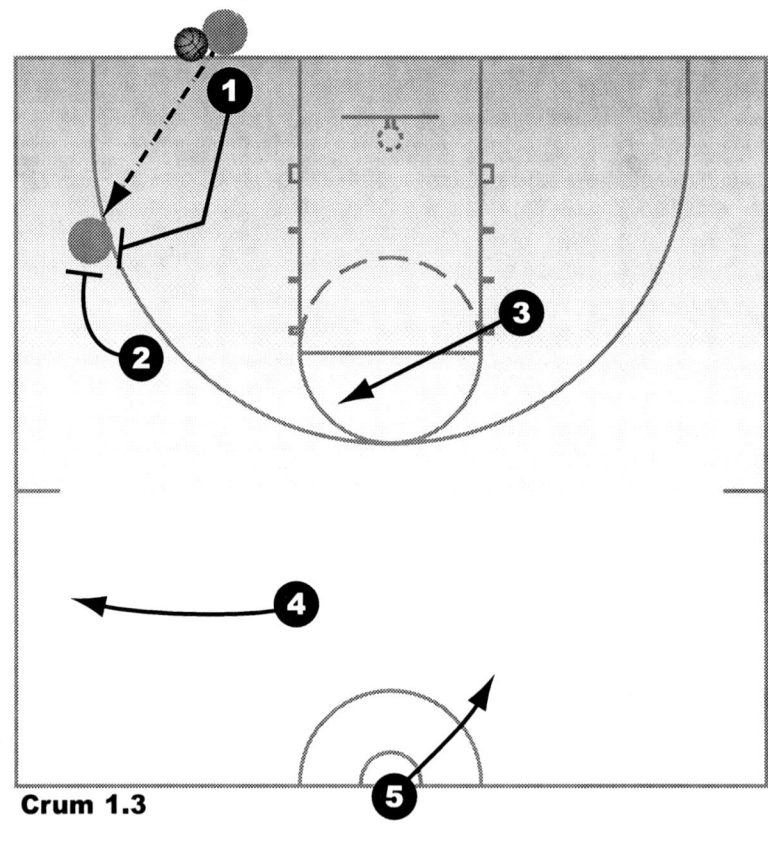

Crum 1.3

THE 1-2-1-1 PRESS

The 1-2-1-1 press is designed to get a quick trap and keep pressure all over the floor. In the 2-2-1 press, you have to have only one good anticipator. In the 1-2-1-1 press, you have to have at least two. **Diagram 1.3** shows the alignment of this press. X1 is usually one of your bigger players. You often can hide somebody at the X1 spot who isn't a good defensive player. X2 and X3 must have good quickness, and they have to be able to play good tough defense. They must be able to cover the middle on a diagonal cutter and make the ball be reversed. X4 and X5 must be good anticipators, must be interchangeable, and must cover the back of your zone effectively.

This press is designed to trap. Trapping does not mean fouling. I believe you can trap without fouling. Once the ball is stopped, we tell our players to get at arms length and stay there. The closer the defense gets to the trapped player, the easier it is to get the ball by him. Anytime you are double teaming, you are gambling, and you know that when they beat the trap, they will outnumber you.

FALLING BACK INTO YOUR HALF-COURT DEFENSE

At the end of the press, we transition into a switching man-to-man defense by matching up with the nearest opponent. If the screen is set on the ball, switching is automatic, regardless of what the offense does. The defensive player on the screener calls the screen and jump-switches immediately. Very few teams switch on defense like we do. Since our opponents are not used to this type of defense, we can confuse them easily. We play man-to-man defense with zone principles, so that we take away what our opponents want to do. We try to deny their ball reversal and force the backdoor move. We follow the following defensive rules:

1. Deny the strongside, one pass away from the ball
2. Deny ball reversal
3. Front all post players
4. Sag hard from the weakside two passes away from the ball
5. Switch on all screens on the ball
6. Switch on all screens away from the ball

KEY TEACHING POINTS

In any kind of press you must teach your players not only to react, but also to anticipate. The way you do that is to take the things that most people do ninety percent of the time against a press, and you put them into drill situations. You take the people who are going to play for you and teach them these situations and how to handle them.

One of the things that you've got to teach your players is to always watch the eyes of

LESSONS FROM THIS LEGEND...

the player with the ball. There are players who would be good anticipators if they knew where to look. If I have the ball in my hands, in order to pass the ball to a teammate effectively, I must see him. I think that you have to look in order to get the ball to another player. Because we believe this, we teach our players to watch the eyes of the player with the ball. You have to teach X4 and X5 to watch the eyes of the man with the ball and anticipate the next pass. If the long pass is thrown, it should be easy to anticipate and intercept.

I think that everybody can press, but in order to do so effectively, you must evaluate your personnel. If you don't have good quickness, don't try to use a gambling press. You can put pressure on people using a press even with slower players. Don't be afraid to press just because you are not real quick. You can still control tempo. You can slow down a game just like you can speed it up. If you press man-to-man, you speed the game up. If you press with a zone, you can slow it down. A press is designed to be used according to what you are trying to get out of it. I believe everybody should have a good press.

Pressing has changed a lot in the last few years. I happen to feel that it is not as effective as it used to be. Analyze this comment: If the press gets the ball for you now only three times where it used to get the ball ten or fifteen times, what does it mean? This means that the steal is that much more valuable now. If you can't get the ball as much as you used to, the value of the ball has risen. Each possession today is worth one point. The press is more important now than it used to be, but not as effective.

SOURCE

Crum, Denny. (1975). Pressing Defenses. *The Basketball Bulletin (Winter Edition)*.

LEGACY OF
Clarence "Big House" Gaines

- Mentored by John McLendon, the "Father of Black Coaches," and was one of the first coaches to break the color barrier in collegiate basketball.

- Spent 47 years at the same school and is the namesake of the C.E. Gaines Center at Winston-Salem University.

- Retired as the second winningest coach in college basketball history.

- Under Gaines' tutelage, his teams were nationally acclaimed for their up-tempo, fast-breaking style of play.

- Led Winston-Salem to the NCAA College Division national championship in 1967.

- Respected as an outstanding humanitarian who truly cared about his students and players.

- Enshrined in eight Halls of Fame.

CLARENCE "BIG HOUSE" GAINES

"Coaches come and go. Records come and go. But if you touch peoples' lives, they remember you."
—Clarence "Big House" Gaines

BIOGRAPHY

Born: May 21, 1923 in Paducah, KY

Inducted into the Naismith Basketball Hall of Fame in 1982

Clarence Edward Gaines was born just before the Great Depression of the 1930s. He attended Lincoln (Paducah, KY) H.S. and was a star football and basketball player. Gaines attended Morgan State (MD) College, where he played basketball for four years and excelled as a football tackle. After graduation in 1945, Gaines accepted a job at Winston-Salem College as an assistant coach in three sports: football, basketball, and track and field. In 1947, he was promoted to head coach in all three sports and eventually became athletic director, professor of physical education, and director of the physical education department. Gaines spent his entire career (47 years) at Winston-Salem, where his basketball teams were 828-447. By 1981, Gaines had become the nation's winningest active coach. His teams won 20 or more games 18 times and captured the Central Intercollegiate Athletic Association (CIAA) championship 12 times. In 1967, the team compiled a 31-1 record and became the first historically black school to win a NCAA national basketball championship (College Division). Gaines retired in 1993 with 828 wins, making him the second winningest coach in NCAA history at the time (behind legendary Adolph Rupp). He has been inducted into eight Halls of Fame, served as president of the NABC, and was selected National Coach of the Year in 1967. Gaines was enshrined in the Naismith Memorial Basketball Hall of Fame in 1982.

Clarence "Big House" Gaines...

Clarence Gaines came from Kentucky Bluegrass Country with humble beginnings in Paducah. He played a lot of basketball as a youngster, even though he didn't have a real basket or even a ball. Gaines' father nailed a barrel hoop on a coal-house door, and they would shoot baskets with any kind of ball they could find.

Gaines starred in football and excelled in basketball at Lincoln (Paducah, KY) H.S. His inspiration was his mother, Olivia. She was an outstanding athlete and would play against Clarence in basketball, softball, and tennis. "I could never beat her," stated Gaines (2003). "Plus the most important thing was that she insisted that I practice and master the basic fundamentals of basketball."

As a young child, Gaines was taught to adhere to the Golden Rule. "My parents emphasized three key points," said Gaines. "Don't lie, don't cheat, don't steal. I've carried these values with me throughout my entire life."

After graduation from high school, Gaines enrolled at Morgan State (MD) College. He left home with 50 dollars in his pocket, driving an old Ford. Upon his arrival at the campus, Clarence stopped at the administration building to ask for directions from the school's business manager, Jimmy Carter. Upon seeing Gaines he remarked "I've never seen anything bigger than you but a house." Thus, the frame produced the name "Big House," and it stuck. He left with a degree in chemistry and Little All-American status in football.

Following his graduation in 1946, "Big House" packed his bags for Winston-Salem State College in 1946, where he was to be assistant coach in football, basketball, and track and field. He planned to stay one year, just long enough to save money for dental school. Forty-seven years later, he was still at Winston-Salem (now a university). "I don't think I was meant to be a dentist," says Gaines, "Coaching is what the Lord called me to do."

What a fantastic forty-seven years it became. Gaines spent only two years as an assistant coach before being elevated to head coach of all three sports, common in those days. His stated goal became to "succeed not only as an athletic coach but also as a respected and significant asset to the university and community." He did that and more. At the time of his retirement, Gaines was the second winningest coach in college basketball history. He also held the positions of athletic director and chairperson of the physical education department and had attained the academic rank of professor of physical education.

In addition, he became a champion of youth sports, not only in the Winston-Salem area, but also in North Carolina. Clarence became a fixture in local youth sports programs and civic organizations. He was truly an educator who reached out to touch the lives and make a difference in the lives of his athletes and students but also young people and others in his community.

"The greatest pleasure I got out of athletics was to see all the guys we work with, who weren't supposed to make it (by society's standards), grow into successful young men." said Gaines. "I've been around for a long enough time to have coached some of the guys who are now retired, and every time I see one of them, I just smile."

Coach Gaines developed an effective system of play, based on fast-breaking, up-tempo basketball. He emphasized ball movement and wanted his post players to flash toward the ball, rather than standing on the block. Gaines also used the "give-and-go play," one of the first plays ever used in basketball. Gaines said, "We did a lot of practicing with no dribbling allowed. The ball had to be passed, rather than dribbled. Players could not stand and wait for the pass. They had to move toward the ball to meet it."

Gaines also used the "four corners" offense popularized by Dean Smith at North Carolina. Hall of Fame coach John McLendon actually developed the concept and called the strategy "Jack in the Corner." Early in his career, Gaines was befriended and mentored by the legendary McLendon who is called the "Father of Black Basketball Coaches."

Winston-Salem's star player on their 1967 national championship team was future Hall of Famer Earl "The Pearl" Monroe. Under Gaines' direction, Monroe was allowed to develop, perfect, and popularize the "spin dribble." Gaines said, "Earl was truly a 'pearl'—a coach's player. I never had a more conscientious player, a harder worker, or a player with a better personality."

Consistency and level-headedness were characteristics of "Big House" Gaines. He handled both victory and defeat with a level response. If the team won, he commended his players for good execution. If they lost, stress was placed on the part of their execution that could be improved. It was a very evenhanded approach that was one component that produced a local legend and a national treasure. Big House seemed always to praise his players and show appreciation for their efforts. Perseverance and humility were trademarks of his classy, professional approach. On the occasion of

.....SCOUTING REPORT.....SCOUTING REPORT...

New Year's Eve day before his team would achieve win number six hundred for him as a head coach, Clarence was asked how he nervously spent the day. He responded that he "scrubbed the kitchen floor," because his lovely wife, Clara, had asked him to do just that. Win number six hundred followed that night before a sparse crowd and honored only by a private party afterwards.

Clarence Gaines also was respected as a humanitarian. He regularly hosted the visiting coach after their game to get a barbecue sandwich or something to eat. Big House stated that he believed it was just the right thing to do. "We are both coaches of basketball; not going to war, but playing a game." He was so revered that he regularly was asked to speak at sports banquets, as are all coaches, but Clarence was asked to speak to rival schools (unheard of in coaching circles). As a humanitarian coach, he was most concerned about players' academic achievement, focusing on hard work. Gaines was especially honored with the prestigious Paul Robeson Award in this area of achievement.

His forty-seven year coaching career was also noteworthy because it occurred in these challenging eras:

- **1947-57**, the "Dark Years," when the contributions of Black Colleges in the United States were unknown and invisible. Black coaches had the added burden of travel, lodging, and board for movement between campuses and competitions in a very hostile social climate—"like a GI plotting a course through a minefield," avoiding and managing hostile racial confrontations and at the same time, maintaining a necessary role of respect, dignity, and leadership." (McLendon, 1982)

- **1960-70**, the period called the social revolution or protest or the "Turbulent Sixties." Victories were difficult in this time period, but a Gaines team reached the pinnacle of success by winning the 1967 College Division Championship.

- **1970-80**, the period of uncertainty and focus on "me" (the drug generation). Through this period of change (times/athletes/students/administrations/rules), the constant factor was Coach Gaines, a "Big House" on the scene—disciplined, adhering to moral coaching principles, unassailable integrity, and a style of gentle, yet firm, authority with class (McLendon, 1982). It was also said that his abilities as a coach were exceeded only by his integrity and his concern for the welfare and education of his athletes. "Gaines has done more to improve the quality of coaching and general conditions of play among predominantly black colleges than any other person." (Fritz, 1980) Big House, in his own way, was responsible for developing higher coaching standards, as well as higher academic and performance standards.

Throughout his career, Gaines was influenced by several future Hall of Fame coaches. Here are his thoughts on some of the game's greatest coaches:

- "Coach John McLendon was a great innovator, mentor, and fundamentalist."
- "The most impressive clinician had to be Adolph Rupp. He could teach more basketball in 15 to 20 minutes than a lot of coaches could teach in two days. I learned all about the continuity offense from him."
- "Nobody ever wrote as many books and articles or ran more clinics both in the U.S. and abroad than Clair Bee. He also wrote the greatest series of juvenile sports novels ever published—the Chip Hilton series."
- "Everett Dean was another outstanding clinician. He wrote *Progressive Basketball*, which I consider the first 'scientific' textbook on basketball."
- "Another outstanding coach and person is Bob Knight. I believe he is the greatest humanitarian in basketball. He helps a lot of people and gets involved in a lot of good causes, without attracting attention to himself."

Gaines urged coaches today to teach fundamental skills and stress the importance of education. Gaines (2003) said, "The low graduation rates worry me. Education is the answer. Back in the old days, there was no professional basketball for black youngsters. We worked with everyone and stressed the importance of a college degree. We need to get back to emphasizing the importance of education."

Gaines would like to see two rule changes in the game of basketball. First, is the distance of the three-point shot. Gaines would like to push the three-point arc back to the international distance. Second, is the number of personal fouls allowed before disqualification. Gaines would like to give each player an extra foul—six instead of five.

Finally, notice should be made of the universal respect and recognition given to Clarence Gaines for his personal and professional accomplishments. He has been inducted into eight Halls of Fame, including CIAA, North Carolina Sports, Winston-Salem State University, National Association of Intercollegiate (NAIA), and the Naismith Basketball Hall of Fame. Uniquely, his nomination for the Naismith honor was sponsored by a rival institution in the CIAA conference, a real tribute to the respect earned by Clarence.

SOURCE

Fritz, Harry. (1980, May 29). Letter to Naismith Memorial Basketball Hall of Fame.

Gaines, Clarence. Vertical Files, Archives. Naismith Memorial Basketball Hall of Fame. Springfield, MA.

Gaines, Clarence. Interview with Ralph Pim. September 6, 2003.

Gaines, Clarence. (1994, April). Break out at the Big House. *Scholastic Coach*.

McLendon. John. (1982, May 3). Presentation at the Naismith Hall of Fame.

LESSONS FROM THIS LEGEND...

COMBINATION MATCH-UP DEFENSE

By Clarence "Big House" Gaines

I teach the match-up defense to my staff and our players in my own way. I just call it "understanding." One of my most talented teams ended up with a mediocre record, because there wasn't enough communication and understanding between all persons concerned.

The understanding that must be considered is between players and coaches. I think with all the coverage that is given basketball teams by the media, a lot of jealousy exists. If an athlete's performance merits television, radio, and newspaper coverage, or any other plaudits, then he deserves it. But, it is the coach's responsibility to see that this publicity does not interfere with his program, and that ill feelings among the players or the faculty and staff do not result. We have a monumental task to perform in the development of a complete person. Opportunities only come to those who are prepared.

We have used the match-up zone very successfully for the past eight or ten years. I call our zone "a point and something."

The first thing I try to get through to every player is that at one time or another in our defense, everybody's going to be the point man. We line up every time in 1-2-2. The players are numbered 1 through 5 (See **Diagram 1.0**). We get in a basketball position; we don't do a lot of arm waving and that sort of thing. We're always in a basketball position to try to go someplace.

If you look at this thing from a theoretical stand-point, when the ball is out front, we want Number 1 to have a man-to-man attitude, an almost pressure attitude, because we do not want him to allow the ballhandler, their one guard, to have an easy pass. Therefore, I come out with a triangle (See **Diagram 1.1**). Now, when the ball is rotated, I'm going to end up with a triangle and a square.

We're not like most coaches, who hold up cards or call out numbers to call their plays. We don't have any plays. We have four offensive sets, and we try to do what we can according to what the defense does. There's no need fighting it, no need fighting a defense at all. When the ball is rotated to Number 2's territory, or area, our players move (See **Diagram 1.2**). Let them play with it; you'll be surprised how players discover new areas where they actually should be, or learn how to close off the passing lanes when you ask them to change their attitude toward it and let them do the drawing on the board.

What kinds of drills actually go with this sort of thing? The first thing we try to get our guys to understand is the conditioning

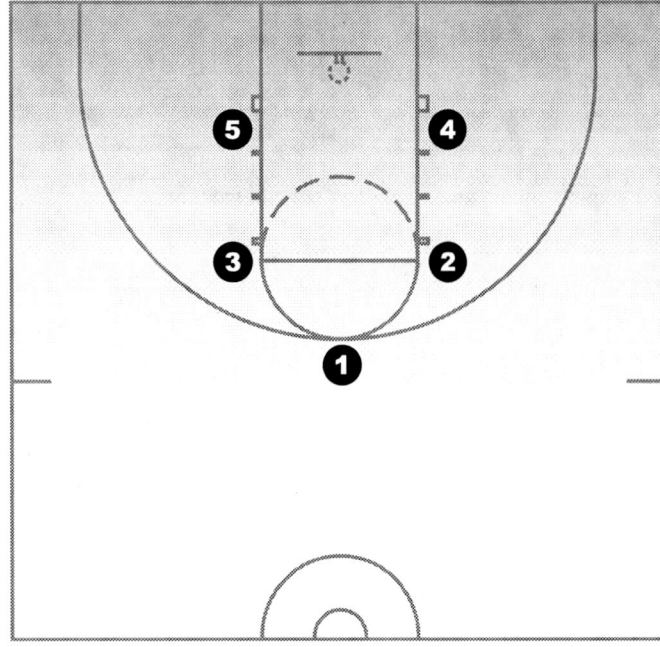

Gaines 1.0

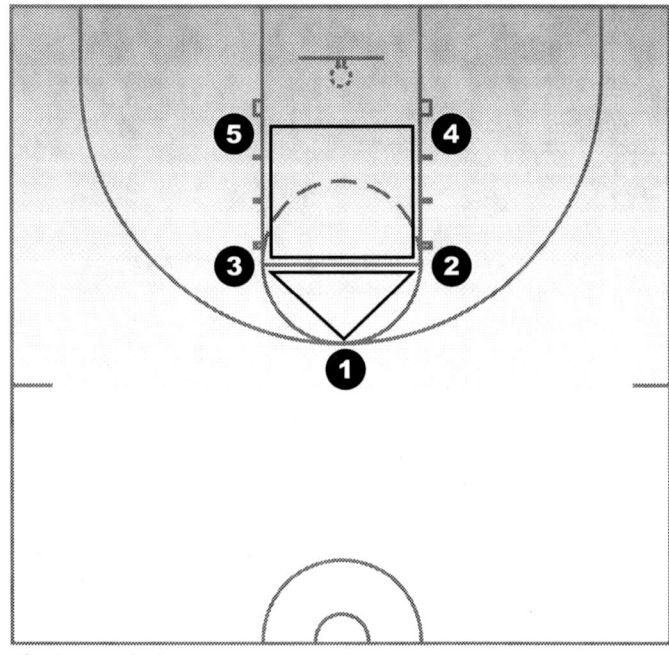

Gaines 1.1

LESSONS FROM THIS LEGEND...

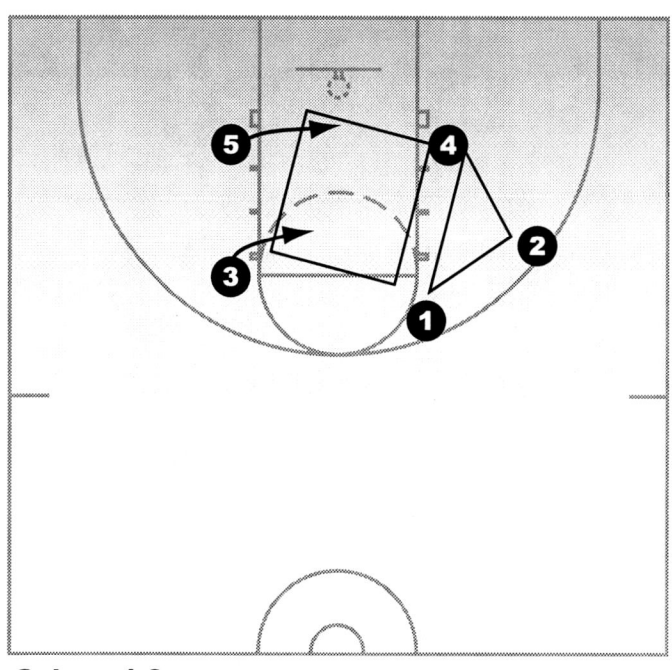

Gaines 1.2

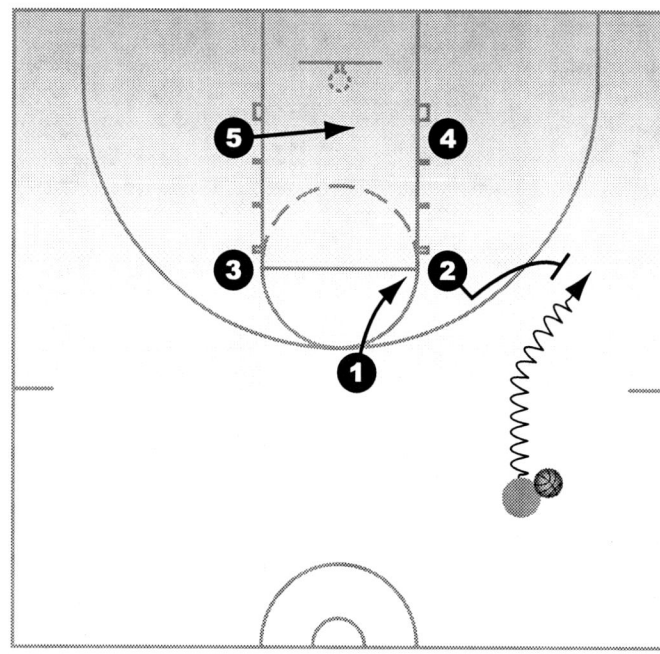

Gaines 1.3

process. They've got to be able to defend a man full-court. For conditioning purposes, we teach the full-court defense and full-court offense before we go into any patterns, and we have the guys dribble one-on-one full-court.

We have a few basic rules that we follow in the matchup. It's really not a match-up zone at all, but rather a combination defense utilizing zone principles and man-to-man principles.

If we get caught in a transition situation, Number 1, who is 5' 11", tries to contain and hold off. During our practice sessions, everybody plays everybody else's spot so they will know exactly what their responsibilities are.

The other thing that bothers us in this setup is that we run across a lot of stack offenses. Our rule states: when the opponent does not place a man in the post and positions someone on the side, we are in a 1-3-1 zone.

We don't want them to get the ball into the middle. We're going to pressure and see that it's as hard as possible for them to do this. Ninety percent of the time when the ball gets inside, it goes to the floor on the dribble, and we drill against it. In practice, every time the ball goes on the floor, we clobber the guy in the middle who puts it on the floor, and it is no foul. After a while when a player gets all the bruises, he figures out that the coach wants rapid ball movement.

In our match-up zone, we teach the players to go hell-for-leather for 27 seconds and force the opponent to take a bad shot. All I've got to get these players to understand is that when they get the ball, they've got to shoot it in thirty-five seconds. I'll tell them to see if they can't bust a gut and get everybody dealing with this sort of thing, and then it's pretty easy to get the thirty-five seconds over with.

Another rule is that if the ball is dribbled to the corner, the moment the other team puts the ball on the floor three times, our defender knows he is in man-to-man defense and follows his man (See **Diagram 1.3**). He takes the man until the series is over. When is the series over? When they take a shot.

Remember, we never plan to widen out our triangle and square too much, because we don't want the offense to find an easy way to get the ball into the middle.

SOURCE

Krause, Jerry and Ralph Pim. (2002). *Coaching Basketball*. New York: McGraw-Hill.

LEGACY OF
A.T. "Slats" Gill

- Possessed the highest moral-ethical values, and his integrity could never be doubted.

- His gracious and gentlemanly manner made him one of the most well-liked and respected coaches in the nation.

- Developed winning teams known for their strong defense and ball-control offense.

- Led Oregon State to Final Four appearances in 1949 and 1963.

- The coliseum on Oregon State's campus named in Gill's honor.

- Earned All-American honors as a player at Oregon State in 1924.

A.T. "SLATS" GILL

"A defender must counter every move of an offensive player with a retreating step."
—A.T. "Slats" Gill

BIOGRAPHY

Born: May 1, 1901 in Salem, OR

Died: April 5, 1966

Inducted into the Naismith Basketball Hall of Fame in 1968

Amory "Slats" Gill was the head basketball coach at Oregon State from 1929 to 1964 and compiled a 599-392 record. His teams won five Pacific Coast Conference championships and earned nine PCC Northern Division titles. Gill led the Beavers to Final Four appearances in 1949 and 1963 and coached 11 All-Americans. He was president of the NABC in 1957-58 and was selected to coach the NABC West All-Star team in 1964. Gill received the Hayward Award as the top sports personality in the State of Oregon in 1955. He was a coach at the U.S. Olympic trials in 1964. Gill served as the school's athletic director from 1964 to 1966, and the coliseum on Oregon State's campus was named in Gill's honor. In 2002, he was inducted into the Pacific-10 Conference Basketball Hall of Honor. His 276 conference wins were second only to legendary UCLA coach John Wooden. Gill was enshrined in the Naismith Memorial Basketball Hall of Fame in 1968.

...SCOUTING REPORT.....SCOUTING REPORT.....

A.T. "Slats" Gill...

A.T. Gill was affectionately known to his friends and admirers as "Slats" because of his slim build. He was raised in Salem, Oregon and was the youngest of three brothers. All three boys excelled in football, basketball, and baseball at Salem H.S. (OR). They continued their athletic careers at Oregon State, and each of the boys specialized in a sport: Whitney, was captain of the baseball team, Eugene captained the football team, and "Slats" was captain of the basketball team.

"Slats" Gill earned first-team All-State honors in basketball in 1919 and 1920 and led his high school team to the state basketball championship in 1919. At Oregon State, Gill was selected twice to the All-Pacific Coast Conference basketball team and earned All-American honors in 1924. Gill and All-American teammate, Marshall Hjelte, led the Beavers to a 21-2 record in 1922 and a second-place finish in the Pacific Coast Conference.

After graduation from Oregon State in 1924, Gill coached two years at Oakland H.S. (CA). He then returned to Oregon State as freshman basketball coach. In 1928, Gill was named head basketball coach, and he served in that capacity for the next 36 years.

A turning point in Gill's coaching career occurred in 1933 when the Beavers were the first Oregon State team in any sport to win a championship. Gill looked back at the early 1930's as among the most difficult years of his career. There was a movement led by Oregon State alumni to force the firing of Gill. Ed Lewis, whose jersey was retired in 1999 and who has often been described as the Pete Maravich of his generation, remembered the incident in these words. "There was a movement in Portland to get rid of him in 1932. It made a real impression on me. It forced me to change my mind about what I wanted to do for a living. I had decided I wanted to be a coach, but after watching what "Slats" had to go through, I changed my major to business." (Edmonston, 2003)

Very likely, Gill's 1933 team and their championship performance saved his coaching career and saved OSU from a men's basketball legacy that could have been very different. In 1933, Washington had won five PCC championships in a row and was the overwhelming favorite to repeat. At the season's end, with the divisional title on the line, Oregon State won two games at Washington to finish on top of the Northern Division. Gill's team then faced the USC Trojans, coached by future Hall of Famer Sam Barry, in a best-of-three series to determine the conference champion. It proved to be one of the greatest series in Oregon State history. In the first game, Ed Lewis led the Beavers to a 35-33 victory. The Trojans won the second game 39-28, and it was down to one final contest. In a carefully played third game, Oregon State prevailed 24-19.

Gill's gracious and gentlemanly manner made him one of the most well-liked coaches in the nation. His team mirrored his disposition and sparked the popularity of college basketball at Oregon State.

Gill believed athletics developed boys into men, and good men into better men. He viewed competition as a demanding, but healthy, teacher. He possessed the highest moral character and integrity that could never be doubted. Gill's excellence in leadership was displayed by the outstanding achievements of his players after their graduation from college.

Merle Taylor played on the 1933 championship team and said "The thing I remember most about "Slats" is how great a man he was. After my first year, I had no money to continue in school, so I was planning to leave OSU. My folks were farmers, and one day while I was working in the field, I saw this man walking across our place headed toward me and wearing a suit. It was "Slats" and he asked, 'Merle, do you want to go to school?' I answered him 'yes' and he said that if I would come back, he would give me a scholarship and a job. It changed my life." (Edmonston, 2003)

.....SCOUTING REPORT.....SCOUTING REPORT...

SOURCE

Edmonston, George P. Jr. (2003, February 9). 1933: The Beginning of OSU Basketball's Legacy. *Corvallis Gazette-Times*.

Hobson, Howard. (1968, April 12). Letter to the Naismith Basketball Hall of Fame.

Gill, A.T. Vertical Files, Archives. Naismith Memorial Basketball Hall of Fame. Springfield, MA.

Ed Lewis expressed similar feelings about Gill: "I lost my dad when I was young, so I grew up without a dad. "Slats" was the closest thing I ever had to a father. He was a great man." (Edmonston, 2003)

"Slat's dedication to the game was unmatched," said former assistant Paul Valenti. Hall of Fame coach Howard Hobson agreed and stated, "I have never known a man more dedicated to the game of basketball." (Hobson, 1968)

In addition to compiling an outstanding coaching record, Gill was a highly respected citizen and contributed greatly to his community, state, and university. He was prominent in educational services and was chairman of the Corvallis School Board. Gill was a member of the Oregon State University chapter of Phi Delta Theta, served on the Board of Directors for the NABC, and was that organization's president in 1957-58. Gill was honored as the Senior Citizen of the Year in Corvallis and was selected the most outstanding sports figure in Oregon in 1955.

LESSONS FROM THIS LEGEND...

INDIVIDUAL DEFENSIVE PLAY

By A.T. "Slats" Gill

Don't believe the old saying that a good offense is the best defense. A good offense is a good offense; a good defense is a good defense. The key is this: when two equally good offensive teams play each other, the loser is the one with defects in its defense.

We take pride in our defense at Oregon State. Here are some of our thoughts on defensive play.

1. **INDIVIDUAL DEFENSE**
   - Keep between your man and the basket.
   - Have one foot forward, which allows facing the ball.
   - The hand, corresponding to the foot that is forward, is held high over the head.
   - Counter every move of an offensive player with a retreating step.
   - Keep weight on the rear foot.
   - Keep direct vision on the man, indirect vision on the ball.
   - Gain an advantage on an offensive man by using a quick step away as he passes.
   - Develop the ability to play the offensive man away from the ball.

2. **DEFENDING THE GIVE-AND-GO**
   - On the pass, give ground and move toward the ball.
   - The natural defensive movement against the give-and-go is for the defender to give ground directly toward the basket. This is wrong, because it allows the cutter to move in front of the defender and receive the pass. Retain position on the offensive player on the side toward the ball; this necessitates the pass being made over the head of the defensive player to the cutter.

3. **DEFENDING AGAINST THE STAR PLAYER**
   - Overplay the best move of the star player.
   - Force him to pass off.
   - Never take your eyes off of him.
   - Play him tight and harass him if you have plenty of help behind.
   - If the star player beats the defender, a defensive switch must occur. The other defenders must also help.
   - If he is a good rebounder, block him out; play him at all times.
   - Stop the give-and-go cut. Drop away toward the ball when the star player passes.
   - We keep our defensive player outside the post as the offensive star player moves into position with the ball.
   - In most cases, it is possible to keep the defensive player behind the post when the star offensive player goes outside without the ball.

4. **DEFENDING AGAINST THE DRIBBLER THAT GETS PAST YOU**
   - Many coaches feel a defensive player should move with a boxer step at all times. We think the defensive player must turn, run, and catch up if in difficulty.

5. **DEFENDING THE REVERSE ACTION (FORWARD-TO-FORWARD SCREEN & CUT)**
   - The main precaution here is to be in a floor position according to the distance between your assigned offensive player and the ball.
   - If the ball is on the opposite sideline, the defense can be very loose.
   - As the ball moves closer to your assigned offensive player, take a tighter position.
   - Against this offensive pattern, we try very hard not to switch because it makes the defense vulnerable to the "backout" for the center (the "backout" is the fake screen by the center who moves away from the basket during the interval of the switch of the two defensive players involved).

   Authors' Note: The reverse action or forward-to-forward is a term used to describe a forward on the helpside cutting across the lane toward the ballside forward. At the same time, the center is moving away from the ball and setting a screen for the cutter.

6. **DEFENDING THE SCREEN WHEN THE BALL IS NOT INVOLVED**
   - It is a defensive problem to try and switch when the ball is not involved.
   - Sag and move through screens on the weakside.

LESSONS FROM THIS LEGEND...

7. **DEFENDING THE CUTAWAY OR ROLL**
   - We either switch and move up to play in between the ball and the cutter, or we sag with our deep player who momentarily plays a zone until play slows.
   - If none of these methods is successful, we send a third player in to stop the player rolling through the middle, and sag our other two players as quickly as possible.

SOURCE

Gill, A.T. (1962). *Basic Basketball.* New York: The Ronald Press.

Gill, A.T. (1966). Tips of Individual Defensive Play. Compiled by the Editors of The Coaching Clinic, *Best of Basketball from the Coaching Clinic.* West Nyack, NY: Parker Publishing.

LEGACY OF
Marv Harshman

- Compiled 642 wins at Pacific Lutheran, Washington State, and Washington.

- Selected NCAA Division I Coach of the Year in 1984.

- Respected as a teacher, philosopher, and strategist.

- Directed basketball programs that reflected dignity, honesty, and class.

- Originated the match-up zone defense in the Northwest.

- Considered an offensive genius for his high-low system of play.

- Led Pacific Lutheran to NAIA Finals in 1959.

- Served on the U.S. Olympic Committee from 1975 to 1981.

MARV HARSHMAN

"Players know how to dribble, shoot and pass. The challenge is to teach them why they should do it a certain way, and when they should do it."
—Marv Harshman

BIOGRAPHY

Born: October 4, 1917 in Eau Claire, WI

Inducted into the Naismith Basketball Hall of Fame in 1985

Marv Harshman lived in Wisconsin, Montana, and Minnesota before his parents, Claude and Florence, settled in Lake Stevens, Washington. Harshman attended Lake Stevens (WA) High School from 1931 to 1935 and was a four-year starter in football and a three-year all-conference performer in basketball. He briefly attended the University of Washington in 1935-36 before dropping out to work and help at home. Marv went back to college and graduated from Pacific Lutheran in 1942. He was a star performer in football and received Little All-American honors in basketball. Harshman was in the Navy during World War II and then returned to Pacific Lutheran to begin his coaching career. In a distinguished 40-year career, Harshman won 642 games at Pacific Lutheran (241-121), Washington State (155-181), and Washington (246-146). At Pacific Lutheran, Harshman's 1957 team finished 28-1, and his 1959 squad finished runner-up for the NAIA national championship. At the University of Washington, four of his teams won 20 or more games, and he was selected PAC 10 Coach of the Year in 1982 and 1984. Harshman is a member of the NAIA National Hall of Fame and was enshrined in the Naismith Memorial Basketball Hall of Fame in 1985.

...SCOUTING REPORT.....SCOUTING REPORT.....

Marv Harshman...

Claude and Florence Harshman were hardy and hardworking German-Dutch folks who had four children; one of which was born October 4, 1917 in Eau Claire, WI. They named this boy, Marvel Keith, who later became known as Marv for obvious reasons. Father Claude moved throughout the upper Midwest, until finally bringing his family west and settling in Lake Stevens, Washington, on a small farm of eight acres, just as the Great Depression began. Marvel and older brother, Sterling, dominated the sports scene at Lake Stevens High School and excelled in football, track, and basketball. Marv stated, that his Lake Stevens years were in a "do-it society that gave you the appreciation of things you were able to do, but also what your neighbors and others had done. It was a genuine appreciation because you recognized how much they had put into it." (Mosher, 1994)

Harshman was a marvelous athlete who was 6 foot 1 inch and 210 lbs. and could run a 100-yard dash near 10 seconds flat. His hard-working heritage and athletic prowess made him an all-sport performer in football, baseball, and track—one of the best in the history of Lake Stevens, from where he graduated in 1935.

Marv or Harsh, as he was called, entered the University of Washington to play basketball and football in 1935-36, but dropped out mid-year due to academics and financial pressures at home. He worked for the Civilian Conservation Corps (CCC) and lumber mills before returning to college, this time at Pacific Lutheran College where he excelled in basketball, football, track, and baseball. In basketball, he was All-League for three years and Little All-American in 1941, his senior year. Harsh was especially noted for football, where his 1940 PLC team went undefeated, defeating powerful Gonzaga University (16-13), who were led by All-American Tony Canadeo, in a special postseason game played in Tacoma, Washington before 15,000 fans. In three seasons, PLC football teams lost only one game.

But, he was also an excellent basketball player. "He reminded me of Elgin Baylor, Seattle University All-American. He was long and slender and could jump like a deer. He was just fabulous—behind-the back passes and one-hand shots," said one observer. Still, he was drafted by the old Chicago Cardinals in football.

WWII interrupted those plans, so he spent the next three years in the Navy. He returned to Pacific Lutheran College, where he became head coach in three sports, athletic director, and instructor in physical education— he remained there 13 years.

His PLC teams were 242-121 and won four district championships; he took his teams to the NAIA National Tourney in Kansas City four times. His 1957 team came within a whisper of winning it all, losing by one point in the semifinals to eventual champion, Tennessee State, who won three consecutive championships under future Hall of Fame coach John McLendon. PLC led all the way, until All-American Dick Barnett hit a shot in the final seconds to win 71-70. Tennessee State easily won in the finals the next night.

Harshman was selected as NAIA District I Coach of the Year seven times, even though his teams won only four championships. It was a sign of the respect he was earning; his NAIA tourney team in 1948 was the first to use his unique contribution to the game—the high-low post offense. It captured the fancy of fans in the 32-team tournament. Harshman exploited defenses by placing two

.....SCOUTING REPORT......SCOUTING REPORT...

offensive players in a high-low formation. Then, he taught players how to play, why they are doing things, and when to do them. He said, "My golden rule of offense is that a defense tells you what to do. The formation dictates where the defense has to be, and then you make the right move at the right time."

From 1958 until 1971, he coached at Washington State University, where he produced three second-place finishes during the Wooden era at UCLA, when only the champion could go to postseason play. It was a challenging place to recruit players, located in a remote spot in Eastern Washington, at the very edge of the state line in the rolling hills of wheat country. In his second year, after getting drubbed by eventual NCAA Champion California, 37-61, at home, Harshman was humiliated and disconsolate. Future Hall of Fame coach Pete Newell came by and sat down with him. "Coach, there is nothing wrong with what you are doing. You just don't have any players. It doesn't matter how much you know about the game—what you are doing is very good." In 1965, Jud Heathcote arrived from West Valley High School in Spokane, and the recruiting level went up. Marv's teams were always competitive after that, and WSU became well known for "getting the most" out of their talent. His WSU teams were the first to beat Wooden at UCLA (Wooden's first year) and the last to beat him in 1975. John Wooden and Harshman became respected friends, with Wooden one of his biggest boosters. Wooden said, "Marv Harshman qualifies for what our favorite American, Abraham Lincoln, once said, "There's nothing stronger than gentleness. In his quiet way, that was Marv, and will always be Marv." Heathcote gave him the highest compliment, "He's the best friend a guy could ever have, and he's the best guy a friend could ever have."

Marv Harshman made a difficult departure from his beloved Cougarville to become coach at archrival University of Washington. It was caused by changes in the WSU administration, both athletic and presidency. His Washington teams were 246-146 in his 13 years there; four teams won 20 games, and claimed two PAC 10 titles. He was selected Conference Coach of the Year three times and NABC National Coach of the Year in 1984. Harsh coached the USA team to the Pan-American Games gold medal in 1975 and was NABC President in 1981. Marv Harshman was a player's coach who earned player respect. He said, "the basis of respect is honesty. Players make their own decisions, based on our actions and how you treat them and how you conduct yourself in the whole situation." He did earn that respect with dead honesty, warmth, high moral convictions, and the straightforward philosophy developed from his humble beginnings. (Mosher, 1994)

He was quoted in 1994 as saying, "If anybody remembers me at all, I think it'll be as a good teacher. I think the thing I've done is teach some people to be better than they might have been in basketball, and, hopefully as people." He also stated that he felt sports is only important if and how they help people. His career has validated this value of sport.

SOURCE

Harshman, Marv. Vertical Files, Archives. Naismith Memorial Basketball Hall of Fame. Springfield, MA.

Harshman, Marv. Interview with Jerry Krause, 2003.

Heathcote, Jud. Interview with Jerry Krause, 2003.

Mosher, Terry. (1994) *Harsh: The Life, Times, and Philosophy of Hall of Fame Coach Marv Harshman.* Mo Books.

LESSONS FROM THIS LEGEND...

ZONE DEFENSE

By Marv Harshman

The primary reason we play zone defense is that we think it can change the tempo of the game. We might also play zone if we have foul trouble, if our players are fatigued, or if we are mismatched for quickness in some areas.

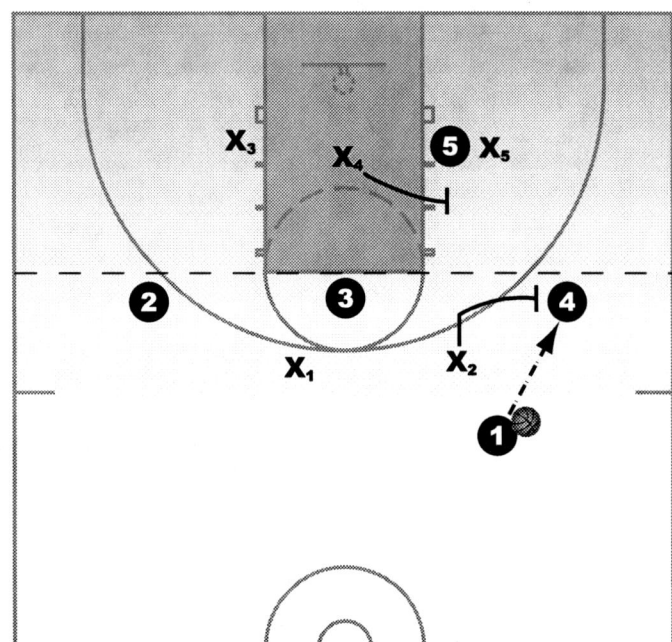

Harshman 1.0

In our defensive play for a 2-3 zone, we want to deny the ball in the shaded area (See **Diagram 1.0**). We position our center to play the shaded area. When we have very big centers, unless the offense was in the low-post area, we side-play the post, rather than front.

If the ball is above the free-throw line extended, we have our guard defend that area. If the ball is below the free-throw line extended, our baseline player defends. If the high post receives the pass, we have our center come up and play man-to-man defense (See **Diagram 1.1**).

We play X1 and X2 to the inside. That is, we are protecting the middle. On a pass to the wing, X2 dropsteps first and then attacks to threaten. The best position we want to give up is the foul-line extended. X2 does not run immediately toward the ball. As X2 leaves to attack, our center, X4, has time to protect a pass to a possible slide by the high post (See **Diagram 1.1**).

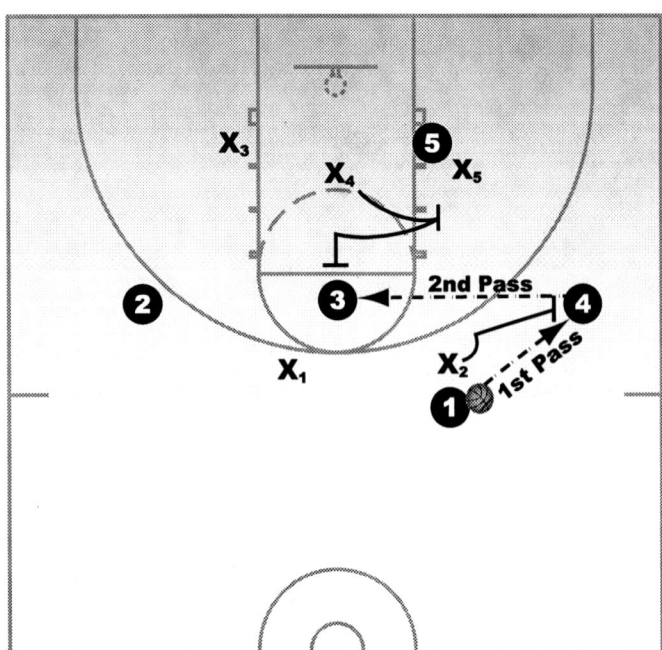

Harshman 1.1

LESSONS FROM THIS LEGEND...

If we are are behind, we try to force the ball into certain areas. Our guards will pressure the ball more, and our centers will side the post up high. We want the ball to be passed to the corner, where we will go for a trap. X5 will not come out too quickly. X2 attempts to seal 5 from above so that he can double-team. If there is another offensive guard, our off guard will challenge him. X3, our weakside, comes to helpside low. Our rule is to deny the three closest people to the ball (See **Diagram 1.2**).

If X5 leaves, X4 must come over to protect the lane area. We are giving up a long pass to 2, hoping for a deflection or interception. Another type of zone we run is "gamble." We do not trap here. Our man plays the ball very hard. Everyone else fronts in order to invite the long pass. When we play gamble, the man who goes after the pass is then committed to go downcourt.

The two adjacent players closest to where the ball is going know our player is going for the pass. If he subsequently gets a hand on the pass or deflects it somehow, those two know they will probably get the ball. The deflector will be going downcourt for a pass and layup. We have been able to score a lot of times from this gamble defense.

The zone defenses we run are very simple and that is the way we teach. Our players know they must learn to "just adjust" by determining the position of the ball and the degree of threat of scoring.

Furthermore, rebounding position in a zone defense is difficult due to the overload. One defensive man must often rebound against two offensive players in his weakside area of the zone. We tell our players they must seal the gaps until we get the basketball.

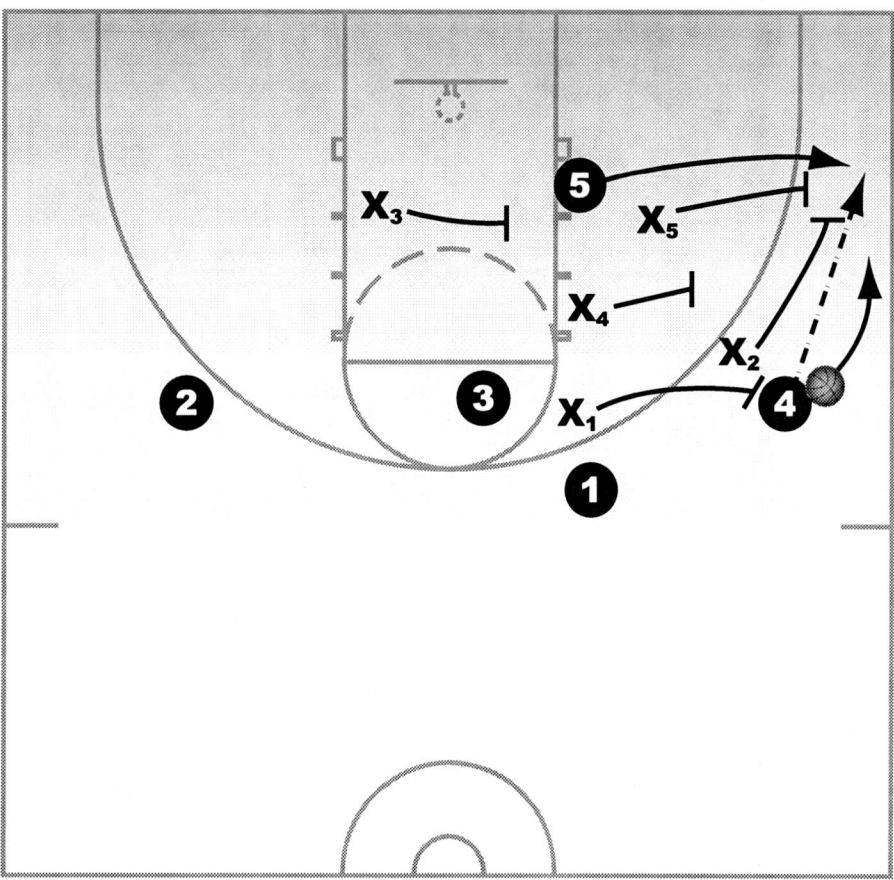

Harshman 1.2

SOURCE

Krause, Jerry and Ralph Pim. (2002). *Coaching Basketball*. New York: McGraw-Hill.

LEGACY OF
Don "The Bear" Haskins

- Led Texas Western past Kentucky for the NCAA championship in 1966 in a game that officially shattered the limits of African-American participation in college basketball.

- Employed a hard-nosed, tenacious defense.

- Nicknamed "The Bear" because of his physical stature and the way he prowled the sidelines.

- Served as an assistant coach on the 1972 U.S. Olympic team.

- At the time of his retirement, he was tied for fourth place among the NCAA's winningest active coaches.

DON "THE BEAR" HASKINS

"My teams are built around tough defense, stingy shot selection, and being hard-nosed."
—Don Haskins

BIOGRAPHY

Born: March 14, 1930 in Enid, OK

Inducted into the Naismith Basketball Hall of Fame in 1997

Don Haskins began his coaching career in 1955 at Benjamin High School (TX). After six successful seasons at several Texas high schools, Haskins accepted the job at Texas Western College (now the University of Texas at El Paso). He coached 38 years at UTEP and compiled a 719-353 record. Haskins led 14 of his teams to the NCAA tournament, and his 1966 squad upset Kentucky to win the NCAA championship. He is the only coach ever to bring an NCAA basketball championship to the State of Texas. Haskins coached future Hall of Famer Nate "Tiny" Archibald and former NBA All-Star Tim Hardaway. He served as an assistant coach for the 1972 Olympic team. During his college playing days, he was an All-Conference performer for future Hall of Famer Hank Iba at Oklahoma A&M (now Oklahoma State) and served as team captain. UTEP recognized the accomplishments of Haskins by naming their basketball facility, the Don Haskins Center. Haskins was inducted in the Texas Sports Hall of Fame in 1987 and enshrined in the Naismith Memorial Basketball Hall of Fame in 1997.

...SCOUTING REPORT.....SCOUTING REPORT.....

Don "The Bear" Haskins...

Don Haskins learned at an early age how difficult life can be. When he was only one-year old, Haskins rolled over onto a flat iron and severely burned his leg. For the first 15 years of his life, Haskins was handicapped with a limp. He strengthened his leg by lifting a homemade weight device and walking as many as 15 to 20 miles while hunting with his father. Haskins slowly developed his burned leg, but running posed a problem. He was cut from the school's basketball team in seventh and eight grade. This only made Haskins more determined, and he would sneak into the gymnasium at nearby Phillips University and shoot for hours. He claimed that any success that he achieved was due to sheer stubbornness.

Haskins' perseverance paid off, as he led Enid High School (OK) to the state tournament his sophomore and senior years. His life was so consumed with basketball that instead of socializing and dancing during his junior-senior prom, Haskins practiced shooting. "There was a giant curtain. On one side was the basketball court and on the other side was the dance floor. There I was shooting baskets by myself for three or four hours. I thought everybody on the other side of the curtain was nuts. I was perfectly content. I had no desire whatsoever to be on the other side of the curtain," stated Haskins. (Haskins, 1987, p. 21)

Haskins was among the first high school players in Oklahoma to perfect the jump shot and was selected to the All-State team. Upon graduation, he decided to play for the legendary Hank Iba, at Oklahoma State. Iba emphasized a ball control offense and wanted his teams to pass around the perimeter and get the ball inside. Haskins wanted to shoot the perimeter jump shot and constantly received the wrath of Iba. "I got chewed out for four years, which I needed," remembered Haskins. "Mr. Iba was a taskmaster. It was a nightmare playing for him, but I wouldn't have achieved what success I have as a coach if I hadn't gone there. I consider Mr. Iba one of the greatest people in the world now, but I hated him then." (Haskins, 1987, p. 25)

At the end of his senior year at Oklahoma A&M, Haskins did not graduate because he was lacking 12 credit hours. It provided a valuable lesson that was passed on to Haskins' players throughout his coaching career. "I did get a degree years later at West Texas State," stated Haskins, "but not having one cost me a lot of money when I became a high school coach. That's why I've been so insistent that my players at the University of Texas at El Paso (UTEP) graduate." (Haskins, 1987, p. 34)

Haskins was a natural athlete. He succeeded in everything including baseball, golf, and pool. Bob Knight compared Haskins to the old-time hustlers and nicknamed him "El Paso Ed," from Jackie Gleason's portrayal of Minnesota Fats in the movie The Hustler. Haskins' first job as a young man was racking balls at a basement pool hall. He got so good shooting pool that he hustled his way through college and also supported himself and his wife when they were newlyweds with money he made in pool halls.

Intimidation was an important part of Haskins' success. He believed that you could beat an opponent just by the way you carried yourself. Haskins urged his players to dunk whenever possible, because it intimidated and humiliated the opposing team. He also instructed his players never to allow an opponent to drive to the basket. Nevil Shed, a key player on the 1966 Texas Western championship team, said, "If anyone drove the lane on us, we'd knock his lights out. For the brave ones, it used to get cloudy in there real fast." (Fitzpatrick, 1999, p. 163)

After college, Haskins played several seasons in the National Industrial Basketball League before accepting his first coaching position at Benjamin H.S. (TX). He also coached at Hedley H.S. and Dumas H.S. in Texas and compiled a six-year prep coaching record of 169-41. Haskins also set a state record for the most technical fouls in a game. "I was trying to intimidate the referee, and I walked out on the floor. He gave me a technical for every step I took. Sixteen steps, sixteen technicals," said Haskins. (Haskins, 1987, p. 42)

.....SCOUTING REPORT......SCOUTING REPORT...

In 1961, Haskins became the head coach at Texas Western College. He immediately started his players on a rigorous training program. "I really worked them hard," said Haskins. "I had four players leave even before school started, and I wasn't even supposed to be practicing." (Haskins, 1987, p. 51)

Haskins preached hard work, intensity, and defense, and immediately started winning basketball games. Nolan Richardson, who coached Arkansas to the 1994 NCAA championship, was a member of Haskins' first team at Texas Western. "People talk about Bobby Knight," Richardson said. "Bobby Knight is a pussycat compared to the way Coach Haskins was back then. He did what he had to, changing attitudes toward winning instead of losing. He made us mentally and physically tough." (Knight, 1997, p.54)

"He (Haskins) was a screamin' demon bag of nerves," said Nevil Shed, "but I'll tell you what. Pressure was nothing to us in games. Nothing was tougher than having coach Haskins yelling at us in practice." (Knight, 1997, p. 54)

Haskins admitted that he was, at times, pretty tough on his players. Prior to their opening game one season, Haskins had his team scrimmage at Texas Tech. "They had a good team and beat us pretty bad," said Haskins. "I worked my guys until five in the morning. It was unbelievable how hard I worked them. It was unmerciful. But, by the time their first game came around, they were ready." (Haskins, 1987, p.51)

Haskins was a man of large stature. He was given the nickname, "The Bear," because of the way he prowled the sidelines and growled his displeasure with his players. His intimidating glare and scowl at officials was commonplace during games. University of Arizona coach Fred Snowden believed that Haskins changed the course of many games, just with his presence.

Texas Western defeated Kentucky for the NCAA championship in 1966 in a game that is remembered as a watershed moment in sports history. Haskins officially shattered the limits of African-American participation in college basketball. For the first time in NCAA championship history, one of the teams had five black players start the game. It still stands as the only time in major American sports that one team composed of entirely black starters and another team composed of entirely white players, competed for a national championship.

"I've been called a champion of civil rights," stated Haskins. "Pat Riley has been quoted as saying I took part in the Emancipation Proclamation of 1966.

But nothing like that was on my mind when I started five black athletes on our Texas Western College team against the University of Kentucky in the finals of the NCAA basketball tournament. I started the five players I thought would have the best chance of beating Kentucky. That they were all black and that it was the first time five black players had started in an NCAA finals was strictly incidental to me." (Haskins, 1987, p.15)

Authors' Note: Pat Riley was a starter for Kentucky and scored nineteen points in the 1966 championship game.

SOURCE

Fitzpatrick, Frank. (1999). *And the Walls Came Tumbling Down.* New York: Simon & Schuster.

Haskins, Don. Vertical Files, Archives. Naismith Basketball Hall of Fame. Springfield, MA.

Haskins, Don and Ray Sanchez. (1987). *Haskins: The Bear Facts.* El Paso: Mangan Books.

Knight, Bill. (1997). The Bear. *Naismith Memorial Hall of Fame Enshrinement Program.*

LESSONS FROM THIS LEGEND...

DEFENSIVE BASKETBALL GUIDELINES

By Don Haskins

I've been regarded as a defensive coach, and that's right. My philosophy is that defense wins in any sport.

I've been asked what I look for in a player so far as defense goes. I answer that defense is a team thing. We have had some great individual defensive players, but what we look for is players who are willing to work hard together. Defense is hard, hard work. Defense is five people learning to play together.

If one man doesn't play well, it won't work. If the player guarding the ball isn't working any harder than the other four trying to help him, you can forget it. It's a philosophy that I learned from Henry Iba. I saw it work, and I came to be a believer in it.

There are many coaches who have learned the same philosophy. That's what makes coaching so tough now. You don't find teams that are poorly coached anymore. There are too many clinics, too many seminars, and too many smart people in the ranks. These new young coaches are something. They all have three-piece suits, they're ambitious, and they're willing to work hard.

I never used to think I'd use a zone defense. I played man-to-man with no switching under Mr. Iba, and I loved it. But I've had to adjust, and I think we play it pretty well. I started putting in the zone in practices some years ago and found it worked, especially against good perimeter players. There are a lot of those around now, and they force you to play a zone.

Speaking of players, there are so many good ones now that it's unbelievable. There are players in high school now who can't get on a college team who would have been starters ten years ago.

Another of my coaching philosophies has to do with high schools. We look for players who come from winning high school teams. There are exceptions, but we've found that players develop habits early, and winning can be one of them. Most of our successful teams have been made up of players who were winners in high school. Successful players love to compete, and they want discipline from their coaches. We will sometimes take a player of lesser ability, if he has the qualities that we want.

The prerequisites for a strong defensive team are: 1) control the tempo; 2) protect the basket area; 3) shoot high-percentage shots; and 4) exercise patience on offense.

CONTROL THE TEMPO

It is important to control the 10-second line. By this I mean, that the dribbler should be stopped at mid-court. All five players must get in front of the ball as quickly as possible. This is why during practice, we rarely play half-court. I want our drills to be game-like and use the entire court.

PROTECT THE BASKET AREA

As shown in **Diagram 1.0**, the front-court is divided into three areas. No shots should be allowed in Area A. We force teams to shoot beyond their favorite spots on the floor. A team's shooting percentage goes down when they are forced to shoot from Areas B and C. We use shooting charts not just to calculate shooting percentages, but also to determine how many shots are taken in each of the prescribed areas.

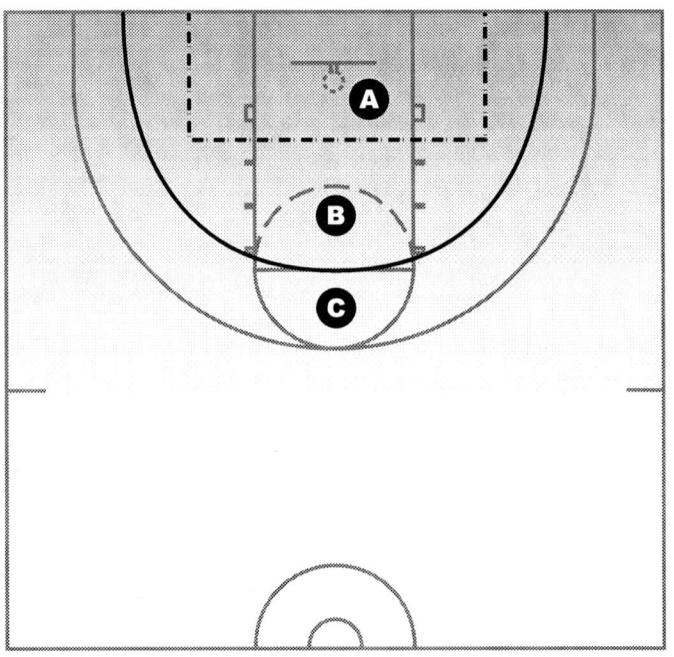

Haskins 1.0

LESSONS FROM THIS LEGEND...

SHOOT HIGH PERCENTAGE SHOTS

As far as shot selection is concerned, we definitely describe what is a good shot for each player. This not only includes the distance from the basket, but also the score and time left in the game.

EXERCISE PATIENCE ON OFFENSE

Execution of your offense and having patience are very important as far as your total offense is concerned. Quick shots from undesirable spots on the floor often result in fast-break opportunities for your opponent. On many occasions, we will use a slow-down or delay type game, especially when we are playing on the road, or when our overall talent is less than our opponents'. By using this particular offensive strategy, it will make the offense better, keep the score closer, and increase our chances for victory.

INDIVIDUAL DEFENSIVE RULES

1. Good defense begins with transition. We emphasize getting our defenders back to the baseline. Always stay in front of your man. We never want to be outnumbered by our opponent.
2. Attack the ballhandler by getting your head and shoulders as close as possible to your opponent.
3. Use a stride stance, rather than a square stance, because it is more difficult for the dribbler to go by you. The back foot is the important one in stopping dribble penetration.
4. Stay with an offensive dribbler by running, rather than sliding. It is our philosophy that as soon as an offensive player moves, the defender should run, rather than use a defensive slide. The reason for this is we want the defender to get from one position to another as quickly as possible. The only way to accomplish this is by running.
5. When guarding a man with the ball, watch the offensive player's waist rather than the ball.
6. Do not fight the ball when it is being dribbled. Always maintain balance, and do not continually go for steals.
7. When playing post defense, do not make contact with the post player. Stay at least three feet away and be closer to the ball than the person you are defending.
8. When playing helpside defense, stay below an imaginary line drawn between the player you are defending and the ball. Always see both the ball and your man. If you have to lose sight of one of them, it is imperative that you lose sight of your man and not the ball.
9. When defending cutters, always stay to the ballside of your man.
10. Do not switch. Communicate and get through screens.

DEFENSIVE DRILLS

1. SPOT DRILL

In this drill, all four offensive players remain stationary, and the ball is passed along the perimeter (See **Diagram 1.1**). The defensive concept that we are teaching is that the defender furthest from the ball must protect the middle of the floor.

KEY TEACHING POINTS

- Offensive players must stay in their general area (no cutting).
- On every pass, each defender must quickly change his floor position.
- Run to the new floor position, don't slide.
- Always see both your man and the ball.
- Don't deny the pass (let the ball be thrown around the perimeter).
- On the helpside, sink away from the ball and protect the middle.
- Always protect the baseline.

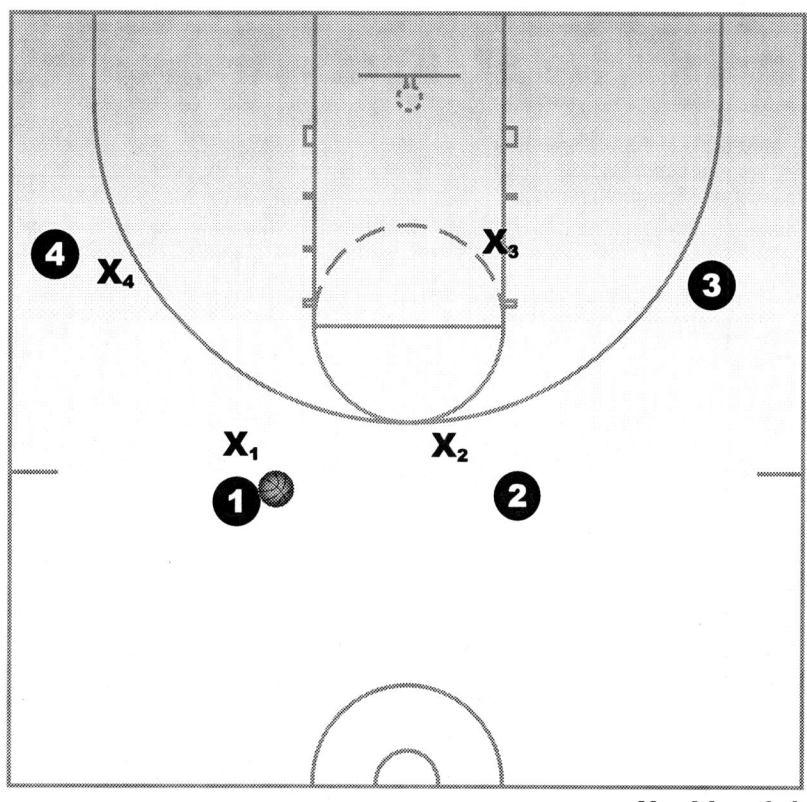

Haskins 1.1

LESSONS FROM THIS LEGEND...

2. Pick and Help Drill

This is a two-on-two drill with a screen on the ball (See **Diagram 1.2**). The defender on the screener must step out and slow down the dribbler. This allows X1 an opportunity to either get over or behind the screen. We do not want to switch.

Key Teaching Points
- Do not switch.
- X2 must quickly step out in the path of the dribbler to allow X1 an opportunity to get either over the top or behind the screen.
- Our first choice is for X1 to go over the top of the screen.

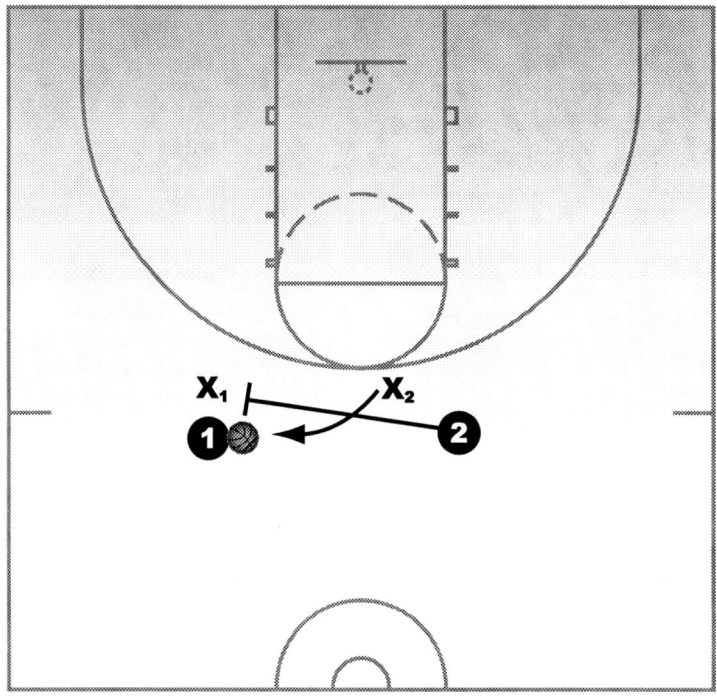

Haskins 1.2

3. Guard and Cutter Drill

This is a four-on-four drill designed to defend against a give-and-go cut (See **Diagram 1.3**). It also reinforces the correct helpside positioning for a guard and a forward.

Key Teaching Points
- X2 must jump toward the ball and not allow a return pass to his man.
- X2 does not allow his man to cut in front of him.
- X1 and X4 quickly move toward the middle of the floor and see both their man and the ball.

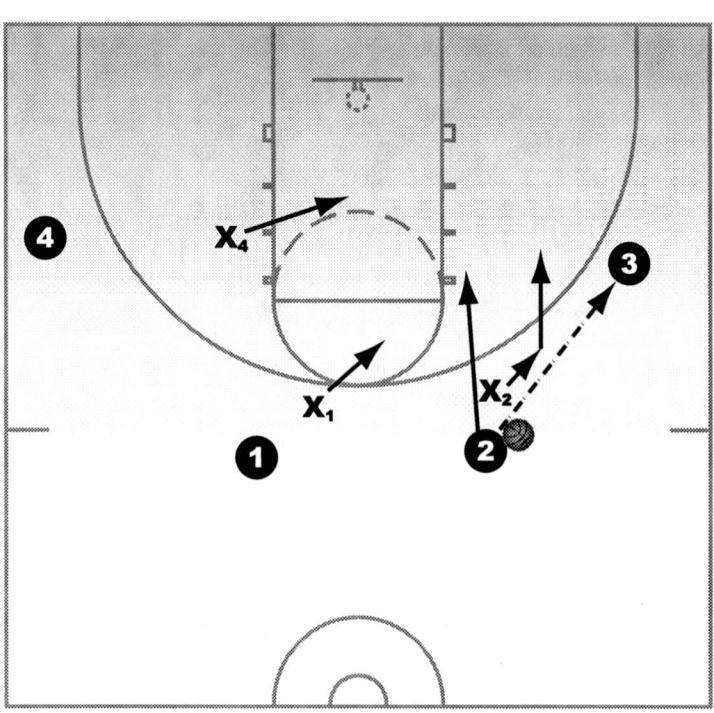

Haskins 1.3

LESSONS FROM THIS LEGEND...

4. THREE-ON-THREE DRILL

This drill is designed to stop a series of movements by the three perimeter players (See **Diagram 1.4**). The offensive players can pass and screen away, pass and cut down the lane, pass and screen on the ball, or dribble and hand-off. It is the toughest drill in basketball.

KEY TEACHING POINTS

- Against the pass and screen away, X1 stays in the middle of the floor and helps his teammate avoid the screen.
- Against the pass and cut, X1 jumps toward the pass and does not let his man catch a return pass.
- Against the pass and screen on the ball, X1 steps out to slow the dribbler and helps his teammate stay with the dribbler.
- Against the dribble hand-off, X1 jumps back and allows his defensive teammate to slide through.
- All defenders away from the ball must stay between their man and the ball and sink to the level of the ball on any penetration.

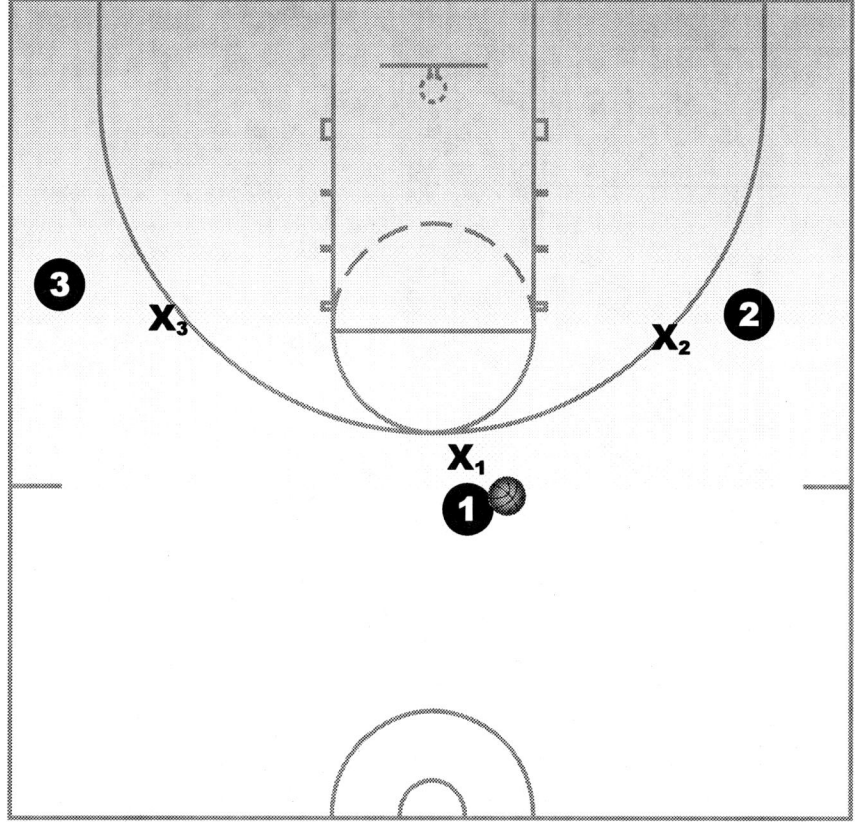

Haskins 1.4

5. FIVE-ON-FIVE DRILL

The offense will have the ball for three minutes with no screens, no dribbles, no shots, and no screens. They can just catch the ball and move to an open area. The defenders must stay between the ball and their man and always be ready to help if necessary.

SOURCE

Haskins, Don. (Winter 1978). UTEP's Man to Man Defense. *The Basketball Bulletin (Winter Edition)*.

Haskins, Don. (1986). Defensive Basketball. *The Basketball Bulletin*.

Haskins, Don and Ray Sanchez. (1987). *Haskins: The Bear Facts*. El Paso: Mangan Books.

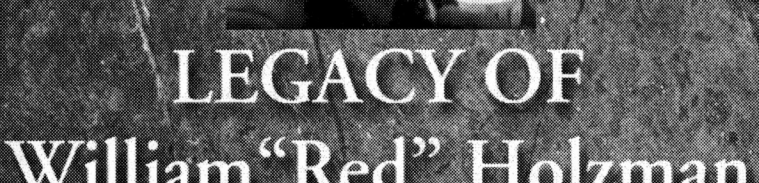

LEGACY OF
William "Red" Holzman

- Led the New York Knicks to the NBA championship in 1970 and 1973.

- Named the NBA Coach of the Decade for the 1970's.

- Considered a master strategist who emphasized unselfish play and team defense.

- Built championship teams by maximizing the strengths of his players.

- Designed his offense based on the concepts of moving without the ball and passing to the open player.

- Demonstrated that coaching can make a difference in the pro game.

WILLIAM "RED" HOLZMAN

"If you play good, hard defense, the offense will take care of itself."
—William "Red" Holzman

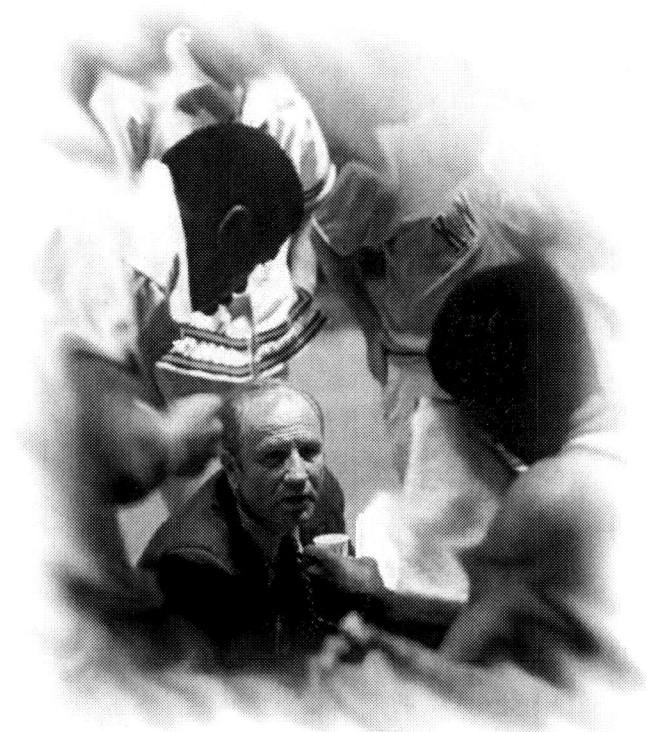

BIOGRAPHY

Born: August 10, 1920 in New York, NY

Died: November 13, 1998

Inducted into the Naismith Basketball Hall of Fame in 1986

William "Red" Holzman began his coaching career as a player-coach in 1953 with the Milwaukee Hawks and stayed with the franchise when it moved to St. Louis. After serving as an assistant coach and chief scout with the New York Knicks for ten years, Holzman became their head coach in 1967. His record with New York was 613-384. Holzman led the Knicks to the NBA championship in 1970 and 1973. He was the NBA Coach of the Year in 1970 and was selected as the NBA Coach of the Decade for the 1970s. Holzman played professional basketball for nine years, eight of which were spent with the Rochester Royals of the BBL, BAA, and NBA. He was selected NBL All-Star First Team in 1946 and 1948. Holzman led the Royals to the NBL championship in 1946 and the NBA championship in 1951. As a collegiate star at CCNY, Holzman played for Nat Holman and earned All-American honors in 1941 and 1942. Holzman was enshrined in the Naismith Memorial Basketball Hall of Fame in 1986.

...SCOUTING REPORT.....SCOUTING REPORT.....

William "Red" Holzman...

William "Red" Holzman's basketball education began in the schoolyards of Brooklyn, where he learned that you had to be good if you wanted to stay in the game, because players on the losing team were forced off the court. It was in these games that Holzman started to learn the value of team play and moving without the ball.

As a young man, Holzman was given the nickname "Red" due to his flaming red hair. He was a hard-nosed, aggressive player at Franklin K. Lane H.S. (NY) and earned All-American honors at City College of New York under the legendary Nat Holman. Holzman played eight seasons with the Rochester Royals and was a two-time All-Star first team selection.

Holzman was player-coach for the Milwaukee Hawks for the 1953-54 season and stayed with the franchise when it moved to St. Louis. The Hawks qualified for the playoffs in 1956, and Holzman was credited with developing future Hall of Famer Bob Pettit.

In 1958, Holzman became chief scout for the New York Knicks. During his ten-year scouting stint, Holzman assembled a group of players who took New York to the top of the basketball world. Through his recommendations, the Knicks drafted future Hall of Famers Willis Reed, Bill Bradley, and Walt Frazier.

On December 27, 1967, "Red" Holzman replaced Dick McGuire as head coach of the Knicks. He initially refused the offer, but finally agreed to finish out the season with the provision that he could return to scouting the following year. The Knicks were 15-23 at the time and had not made the playoffs in seven of the previous eight years. On his very first day, Holzman started his new regime by fining four players for being late to practice. He introduced team defense and emphasized the importance of team unity, both on and off the court.

New York lost their first two games under Holzman and then soared to a playoff berth and their first winning season since 1959. At the conclusion of the season, Holzman agreed to stay on as head coach.

"Red brought an aggressive philosophy to the team," said team captain Willis Reed. "He gave us positive thinking, always doing everything he could to build our confidence, even in defeat. Don't kid yourself, that's an important attribute, even in the pro ranks". (Goldaper, 1968)

Holzman turned the Knicks into relentless, aggressive, defensive-minded players. They pressured opposing guards, created turnovers, and positioned themselves to help a teammate whenever necessary.

Holzman's offensive teachings were based less on set patterns and more on constant motion, alertness, and unselfishness. He used phrases such as "move without the ball" and "hit the open man." He taught players how to work together to create scoring opportunities, and they were unselfish to an almost unbelievable extreme. "The Knicks try so hard to set each other up that, if anything, they pass occasionally when they could shoot," said Boston playmaker Bob Cousy. "But that's a fault that every coach would love to worry about." (Newsweek, 1969)

"As a team, everybody's moving and taking part in every play," said Bill Bradley (Newsweek, 1969). "When one of us moves, the other four adjust. The joy comes from playing this game the way it should be played."

"Red's style is soft and gentle," said former Knick player Phil Jackson. "Red is also very slick, and he can con a man into playing well. He is a gentleman, and the attitude he communicates is that the Knicks can win basketball games only if the players do the best job they are capable of doing. Red is a diplomat rather than a tyrant, and the Knicks bear his imprint." (Goldaper, 1977)

On the bench during games, Holzman barked out instructions and moved players around like chess pieces. He often looked more like a businessman than a coach. If all were going well, he would sit back, either with his arms crossed or his chin cupped in his hands. At other times, he leaned forward, studied the action, and then gave directions to his players. When the game came down to the end, Holzman usually directed the team from his famed kneeling crouch.

In Holzman's second full season, the Knicks were the class of the NBA and won their first championship. Three seasons later, they were back for another NBA championship.

Holzman downplayed his role in the success of the Knicks. He tried to hide his talents behind a guise of ignorance, luck, and chance, rather than personally taking credit. Holzman told reporters that he was dull and rarely said anything worth quoting. He responded to their questions with answers such as "It's just one of those things," or "It's no big deal." He was cordial and friendly, but always avoided the dramatics.

When asked by reporter Jim Benagh (1977) what he thought he had accomplished as a coach, Holzman gave

.....SCOUTING REPORT.....SCOUTING REPORT...

one of his characteristic answers: "I don't know what I have done—I guess it depends on how others have seen it. I don't think there is such a thing as a coaching genius, just hard workers."

Holzman's credo was "never worry about something you have no control over." (Lipsyte, 1969)

"Red" Holzman destroyed the myth that pro coaching was nothing more than calling a time out or making a substitution when somebody was tired. He demonstrated beyond a doubt that coaching can and will make a difference in the pro game.

Each player on Holzman's team was an integral part of the machine. He was driven by an incredible sense of understanding his players' weaknesses and strengths and always seemed to know when to make the right substitution.

"The real genius of Holzman lies in his handling of players," said Bill Bradley (1995). "He never tells players exactly what he wants them to do beyond the general rules of 'seeing the ball' on defense and 'hitting the open man' on offense. He prefers to shape a player as he performs. Toward some players he is stern; others he cajoles and flatters. A few he abuses verbally. Each of his moves is calculated to manipulate the player toward action, which Red thinks, will bring victory."

SOURCE

Benagh, Jim. (1977, April 10). NBA Genius Bows Out at Cobo Arena Today. *Detroit Free Press.*

Bradley, Bill. (1995). *Life On The Run.* New York: Knopf Publishing.

Goldaper, Sam. (1968, December 25). Knicks Are Rebounding for Holzman. *New York Times.*

Goldaper, Sam. (1977, April 10). For the Knicks, the End of an Era. *New York Times.*

Lipsyte, Robert. (1969, April 19). The Ordinary Man. *New York Times.*

The Dazzling Knicks. (1969, December 15). *Newsweek.*

LESSONS FROM THIS LEGEND...

INDIVIDUAL DEFENSE

By William "Red" Holzman

PHILOSOPHY

Shooting is enjoyable; defense is hard work. Team defense is as good as the desire of the players. Most young athletes grow up with the idea that defense is not fun. The Boston Celtics changed that in the Bill Russell era by making defense popular and enjoyable, because it was so clearly related to their fabulous run of eleven championships in thirteen seasons.

The Knicks have established a similar pride in their defense. They became more receptive to the hard work that is demanded when they realized how much it meant to winning. They discovered it was fun to keep the other team under 100 points.

From a team viewpoint, a player must approach the situation with a determination to stop his man, while being prepared to help a teammate. It takes the proper attitude to sometimes sacrifice a desire to hold an opponent scoreless when it is more important to contribute to team defense. There are many times when Bill Bradley may be playing a good shooter such as Jim McMillan but has to drop off and help Jerry Lucas with Wilt Chamberlain.

A strong defensive team generates a brand of confidence that rubs off on the rest of the game. It takes outstanding teamwork to blend individual skills into a unit that instinctively reacts to every move by the opponents. It is much like a game of chess. Each chess piece is a weapon used to block the attack on the "king" by the opponent. In basketball, the "king" is the basket, and the players are the pawns. By sliding one piece over, a player manages to impede the progress, as well as the strategy, of his opponent.

THE IMPACT OF BILL RUSSELL

Anyone can identify the player who created the greatest defensive impact on pro basketball. Yes, it was Bill Russell. He was not only good; he was shrewd. He played defense from the book but added a few chapters of his own.

He had the physical equipment. He had the mind. He had the knowledge. He had the ability to analyze and react. He was the perfect blend of what it takes to play sound, fundamental defense.

He was pretty tricky. He would contest almost every shot until the Celtics would get too far in front to lose. Then he would let the other team drive in for lay-ups. He would permit them to build their confidence when it did not matter and then jam shots when it did. He was a poolroom hustler on defense.

Russell was born with certain qualities that enabled him to apply the fundamentals of defense more naturally than those not equally endowed. But, defense can be learned. Defense can be taught.

BASIC DEFENSE

No matter what defense is employed by a team, it inevitably boils down to a 1-on-1 confrontation. Sometime, somewhere, one player winds up on another player and has to stop him from scoring. It doesn't matter if a team uses the zone, zone press, or whatever, it always boils down to one man against another, and that is when a player must know what to do. In order to play good team defense, a player must know the intricacies of individual defense.

Defense is motion, constant motion. The worst thing a defensive player can do is relax or sneak a look at what is going on around him. A defensive player who does not concentrate on the job and the fundamentals will get into trouble. Sharp opponents will easily trick him.

Never rest on defense. If you are tired, learn to pace yourself by catching your breath while your team is changing over from defense to offense. If you are very tired, do not be afraid to ask the coach to take you out for a rest.

On the Knicks, we like to pick up a man no further than mid-court, most times deeper, depending on the game situation. If we are fighting for time in a close game, we pick up the other team at the endline.

THE SCORING AREA

The closer a team moves the ball to the basket, the tighter the defense. You can give a man room on the outside, but the space dwindles when he moves inside. The amount of room you give a man depends on how much room you need to react to any move he makes without fouling him.

Every player should be aware of where he is on the court at all times. He should protect the scoring lanes, which can be determined by the markings on the floor. He should be prepared to make a shooter go over him, rather than let him drive for an easier basket. If a man is in the corner, it is wiser to make him drive toward the middle and traffic, rather than travel the shortest distance between two points along the endline.

THE DRIBBLER

Always protect against a man dribbling past you. As in all cases of fundamental defense, stay between your man and the basket.

LESSONS FROM THIS LEGEND...

Don't reach for the ball; once you shift your weight forward, it is easier for the dribbler to get around you. Maintain a well-balanced position, with your weight distributed evenly enough to match any move the dribbler makes.

If the dribbler stops, that is the time to close in. Be careful not to walk into a trap—where the dribbler gives off and cuts past. As long as the dribbler moves laterally, the man guarding him can maintain some spacing.

Pro teams invariably try to force the dribbler to the sidelines. It reduces the area of maneuverability and places him in a greater risk of being trapped. The guarding man should never yield the inside. If the dribbler goes down the sideline, force him into the corner, but do not let him get around you. Try to break his rhythm by making some feinting moves, as though you are trying to steal the ball. If he decides to drive for a lay-up, play to block the shot and not steal the ball.

Floor Position

It is not always advantageous to stay between your man and the basket. Against a left-handed dribbler, try to make him dribble right. That means overplay his left hand. There are times when a team can play a floating defense, which means the forwards will gamble and cheat on their men to protect the middle. You do not have to guard a man that closely if he doesn't have the ball.

In any defense, it is up to the guard to cover as much territory as he can to close the passing lanes. He is responsible for his man when he is dribbling the ball, but he must also be alert and active enough to help out.

Know where the ball is at all times so you can work on the passing lanes. Do not turn your head to look for the ball. Sneak a glance out of the corner of an eye, but never lose sight of your man.

Use peripheral vision. Like a driver in an automobile, try to see more than the car in front of you. You use your side-view mirror and your rear-view mirror, and be alert to traffic on your weakside—but you never lose sight of the car in front. In basketball, you play your man first, but you must know what is going on around you, which is where peripheral vision is necessary.

If you are two or more passes away from the ball, you can move one step closer to the middle to help clog the cutting and passing lanes. If you are one pass away, you must be close to or within one arm's length away from you opponent.

Footwork and Stance

Balance is the key. The defensive man must be in position to react to the offensive man, who has the advantage of making the first move. The feet should be fairly close—slightly less than the width of the shoulders. The weight is distributed evenly—not back in the heels or up in the toes.

No matter what happens, do not cross the legs. That is a fine way to trip yourself while the man goes around you. Slide left and right, according to the direction he is going. If he goes left, slide the right foot out and move that way. If he drives at you, a step backward will leave you in a secure, balanced position.

When guarding a man without the ball, crouch a little and be prepared for a fast start. When playing the man with the ball, do not go for the fake. Wait until he actually is in the act of shooting before leaving your feet in an attempt to block the shot. Some players key on the shooter's chest to avoid going for the head-and-shoulder fakes.

Use of Hands

Walt Frazier, Jerry West, and Lenny Wilkens have the fastest defensive hands in pro basketball. Make a mistake against them, and you no longer have the ball. They have busy hands, which should be used when playing defense. Hands should be used to distract a shooter.

Wilt Chamberlain extends his arms on defense. I hope you can appreciate what that does to the passing lanes for a team trying to work the ball in close. It is wise to keep one hand high and the other extended when a man is driving at you. That way, you can harass a shot and, possibly, impede a pass if your man is trying to give the ball to someone else.

Use of Eyes

"I watch a man's eyes a lot," says Walt Frazier. It is extremely difficult to shoot, pass, or dribble without looking in the direction to be employed. That does not mean the defensive player should stare himself into trouble. Actually, if you are playing 1-on-1, the hips will tip off where your opponent is going better than anything.

Never lose sight of your man, and never lose sight of the ball, either. If you are playing away from the ball, assume a position (or angle) between your man and the ball. Use peripheral vision to see both. That way you will be in a position to keep your man from sneaking off, and you can steal a pass or help a teammate.

Switching

This is a technique that is generally employed in the pros, where man-to-man defense is emphasized. I always like to combine switching with talking on defense. They go together.

A man switches because he is unable to keep up with his opponent on a play. He runs into a blind pick. He gets caught behind a screen. In some cases, when he has time to recognize what is developing, he should yell to a teammate to switch and take his man. The responsibility of yelling for the switch rests with the man closest to the basket, since he can see what is happening to his teammate.

It is not necessary to switch unless the ball is involved,, and the defense gets into trouble. There is too much of a risk switching off a big man, unless, it is absolutely neces-

LESSONS FROM THIS LEGEND...

sary to stop another player driving for the basket. Switching is not too difficult when used in a team defense against screening, because switching is generally automatic under those conditions. The thing to remember is to try and switch back to your man if you get caught in a mismatch you cannot handle.

SPACING

How close you play an opponent depends on him. Never play far enough off a man to permit him an easy shot. It is a good idea to determine a shooter's range and play him accordingly.

In the pros, if we find an opponent who does not hit from outside, we drop off and help protect the more vulnerable inside area.

A good gauge would be to stay within three feet of an opponent on the outside when he does not have the ball. As soon as he gets it, close in to a position that enables you to respond to any direction he decides to take. The Knicks play a lot of 1-on-1 after regular workouts to drill themselves on defensive reactions.

MAN WITHOUT THE BALL

Determine everyone's strength, and then act accordingly. If the man you play is not a good outside shooter, you can float until he gets the ball in close. If the man is the playmaker, you must play him closer. If he is an excellent shooter, play as tightly as possible and attempt to discourage getting the ball to him.

A player, any player, becomes more dangerous with the ball, but you still must be careful of those players without it. If you drop off and float, keep your hands and body busy to make sure he has no clear passing lane. It is possible to be caught a little too far away when your man gets the ball. In that case, don't rush right at him. Close in and keep your center of gravity low, should he try to drive around you. You will be able to change direction faster that way.

MAN WITH THE BALL

Don't try to out-guess him. He knows where he is going. If he is not a good outside shooter, he is more inclined to drive on you. Retreat a little before he moves, then pressure him when he goes. The idea is to try and force a bad-percentage shot or cause him to pass.

TALKING

The voice is important on defense. I don't know why, but it seems as though the toughest thing to get across to a player is talking on defense.

Defense does not begin and end with individuality. An individual may think his responsibility is fulfilling his own assignment, but he is only one part of a machine. It is nice to know that a player has been letter perfect against his own opponent, yet, he should never forget his teammates. There are times when they need help, as there will be times when he will need it.

We have our defense talking all the time. Basketball is a game where the use of the mind, body, and voice are equally important. If it means helping your team win—and it often does—talk.

REBOUNDING

Position is the most important consideration. Boxing out is the secret. Jerry Lucas is one of the finest rebounders the pro game has known, considering the results and his size. When he gets position, it is virtually impossible for much taller players to get the ball, unless it bounces over his head.

When a shot goes up, the defensive rebounder must first determine where his man is before looking for the ball. Lucas will turn directly into his man, boxing him out, then look for the rebound. While Lucas is waiting for the rebound, he takes up as much room as possible. He keeps his man as far away from the board as he can and concentrates on not letting him escape the trap. He leans into his man but is ready to time his jump when the ball comes off the board.

Winning teams usually control the rebounds. It certainly makes it more difficult to win if you let the other team get two, three, or four shots at a time, because someone on your team does not know how to rebound.

The idea is to leap as high as you can. Get the arms up as high as possible. Grab the ball with two hands and bring it into the body for protection. Do not wave the ball out in front of you or over your head. It is too easy to steal that way.

Stay as low as possible after rebounding until you are sure you have control. Then turn and look to pass to a deep man or a teammate alongside. Teammates breaking down court should always be alert to the possibility of having to come back and help a rebounder if he gets into trouble.

THINGS TO REMEMBER

1. Stay between your opponent and the basket at all times.
2. Stay down, with knees flexed, so you can react. Keep your center of gravity low in the defensive stance.
3. Make the ballhandler or shooter commit first. Do not go for the fake. Remember the offense must make the move, and then the defense must react.
4. Learn to cover quickly on a turnover. Do not waste time thinking. Know what you should do before anything happens.
5. Get back on a fast break. Do not worry about match-ups. Pick up the man nearest to you. Switch to your man only if your teammates can get set.
6. See the ball. Know where it is at all times.
7. Do not turn your head. Assume an angle where you can see the ball and your opponent. Keep both in view so your man cannot sneak away while your head is turned.
8. Don't be lazy. Play your opponent aggressively whether or not he has

LESSONS FROM THIS LEGEND...

the ball. Attack on defense. Loosen up only if you are playing a poor shooter from outside.

9. Be prepared to switch at all times, and let your teammates know by yelling.
10. Talk on defense. Communicate everything to teammates who cannot see what is developing. If you are the back man, let your teammate know where they are setting a pick on him.
11. Don't leave the backcourt uncovered after your team shoots. Someone must protect against an opponent sneaking away for an easy basket.
12. Don't play the ball unless you have good defensive teammates, or a Bill Russell, to cover for you.
13. Try and move your man laterally—away from the basket. Try and force dribblers along the sidelines and into the corners. Don't let an opponent drive the baseline. Force everything to the outside.
14. Keep your hands busy. Use them to distract the ballhandler and shooter. Extend them into the passing lanes.
15. Play a pivot man on the side where the ball will be coming to him. If he is much bigger and stronger, and takes you inside, get in front of him. Pressure all big men to move away from the basket for poorer-percentage shots. Work from the basket up toward the foul line.
16. When an opponent shoots, box out your man first. Know where he is and turn into him before you look for the rebound.
17. Pick up your man as soon as possible. Don't let him move unmolested to the area on the floor he desires. Annoy him.
18. Go with the dribbler, don't slap at him. Don't reach for the ball. Maintain defensive balance at all times so you can move in any direction without wasting motion.

SOURCE

Holzman, Red and Leonard Lewin. (1973). *Holzman's Basketball: Winning Strategy and Tactics.* Co., New York: Macmillan Publishing.

LEGACY OF
Henry "Hank" Iba

- Compiled a record of 767-338 during his 41-year career.

- Retired as the second all-time winningest coach in NCAA history.

- First coach to win consecutive NCAA national championships (1945, 1946).

- Only coach in history to win two Olympic gold medals (1964, 1968).

- Taught a man-to-man defense, utilizing zone principles away from the ball, that he called the "swinging gate."

- Advocated a methodical, ball-controlling offense based on passing and player movement, which is the forerunner of today's motion offense.

- A strict disciplinarian who did not tolerate anything less than all-out effort and good manners.

- Earned a reputation as a great teacher of the fundamentals.

HENRY "HANK" IBA

"You must be sure that you give back something that's beneficial to the game. Any of the teaching you do must be for the benefit of the men who play".
—Henry "Hank" Iba

BIOGRAPHY

Born: August 6, 1904 in Easton, MO

Died: January 15, 1993

Inducted into the Naismith Basketball Hall of Fame in 1969

An all-around athlete in grade school and high school in the small town of Easton (MO), Henry Iba attended Westminster College (Fulton, Missouri), where he played football, basketball and baseball. He coached two years at Classen High School in Oklahoma City, then graduated from Northwest State Teachers College, Maryville (MO) in 1929. Iba's record at Classen was 51-5, and he led his team to the state championship and to the title game of the national high school championship tournament in 1929. On the collegiate level, Iba coached at Maryville (MO) Teachers College (1929-33), the University of Colorado (1933-34), and Oklahoma State University (1934-70). He compiled a record of 767-338 during his 41-year career. At the time of Iba's retirement, he was the second all-time winningest coach in NCAA history. He led Oklahoma A&M (now Oklahoma State) to consecutive NCAA national championships in 1945 and 1946 and a runner-up finish in 1949. Iba coached the USA team in three Olympiads and won two Gold Medals. He coached the USA team in 1972, when they suffered their first Olympic defeat in a controversial loss to the Soviet Union. Iba was selected National Coach of the Year of 1945 and 1946. He was enshrined in the Naismith Memorial Basketball Hall of Fame in 1969.

...SCOUTING REPORT.....SCOUTING REPORT.....

Henry "Hank" Iba...

Henry Iba started his life and sports career in the small Missouri town of Easton, where he lettered in the only sports the school had—basketball, baseball and track. He attended and took most of his classes in Fulton (MO) at Westminster College. He left before graduating to take a head basketball coaching position at Classen High School, Oklahoma City. He later graduated in the summer of 1929 from Northwest State Teachers College in Maryville, MO, where he was then hired as basketball coach—his first team went 31-0 and his coaching career was on its way.

Iba's coaching philosophy was highly influenced by a game that he participated in as a youth. In his first year in high school, he played in a game to welcome home the troops from WWI and was on the losing end of a 62-14 score. He thought at that time there must be a better way to play the game. Iba said "there's no way you can get beat that bad." This must have left an indelible impression that shaped the way he later would coach the game. Iba did find a better way. He nurtured it, he polished it. He perfected it, he preached it. And in the process, he became a basketball legend.

Iba's Northwest Missouri team followed the unbeaten 1930 season with 32-6, 26-2 and 12-6 records, while becoming National AAU Tournament Runner-up in 1932. After a one year stop in Colorado, he went to Oklahoma A & M in 1934 as basketball coach, baseball coach, and athletic director. He remained there until 1970. As athletic director, his school was second only to the University of Southern California in national titles garnered during his tenure.

Iba's strong leadership greatly influenced the game of basketball. He was very active and instrumental in rules formation and served as president of the NABC. Iba served as a mentor for thousands of disciples of the Iba system of basketball.

This system of play served him well in international play; his widely held stature earned him the unique distinction of coaching the USA team in three Olympiads (two Gold Medals and a disputed Silver Medal in 1972). This was done using college/amateur players who were generally considered of lesser overall talent and brought together for a shorter time period than most other countries. The Iba system still prevailed and produced a legion of followers.

The Iba system was based on the following essentials:
- Discipline and fundamentals
- Ball-control and exceptional ballhandling (the forerunner of modern motion offense)
- Man-to-man defense (played with Iba fervor and tenacity)

The "Iron Duke" of basketball was aptly named—his teams were renowned for discipline, both on and off the court. Discipline was the first component on Hank Iba's list of those necessary for success in basketball. It was a disciplined state of mind that all good coaches seem to develop in their players. Iba grew up and began coaching in the 1930s—the heart of the Great Depression, when discipline was needed for survival. In basketball, ball-control and discipline went hand-in-hand. The ball was like gold, and one didn't throw it away. This made sense to Iba, who claimed he decided to stick to the disciplined, controlled, patterned, defensive style of play because, "I was taught that you never should let a boy get beaten badly. And that's why we use the system we do." Since teams trade possessions after every score he concluded, "success was a matter of eliminating mistakes." He reasoned you should be able to control the tempo of the game with proper self-discipline.

Discipline starts with the coach and each player knowing themselves. He claimed "if you understand yourself, chances are you'll be honest. And if you're honest, it's pretty easy to have discipline."

Through acceptance and embracing discipline, he was able to execute his ball-control offense (which later became the motion game or passing game offense) and tight man-to-man defense. Iba said, "The run and shoot style of play is the best game to watch. But, if you can't do

.....SCOUTING REPORT......SCOUTING REPORT...

that you better have something to go against it, and that's what we did." He believed in giving his players the best chance to win by equalizing the material on any given night. Mr. Iba believed he didn't have the material to run, so he made it a game of ballhandling and defense. As he stated, "they (the other team) sure can't run if I have the ball." So his teams always were great ballhandling teams, who took care of the ball, took high-percentage shots, hustled, and reduced or eliminated mental mistakes while they played tenacious defense. Iba said, "offense is exciting, but defense wins the big games."

Iba believed there was no greater sin than taking a bad shot. "I'm not against shooting," he once said. "I'm against bad shooting. I want my boys to shoot. I love my boys to shoot. But glory be, make it a good shot."

During his 41-year coaching career, Coach Iba felt that developing discipline became more challenging. Early on, he felt it could be developed easier and more as a group. As society changed with the decline of the family, Iba believed that much more time and individual approaches were needed to develop his staple ingredient—discipline. Interestingly, he also concluded that selfishness that destroys team play is usually caused by the lack of discipline.

The respect shown by players, coaches, and peers who used to address him as Mr. Iba was said to have started in his early years of coaching. During the first week of practice his first year at Oklahoma A & M, a player addressed Iba as "Henry." The 30-year old Iba snapped back "Hey boy, you don't know me that well." And so it became "Mr. Iba" after that. Then, the play of his teams earned him the respect of his peers, who also used the term.

Henry Iba also set high coaching standards in dealing with players. He said "my first responsibility is to the boy I'm coaching. When parents sent their sons to play under me, I felt it was my responsibility to send him back a better man." He also believed that the secret of successful teams is sound leadership by older players. "When they are willing to help younger players every day, then you've got the right environment to build a winner," said Iba. This fit into his concept of giving back something that benefits basketball. He stated that any teaching done must be for the benefit of your players.

The presenter for Henry Payne Iba at the Naismith Hall of Fame enshrinement was Robert Kurland, who along with George Mikan, ushered in the advent of the tall player in basketball. He was the foundation for the back-to-back national championship teams in 1945 and 1946.

In his presentation address, he said that Mr. Iba was a hard, but extremely fair, man. "If young people today want to know about Mr. Iba, it is very simple," said Kurland (2002). "Take the first letter of his last name, and the "I" stands for integrity. That was Mr. Iba." Kurland also said that he could testify to Mr. Iba:

- Conducting long, hard practices
- "Peeling our hides" verbally when we didn't put the team first
- "Chewing our ears" off when we didn't act and dress like gentlemen
- Kicking us out of practice if we ever gave less than the maximum effort
- Insisting that education was more important than basketball
- Prioritizing family first, then school, team, players, and self

In essence, Henry Iba had a long and storied career. He did it his way; railing against basketball corruption and coach timidity until the very end. Some said his system was not artistic, just successful. That is a good description of Mr. Iba's career.

Legendary John Wooden called Iba "the greatest friend basketball ever had and its most admired gentleman."

SOURCE

Bischoff, John. (1980) *Mr. Iba: Basketball's Aggie Iron Duke.* Oklahoma City: Western Heritage Books.

Iba, Henry. Vertical Files, Archives. Naismith Memorial Basketball Hall of Fame. Springfield, MA.

Kurland, Bob. Interview with Ralph Pim. September 28, 2002.

LESSONS FROM THIS LEGEND...

OKLAHOMA A&M'S MAN-TO-MAN DEFENSE

By Hank Iba

Authors' Note: The concept of tight, tough man-to-man defense with no switching allowed was fostered in the post WWII era by Mr. Iba. In fact, he was such a staunch believer in this type of defense for winning championships that he refused to allow his team to play zone defense even once his 41-year coaching career.

While relatively few boys possess the natural ability to become great offensive players, any boy with the proper mental attitude and a reasonable amount of physical attributes can learn to play good defense.

Few kids like to play defense. Soon as they become big enough to handle a ball, they want to do the shooting. It's perfectly natural. There isn't much excitement or glamour in keeping the other fellow from scoring.

Defensive-consciousness is something that must be built up within each boy and each team. It takes time and a lot of work every day in practice. But it definitely is worth it.

Good defense has become a tradition at Oklahoma A & M. It is a great help not only in developing winning teams, but also in inculcating desirable character traits.

Odd as it may seem, our boys take as much pride in preventing an opponent from scoring as they do in scoring themselves.

It makes no difference how well a boy has done offensively on any given night. If the man he was assigned to cover has scored well, our player feels that he had a bad night, and he will be a long time forgetting it.

Why the great emphasis on defense? We feel that the answer is obvious. The finest individual player or team will have "off" nights.

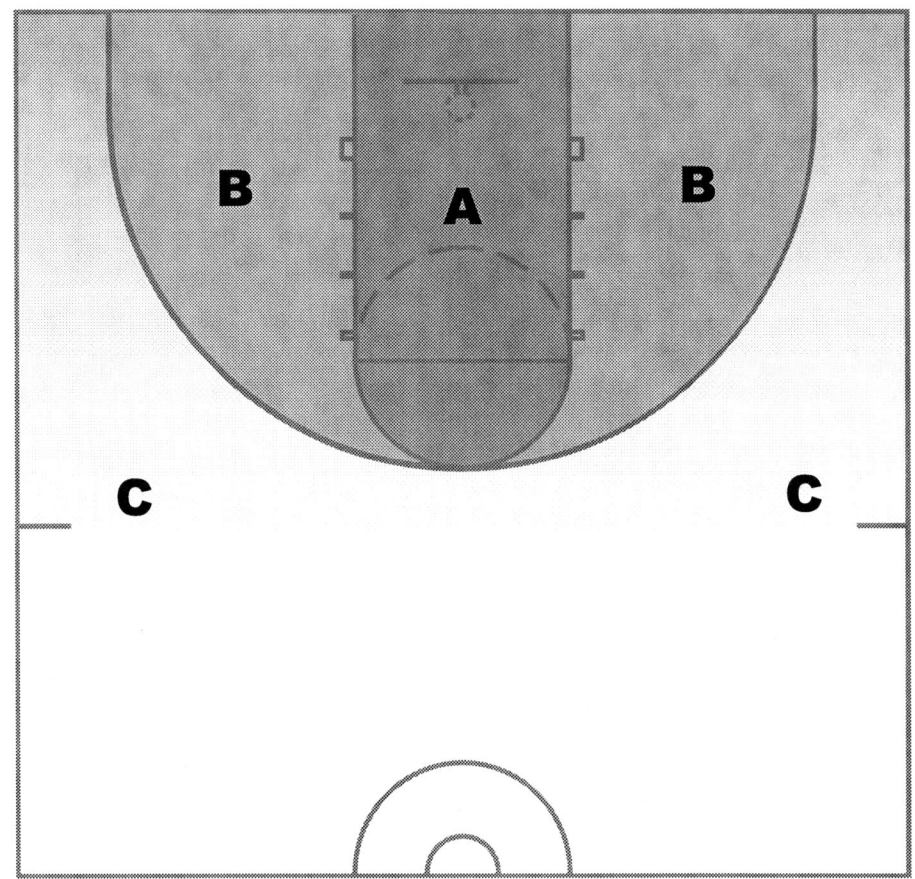

Iba 1.0

It makes no difference the sport. There always comes a time when the good batters just can't connect with the ball, when the forward passers can't hang those passes out on a line, and when the All-American forwards can't seem to hit that basket.

When these hard times come, a team should have something in reserve. Defense is the answer. Defensive play of a man or a team varies little from game to game. A good defensive player can be depended upon to play a good defensive game practically every time out.

It isn't unusual any more to find two teams playing each other on successive nights. Team A will win the first game by as much as 10 or 15 points, while Team B will win the second game by the same margin or more.

How do you account for this? The same playing arena, the same personnel, the same officials, but the score reversed. The answer, we feel, is hot-and-cold shooting with neither team having a strong defense to help its cause on the cold night.

LESSONS FROM THIS LEGEND...

In the teaching of individual defense, several points must be stressed:

1. Stance—feet comfortably apart, with one forward, never parallel, and weight slightly back.
2. Footwork—never cross the feet, slide them. This corresponds to the boxer's step or shuffle.
3. Movement—your first movement on defense always is backward. That is why the weight must be kept slightly back in the stance. The thought in your mind should be that the offensive man will drive. So, your first move is back when he moves. In other words, give way on the outside shot, but never let a man drive for a short shot.
4. Defensive Zones (See **Diagram 1.0**)

   In Zone A: Don't allow the offense to handle the ball. The ball must not be allowed to come into this zone without the defense contesting it. Neither the pivot man nor any other offensive player must be permitted to catch or play the ball within this area.

   In Zone B: Cover the point of the ball and lay back on the offside. When your man is handling the ball in this zone, get up on him tightly, so that he may not get a shot away. If he does not have the ball, stay away from him. The farther he is from the ball, the farther you may stay from him, but always be in position to move up as the ball moves in his direction.

   In Zone C: Stay completely away from the man, unless you know he is an excellent shooter in this zone. If he is, you must move out on him.

I once made the statement that there can be no fast break in basketball...if the defense is played correctly. I still firmly believe this.

There should always be three men in position to rebound on the offensive backboard. That leaves two men in position for defense. There can be no successful break if these men have been taught correctly.

In short, the instant the shot goes up, each man should know his responsibility. If he is inside the free throw circle and in position to rebound, he should do so. If not, his only move is toward the defensive end of the court. Whenever we lose possession of the ball, every man's concern should be defensive position, and that is all that should be on his mind.

We do not attack the ballhandler or try to intercept the ball. Instead, we get position between the ball and the basket and then pick up our man.

Therein lies the secret of a good defense. How quickly can you revert from an offensive to a defensive position?

Authors' Note: Offense-to-defense transition. If it takes you the count of three or four or more, that is too late. You must be able to realize the change instantly and make your movements accordingly.

Now that you are on the defensive, your only concern must be in keeping the opponent from scoring. If your mind is taken up with thinking about breaking to the offense and intercepting passes, mistakes will be numerous and costly.

When the opponent's shot goes up, each man on the defense must fold back around the lane area and set what we term "a defensive cup." If we have all five men in that cup, even if we do not get our hands on the ball, we will be in a position to keep any opponent from tipping it or going back for a second shot.

We call our particular type of defense "man-to-man with a sinking, or sliding, off-side." By this I mean wherever the ball is, that man must be covered tightly unless he is outside Zone B. On the off-side of the ball (opposite side of the court from the ball), every defensive man is sinking or sliding to the middle in order to stop any driver or help his teammate.

How effective this may be depends upon how quickly the sinker can get back up on his man as the ball moves in his direction. This, of course, is dependent upon the individual. If he is quick and his reactions are fast, he will be able to furnish more help in the middle. This man-to-man defense encourages individual responsibility and the desire to out-play an opponent. It is easily adaptable to all types of offense and makes it possible to match speed against speed and height against height.

We do not believe in the switch, or shift, when a man is about to be screened. If a boy knows that he can shift any time, he will be inclined to become a little lazy. But if he knows that he must "come through a screen" in order to stay with his man, he will develop more scrap.

Every player should be ready to help a teammate, but only if he has made a mistake and cannot possibly cover his man.

Many coaches feel that certain weaknesses exist in this type of defense. Here is the way we look at them:

1. Susceptible to screen plays. This type of defense need not be susceptible to screen plays if the man covering the screener plays away from him and stays alert to the driver. We teach this man never to play the screener tightly, but rather to step back and be ready to help in case his teammate does not get through the screen.

   Many screens are set on the side of the court away from the ball, with the screener moving from the inside to set his screen on the outside. Our defensive men on the off-side of the ball are required to sink as much as possible. When they do so, they make it almost

LESSONS FROM THIS LEGEND...

impossible for the offense to set an effective screen.

2. Does not afford opportunities for a fast break. This defense stresses position, rather than interception. In fact, we teach our players, especially the young ones, to forget about the ball entirely and concentrate upon position.

   Won't such defense discourage interceptions and offer little opportunity for quick breaks? Not if the sinking (off-side) is correctly done. With good execution, the defense will intercept as many passes without losing position as it would by deliberately concentrating on interceptions.

   As I stated before, we do not believe it is possible to fast break against a correctly played defense. Whenever we find the opposing defense out of position, we naturally will go for the fast break. But, we feel that our position on the defensive end of the court is more important than trying for the break.

3. It is more tiring and requires the players to be in better condition. This definitely is true. Many consider this a weakness, but, to us, it is a strength, as we know that our players are going to be in top condition.

   Here again, the question of responsibility enters. If a player knows what the system demands of him and what he must do to be a part of it, he will make every effort to condition himself to meet his responsibility.

SOURCE

Iba, Hank (1949, December). Oklahoma A.&M.'s Man-to-Man Defense. *Scholastic Coach*.

LESSONS FROM THIS LEGEND...

THE DEFENSIVE STANCE

By Henry "Hank" Iba

Believe in Your System
It is my belief that before something can be taught effectively, the teacher must believe in what he is teaching. Players can sense whether their coach is really sold on the importance of defense. A coach should never try to fool his players. The reason for this statement is the fact that if a coach is only half-sold, that is about all the enthusiasm he will have in his teaching and about all the enthusiasm that his team will demonstrate in their defensive play. First and foremost, coaches must believe in what they are teaching.

Defense is Hard Work
Players must realize that attaining defensive ability requires lots of determination and concentration. Fundamentals are important and a must, but they are worthless without the two qualities mentioned above. A good defensive player must be tenacious and enjoy shutting down his opponent. We feel any player who has the desire can become a proficient defensive player. Let's not fool ourselves. It takes lots of hard work to become a defensive standout. We tell our players that they must work as much on their defense as they do on their offense.

Staggered Stance
The defensive stance is our starting point when we teach defense. We start from the floor with the feet and then work our way up. The feet must be staggered, with either the right or the left foot in front. We do not want the player's feet to be parallel. The width of the feet should be about shoulder-width apart. If the feet are too close, balance will become a problem. If the feet are too wide, the legs have a tendency to tighten up, and then movement becomes a problem.

Stay Low
The knees must be flexed. No player can make a quick start with his knees straight or locked. We want the trunk bent slightly forward with the buttocks pulled down a little. By doing this, we feel as though it makes the center of gravity a little lower, and the player can move with better balance and not be top-heavy.

Keep the Head Stationary
The head and shoulders must be stationary. If the head and shoulders move from side-to-side with fakes, the body weight will shift from side-to-side, and this will result in the man being faked out of position.

Eyes are Focused on the Midsection
We want the eyes fixed on the offensive man, about at the belt buckle and not on the ball. If the eyes are on the ball, there will be a tendency for the head and shoulders to move with the ball.

Quick Hands
The only parts of the body left are the hands and arms. These we allow to be carried in a comfortable position. We do not want the hands raised above the shoulder, for this tends to bring the weight too far forward, resulting in a man not being able to go backward quickly enough. Reaching with the hands is not encouraged. Most players will not move their feet if their hands are moving. Of course, the player with extremely quick hands is encouraged to use his quickness as long as he moves his feet.

Defensive Movement
The defensive stance goes along with the first movement of a defensive player, and these two are taught together. The back foot must move first. The first two movements are somewhat like a boxer's one-two punch; by this we mean the quickness of them. The step back is executed with both feet and is not a hop. The back foot moves first and then the front foot.

We have tried to explain the things we emphasize to our players at Oklahoma State University regarding the defensive stance. It is our belief that all of the individual defensive fundamentals can be and should be worked on during the off-season. Anytime two players get together on a court, one player should be working on his defense, while the other is working on his offense. Then, they should reverse roles so that both players can improve their all-around game.

Source

Iba, Henry. (1966, November). Individual Defense. *The Basketball Mentor.*

LEGACY OF
George Keogan

- Led Notre Dame to the Helms Foundation national championship in 1927 and 1936.

- Popularized the defensive switch, which he called the "shifting man-for-man defense" to combat the popular offense of that time, the "figure 8."

- Directed Notre Dame to 20 consecutive winning seasons—his whole tenure at Notre Dame.

- Won 77 percent of his games during his coaching career.

- Hired at Notre Dame in 1923 by football legend Knute Rockne as an assistant football coach.

- Built his teams on speed, aggressiveness, and strong pivot play.

GEORGE KEOGAN

"Players should respect their opponent but always consider themselves equal or superior."
—George Keogan

BIOGRAPHY

Born: March 8, 1890

Died: February 17, 1943

Inducted into the Naismith Basketball Hall of Fame 1961

George Keogan directed Notre Dame to 20 consecutive winning seasons from 1923 to 1943. At the time of his arrival in 1923, basketball was not highly regarded at Notre Dame. Keogan quickly changed that way of thinking and led the Fighting Irish to the Helms Foundation national championship in 1927 and 1936. His coaching record at Notre Dame was 327-96-1, for a .771 winning percentage. Prior to Notre Dame, Keogan coached on the college level at Charles City (IA), Superior State (WI), St. Thomas (MN), Allegheny (PA), and Valparaiso (IN). His overall collegiate record was 412-124-1. Keogan's innovative and visionary style of play featured the defensive switch and strong pivot play. He was a student of the professional game and built his coaching strategies from the Original Celtics and the Buffalo Germans. Keogan coached future Hall of Famers Edward "Moose" Krause and Ray Meyer. Keogan died of a heart attack during the middle of his 20th season as head coach of the Fighting Irish. Keogan was enshrined in the Naismith Memorial Basketball Hall of Fame in 1961.

...SCOUTING REPORT.....SCOUTING REPORT.....

George Keogan...

George Keogan was born and raised in Minnesota Lake, Minnesota. He graduated from Detroit Lakes (MN) High School and began his coaching career at Charles City (IA) College. He had coaching stints at Lockport (IL) H.S. and Riverside (IL), before leading Superior (WI) State Teachers College to a 17-5 record.

Keogan attended the University of Minnesota and St. Louis University. While attending St. Louis, Keogan took several dentistry courses and was referred to as "Doc." He also coached the basketball team to a 13-5 record.

After serving as an instructor in World War I, Keogan coached at St. Thomas (MN), Allegheny (PA), and Valpariaso (IN). While at Valpariaso, Keogan's football team battled heavily favored Notre Dame to a relatively close game. Legendary football coach Knute Rockne was so impressed with Keogan's coaching effectiveness that he offered him a position on Notre Dame's football staff. Keogan's responsibilities at Notre Dame also included being the head basketball and baseball coach.

When Keogan took over at Notre Dame in 1923, the team's record the preceding six years was a dismal 35-64. The program was not highly regarded, and the facilities and equipment left much to be desired. Instead of a sharply lined hardwood court, Keogan had nothing but a dirt base with dry lime markers to form the outline of the court. The uniforms were of various colors.

Keogan quickly turned things around and built a nationally acclaimed program. He led the Irish to back-to-back 19-1 seasons in only his third and fourth seasons as coach. In twenty seasons at Notre Dame, Keogan won 327 games, second in Irish history, while losing just 97, for a .771 winning percentage. The Helms Foundation named Notre Dame national champions in 1927 and 1936.

Keogan was one of the game's more notable innovators. To defend against the figure 8 offense, which used screening and blocking tactics, Keogan popularized the screen-switch defense. He called it the "shifting man-to-man" defense. Keogan instructed his defenders to switch opponents whenever a block or screen was encountered. This enabled the defenders to be in a better position to stop an uncontested shot.

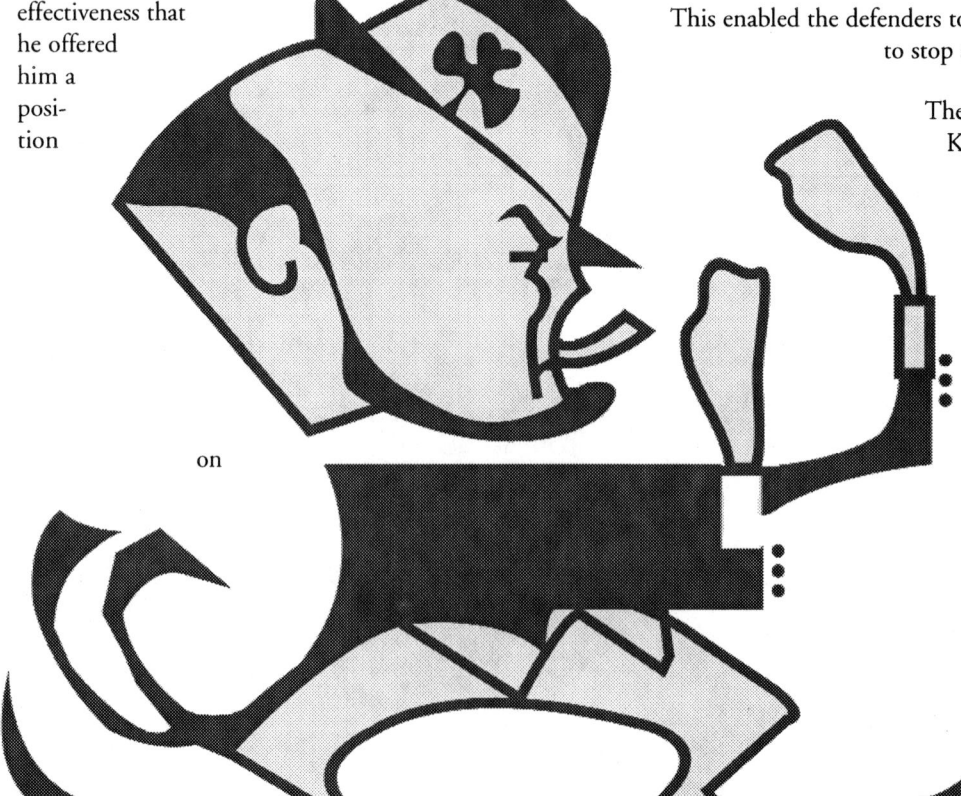

The three characteristics that Keogan insisted upon were speed, aggressiveness, and alertness. He wanted his players to "love basketball, live clean, work hard, and play with all that they had."

He constantly studied the game of basketball and always looked for new ideas. When future Hall of Fame player Ed "Moose" Krause enrolled at Notre Dame, Keogan combined ideas from the Original Celtics and the Buffalo Germans in order to better

...SCOUTING REPORT......SCOUTING REPORT...

use the talents of Krause. The Original Celtics utilized a play where their star pivot man, Dutch Dehnert, stationed himself on the foul line with his back to the basket. His teammates would pass to him and then cut off of him, trying to run their defenders into a screen. Keogan designed an offense combining the Original Celtic's pivot man with the cross-court offense that he had developed from the Buffalo Germans.

Describing his offense, Keogan said: "Picture, if you can, a basketball court hung on the wall like a clock. The pivot man under the basket is the top of the pendulum. The rest of the team is the weight on the pendulum. They swing back and forth across the court, passing the ball to one another until they see an opening. Then, they pass the ball into the center man, who either shoots, passes, or fakes a pass to one or more men breaking for the basket." (Petritz, 1932)

Adolph Rupp, whose Kentucky teams were defeated the first six times they met Notre Dame, said, "He (Keogan) taught me a rugged kind of basketball. I'm sure our teams are much better because of the whippings we took from Notre Dame."

Hall of Fame coach Tony Hinkle from Butler stated, "Notre Dame is the most powerful under-the-basket team I have ever seen anywhere." (Petritz, 1932)

In 1936, the Helms Foundation named Notre Dame national champions with a record of 22-2-1. The tie occurred on December 31, 1935 in a game played at Northwestern's Patten Gym. Late in the game, future Hall of Famer and Irish star Ray Meyer went to the free-throw line and made two free throws. The scoreboard at one end of the gym read 20-19 in favor of Notre Dame. At the other end of the gym, the scoreboard read 20-19 in favor of Northwestern. As time expired, both teams left the floor celebrating and thinking they had won the game. There was much confusion. After newspapermen rechecked their books, it was discovered the score was 20-20. But by this time, the players had showered and were dressed in street clothes. It was then decided to leave the game tied at 20-20.

"There are two ways of coaching," stated Keogan "They'll play for you because they hate you or because they love you." (Meyer, 1987)

Ray Meyer (2003) said, "Coach Keogan was the best at preparing a team for a game. If I could select only one coach to get a team ready for a game, I would definitely select George Keogan. He was an outstanding coach. He was also very demanding and particular. He expected his players to have their hair cut, dress accordingly, and represent Notre Dame in the proper way. It was very simple. You did what he said or you didn't play. Period."

Keogan and "Doc" Carlson from Pittsburgh were archrivals and had many fiercely contested games. Meyer remembered the game that occurred during his freshmen year in these words. "Notre Dame was leading by eight or ten at halftime. The second half started, and we had played around ten minutes, when it was discovered that the clock had not started. Keogan went up to the officials and said that we had played about ten minutes and the clock should be adjusted accordingly. Carlson disagreed and said that the clock indicated that we had not played at all so they should start the half from the beginning. We ended up playing the whole half over again, and Pittsburgh won the game. Keogan was so mad that he took the clock and threw it against the wall and it broke into a thousand pieces. There were many other times that "Doc" Carlson drove Keogan crazy. Notre Dame would have a great team, and before the game, Carlson would announce that he didn't think the Irish were that good and that he was going to start his second team. Keogan would come into the lockerroom, and he would be raving mad. Carlson did it just to torment him."

Basketball lost a great coach and leader when George Keogan died of a heart attack at the age of 53 during the 1943 season.

SOURCE

Keogan, George. Vertical Files, Archives. Naismith Memorial Basketball Hall of Fame. Springfield, MA.

Meyer, Ray. (1987). *Coach.* : Chicago: Contemporary Books.

Meyer, Ray. Interview with Ralph Pim. September 5, 2003.

Petritz, Joseph. (1932, March). Release from Department of Sports Publicity, University of Notre Dame.

LESSONS FROM THIS LEGEND...

A DEFENSE TO STOP THE FIGURE 8 OFFENSE

By George E. Keogan

Certain coaches like and employ the straight man-to-man defense, the first defense known to basketball; some employ the shifting man-to-man defense, while still others like and employ the zone defense. Every coach to his own likes and dislikes! But, there is one thing very certain—no matter what type of defensive set is used, the success or failure of that defensive set depends entirely on the proper teaching and execution of the defensive fundamentals. The set means nothing if the fundamentals are lacking in the players supposed to carry it out.

In this article, I will try to explain how to defend against a team using two-man screen plays as the foundation of their offense. The offense made up of these plays may be called "the in, out and over," or it may be called the "figure 8 offense."

The two-man moving screen, in itself, is very simple. It merely means that the passer moves over and legally gets in the path of the guard of the man receiving the pass, which allows the latter to get free for a shot or a dribble in to the basket. If a straight man-to-man defense is used against this type of attack, the defense is doomed to failure. If a shifting man-for-man defense is used, better success will be the result, provided the defensive men are equal physically in speed to their opponents.

Authors' Note: Keogan's shifting man-for-man defense is now called the defensive switch.

In **Diagram 1.0**, the defensive team is employing a straight man-to-man defense. O1 has the ball and is defended by X1. O2 is the receiver and is defended by X2. O1 passes to O2, and after the pass, cuts toward O2. He slides his body in front of X2. X1 follows his man. When O1 crosses in front of O2 and gets his body between X2 and the ball, O2 dribbles around O1, X1, and X2, and goes to the basket. No contact must take place between O1 and X1. X1 carries himself out of the play by staying with O1.

To this point, the situation has been reasonably simple to explain and simple to handle. The difficulty comes when two-man screens are used successively, necessitating rapid shifting by three or possibly four guards.

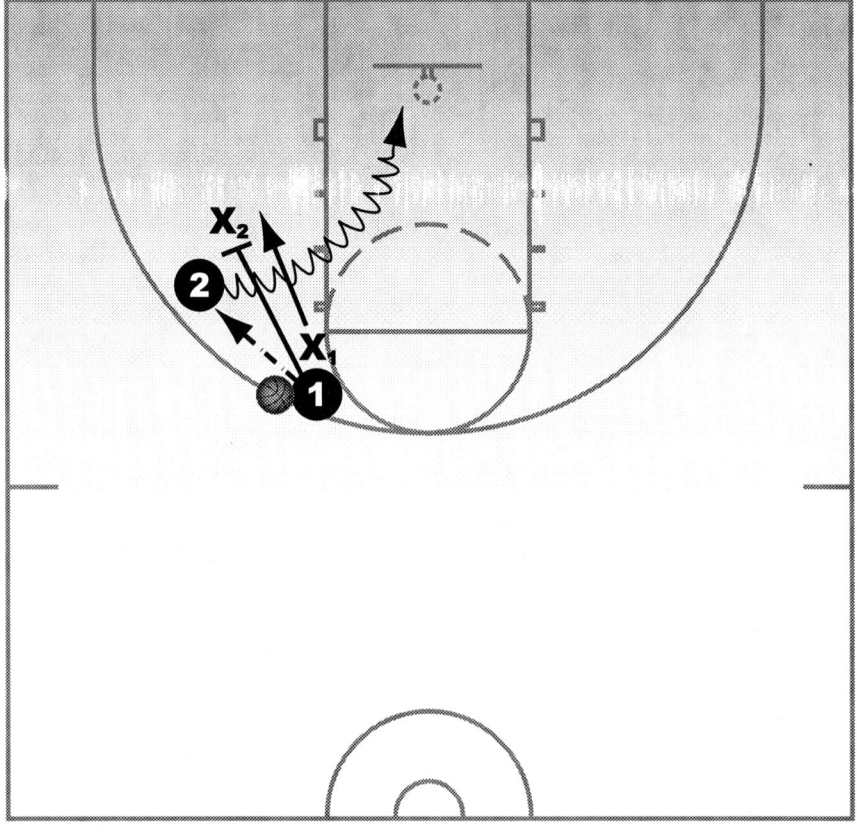

Keogan 1.0

LESSONS FROM THIS LEGEND...

Keogan 1.1

To defend against such an offensive maneuver, we employ the shifting man-for-man defense. This defense is shown in **Diagram 1.1**. O1 passes to O2 and takes the path indicated to screen out X2. The two guards, employing a shifting man-for-man defense, immediately sense a screen play. X1 starts to follow O1. X2 yells, "Shift!" X1 immediately picks up O2. X2 steps back and stays with O1. Therefore, when O2 dribbles out of the screen, X1 has him guarded, and X2 covers O1. Both offensive players are covered. This maneuver takes much practice, but players grasp such things readily.

A successive two-man screen is explained in **Diagram 1.2**. O1 passes to O2 and then cuts in to screen X2. X2 yells, "Shift!" X1 then cuts back and picks up O2. X2 stays with O1. As O2 dribbles in, he is covered by X1. O3, who is guarded by X3, then immediately breaks from the side of the court toward O2. O2 passes to O3 and cuts across to screen X3. X3 yells, "Shift!" X1 slides back and picks up O3. X3 stays with O2. O3 tries to dribble in for a shot. If he sees it cannot be made, he passes the ball to O1, who remains on the opposite side of the court, and the same routine is repeated.

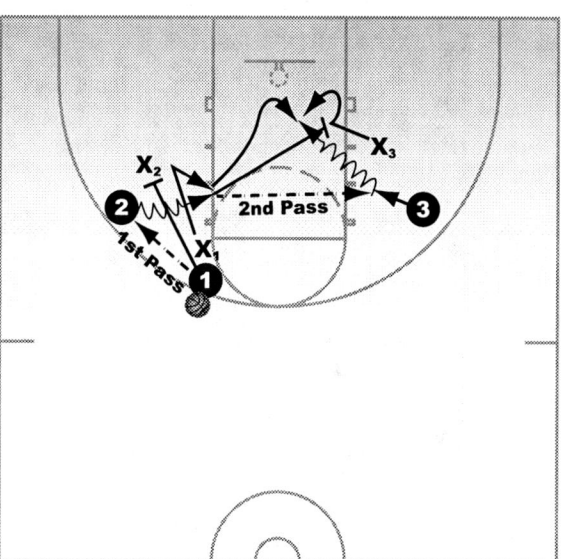

Keogan 1.2

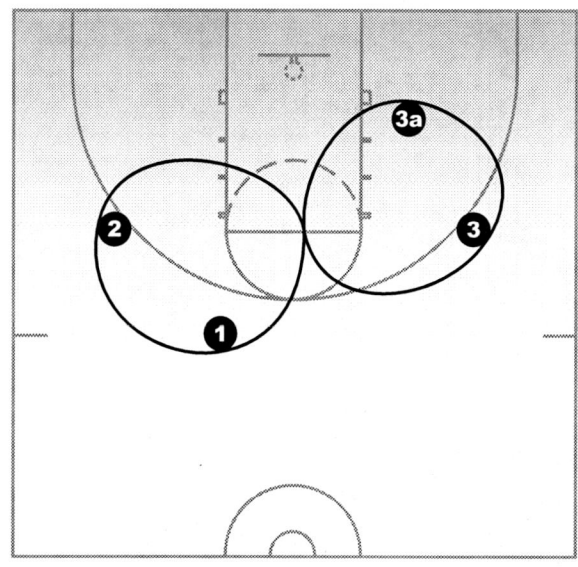

Keogan 1.3

Now, draw lines from O1 to O2 and from O2 to O3, then through O3a, the secondary position of O3, and back to O1 (See **Diagram 1.3**). You will find these lines resemble a figure 8. Hence, the name "figure 8 offense," which is in reality only a succession of two-man screens.

The repeating of these two-man screen maneuvers may eventually be successful by a guard's failure to pick up his offensive man. This would allow an offensive player a free lane to the basket and a shot.

I have tried to explain in detail how to stop the in, out, and over, or the "figure 8 offense," by using a shifting man-for-man defense. Of course, it would be much more simple to employ a zone defense. Against this latter type of defense, screening is almost impossible.

SOURCE
Keogan, George E. (1934, December). A Defense for the Figure 8 Offense. *The Athletic Journal*.

LEGACY OF Bob Knight

- Highly principled coach who believes his primary role is to prepare his players for success in life.

- Led Indiana to three national championships (1976, 1981, 1987).

- One of only three coaches to win the "Triple Crown" of coaching.

- Regarded as one of the all-time best teachers.

- One of the top five winningest coaches in the history of basketball with more than 800 wins.

- Demands the absolutely best effort possible from his players.

- Played on the 1960 national championship team at Ohio State.

BOB KNIGHT

*"The will to win is not as important as
the will to prepare to win."*
—Bob Knight

BIOGRAPHY

Born: October 25, 1940 in Massillon, OH

Inducted into the Naismith Basketball Hall of Fame in 1991

Bob Knight earned the reputation as one of the top coaches of all-time and has won three NCAA championships (1976, 1981, 1987). He won 763 games at Indiana University and the United States Military Academy and is currently the head coach at Texas Tech. In 2003, Knight earned his 800th college victory. His Indiana teams won eleven Big Ten Conference titles and made five Final Four appearances. His Army teams led the nation in team defense for three consecutive years. Knight is one of only two coaches to both play on and coach national championship teams. As a player, he played at Ohio State for Hall of Fame coach Fred Taylor. Knight was selected National Coach of the Year in 1975, 1976, 1987, and 1989. He coached the U.S. Olympic team to a gold medal in 1984. Knight was enshrined in the Naismith Memorial Basketball Hall of Fame in 1991.

...SCOUTING REPORT.....SCOUTING REPORT.....

Bob Knight...

Bob Knight learned the game of basketball while playing at Ohio State University for future Hall of Fame coach Fred Taylor. A native of Orville, Ohio, Knight was a member of Buckeye teams that won Big Ten titles in 1960, 1961, and 1962. Ohio State posted an overall record of 78-6 during those three years and won the 1960 national championship. In 1961 and 1962, the Buckeyes finished second in the NCAA tournament.

After graduating with a degree in history and government, Knight was an assistant coach at Cuyahoga Falls, Ohio one year before entering the U.S. Army, where he was assigned to assist Coach Tates Locke at West Point. When Locke became head coach at Miami University (OH), Knight became the head coach at West Point in 1966, earning the distinction of becoming the youngest head coach in major college history at the age of 26. Knight's Army teams finished 102-50, led the nation in team defense three consecutive years, and participated in four NIT tournaments in five seasons. Among his players at West Point was future Hall of Fame coach Mike Krzyzewski.

When Knight left West Point in 1971 to accept the position at Indiana University, he called the decision "the toughest in his life." During his first decade, Knight's coaching strategies changed his style of play, from run-and-gun to ball control. His hard-nosed approach reaped large benefits. During his 29-year stint at Indiana, the Hoosiers won 662 games, including 22 seasons of 20 or more wins. Indiana won 11 Big Ten Conference titles, three national championships, and one NIT championship.

Knight became the head coach at Texas Tech in 2000 and immediately turned the program around during his inaugural season. The Red Raiders compiled a 23-9 record and earned an NCAA berth during Knight's first season. The year before Knight's arrival, Texas Tech won only nine games.

On February 5, 2003 Knight earned his 800th victory. Only Dean Smith of North Carolina (879), Adolph Rupp of Kentucky (876), and Jim Phelan of Mount St. Mary's (827) have won more than 800 men's games in Division I.

Coach Knight stands for high principles. He demands excellence and possesses the uncanny ability to extract the full potential from his teams. He is demanding of himself, his players, and the officials. Knight does not demand victory; he demands the absolutely best effort possible. He has said that you aren't just playing against opponents, but the higher calling is to play against the game.

Knight believes that the majority of players never understand how to win. "When players understand what has to be done to win, then you've got a chance to be pretty good. And the very first thing that has to be done to win, in any team sport, is playing well defensively. I mean, there's never been a team that has won championships, in whatever the sport, that has not been very good defensively." (Packer, 1999, p. 102)

"From a coaching standpoint, the greatest fear I've ever had is that in some way I might not have prepared my team as well as I could have," said Knight (2002). "I'm

.....SCOUTING REPORT.....SCOUTING REPORT...

always afraid I've left something out, or overlooked something. If you've done that, you've shortchanged your players. They're not as well prepared as they should be."

Discipline is an important component to Knight's success. "To a lot of people, discipline is a very negative word," said Knight. "I've always felt it was a positive word, and I defined it in that vein a long time ago. I said discipline is doing what has to be done when it has to be done. You do it as well as you can do it, and you do it that way all the time. That's what a disciplined person does, and that's how a disciplined person plays." (Packer, 1999, p. 114)

Coach Bob Knight is truly a legend. He is a four-time National Coach of the Year, and he is one of only three coaches to win the "Triple Crown" of coaching—winning NCAA and NIT titles and an Olympic gold medal. He has been an outspoken critic of illegal recruiting practices and prides himself on his violation-free programs at Indiana and Texas Tech. Knight takes immense pride in the graduation rate of his players. All but two of his four-year players completed degrees, a ratio of nearly 98 percent. Equally impressive is the fact that 27 former players and assistants have gone on to become successful head coaches.

When asked about the changes in college basketball during his career, Knight (2002) responded in these words. "Certainly, the pay is enormously better. But, that's about the only change I'd consider positive. I hate the elements that recruiting has brought into college basketball—the know-it-alls, but know-nothings, who have made fortunes by feeding the national recruiting frenzy with gossip and guessing that is passed off as inside information; way out-of-control AAU summer programs; shoe-company financial involvement that attracts unqualified and sometimes undesirables into basketball. The worst effect of all this may be the damage done to the egos of sixteen and seventeen-year-old kids, in way too many cases, convincing them they're far better than they are."

Regarding rule changes, Knight (2002) said, "I don't like the three-point shot and the shot clock. Those two changes take away some of the control I felt I had on the outcome of the game. The three-point shot exclusively favors raw talent—the ability to shoot the basketball, period. I think the intent of the rule was to take the zone defense out of college basketball by awarding three points for an outside shot over the zone. I don't think rules should ever be made to favor the team with the most talent. And in my opinion, both the shot-clock and the three-point shot are talent-oriented rules. I think the three-point shot has taken a lot of the science of coaching from the game."

SOURCE

Knight, Bob. Vertical Files, Archives. Naismith Memorial Basketball Hall of Fame. Springfield, MA.

Knight, Bob and Bob Hammel. (2002). *Knight: My Story.* New York: Thomas Dunne Books.

Packer, Billy and Roland Lazenby. (1999). *Why We Win.* Chicago: Masters Press.

LESSONS FROM THIS LEGEND...

DEFENSIVE RULES

By Bob Knight and Pete Newell

We spend 70 percent of our time during the first four weeks of practice on defense. Approximately fifty percent of each practice session from the fifth week until the end of the season will be devoted to defensive work.

Webster defines aggressiveness as "the disposition to dominate." For us to win, we feel that our defense must dominate the offense. We want the offense doing what we want, not what they want. Therefore, just as some defenses are built on quickness, size, or strength, ours is built on aggressiveness. This idea permeates all of our defensive thinking, and the players are well aware of this. We believe, that while not everyone can be quick, or big, or strong, there is no reason why each of our players can't be extremely aggressive.

There are three things you must teach defensively. We don't care what defense you play. We don't care if it is a press, a zone, three-quarter, half-court, or anything else.

PRESSURE ON THE BALL

A defense cannot be effective if it allows the ball to be moved without pressure on the ball and on the people who are going to receive the ball. As a coach, there are two words that you must be careful about using—"never" and "always."

You have to understand that these words just won't happen in the game of basketball. We are trying to get as close to this as we possibly can. The closer we get to either of those words, the better we are going to be. We have a little thing in our locker room that says, "victory favors the team that makes the fewest mistakes." This is sort of the basis for our teaching of the game. We don't think anyone plays this game well. This is the greatest game in the world from the standpoint of total involvement of everyone. You must play both ends. You must incorporate all the skills of the game. Everyone has to be able to play the game of basketball, so it becomes a very complicated game. Consequently, it becomes a game of mistakes.

Everything that we have to do involves two thoughts. One of these thoughts is simplicity. The more complex you are, there is a greater chance for error. The second thought is to eliminate mistakes. Once again, "victory favors the team that makes the fewest mistakes." So, if we get pressure on the ball and if we pressure where the ball is going, this really is an asset to our defense.

FORCE THE BALL TO THE CORNER

Scouting can set up getting the offense to do something they don't want to do. If they like to set up on the right side, you make them set up on the left side. If they like to start out by hitting the high post, you deny the ball to him.

It is imperative we figure out what they like to do and then try to take it away from them. Again, it is not always going to happen, but we must try to force them to do something different. We try and force the ball to the corner.

We put lines down about seventeen feet from the basket at the baseline and tell our players we don't want the ball to get past this point. This is where they are going to be forced out-of-bounds. Again, this isn't always going to happen, but if we set up a situation in practice that is much harder than the game, we have a better chance at accomplishing it in a game.

You have two great defensive players—the baseline and the sideline. It is up to the defense to take advantage of them. By forcing the ball to the baseline, we have taken away an option they like to do. The only way for a pass to come back out is to the middle, and we can be ready to defend against it.

If we get an offensive player to pick up his dribble, we want the man guarding him to get all over him on his high side. That is the only place for him to throw the ball to avoid the pressure. We want to force him to make the pass back to the baseline and try to take away the pass back to the top of the circle or middle of the floor.

SEE THE BALL

The third thing any defense must be able to do is keep track of ball location. Location of the ball is extremely important at all times. There are two old axioms that used to be taught that we don't agree with any more. One is the cross-court pass. In earlier years, we were told never to throw the cross-court pass because it could be picked off too easily. One of the most effective weapons against the zone defense today is the cross-court pass.

The second axiom that we don't agree with anymore is that a defender must never turn his or her head. A defensive player must be constantly turning his head. This applies to the person playing the ball, as well as anyone else. If you are contesting a pass, you must have your head moving to see what is going on. Turning the head is extremely important as a defensive player, particularly as a helpside defensive player, to know where the ball is and to then adjust accordingly. Any defense has, first of all, a priority

LESSONS FROM THIS LEGEND...

of pressuring the ballhandler and making it difficult for the ball to be moved. If players are not aware of ball location, it is questionable where they are going to be in terms of defensive positioning.

We don't think there is an offense that involves more than three people at any one time. There may be a screen away or something like that, but the ball cannot involve more than three people. If we pay attention to ball location defensively, we are going to set up so that we always have a five-on-three or five-on-two situation, favoring the defense. Consequently, if five players are paying attention to the ball, knowing where it is at all times, we have a chance to stop penetration.

DAILY REQUIREMENTS

In addition to three general points of interest defensively, we have identified five areas that we believe must be covered in one way or another in daily practice sessions:

1. Pressure on the ball:
   a. The focal point of our defense is the ball itself. Each of our five defensive players has as his primary responsibility the job of stopping ball penetration.
   b. The defensive player should be close enough to the player with the ball so that he can put the palm of his hand on the offensive player's chest.
   c. The defensive player must always have his head directly between the ball and the basket. Emphasis on the ball, rather than on the player's stomach, will keep the defensive player in position to always get pressure on the ball with his hands.
   d. The hands apply constant pressure to the ball. The defensive player, playing palms up, pressures the ball with the hand nearest the direction the offensive player is going, i.e. if the offensive player goes to the right, use the right hand. The back hand is used to pick up the crossover dribble.
   e. If the offensive player turns his back on a reverse dribble, the defensive player must retreat one step to avoid getting caught by the offensive dropstep and hook.
   f. When the offensive player with the ball shoots, our rule is: you leave your feet as soon as he has left his. We want the defensive player's hand on the ball, not in the shooter's face. We believe that forcing the shooter to adjust his shot is more detrimental to good shooting than obstructing his vision.

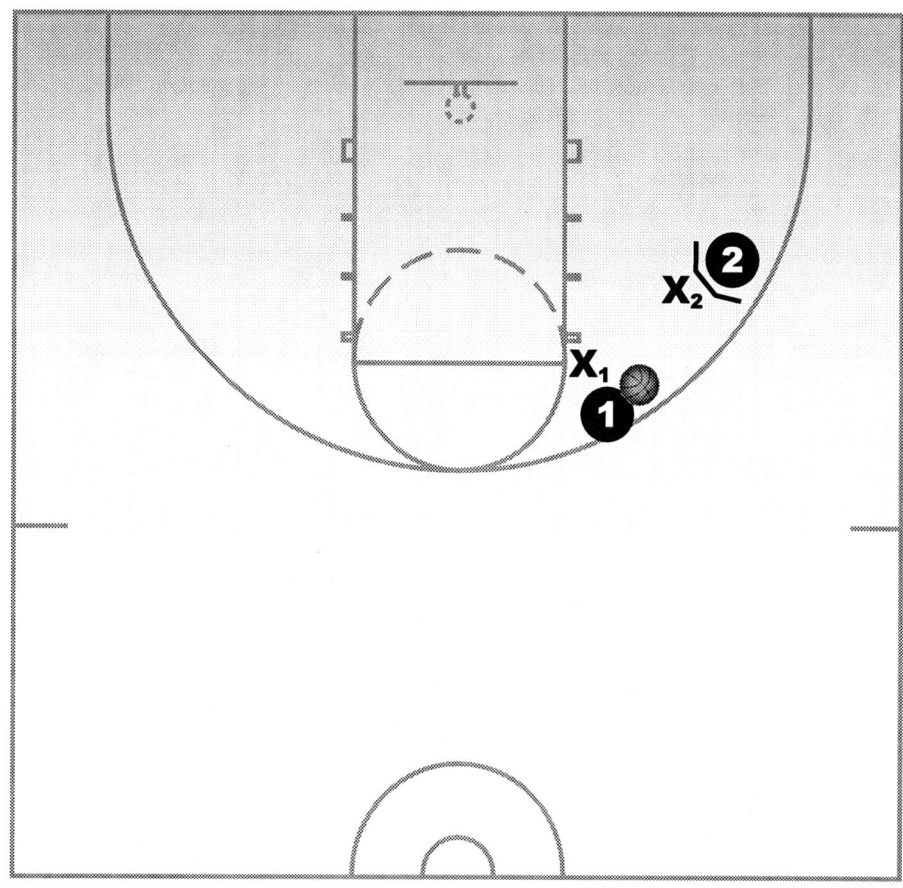

Knight 1.0

2. Pressure the passing lane:
   a. We must work on making it tough for the offense to move the ball from one position to another.
   b. We try to make it as tough as possible to get anything done on the ballside. As shown in **Diagram 1.0**, X2 must always keep his head between the man he is playing and the ball. This will take away the passing lane and prevent a quick cut into the post.
   c. X2 must also learn to ignore the first step toward the basket taken by O2. If he does not, O2 can step right back for the ball. Keep in mind that the guard-to-forward pass for a successful back-cut

LESSONS FROM THIS LEGEND...

is difficult to complete, and help will be reacting to it.
  d. The next thing we try to do is to keep the ball from being reversed. (See **Diagram 1.1**)
3. Help and recover:
  a. We want our players to realize that basketball is a game of continuous action where they complete one job only to move immediately to another.
  b. The phrase "help and recover" is one our players hear many times each night. It refers to a player getting into position to help stop penetration of the ball and then recovering to his own man.
  c. A defensive player who has helped stop penetration but does not recover in time to prevent his man from scoring is not doing his job.
4. Block-out:
  a. We approach this aspect of our defense by telling our players that the two most overrated things in basketball are size and jumping ability. Position is by far the most important part of our rebounding.
  b. Make contact. We feel it is essential to make contact with the offensive player to keep him off the board.
  c. The direction your man goes establishes your pivot foot. If he goes to your right, you pivot on the right foot. We use the reverse turn because it gives us more time to make contact and enables us to get the man if he changes direction.
  d. As the pivot is being made, we want the elbows as high as the shoulders, with the hands raised. This greatly widens the blockout surface and puts the hands in a position where they can't hold.

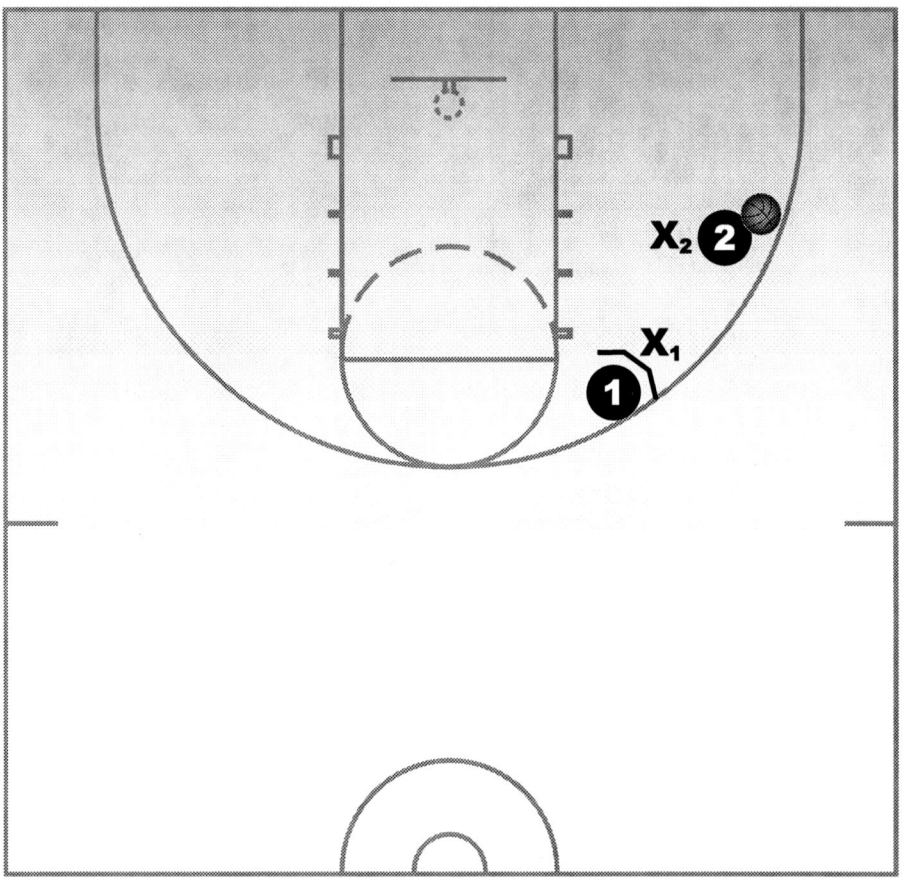

Knight 1.1

  e. From the time the shot is taken until it can be rebounded, approximately three seconds will elapse. We want our defensive players to be able to hold the blockout for five seconds.
  f. We say the perfect rebound is one that hits the floor and bounces into your hands.
5. Post defense:
  a. Post defense is really the heart of defensive play. We feel that if we can take away or, at least to a great extent, hinder the effectiveness of the offensive post player, we are forcing the offense to move away from the basket.
  b. We have two rules for ballside post defense. The first rule is to play on the highside of the post player as long as you can keep the pass from coming into him without fronting him. The second rule is to play on the low or baseline side of the post player when the ball is being fed from below.

SOURCE

Knight, Bob and Pete Newell. (1986). *Basketball According to Knight and Newell, Volume 1.* Seymour, IN: Graessle-Mercer.

LESSONS FROM THIS LEGEND...

FIVE-ON-FOUR DEFENSIVE DRILL

By Bob Knight and Pete Newell

Defensive quickness is necessary for a team to be successful. It is our belief that the best way to develop team defensive quickness in both thought and action is to put the defense at a disadvantage. In the Five-on-Four Drill, we use four defensive players against five offensive players. The defense leaves the player furthest from the ball unguarded. (See **Diagram 2.0**)

When the unguarded player moves into position to receive the ball, the four defensive players quickly adjust to the new situation by picking up that player. When there is ball movement, the defenders must change their floor positions and leave the least dangerous player open. (See **Diagram 2.1**) The theory to our Five-on-Four Drill is that the defense will have to be constantly talking, helping, and recovering to pick up the free player, who could be any of the five offensive players.

The five offensive players should run their normal offensive patterns so that the four defenders must be continually adjusting to new situations. Remember, you don't form habits through discussion—you form them through work. We use this drill every night in practice, because we feel it has done a great deal in developing quickness and second effort in our defensive play.

TEACHING POINTS

The defenders must:
1. Communicate.
2. Jam the passing lanes.
3. Keep the ball from going inside.
4. Force the ball to the outside.

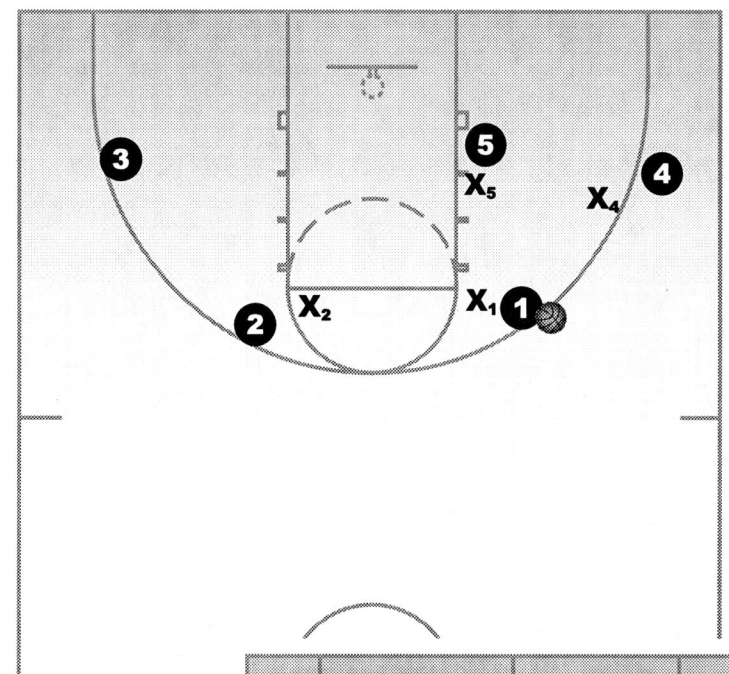

Knight 2.0

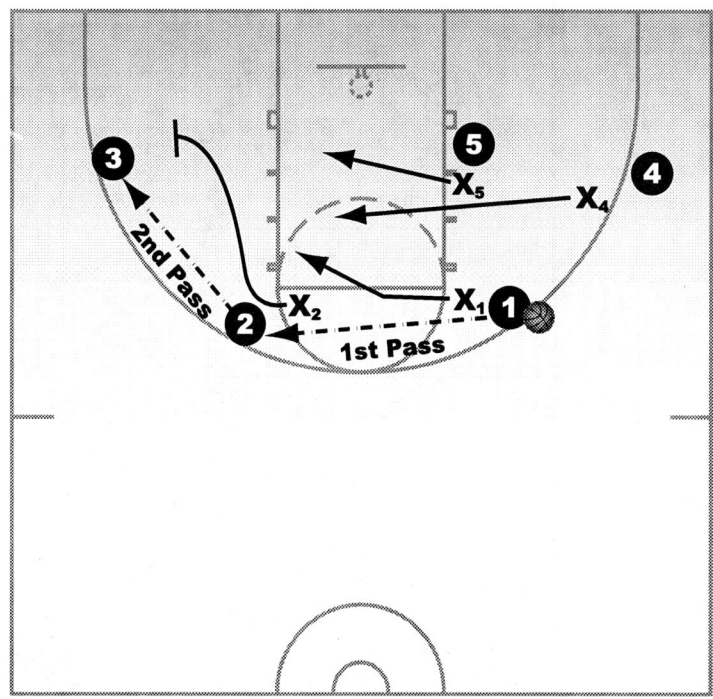

Knight 2.1

Source

Knight, Bob and Pete Newell. (1986). *Basketball According to Knight and Newell, Volume 1.* Seymour, IN: Graessle-Mercer.

LEGACY OF
Mike "Coach K" Krzyzewski

- Led Duke to three NCAA national championships (1991, 1992, 2001) and ten Final Four appearances.

- Considered one of the all-time great leaders in the history of coaching.

- Graduated from West Point and played for Hall of Fame coach Bob Knight.

- Established programs built on hard work, commitment to excellence, teamwork, and attention to detail.

- Regarded as an excellent teacher and a person of the highest character.

- Believed the primary responsibility of a leader is to inspire.

- Selected NABC Coach of the Decade for the 1990s.

MIKE "COACH K" KRZYZEWSKI

"When our goal is to try to do our best, when our focus is on preparation and sacrifice and effort—instead of numbers on the scoreboard—we will never lose."
—Mike Krzyzewski

BIOGRAPHY

Born: February 13, 1947 in Chicago, IL

Inducted into the Naismith Basketball Hall of Fame in 2001

Mike Krzyzewski has been one of the most dominant college coaches during the past two decades and was selected the NABC Coach of the Decade for the 1990s. Krzyzewski led Duke to three NCAA national championships (1991, 1992, 2001) and ten Final Four appearances. His three national championships place him third on the all-time list, tied with mentor Bob Knight and trailing Adolph Rupp (4) and John Wooden (10). "Coach K" is the winningest active coach in NCAA tournament play with 64 wins and is only one game behind the leader Dean Smith. His ten Final Four appearances place him second on the all-time list behind John Wooden (21). Krzyzewski won a Gold Medal in the 1992 Olympics, serving as an assistant coach. He is a graduate of the United States Military Academy, where he played for future Hall of Fame coach Bob Knight. Krzyzewski returned to West Point and began his head coaching career in 1976. He led Army to an NIT appearance, before accepting the position at Duke in 1980. He has been named National Coach of the Year 11 times. Krzyzewski was enshrined in the Naismith Memorial Basketball Hall of Fame in 2001.

...SCOUTING REPORT.....SCOUTING REPORT.....

Mike "Coach K" Krzyzewski...

They still can't spell or pronounce his name (Krzyzewski which sounds like Sha-shef-ski), but they know that "Coach K" is associated with the highest level of success in the college basketball world. But, what sets him apart from thousands of coaches striving for success in the basketball coaching fraternity? It is one word—"leadership." He believes that the main job of a coach is to motivate, and the primary job of a leader is to inspire, and how well he does that. Grant Hill, former Duke All-American player, said it best. "My first team meeting in 1990 was an awesome day. I remember being excited, anxious, and nervous when Coach K. walked in; the first thing he said was that we're going to win the national championship. That's one of his most valuable qualities. He's inspiring. He makes you a believer." (Krzyzewski, 2000) An even more important question is how he became such an exceptional leader?

Mike Krzyzewski had humble beginnings, filled with early involvement in sport and a strong support system; father, William (an elevator operator at Willoughby Tower in downtown Chicago), mother, Emily (a homemaker and cleaning woman at the Chicago Athletic Club), brother, Bill, and best friend, Moe Mlynski. There were few material things but lots of love and pride in the family. The family sacrificed so Mike could attend Weber High School, a private all-boys Catholic school in Chicago. This may be why he has developed such a strong sense of confidence in what his family/his teams can accomplish together. His strong sense of unconditional support and commitment to success he attributed to his mother; he stated that his happiness, commitment to family, and not being afraid to fail came directly from her. In fact, before each game, he puts his hand over the pocket where he carries his mother's rosary and says this prayer, "Please God, help me to do my best, help me be myself, and help me lead from my heart."

When Mike decided to attend the United States Military Academy at West Point, a difficult decision, it was again because of his parents. Even though he didn't want to go, he had the discipline to believe and trust in his parents at a moment's notice. This is another coaching trait he felt was important for success. During his four years at Army, he was exposed to the teachings of future Hall of Fame coach Bob Knight, as well as being absorbed in the Academy, and it's claim as one of the best leadership development programs in the world. Not only did he assimilate the West Point honor code: "I will not lie, cheat, or steal—nor tolerate those who do," but he took to heart the academy purpose "to develop leaders of character for service to the nation." His coaching videos stress absolute honesty (instant belief in each other), complete responsibility for your own actions (no excuses), and shared experiences (the Army code of soldiers depending on each other). When Mike left West Point as an officer/leader, he went on to another military service leadership development experience that led to his eventual promotion to captain. He still attributes his developmental years at USMA as a strong factor forming his character in the West Point crucible of leadership.

Finally, Coach K. views coaching being focused on two essentials:

- **TEACHING**—he states that "I am a teacher and a coach". Our whole approach to coaching revolves around teaching. "We need to always find better ways to become better teachers. Teaching is what I love most." (Krzyzewski, 2000) He also believes in exposing his players to teaching; to force them to learn themselves and serve others; and to teach is to learn twice. Coach K. has said that teaching is the heart of his coaching style.

- **LEADERSHIP**—like most coaches, he believes strongly that the coach is a leader, but his background and development has forged a new definition of leadership in the coaching world. The lessons learned from his family, the Academy experience at West Point, and the leadership laboratory in the Army, plus his varied coaching experiences have produced a new leadership model. This is reflected in his belief that leaders need to do their best, learn their limits, and try to extend them as a proper leader perspective. He believes that the main job of a coach is to motivate, and the main job of a leader is to inspire. (Krzyzewski, 2000) These are sound principles for all to follow.

.....SCOUTING REPORT.....SCOUTING REPORT...

This emphasis on leadership and teaching has produced the following milestones at Duke:

- Three national championships (1991, 1992, 2001)
- 11 National Coach of the Year honors
- 20 NCAA tournament bids
- Ten Final Four appearances (third all-time)
- Seven ACC tourney championships (first to win four straight in 2002)
- Nine ACC season championships
- Winningest active coach in NCAA Tourney victories with 64 (behind Dean Smith at 65).
- NABC Coach of the Decade (1990s)
- Coach K. Court naming honor at Cameron Indoor Stadium in 2001
- Duke's all-time winningest coach
- Naismith Basketball Hall of Fame in 2001
- John Wooden Legends of Coaching award in 2000
- NABC President in 1998-1999
- Named "America's Best Coach" by Time/CNN in 2001
- Coached players selected as National Defensive Player of the Year seven times
- Registered during his career 64 NCAA wins and an overall 665-234 record.

SOURCE

Krzyzewski, Mike. Vertical Files, Archives. Naismith Memorial Basketball Hall of Fame. Springfield, MA.

Krzyzewski, Mike. (2000). *Leading with the Heart: Coach K's Successful Strategies for Basketball, Business, and Life.* New York: Warner Books.

Krzyzewski, Mike. Interview with Jerry Krause. 2001.

LESSONS FROM THIS LEGEND...

MAN-TO-MAN DEFENSE

By Mike Krzyzewski

I've been using the man-to-man defense and the motion offense for my ten years as head coach, five at Army and five at Duke. I think it's a fun way of playing, but it's a different way of playing.

I'd like to start with our man-to-man drills. Some people say that we do exactly the same thing as Indiana. That's not so. I played for Coach Knight (at Army) and worked under him at Indiana, and a lot of the things that we do come as a result of my association with him, but I think that the main thing that you must do in setting up your own system is to be flexible. I remember after coaching at the West Point Prep School, which is like a very good high school job, I went to Indiana, and we had done things in the man-to-man defense exactly the way that I had done them as a player when I had played for Coach Knight. Everything was the same. The drills were the same. I said that if he had that much success doing it that way, maybe I could have success also.

But, when I went out to Indiana, the year before they won the national title, at my first practice in Indiana, I was helping out, and after practice, I was somewhat mystified because a drill that we used everyday at Army had not been utilized. It was called the zigzag drill. That's where you and a partner get together at full court 1-on-1, with a defensive man sliding the length of the floor back and forth in a zigzag fashion. We did that every day at West Point. Every one of my teams up until that time did it everyday.

I was mystified, but wasn't brave enough to ask Coach Knight why he hadn't used this drill. The second practice we go again, and again the drill isn't used. We are in the locker room afterwards and Coach Knight is in a good mood, so for all the Army players who got down in that stance everyday and who worked their fannies off, I have to ask why. So, I asked if I could ask a question. Coach Knight said, "Sure Michael, what do you want?" I said, "How come we aren't doing the zigzag? We did that drill over and over and over again." Coach Knight came over to me and I said to myself, "you are a dumb Pollack." He puts his hand on my shoulder and says, "Michael, there is a little lesson that you must learn in life. There is a big difference between you and Quinn Buckner." And that's true.

The point is that we must adjust to the type of people that we are coaching. You

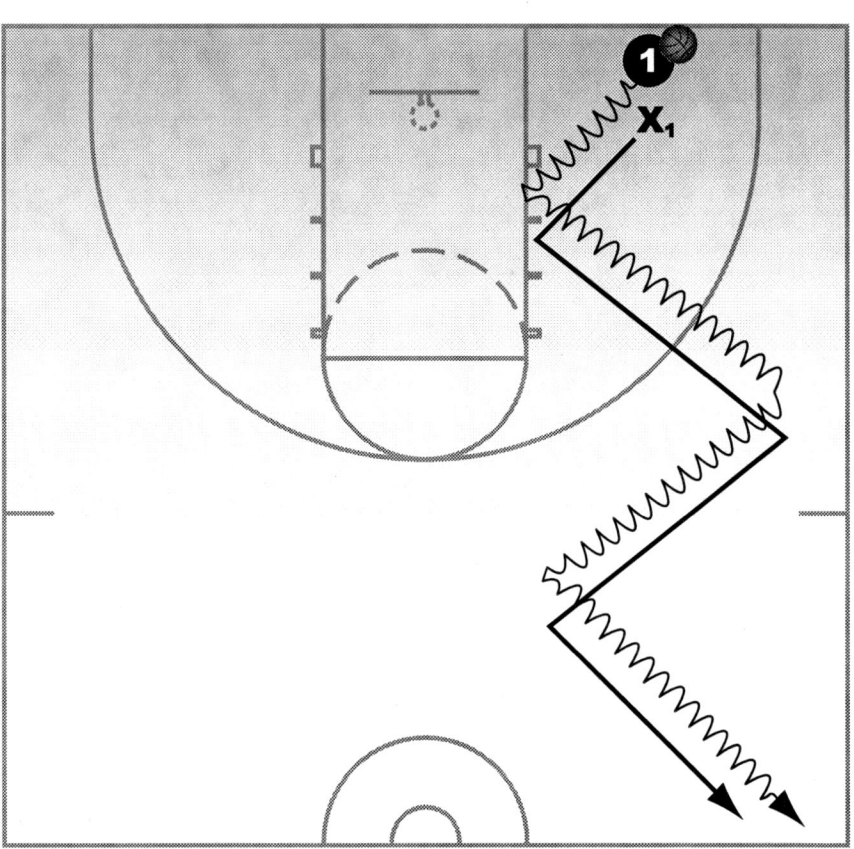

Krzyzewski 1.0

must look at your team from year to year and figure out what is the best for them. You can play man-to-man defense. You can play motion offense, but how does it best suit your team? And, that is a big lesson I learned at that time in my coaching career. This year at Duke, we played man-to-man, but we did play some zone, and we did press. The difference is that if you watch Indiana, they play a sloughing man-to-man. It is difficult to get anything in the three-second area. After a shot was taken, Indiana gave very few second shots. At Duke, we have a little more quickness, so we put pressure on the ball and used more of the court. Here is what we do in drills to try to get this across.

LESSONS FROM THIS LEGEND...

ZIGZAG DRILL

We do the normal zigzag drill (See **Diagram 1.0**) Our defensive man is in a heel-to-toe stance, with the head on the ball. We emphasize keeping the shoulders square as the man is dribbling. The defense must beat the dribbler to the sideline. We have a coach go down the court with the man. We do this almost every day.

You can change this drill several ways. One, we put a coach in different spots (See **Diagram 1.1**). The dribbler can pass ahead at any time. Since we do a lot of full court pickup, we are trying to make our drills more game-like. That's one of the main things that I would like to get across, make your drills game-like. Create drills to fit the game situation for your team. What we emphasize in this drill is to retreat to the line of the ball after the pass is made, quickly. The offensive man continues down the floor, and we front the cutter all the way. We try to keep the man from getting the ball back. If he gets it back, then the drill continues 1-on-1. The coaches will vary their positions along the sideline.

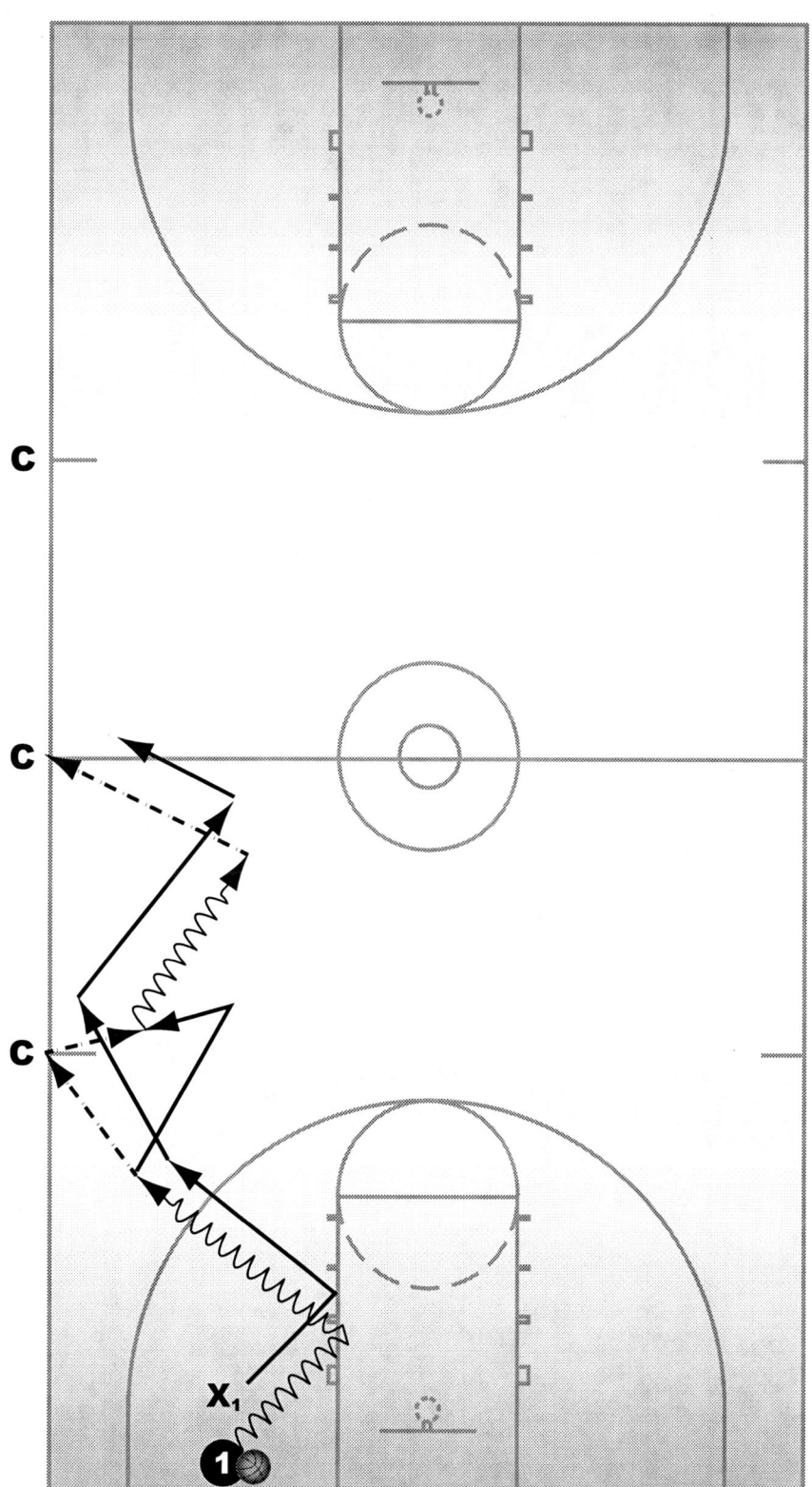

Krzyzewski 1.1

LESSONS FROM THIS LEGEND...

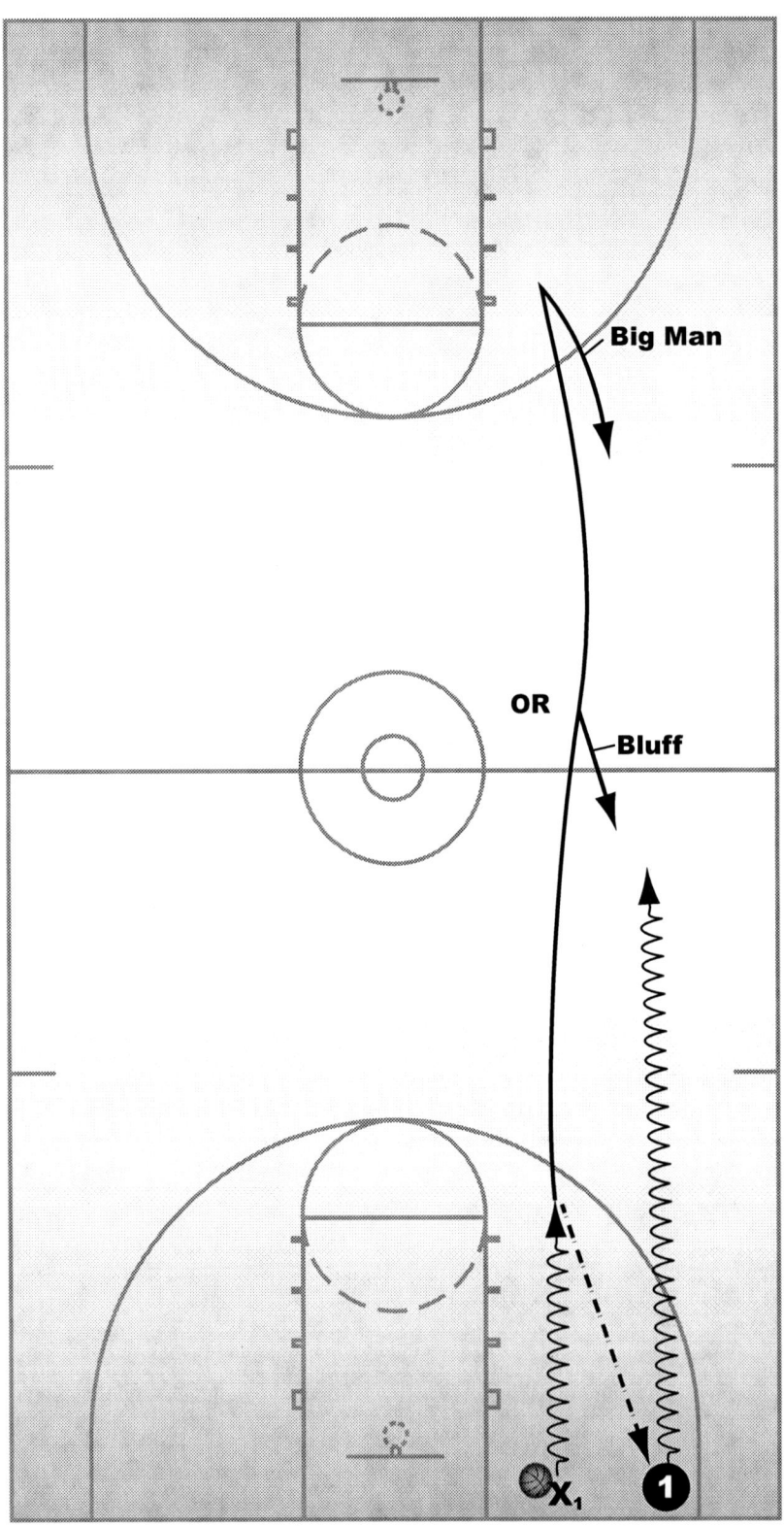

Krzyzewski 1.2

INFLUENCE DRILL

We call this the influence drill (See **Diagram 1.2**). The defensive man starts out with the ball. He dribbles to the free-throw line and passes the ball back to a trailer, O1. When he passes the ball back, if he is a guard, he will sprint to half-court. If he is a big man, he will sprint to the foul line. We call this the fake trap. One of the toughest players to defend is the one who is coming full speed right at you. The defensive man is taught to fake at the offensive man, so that the man with the ball will slow down and react instead of laying back and letting the offensive man dictate what to do. If you are going to do some pressure defense, I think that you must have this drill. Then, it is a 1-on-1 drill all the way to the basket. The reason that we have the big men go all the way to the foul line is that this is their position on our press, where they must defend against a 2-on-1 with the quick guard. They are protecting the basket. So, this is a realistic situation on the court. This drill has really assisted us in the teaching of our defense.

LESSONS FROM THIS LEGEND...

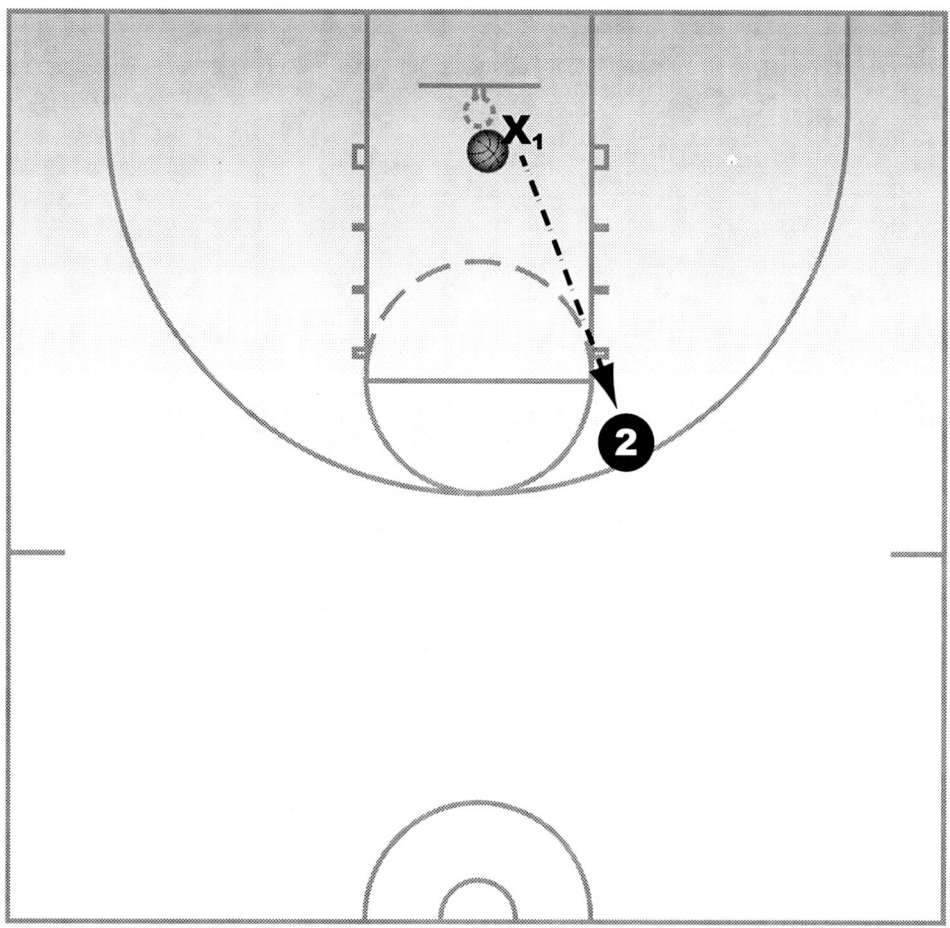

Krzyzewski 1.3

CLOSE OUT DRILL

The close out drill (See **Diagram 1.3**). X1 passes the ball to O2. O2 can shoot or make a move. X1 must play defense. If you are playing a man defense, you are involved in many help and recover situations. And in many of these, you must block out a player who is in a different spot on the floor. If I am sagging and the ball is passed to my man, I must "close out" to my man. Sometimes you see a player fly by his man instead. In this drill, and in our defense, we sprint half way to the man, and then come up to the man with the foot and hand nearest the middle of the court forward. We force to the outside in our defense. You should give some direction to your defense.

I think that this type of drill is extremely important. One change we made is the hand position while guarding the player with the ball. In our normal defense, the hands and palms are up, waist high. Once the pass is made from the point to the side, we then pressure the ball with the inside hand up. (Inside hand means the hand closest to the middle of the court.) We found that many teams use the two-hand overhead pass, and this defensive position stops that. The other hand is at waist level. We feel that this puts extra pressure on the ball. As soon as the ball is dribbled, we go back to the original defensive position.

LESSONS FROM THIS LEGEND...

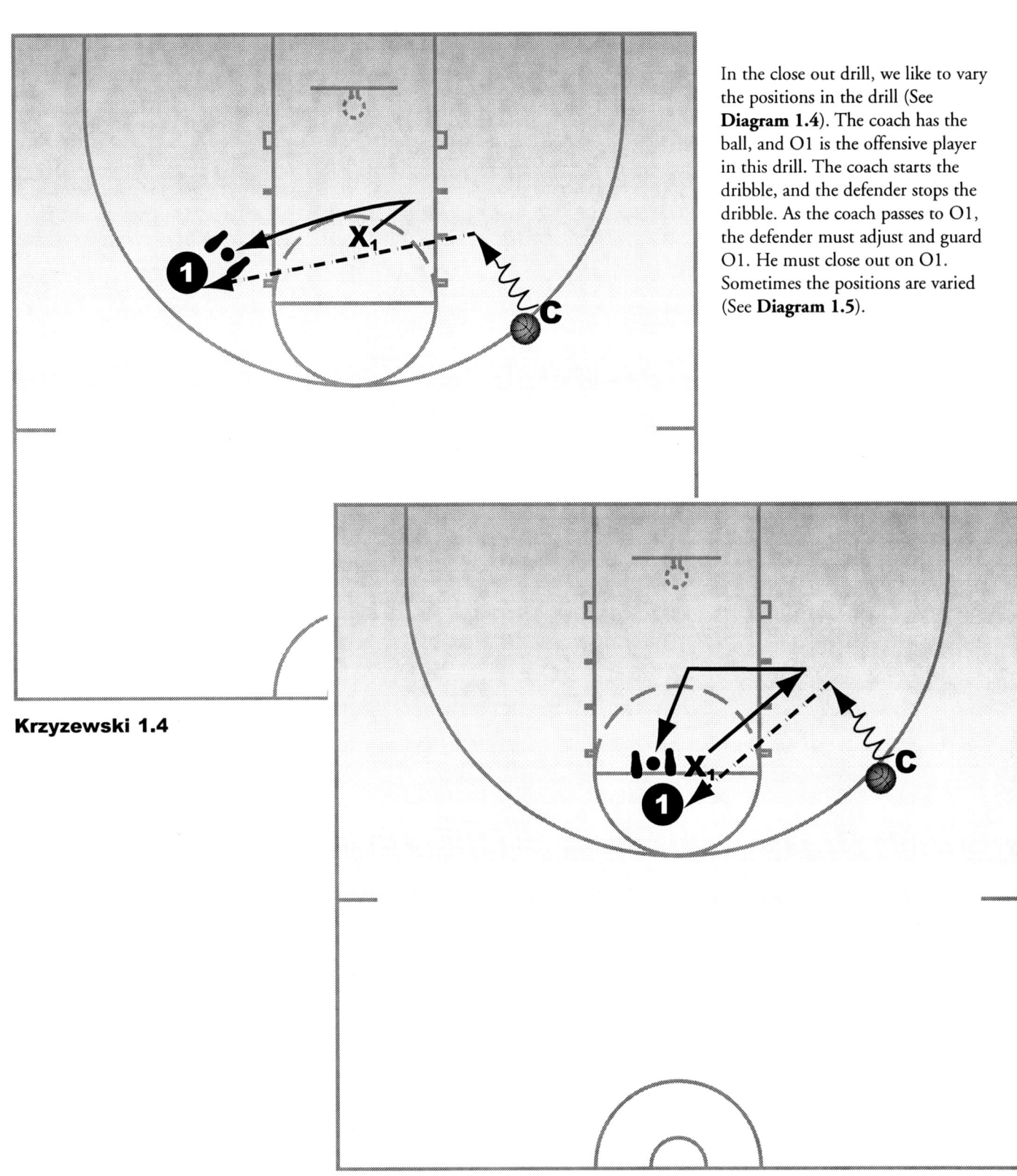

In the close out drill, we like to vary the positions in the drill (See **Diagram 1.4**). The coach has the ball, and O1 is the offensive player in this drill. The coach starts the dribble, and the defender stops the dribble. As the coach passes to O1, the defender must adjust and guard O1. He must close out on O1. Sometimes the positions are varied (See **Diagram 1.5**).

Krzyzewski 1.4

Krzyzewski 1.5

LESSONS FROM THIS LEGEND...

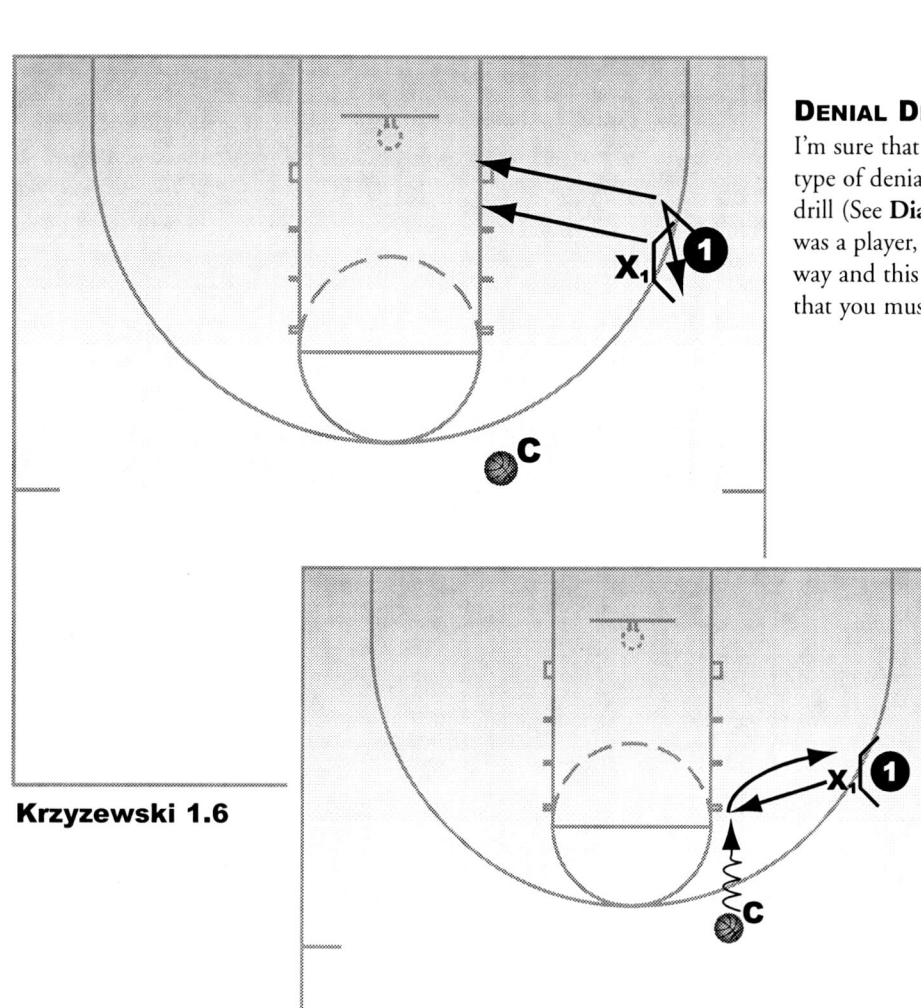

Krzyzewski 1.6

Krzyzewski 1.7

DENIAL DRILL

I'm sure that all of you do some type of denial drill, a contesting drill (See **Diagram 1.6**). When I was a player, we always did it this way and this way only. But, I think that you must change these drills.

So, we added the possibility of the coach driving to the basket (See **Diagram 1.7**). Now, X1 must fake trap from the contesting defensive stance without committing to the dribbler. X1 must help and then recover back to O1.

Another option is that the coach can shoot the ball during the drill (See **Diagram 1.8**). We do this in our 1, 2, 3 and 4-man drills. Anytime during the drill, the coach can take a shot, and the defenders must block out and rebound.

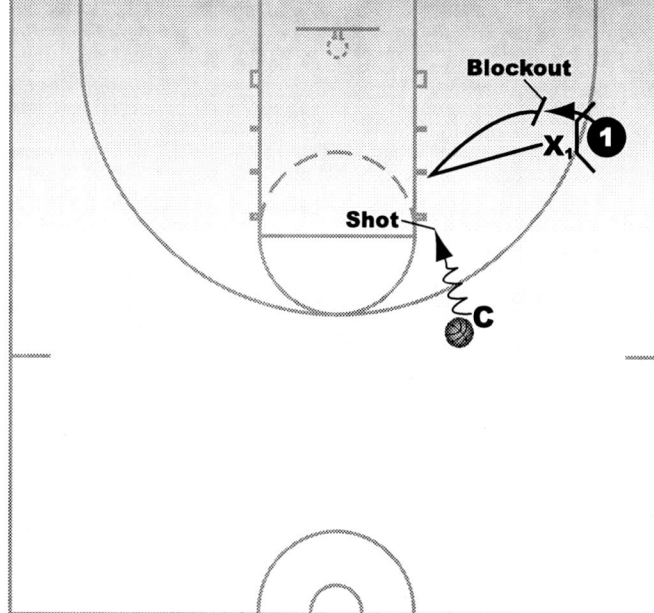

Krzyzewski 1.8

LESSONS FROM THIS LEGEND...

Test your rebounding at that time. We all have good rebounding drills, but in addition to those drills, make them rebound in a game-like situation. How do you react? Keep adding things to your drills that make them more realistic. Take a look at your drills and see how you can improve them. At the end of last year, we took a look at all the drills that we used. And we asked ourselves as a staff, how can we improve this drill? I divided the drills between our assistants, and we studied all of them. I really think that it has helped us. It makes practice move a lot quicker. It makes the players concentrate. They don't know what you are going to do. It makes them think. We also changed this year in another way. We used to run a real quick practice, maybe an hour and a half-to-two hours long. We found that we lost a little of the teaching element. So, early on, instead of running a drill for four minutes or whatever, do it for two minutes longer. This will give you enough time to teach during that drill. Now, don't just lecture. Keep practice moving.

Krzyzewski 1.9

COMBINATION DRILLS

Since defense is a continuous proposition, we like to use combination-type drills. Let's add to the contesting drill (See **Diagram 1.9**). While the drill is being run, the coach will call "clear out." As O1 goes to the other side, make sure that the defensive man X1 stops in the lane. You must be able to switch from the ballside defender to a helpside defender. What rules do you have? Where do you stop in the lane? On occasion, the coach could drive the ball at the defender. The coach could pass from the dribble to O1, and this then becomes a close out drill.

LESSONS FROM THIS LEGEND...

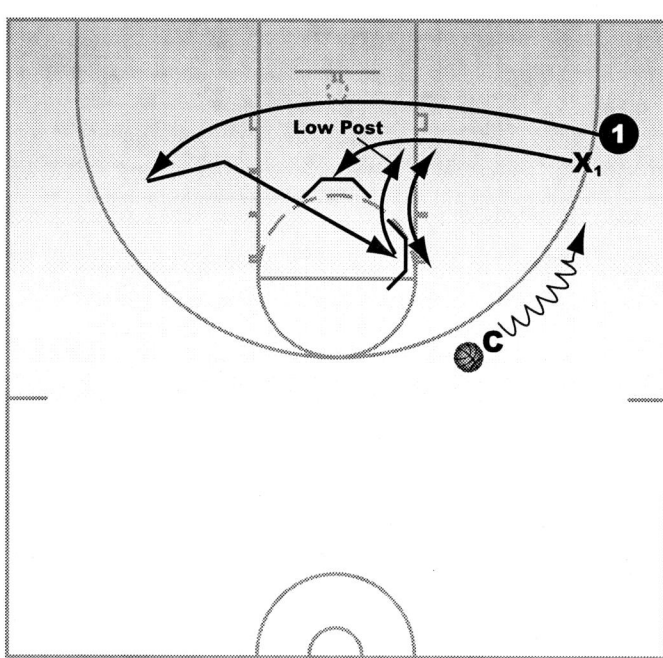

Krzyzewski 1.10

Another option would be to flash O1 back across the lane (See **Diagram 1.10**). The defensive man must deny the flash pivot. O1 could roll into the low post, and the defender would now be required to play low-post defense. So, we have gone through many different things during this drill. We have gone through contesting, ballside and helpside defense, fake trap, close out, denying the flash pivot, and playing the low post. It's important for you to practice those things individually, but it helps to put them in a continuous drill.

Here is a drill for the guards (See **Diagram 1.11**). O1 passes to C, and runs a "give-and-go" cut to the basket. The defensive man must jump towards the ball and front the cutter. O1 posts up at the low post. You must over play to force the lob pass.

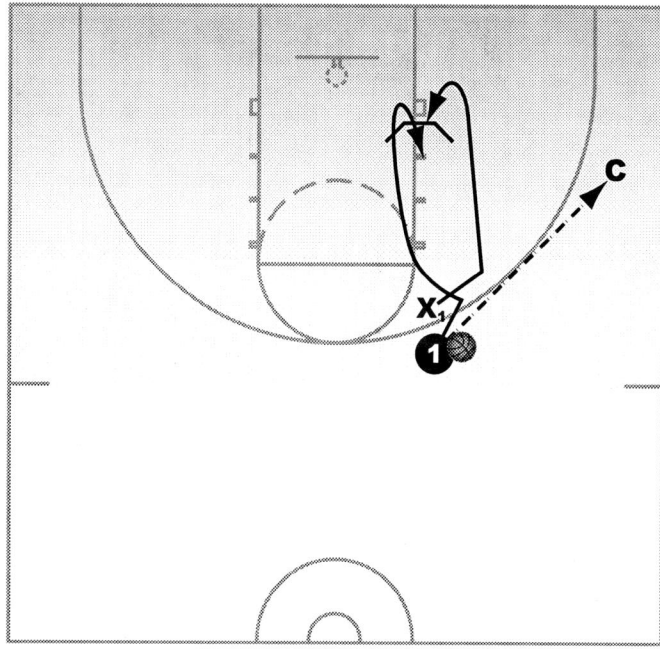

Krzyzewski 1.11

Krzyzewski 1.12

Now, add to the drill (See **Diagram 1.12**). Add another player and have the coach at the top of the key. O1 passes to O2 and cuts to the low post. The defender fronts him all the way. 2 passes back to the coach and screens down. The defender must fight through the screen. Take a look at what other teams did against you last year and design your drills to practice those aspects of the game. This is what you are going to be facing in the games, so include them in your drills.

LESSONS FROM THIS LEGEND...

TWO-BALL DRILL

It is also important to develop drills that are tougher than game-like situations. (See **Diagram 1.13**). We use the "two-ball" drill. This is 4/4 with two players in the corner. The four players on offense can be anywhere. O5 and O6, as soon as they get the ball, take it to the basket. This is especially important to us because we force to the outside. For example, if O3 cuts to the middle and the pass goes from O1 to O5, 5 takes it to the basket. The defender cannot lose visual contact with the ball. He must stop and guard 5. The defender should try and draw the charge. All the defensive men must adjust. You can also add extra men against your zone. Put the players in the vulnerable spots of your zone. Let's see how they are covered.

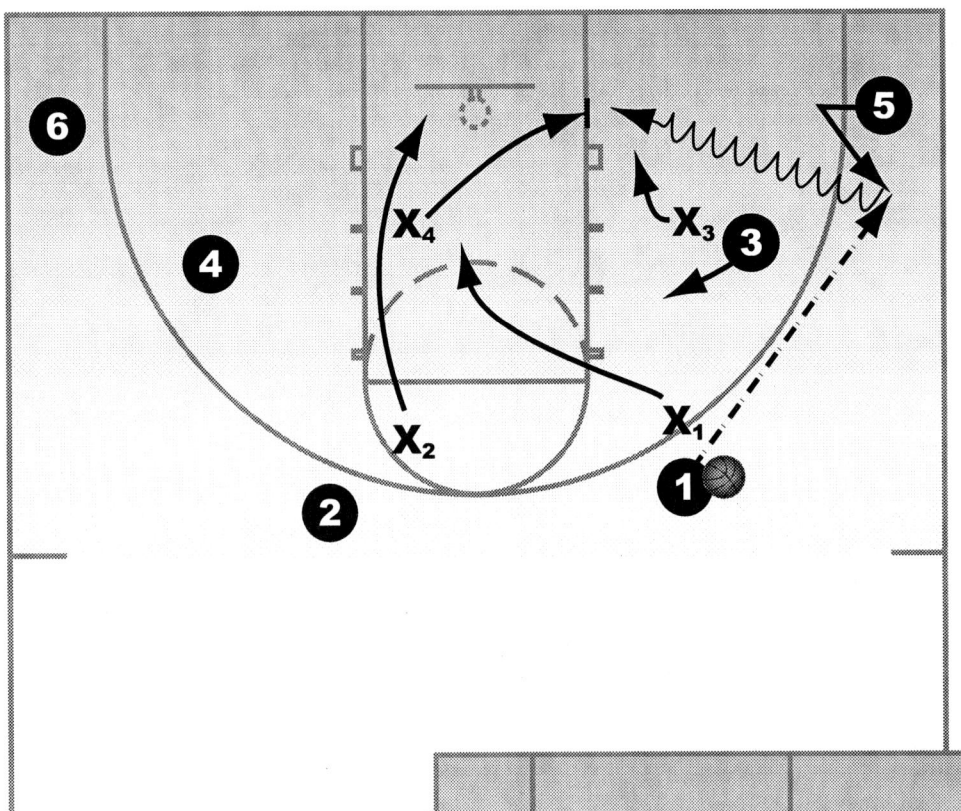

Krzyzewski 1.13

What are your rules for defending the post-exchange action? (See **Diagram 1.14**) How do you defend when O4 goes away from the ball and screens for O5? Do you switch? Do you sometimes switch? Do you never switch? What are your rules? Our rule is this: the helpside man (guarding O5) takes the man high. The ballside man takes the man low. This helps your defense. If the helpside man knows that he is going to take the man high, he's already fighting over the screen on the high side.

Krzyzewski 1.14

LESSONS FROM THIS LEGEND...

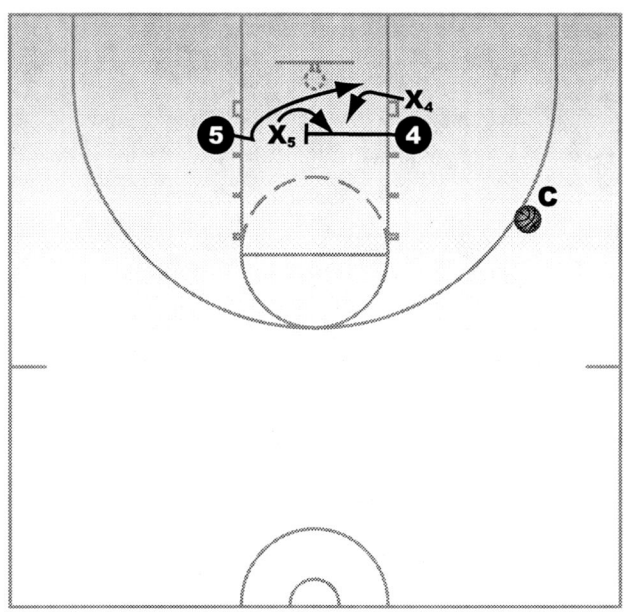

Krzyzewski 1.15

Now, if O5 stays low (See **Diagram 1.15**), X4 switches, because the rule says that the ballside man takes the low man and the helpside man takes the man going high. Now, I'm not trying to convert you to our way of thinking, I'm saying that you must look at these situations and develop rules to help your defense.

RANDOM MOVEMENT DRILL

In some way you must develop toughness in your defense. When I played, we used to have loose-ball drills. We seldom do that now. but we have a "random movement" drill (See **Diagram 1.16**). Random movement is just what it means. The offensive players move wherever they wish. There are three coaches also. As soon as a defensive player is not looking at the ball, the coach throws the ball to him. Wham! You're not going to hurt the player, but you will get his attention. "Look at the ball. See the ball." The ball can also be passed to the offense. The ball can also be thrown badly on purpose for a loose-ball situation.

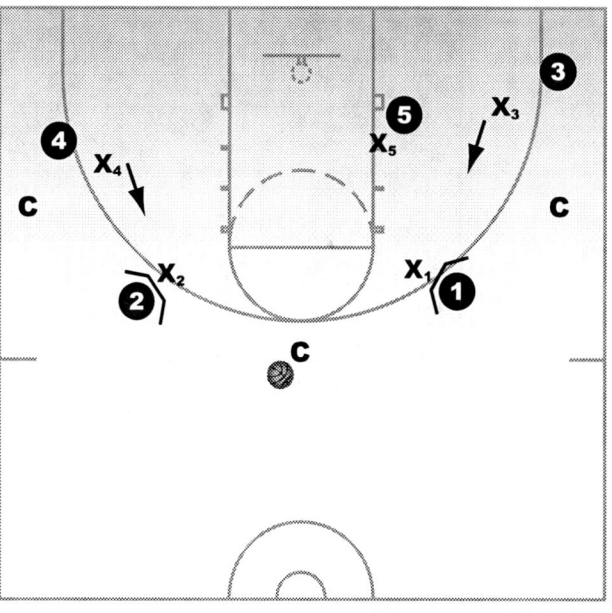

Krzyzewski 1.16

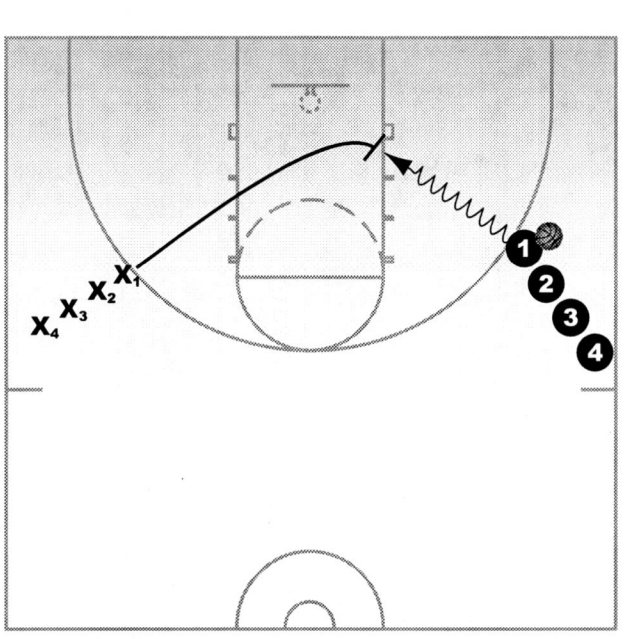

Krzyzewski 1.17

TAKE THE CHARGE DRILL

We have a take the charge drill (See **Diagram 1.17**). At least once a year, we do this drill. We do it once.

SOURCE

Krzyzewski, Mike. (1985). Man to Man Defense. *MacGregor Flashback Notebook (Vol. 11).*

LEGACY OF
Joseph "Joe" Lapchick

- Starred for the Original Celtics and became basketball's first true agile big man.

- Controlled almost every center tap that followed each made basket in basketball's early days.

- Self-educated, charismatic ambassador of the game.

- Compiled a 334-130 coaching record in 20 seasons at St. John's.

- Led St. John's to four NIT championships (1943, 1944, 1959, 1965).

- Guided the New York Knickerbockers to three consecutive NBA championship appearances.

- Believed it was essential to always keep your head up and don't let life get you down.

JOSEPH "JOE" LAPCHICK

"Make a strong effort to help players develop high ideals, a moral sense of correct behavior, and the power to govern emotional control as a player and as a gentleman."
—Joseph "Joe" Lapchick

BIOGRAPHY

Born: April 12, 1900 in Yonkers, NY

Died: August 10, 1970

Inducted into the Naismith Basketball Hall of Fame in 1966

Lapchick was the game's first true agile big man at 6 feet 5 inches. After leaving school before high school graduation, he played for pay to assist his family and signed in 1923 with the first great basketball team, the Original Celtics. Lapchick became the key pivot player for the Celtics, who were disbanded because of their dominance in the 1920s. Lapchick and two other Celtics went to the Cleveland Rosenblums in 1928 and won two straight ABL championships. He played pro-ball from 1917 to 1936 and then was hired to coach at St. John's University in 1937. After 11 seasons, Lapchick left St. John's to coach the New York Knickerbockers and led the team to three consecutive NBA championship appearances. Lapchick returned to St. John's to coach nine more seasons. In 20 seasons at St. John's, he compiled a 334-130 coaching record, becoming the only coach to capture four NIT championships (1943, 1944, 1959, 1965). The NIT was the nation's premier basketball tournament at that time. While at St. John's, Lapchick was twice named National Coach of the Year. He also received the NABC Metropolitan Award in 1965. Lapchick was enshrined in the Naismith Memorial Basketball Hall of Fame as a team member of the Original Celtics in 1959 and as a player in 1966.

...SCOUTING REPORT.....SCOUTING REPORT.....

Joseph "Joe" Lapchick...

Joe Lapchick would seem to be an unlikely candidate to become a legendary head basketball coach at one of the most prestigious universities in New York, let alone coach of the world famous Knickerbockers professional team from the most famous early 1900s city in the United States.

He was born of Czechoslovakian immigrant parents in Yonkers, New York. "Yonkers is the biggest city in the world," Joe used to joke, "next to New York." His father held odd jobs and eventually became a Yonkers policeman, and both parents left a firm mark of humble beginnings on son Joe. He never really left his Slavic roots in Yonkers over a storied career of more than fifty years of basketball, spanning its early years until its evolution as a staple of college and professional sports. Times were hard when Joe, the oldest of seven Lapchick children, dropped out of school to add to the family income, after completing the sixth grade at P.S. #20. The self-educated man, with little formal education, would eventually hold his own intellectually with highly educated college faculty at St. John's University. There, he was held in such esteem that he was awarded an honorary degree upon retirement in 1965. This academic capstone was a fitting tribute to the storied coach. It brought him to tears. His famous successor, Lou Carnesecca, said Lapchick was the best example of self-education he ever knew and described him in these words: "Joe was a tremendous man who never dies. He just stays with you." Lapchick had a credo he learned at an early age in Yonkers: "keep your head up and don't let life get you down. Do your best and that's all that counts." So, the "humble Joe" who coached the St. John's Redmen became the much-loved "Big Indian" of Yonkers forever.

In addition to being the ultimate self-educated man, Joe was also very humble. One writer called him "a guy named Joe." After his mandatory retirement from St. John's at age 63, Lapchick became the summer athletic director at Kutcher's Country Club/Resort north of New York City in the Catskill Mountains of Monticello. It became famous for summer basketball competition between college and professional players from the East Coast. One such game featured future Hall of Fame players Wilt Chamberlain and Lew Alcindor (later to become known as Kareem Abdul-Jabbar). Joe had other duties that kept him busy until after the game had started. By the time he reached the gym, it was "standing room only" and he wasn't able to get in, so he stood behind in the doorway, refusing to use his clout and push through the crowd. One observer noted this and marveled at Lapchick, "How ironic is it that the first great center in the game would not be able to see the matchup of the two reigning centers, because he was too humble to push his way through the crowd?"

Joe began playing the fledgling sport at twelve, along with odd jobs and golf caddying. He learned quickly and, with his size which was so prized in the days of the center jump after each basket, began to play for money at the early age of fifteen. Soon, he was a paid professional of the day, playing each game for the highest bidder. By 1923, he joined the Original Celtics, the dominant white team of the day (along with the black New York Rens). This is where he also became a renowned offensive player. Without a formal coach, Lapchick and his teammates developed some ground-breaking basketball tactics: the "give-and-go," offensive weave, the use of post/pivot play (today called "split the post"), and even switching zone defenses. Joe was in the center (literally and figuratively) of it all—even launching his coaching career as a player/coach when entertainer Kate Smith sponsored the barnstorming Celtics from 1930-36. But, Joe became his own coach prior to that. Before the Celtics tenure, and after work

.....SCOUTING REPORT.....SCOUTING REPORT...

when he didn't have a game, he would practice footwork (unheard of at that time)—starts, stops, sprints, change-of-direction and pivoting.

The legendary center for the "Original Celtics" was the first true agile "big man" in basketball, standing 6'5" tall. He not only was a great ballhandler who could pass and shoot (he could palm the ball), but he also jumped center after every basket and generally got this tips.

Lapchick was a paid professional from 1917 to 1936. His barnstorming years included playing stints with the following teams: Holyoke Reds, Schenectady (NY), Brooklyn Visitations, Troy (NY), and Cleveland Rosenblums, as well as the future Hall of Fame team, the Original Celtics (from 1923-27 and again on entertainer Kate Smith's sponsored barnstorming tour from 1930-36).

In 1936, former Celtics teammate Nat Holman, who left the Celtics in 1933 to become coach at City College of New York (CCNY), recommended Lapchick for the coaching position at already strong arch-rival St. John's. Joe, with only an elementary school education, accepted with some apprehension. He knew the difference between doing and teaching, and feared he would be exposed as a fake. But, his fears were groundless, because he became a coaches' coach—knowledgeable (especially for his defensive innovations), charismatic, and a mentor and maker of coaches. His first nine-year stay at St. John's, called the "Tourney Era," produced two NIT titles (back-to-back in 1943 and 1944) and seven NIT invitations. This was a time when the NIT was the prominent national tourney of the day.

His later years at St. John's (1956-1965) produced similar results and two more NIT titles (his teams were the only ones to accomplish this). Sandwiched between his twenty-year St. John's split career were nine seasons as head coach of the New York Knicks, where he never had a losing season. His 1954 Knick team, alone, produced eight players who went on to coaching careers. He produced scores of other coaches, both at St. John's and with the Knicks. Due to the effects of the high stress of pro basketball on Joe's health, he finally returned to his St. John's home, where he retired in 1965. He was national college coach of the year twice at St. John's. Of his last team that won the NIT title, he said, "It's been a long road, enough action to fill a lifetime, I enjoyed every second—what a way to go."

Joe Lapchick became a link between the dance hall/outhouse days of basketball (when he played) to the international game (both college and professional). Charismatic Joe was considered an exceptional "ambassador of basketball," especially with fans and the media. He said, "I do my best work selling my favorite game after most coaches are asleep. My mission begins then, and it is no chore. The great fellowship happens after the games until 3 AM." Lou Carnesecca related how Joe would talk with anyone at anytime and was revered throughout the country for his humility and commonness—Lou called him a "Saint of Basketball." He may have been.

SOURCE

Lapchick, Joe. Vertical Files, Archives. Naismith Memorial Basketball Hall of Fame. Springfield, MA.

LESSONS FROM THIS LEGEND...

THE COACH PHILOSOPHY

By Joe Lapchick

Authors' Note: The Lapchick lessons are taken from his 1968 book, *50 Years of Basketball*, written just two years before his death in 1970. It addresses two areas that are strong legacies from him—player relations and defense, both of which he mastered. There is a strong flavor of his vast experiences, both as a pro player with the Original Celtics and as a college and pro coach.

The most impressionable years of a man's life are those of his youth. Because I had spent the better part of my youth as a player growing up with the game of basketball, it was natural that I should think in terms of players when I approached my first coaching position. Today, after many years as a basketball coach, my thinking remains unchanged. The players are the essence. The quality of their skills, the pooling of their abilities, and the sum total of their desire, courage, spirit, dedication, and love for the game determine the success of the team and the coach.

HANDLING PLAYERS

The handling of players is far more important than knowing all the mechanics of the game. One player will respond nobly when the coach "chews him out." Using the same approach with another player may break him like a twig.

Fans often ask me the difference between college coaching and professional coaching. In my experience, I have found college coaching more attractive. In college coaching, you drill and drill, and meet twenty-six different opponents. In professional coaching, you drill for six weeks and then play the rest of the teams in the league over and over again. With respect to the players, I have found the professionals just like college youngsters—great to work with.

Championship-winning coaches will be the first to acknowledge that players make the coach. That premise is undoubtedly the chief reason why I have remained aloof from a stereotyped offense and far removed (indeed, almost antagonistic) to the use of any defense, except man-to-man. Celtic players were free to attempt personal plays at any time, and I have always believed that my players should have the same freedom in making "situation" decisions.

During my entire career as a player, I never had the opportunity to come under the influence of a coach, as such. In fact, there were no coaches in professional basketball when I played. You learned basketball from experience and by watching, imitating, and listening to the great players of the time. It was a system of trial and error, with the emphasis on not making the same mistake twice.

Most coaches I have met during my later years in the game played for outstanding high school and college mentors, and carried on with the style of play they had been taught. Other coaches "adopted" the methods of successful "name" coaches and attempted to apply these methods to their own coaching. To my way of thinking, this is a mistake. I feel that a coach should remain in character and apply the type of offense and defense with which he is most familiar. The abilities of the players available are, of course, the determining factors in determining the style of play to be adopted.

The only coaches I knew much about when I accepted my first coaching assignment (St. John's University, 1936) were Nat Holman and Clair Bee. I had, of course, played with Nat when we were Celtic teammates. Since he had coached at CCNY while playing with the Celtics, he was the first man to whom I turned. Nat gave me a lot of fine advice and help.

I was not personally acquainted with Clair Bee, but he was setting some great records with his LIU Blackbirds at that time. I decided to have a talk with him. Clair and I soon became friends and have remained close ever since.

During our conversation, Clair asked how the players addressed me. "They call me Joe," I said.

He shook his head and said, 'That's no good. They should call you Mister Lapchick, or, preferably, Coach."

I never forgot that little bit of advice. To me, respect is an important part of discipline that always goes hand-in-hand with coaching success. During my first year of coaching, a player intensely interested in something might unthinkingly call me Joe. I would smile and say, "Sure Mister 'X'— you're absolutely right." The player always got the point.

COACHING FROM EXPERIENCE

Clair then helped me draw up some practice programs, and just before we parted, he said something which, at the time, passed right over my head.

"Joe," he said, "I am embarrassed that you should come to me for suggestions. Why, when I first started to coach, I used to drive several hundred miles to and from

LESSONS FROM THIS LEGEND...

Cleveland just to watch you and your Celtic teammates play."

Later that statement came back to me, and I realized that I could best teach that which I had learned through personal experience. I had been playing basketball all my life, part of the time with the greatest team of all time. I knew Celtic basketball inside and out, and it had been good enough to beat anyone and everyone. What more did I need?

I carefully reviewed the fundamentals, team techniques, and game tactics I had learned the hard way as a Celtic and then adopted them as my coaching "book." Those Celtic principles of personal and team play have stood by me through nineteen years of coaching the St. John's Redmen and the New York Knickerbockers. They were good enough to win against the best opposition professional and college basketball could offer.

The Celtic game is as good as it ever was, and some of the best college teams in the country are using the style successfully today. Were it not for the 24-second rule (after obtaining possession a professional team in the NBA must shoot before 24 seconds elapse), most of the pro teams would be using the Celtics' passing attack today.

St. John's University has always fielded great teams. Coincidentally, one of the greatest of the Redmen teams—the "Wonder Five," coached by Buck Freeman—used the Celtic style exclusively. In his nine seasons as head coach, Buck's teams won 103 games and lost only 31. My St. John's teams were consistently regular-season winners and record-tournament victors.

All of the St. John's winning successes are, in my opinion, due to the presence of great players at the University. Down through the years, and particularly in recent years, New York City high school coaches have turned out hundreds of well-coached players, and St. John's was fortunate in getting its share of the talent.

PLAYER RELATIONSHIP CODE

Undoubtedly, my personal experiences when breaking in with the Celtics had a great influence on my coaching. At any rate, I developed a sort of player relationship code down through the years. Some of the parts are listed below:

1. Make a strong effort to help players develop high ideals, a moral sense of correct behavior, and the power to govern emotional control as a basketball player and as a gentleman. With this as a starter, fair play, appreciation of the rights of others, and general sportsmanship follow in natural sequence. As a player, I became considerably less effective if I became unreasonably angry with either my opponent or the referee.
2. Take an active interest in the academic standing and progress of every player. The chief objective in the player's life is a good education. Show him that you are interested in his life objectives and his desire for an education.
3. Guard the health and physical welfare of the players. Devote personal attention to injuries and see that treatment is prompt and continued regularly. Make sure that good equipment is issued to every player and that he is given frequent medical checkups and attention. (It is especially important that the players be checked before the gut-ripping drills start.)
4. Keep players at a distance without building a wall of reserve. Express warm concern in matters pertaining to their personal affairs where possible, but show no favoritism.
5. Study and "know" every player. Make him feel that he "belongs" and is important to the success of the team whether he is a starting "star" or the last sub on the bench. Be reasonable and treat little incidents with a sense of humor, but by all means praise generously a job well done. Be a disciplinarian and a teacher, but keep in mind that every player is different. Some players resent strong criticism, while others expect it and will respond to it. In this connection, I have always made a practice of telling a player why I took him out of a game, unless it was merely for a rest.
6. Be friendly and industrious, take pride in your work, and permit no disrespect. Be the boss, but work democratically with your players. A pleasant, but firm, approach to the job will enable the coach to sell his coaching to his players.
7. Show that you expect players to take pride in their behavior and appearance by setting a personal example of cleanliness in speech, dress, and actions.
8. Develop a strong desire in your players to win, but be sure to stress that it is important to win with controlled joy and a degree of humility. Losing is never pleasant, but if something is learned, all is not lost. You can lose with dignity, despite internal pain, if you have played your best and acted like a gentleman.
9. Player discipline is a must, but it is far better to help a player overcome his faults than to make him turn in his uniform for an infraction. It is the coach's solemn duty to first try to save the boy, not because of his importance to the team, but for the good of the boy himself. However, this must never be done at the cost of loss of respect by the other members of the squad.

SOURCE

Lapchick, Joe. (1968). *50 Years of Basketball.* Englewood, Cliffs, NJ: Prentice-Hall.

LESSONS FROM THIS LEGEND...

DEFENSIVE SKILLS

By Joe Lapchick

The difference between the mental approach of the Celtics and other professional players in the early days, compared to that of the modern players, is so marked that I feel it is worthy of comment. The Celtics were never concerned with scoring points. We knew we would get more than our share. Our main objective was to prevent the other fellow from making baskets.

Defensive basketball was the most important part of the game in the early years. Chris Leonard had the nickname "Dog," because he dogged anyone he played against from the first toss-up to the last second. The player who faced Chris knew he was going to have a tough night.

Perhaps the best illustration of the way we old-timers regarded defense would be to use Skeets Wright, of Jersey City, New Jersey, as an example. When Skeets walked out on the floor to shake hands with his opponent, he would grin and say, "I get two points, and you get two, O.K.?"

The other guy would usually smile and nod, so, Skeets made sure he got his two first. Then, when they lined up for the center-tap following the score, Skeets would glare at the other guy and say, "All right, I got mine. Let's see you get yours!" Moving purposefully between his opponent and the basket, Skeets would mutter, "over my dead body!"

When his opponent scored, Skeets would go wild with rage. I remember once how his teammates, enjoying a comfortable lead in the game, plotted a little fun with Skeets. As the other team came down to the attack, a teammate called out, "switch men, Skeets. I've got your man."

Skeets obediently switched and was horrified when his man got away from his teammate and scored. The next time the opponents came down the court with the ball, another teammate called out for Skeets to switch opponents. "I've got your man, Skeets," he yelled. "Take mine."

Skeets squared his jaw and nodded grimly "Sure!" he called, "you go ahead and take him. I've got him too!"

Only a few players possess that type of fierce defensive pride. Sometimes, during the last years of my coaching, I have seen one of my players presumably exhausted, dead on his feet and looking like the next step he took would be his last one while he was playing defense. Then, we got the ball, and the result was astonishing indeed. The old love-light would glow in his eyes, and he would become vibrant, alive, fresh as a daisy, and would dash madly toward our basket calling for the ball.

The Celtics brought the switch into basketball. Before the switch was developed by the Shamrocks, it was man-against-man on an intensely personal basis. The big objective was to hold your opponent to fewer points than you got. The theory was, of course, that if everyone did his part, your team had to win. I had never used the switch before I joined the Celtics and had quite a time mastering the skill well enough to suit the Shamrock players. They not only switched on a "block" play, but they always picked up the closest opponent. Heaven help you if a teammate's man scored on you.

On such adjustments are championship dynasties nurtured. You knew where you had to be or go all the time. At the moment of decision, the champs make the right play. The New York Celtics and the Boston Celtics never defeated themselves when the marbles were down. Only the passing years and lack of good replacements eventually end athletic dynasties, yet the champions always have a reserve of pride and "know-how" that enables them to win "one more big one."

The modern game of basketball is highly geared to telephone-number scoring, and since all players like to see their names in the papers, they concentrate on the offensive skills of the game. However, defense is still a big factor, and it is up to the coach to sell his players on the importance of individual and team defense.

The "great" teams, the teams that win the championships, are those who play good defense. The coaches of the great teams are dedicated to the teaching of defensive play. Their players are always well-grounded in basic defensive fundamentals. That is the secret of their personal greatness, just as individual and team defense was the secret of the Celtic success.

Great baseball hitters often run into slumps when they cannot buy a hit; quarterbacks have days when they cannot generate an attack, and basketball players have nights when they swear the basket has a lid on it. But—if your defense is well-disciplined, you still win in spite of a sputtering offense.

INDIVIDUAL AND TEAM DEFENSE

It is difficult to separate individual and team defense. The two are so closely interwoven that each would fall apart without the other. Mentally, the same qualities are required—pride, desire, determination,

LESSONS FROM THIS LEGEND...

hustle, alertness, aggressiveness, and resourcefulness—in applying continuous concentration.

Most players want to be "complete" players, but few have the guts required to stick with this exacting part of the game. Those who possess the intestinal fortitude to master and apply good defense are the players who win the big games, despite the fact that their contributions are seldom recognized.

Starting with the assumption that the player wants to be a complete player and has disciplined himself to go the hard way in the defensive part of basketball, we can turn to the individual skills.

INDIVIDUAL SKILLS

I like to think of the defensive skills in terms of back-court players (guards), corner men (forwards), and pivot players (centers), because, in my opinion, it is a waste of drill time to teach all players all the position skills. There is a great difference in the skill needs of players in the different positions, particularly with respect to stance and defensive floor alignment.

After there has been a general approach to the fundamentals in the early part of the pre-season workouts, it is probably to the advantage of everyone—coaches and players—to separate the candidates and stress the skills, which apply to the different positions.

STANCE

The boxer's stance, with one foot forward, is preferred, because it provides greater coverage than the lateral (parallel) position. The feet are staggered so they are separated approximately the width of the shoulders, and the arm on the side of the forward foot is raised high and extended toward the opponent. The other arm is held wide to the side.

BALANCE

The weight is evenly distributed on the balls of the feet, with the heels barely touching the floor. The knees are slightly bent, and the back should be straight, leaning forward a bit. The head should be up. When moving laterally to keep up with an opponent, the lifted arm may be dropped to the side.

FLOOR POSITION

The old axiom of keeping between your opponent and the basket has been outmoded by overshifting, the pressure defense, playing between the opponent and the ball, and playing in front of opponents close to the basket (particularly the big man).

SLOUGHING-OFF

Sagging and floating, shifting right or left, beating opponents to positions they prefer, protecting the baseline and switching, all violate the principle of "staying between the opponent and the basket."

When an opponent cuts or dribbles to his right most of the time, the good defensive player will overshift to hamper the other man's moves. However, at no time will the good defensive player turn his head to locate the position of the ball or check the action behind him.

FOOTWORK

Position on the floor and whether or not the opponent possesses the ball govern the stance and the footwork of the defensive player. If the opponent is not in scoring distance, the stance can be adjusted to guard against cutting, passing, dribbling, and driving. Stance and body balance should enable the defensive player to maintain his position.

The shuffle (glide) should be used when possible. Crossing the feet and taking long back steps are to be discouraged, as is leaping in the air when faked. Moving both feet simultaneously in a quick, skipping fashion will enable the defensive player to "stay" with his opponent and prepare him to meet changes, stops, starts, pivots, and drives.

When an opponent drives against the forward foot, it should be swung quickly back by using the shuffle-skip and hop. The first step is back, and the body must be held ready to shuffle in the opposite direction should the opponent use a change or a cross-over.

If the opponent cuts to the back-foot side, the move is again a little shuffle and a hop, with the feet remaining in the starting position. Should the opponent outmaneuver the defensive player, the cross-over step is used, and the hands are raised in line with the cutter's eyes and the position of the ball. The defensive player must stay with his opponent so he will be in position to back up a teammate who switches to help out.

VISION

The defensive player should concentrate on his opponent, but peripheral vision should be used to see as much of the playing court as possible (position of the ball and opponent's teammates). Turning the head to follow the ball is dangerous; smart opponents will quickly spot the weakness and retaliate by cutting to the basket for a pass.

Opening the stance slightly and sagging or floating will enable the defensive player to watch the ball and his opponent without turning his head. The defensive player should watch his opponent's hips, but peripheral and depth vision should enable him to also see the ball and his opponent's teammates.

USE OF HANDS

Quick hands are important in defensive play. The hand on the side of the advanced foot should be kept moving to distract the shooter or hamper his vision, even if it is impossible to block his shots. When an opponent checks his dribble and comes to a stop, the proper use of hands will force the opponent to pivot away and may lead to an interception or a held ball. In this situation, teammates will, naturally, put pressure on their opponents and be poised for interception attempts.

LESSONS FROM THIS LEGEND...

BACKTRACKING

The good defensive player backtracks when retreating from the front-court to the back-court. The ability to run backward will enable the defensive player to direct traffic, point out his own man, and help teammates locate their opponents and get into defensive positions.

A nonchalant retreat with his back turned to opponents who are coming down-court with the ball marks a lazy player. Retreating to a defensive position is the time to be alert and fire up teammates so opponents will not be able to score easy baskets.

TALKING

Defensive players can help out in the general team defense by "talking it up." Warning teammates of impending screens and picks is an important team-defense fundamental. The terms should be short and pertinent: "Hands up!" "Watch the pick!" "Stay!" "I've got number 22 take 34!" "Switch!" "He's dead!" "Ball!" "Low post!" "High post!"

DEFENSE SCREENS

There is some discrepancy regarding terminology when screens are discussed, but for the purposes of this discussion, "outside" screens will be considered as those set behind defensive players; "side" screens are those set on the sides of defensive players, and "inside" screens are those set between an offensive player and his defensive opponent. The following diagrams will illustrate the screens.

The basic defense against inside and outside screens is the "front" (over the top) shown in **Diagram 1.0**, the "slide" (See **Diagram 1.1**), and the "switch" (See **Diagram 1.2**).

In all situations involving screens and picks, the defensive player closest to the basket is responsible for calling the play. It is he who must make the first move in the switch. His move must be positive, and he must make a fast, aggressive switch. The player who is being screened (blocked) must immediately take the responsibility of guarding his teammate's opponent (See **Diagram 1.3**).

On high-post or pivot defensive plays where the ball is in the possession of the post or pivot man, the switch should be made only toward the ball. In defensing post splits, the defensive man guarding the post player often switches to the first cutter, whether the ball is passed or not. Most coaches prohibit this and permit a switch only when the ball is passed.

When the pivot opponent is close to the basket, most defensive players will play in front of him. A switch will occur in this situation only when the two defensive players collide. The rule—no contact, no switch!

In making any switch, the deep (back) defensive player should move quickly forward (jump-switch) and try to force the cutter to move laterally. Forcing the cutter to move laterally prevents him from turning the corner and getting off a good shot "facing" the basket.

DEFENSING THE DOUBLE-SCREEN

When opposing a team which uses the double-screen, a three-man slide may be necessary. This type of defensive move should be practiced in advance; scouting notes will determine the methods to be used. If the opponents make extensive use of the double-screen, a two-man zone, which the defensive player guarding the cutter joins when his opponent cuts off the double-screen, may be used (See **Diagram 1.4**).

DEFENSIVE ROLL

The defensive roll is tied in with the switch. When a defensive player is forced into actual contact with an offensive post or pivot player, the roll (toward the basket) will help him recover from the pick and cover his teammate's opponent (See **Diagram 1.5**).

In all individual guarding practices, the player should ask himself what move the opponent—passer, cutter, dribbler, post or pivot man, player with or without the

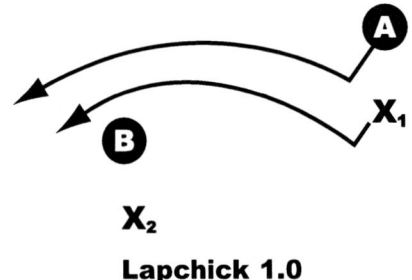

Lapchick 1.0

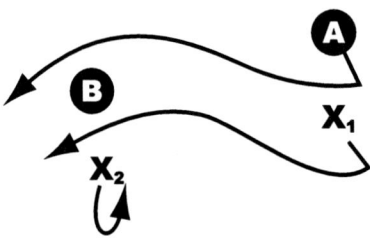

Lapchick 1.1

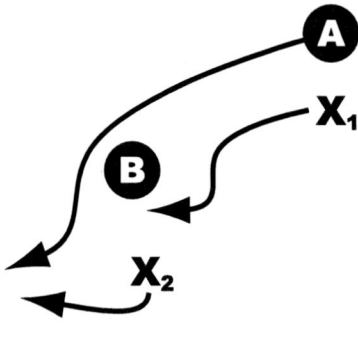

Lapchick 1.2

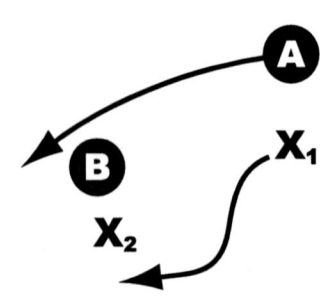

Lapchick 1.3

LESSONS FROM THIS LEGEND...

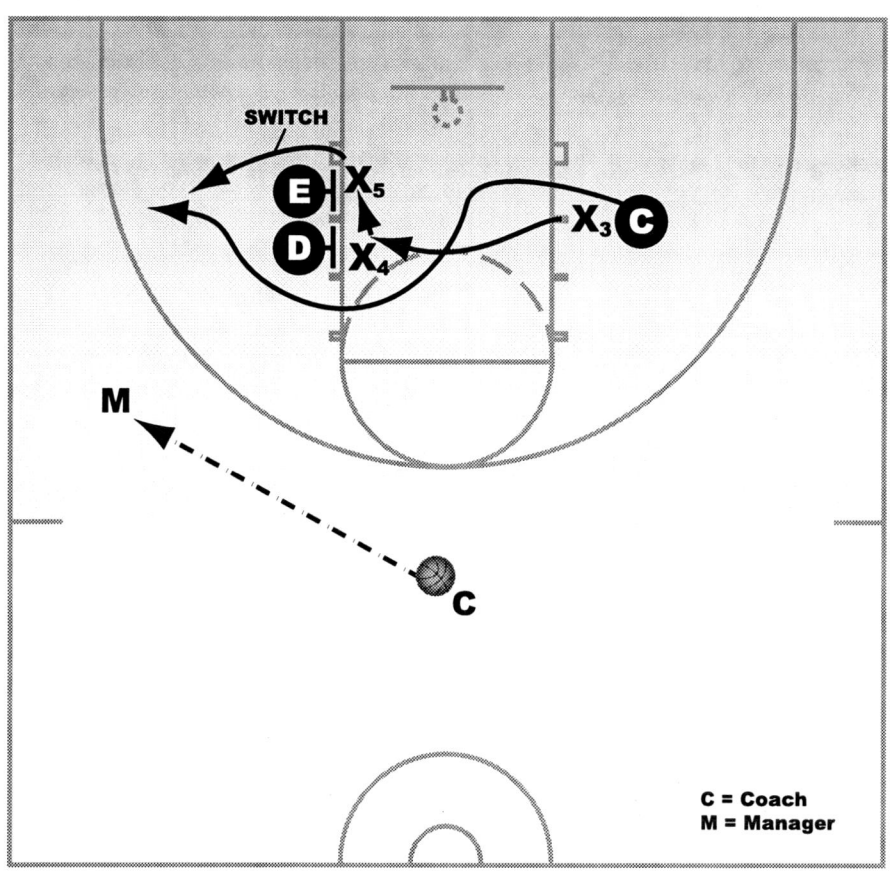

Lapchick 1.4

ball—can make. This will reduce the possible moves to the minimum, and the defensive player will be prepared for them.

GUARDING THE PLAYMAKER (QUARTERBACK)

This player is the key to the opponent's fast break and set attack. Practically all defenses now apply pressure, (play the "point of the ball" tight). This pressure could very well be applied to the playmaker, whether he

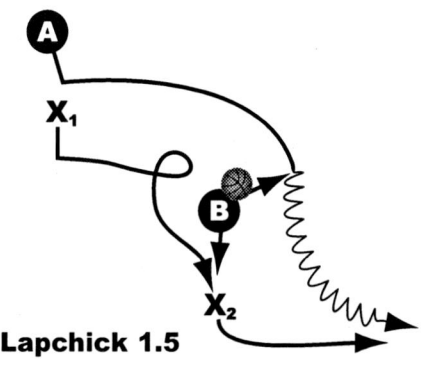

Lapchick 1.5

has the ball or not. If the ball can be kept away from the playmaker a good part of the time, it is a good step in the over-all team defense.

In guarding the playmaker, aggressive pressure with arms moving may restrict his passing or force him to make erratic passes. When this occurs, defensive teammates should, naturally, play potential receivers closely even to the extent of over-shifting and risking "back door" moves. After the playmaker completes his pass, the defensive player should drop back and toward the direction in which the ball has been passed to lessen the quarterback's opportunity to set a screen.

GUARDING THE CUTTER

The defensive player should give the cutter room when he is deep in his back court. Without the ball, he is not as dangerous as he is with the ball, so the defensive man

can drop further away. If scouting notes or game play show he favors one direction, over-shift to that side and try to make him go the other way. If the cutter has the ball, the defensive player gives ground-and-goes. As soon as the cutter passes the ball, the defensive player should drop back quickly and turn his body so both the ball and the opponent may be kept in view.

It is important that the defensive player refuse to fall for the cutter's feints and fakes. Keeping his eyes on the cutter's hips, his weight evenly distributed, and his feet on the floor will help if it is necessary to move laterally. Should the opponent gain a step and appear likely to outrun him, it is permissible for the defensive player to use a half-turn and utilize a running stride to keep up. When in doubt, he should take a half-step backward so he can handle his opponent's moves a little better.

GUARDING THE DRIBBLER

If no scouting information is available, the defensive player should guard the dribbler straight away until he finds out in which direction the player dribbles best. Once determined that he favors a particular side, the defensive player can force him toward the other direction by over-shifting. Give him room, unless he is close to the basket, and be sure to keep your weight back.

The hands must be kept low, and the inside hand used to stab at the ball. The defensive player should never lunge at the dribbler or try to steal the ball. It is better to force the dribbler to go laterally. When the dribbler moves laterally, he will be forced to reverse in order to dribble toward the basket, and this provides the defensive player with an opportunity to knock the ball away. When a reverse is made, the guard should drop back a little and keep his center of gravity low, so he can stay with the dribbler.

When the dribbler goes to his right against a defensive player whose left foot is advanced, the guard should drop his right foot far back and swing his left foot to the left with a double-shuffle of his feet. Again,

LESSONS FROM THIS LEGEND...

the body should be kept low, unless the dribbler swings toward the basket or stops and faces the goal.

GUARDING THE SCORER

The scorer should be played so closely that it is difficult for him to get the ball. Most scorers have favorite areas in which they are dead shots. If the scouting notes reveal these areas, it is wise for the guard to keep him from reaching these spots, with or without the ball. The weight must be balanced and the extended hand held high and "on the ball" when the opponent is in possession.

When the "scorer" keeps the ball low while standing, faking, or dribbling, the defensive player should retreat a half-step. As soon as the scorer stops following a dribble or raises the ball when in a "facing" position, he should be played aggressively—forced to get rid of the ball or made to pivot away.

GUARDING THE MAN WITHOUT THE BALL

The distance from the basket governs the space the defensive player can give his opponent. Generally, the defensive player should overplay toward the ball and make a determined effort to close the possible path of the ball to the opponent for his path to the ball. The opponent should be forced to work to get into position to receive the ball, especially when he is close to the basket. If he is some distance from the basket, it may be more important to sag or float away and help with the general team defense.

SLOUGHING

Sloughing-off is employed by practically all team defenses. When the ball is on the side of the court away from defensive players, they can "float" toward that side to jam up the basket area or help out with general team defense.

When the ball has been passed beyond them and close to the basket, the guards may "sag" back to jam up the middle. In this sag-off, the guards should avoid turning their heads. Shifting a bit off-line will enable them to see the action and still concentrate on their opponents.

DOUBLE-TEAM TRAPS

All pressure and pressing defenses utilize double-teams. The double-team trap may be the result of a planned or an unrehearsed action by two players acting in unison to overwhelm an opponent. The object is to force bad passes, secure held-ball situations, or stall the ball. Usually, the trap is a well-planned "team" action, used as part of the man-to-man or zone presses. In my opinion, double-teaming works best off the man-to-man defense, although a great many teams use it successfully as part of the zone press. At any rate, since it requires two or more players, it may be considered a team effort. It can be applied on the first pass, from out-of-bounds; on the second pass, when the ball is advanced across the ten-second line; following a held-ball situation; or in opposing the opponent's big man.

In developing a "trap," the defensive players should stagger their advance so that the first man can force the opponent to change direction or pivot away. Then, the second defensive player advances until he reaches a position close enough to his teammate to eliminate the possibility of the offensive player dribbling between them. Now, the hands should be raised, and the logical passing lanes closed.

The trap may be applied on a switch play, when opponents screen and cross in their back court; when the ball is passed to the pivot, especially when the big man is inclined to bring the ball down close to the floor; when a dribbler pivots away from an aggressive opponent; or when teammates must cover the loose man by swinging their defense around so the man closest to the basket will be covered.

BEATING OPPONENT TO POSITION

Many players have favorite scoring positions on the sides of the court or under the basket. Scouting material or a diagnosis of the opponent's moves early in the game will often provide the necessary information. Playing the offensive player on the side and in front in certain areas will often force him away from his favorite scoring position.

BOXING-OUT

Each defensive player is expected to keep his opponent from getting position where he may retrieve the ball or score by means of a tap-in. As soon as a shot is taken, the defensive player should hesitate a second to determine where the opposing player will try to move. His path to the ball must be blocked; a cross-over step taken toward the path the opponent is taking to reach the ball may be necessary. Thereafter, by watching the opponent, the proper shifts to the right or to the left can be made to meet a change of direction.

REBOUNDING

In going up for the rebound, the defensive player's weight is carried low, the legs are spread, and the elbows and arms are extended slightly. There is usually some contact under the boards, and the defensive player must make sure he is not forced so far under the hoop that he cannot make the rebound. Players who can leap high often take off for the rebound, only to see the ball sail over their hands. Boxing-out is not a one-man job. It is an integral part of team defense.

Against a high-scoring offensive rebounder, it may be more effective to continue playing the opponent face-to-face. This may succeed in keeping him away from a good rebounding position. Here, of course, recovery of the ball is the responsibility of teammates. Defensive guards should drop away from their back-court opponents to a point near the free-throw line to take care of deep rebounds.

All five players should be expert in boxing-out and in "delaying" opponents until recovery is possible. Normally, the big men can control the area close to the basket, but if the back-court players (guards) are

LESSONS FROM THIS LEGEND...

careless, the "overs" which rebound deep can beat a team well equipped with "inside" rebounders.

BLOCKING SHOTS

Big men today have developed great skill in blocking not only opponents' shots, but those made by their teammates' opponents. Bill Russell of the Boston Celtics is an expert in this department, as are Wilt Chamberlain (76ers) and Lew Alcindor (later Kareem Abdul-Jabbar) of U.C.L.A.

When an opponent outmaneuvers a defensive player and drives for the basket, the only way to block the shot is to follow at full speed and try to stop the shot with the inside hand, just as the shooter releases the ball. This requires timing and practice. Good hustle pays off there.

THE SAVE

Many centers are proficient in making "saves." This means that a teammate's opponent has escaped and is driving in to the basket for a sure score. Again—as in the block—alertness, good timing, and speed of foot and hands are required. This is a spectacular play and an important team defense asset.

GUARDING THE OUT-OF-BOUNDS OPPONENT

The opponent out-of-bounds with the ball should usually be played in a position between him and the basket. The defensive player should turn sideways so he can see the ball and any play that develops on the court. It is well to keep in mind that the player out-of-bounds with the ball is often set up for scoring plays.

FREE BALL

Loose balls are important. The recovery of a teammate's fumble or that of an opponent means a possible four points. In close games, the aggressive players who have the guts to go after the free ball are invaluable to team offensive and defensive play.

ONE-ON-ONE DEFENSE

All teams have one-man plays, and the ability to meet the one-on-one situation is important. This is the ultimate in defensive play because the opponent has the ball and just one idea—to score. Body balance, footwork and heart are important in shutting out the opponent.

TWO-ON-TWO

Two-on-two defense is similar to the one-on-one, except now the defensive players will have the screens and picks to contend with. Front, slide, switch, talk, aggressive play and the use of the double-team moves are important here. Two-on-two offers wonderful training for offensive play, as well as defensive work.

PRESSURE DEFENSE

Pressure defense is based on good body balance, footwork, alertness, and hustle. Practically all teams are using pressure today in one form or another, and coaches must drill their players in the ability to prevent opponents from getting clear to gain possession of the ball and in the tricks of double-teaming. It is important to impress on players that pressure means more interceptions, but can also lead to unguarded scoring shots.

INTERCEPTIONS

Interceptions result from bad plays by opponents. Careless passing (cross-court, soft looping tosses, blind passes, straight-away passes to pivot-men), fumbles, "traveling," and bad shots result from pressure defense. All defensive players should be alert to the opportunities which result from pressure.

GUARDING THE BIG MAN

Big men today are agile, fast, and great shooters. Many of them can play wing and corner positions, and a few can even play in the back-court. Individually, defensing the big man calls for playing him on the side toward the back, in front, beating him to his position, and frequently playing him face-to-face on teammate's scoring attempts. Tip-in experts must be boxed-out, and if the big man is particularly adept at tip-ins, it may be necessary to assign teammates to rebound duty and let the player guarding the big man forget about the ball.

The defensive player should be so active that the opponent's feeders will find it difficult to get the ball to the big man. He should be played aggressively and strongly, and all passes to him should be contested. When the big man is clearly superior and one defensive player cannot handle him, it might be wise to get help from the forwards and guards through sloughing-off or even double-teaming. Use of a zone may be necessary. In this event, it might be wise to remember that the one-three-one was designed by Clair Bee for just this purpose—to hamper the scoring of the opponent's big man.

HELPING OUT

This is a team effort. All players should be alert to helping teammates through talking, deflecting passes, playing the point of the ball aggressively, watching for bad passes, interception opportunities, batting at the ball when a dribbler passes close by, double-teaming, etc. However, the coach must be sure his players realize the importance of defensing their assigned opponents first and "helping out" second. It is silly for a defensive player to gamble for an interception or a "steal" and neglect his own opponent. Scores which result from such plays can be demoralizing, especially in the closing minutes of a game. Only when time is running out and the team is behind should players gamble (40-percent to 60-percent chance) on "steals."

SOURCE

Lapchick, Joe. (1968). *50 Years of Basketball*. Englewood, Cliffs, NJ: Prentice-Hall.

LEGACY OF Harry Litwack

- Introduced the box-and-one defense.

- Developed one of the best 3-2 zone defenses in the country; in 1938, Temple won the first NIT using the 3-2 zone defense.

- Many basketball historians believe that Litwack achieved more success with less talent than any coach in history.

- Promoted sportsmanship and was a coach of the highest character.

- Played professional basketball with the Philadelphia SPHAS for seven seasons and helped them capture championships in both the Eastern and American Basketball Leagues.

- Directed Temple to 13 postseason tournaments, including the NIT championship in 1969 and third-place NCAA finishes in 1956 and 1958.

HARRY LITWACK

"When playing a zone defense, we want to be the aggressor. We don't just stand there and watch the offense attack."
—Harry Litwack

BIOGRAPHY

Born: September 20, 1907 in Austria

Died: August 7, 1999

Inducted into the Naismith Basketball Hall of Fame in 1976

Harry Litwack compiled a 373-193 record at Temple University from 1952 to 1973. He led the Owls to 13 postseason tournaments, winning the NIT in 1969 and finishing third in the NCAA tournament in 1956 and 1958. Litwack created the box-and-one defense, and his teams were nationally recognized for their 3-2 zone defense. Litwack was a two-time MVP and captain during his collegiate playing career at Temple and was one of the top scorers in the East. He coached the freshman team at Temple for 20 years and compiled a record of 181-32. During the 1950-51 season, Litwack coached the freshman team at Temple and served as Eddie Gottlieb's assistant coach with the Philadelphia Warriors. Litwack played professional basketball with the Philadelphia SPHAS for seven seasons and helped them capture championships in both the Eastern and American Basketball Leagues. He was named the Philadelphia Basketball Writers Association Coach of the Year in 1956 and the New York Basketball Writers Association Coach of the Year in 1958. Litwack was enshrined into the Naismith Memorial Basketball Hall of Fame in 1976.

...SCOUTING REPORT.....SCOUTING REPORT.....

Harry Litwack...

Harry Litwack was born in Austria in 1907 and arrived in the United States at the age of five. The son of a shoemaker, Litwack was raised in South Philadelphia, and his family spoke only Yiddish at home. The prominent sport in his neighborhood was basketball. "Every phone pole had a peach basket on it," said Litwack. "Every Jewish boy was playing basketball...and everyone dreamed of playing for the SPHAS." (Entine, 2001) The acronym stood for the South Philadelphia Hebrew Association, and the team was one of the top professional teams of the era. (The SPHAS were co-founded and coached by future Hall of Famer Eddie Gottlieb.)

Litwack became a star player at Southern High School in Philadelphia and then attended Temple University. He was selected captain and MVP during his last two years and was one of the top scorers in the East.

After graduation from Temple, Litwack fulfilled his boyhood dream of playing for the Philadelphia SPHAS. Litwack joined the SPHAS in 1930 and, at the same time, was an assistant coach at Temple. He was paid $15 or $20 a game for playing with the SPHAS, and the season consisted of 85 to 100 games a year, including doubleheaders on Sunday.

With the emergence of Nazism in Germany and an escalation of anti-Semitism in the U.S., the SPHAS often faced incessant racial slurs and biased officials in the small towns in which they played. Litwack said, "Eddie Gottlieb told us the best way to answer them was to be the best team in basketball...we played extra hard, and we had to stick together. One time in Jersey City or Hoboken, the ball went out-of-bounds, and a fan grabbed it. I tried to get it back from him to put the ball into play quickly, and that started a big fight. I was hit over the head with a Coke bottle by an irate fan, and was taken to the hospital. We got into a few brawls, but that's the chance you had to take. You ran into those things."

From 1929 to 1933, the SPHAS won three championships in the Eastern Professional League. In 1933, they joined the new American Basketball League and won championships in 1934 and 1936. Litwack played with the SPHAS until 1936 and then retired. He said, "The most thrilling thing in my career was having the team picture with all the SPHAs put into the Naismith Basketball Hall of Fame."

Litwack coached the freshman team at Temple to a record of 181-32. He perfected a zone defense that revolutionized the college game. With tall players, such as 6'6" Mike Bloom, Litwack developed a 3-2 zone and introduced the box-and-one defense. Litwack taught his tall frontcourt players to stretch their arms to the side, because it was tougher for the offense to get the ball inside. In 1938, Litwack, as an assistant coach to James Usilton, employed his defensive strategy in the first-ever NIT tournament. In the semifinal game, Temple used their trademark defense against Oklahoma A&M (Oklahoma State) and their future Hall of Fame coach Henry Iba. The Aggies struggled against the defense and were beaten 56-44. Temple employed the same type of defense in the NIT championship game against Colorado. The New York Times wrote, "Colorado was helpless...Temple's zone defense was as a rock barrier...Mike Bloom and Don Henderson were the "goaltenders" who batted away everything in sight and clamped down on the Colorado shooters like a net..." Temple soundly defeated Colorado 60-36 to capture the first NIT championship.

As head coach at Temple, many basketball historians believe that Litwack achieved more success with less talent than any coach in history. "Harry Litwack's budget was

.....SCOUTING REPORT.....SCOUTING REPORT...

miniscule, the recruiting limited, his talent lean, particularly in the vital areas of height and depth, but the basketball was always big-league. Temple teams executed, they hustled, and they played with courage, intelligence, poise, and discipline." (Conlin, 1973)

Between 1952 and 1962, Temple had a full-time basketball staff of none. Litwack and assistant coach Skip Wilson taught in the Philadelphia public school system and would rush over to Temple to conduct practice. An extravagant recruiting trip was a 20-mile drive to a high school game in New Jersey.

Former Notre Dame coach Digger Phelps said, "Harry's the best. He's done so much for college basketball. He's a legend. He goes down with the best of them—the Adolph Rupps and the Hank Ibas." (Dell, 1973)

Litwack led Temple to three consecutive third-place finishes in national tournaments between 1956 and 1958. The Owls were led by two-time All-American Guy Rodgers, who has been called the greatest dribbler and passer that the city of Philadelphia has ever produced. In 1956, Rodgers combined with teammate Hal Lear to form the nation's best backcourt. Rodgers and Lear combined to score 74 percent of Temple's points in the 1956 Final Four. Lear scored 32 points in the semi-final loss to Iowa and 48 points in a victory over SMU in the NCAA third-place game. In 1957, Temple defeated St. Bonaventure for third place in the NIT. In 1958, Temple lost a heart breaker to Kentucky in the NCAA semi-finals and beat Kansas State to capture third-place.

The 1958 NCAA semi-final game between Temple and Kentucky was probably one of the most eagerly awaited Final Four games of the decade. Earlier in the season, Kentucky had defeated Temple by one point in three overtimes. Kentucky converted a free throw at the end of regulation to send the game into overtime. The Wildcats escaped again and scored with one second remaining on a 47-foot shot to send the game into the second overtime. Kentucky eventually won the hard-fought game that was played on the Wildcat's home court 85-83. In the NCAA semifinal rematch in Freedom Hall, Temple looked like the eventual winner, leading 60-59, when Rodgers stepped to the line for a one-and-one with 27 seconds to go. The usually reliable Rodgers missed the first shot, and Kentucky secured the rebound and called a time-out. Kentucky then scored on a baseline lay-up and hung on for a 61-60 victory.

Litwack's outstanding sportsmanship and flawless character made him a coaching legend in Philadelphia. He was nicknamed "Chief" because it was a catch phrase he used when meeting new people. He was also known as "The Suit Salesman."

Litwack was named by many of his contemporaries as the best college coach during the decade of the 1960's. Lou Carnesecca summed up Litwack's coaching ability when he said, "playing a Litwack team is like attending a clinic. He shows you an entire course in coaching, while he is beating your brains out."

Other coaches described Litwack in statements such as, "trying to beat a Litwack team is like trying to stuff a marshmallow into a piggy bank," or "Harry's defense is easy; his players kill your man with the ball." But, the accolades go beyond Litwack's coaching ability. Litwack was a true sportsman and gentleman. Hall of Fame coach Joe Lapchick said, "I know he's a fine coach but Harry's a gentleman, a real gentleman, and that's what counts more."

Litwack died at the age of 91 in 1999.

SOURCE

Cohen, Steve. (Date Unknown). The Little Team That Could. *Jewish Exponent.*

Conlin, Bill. (1973, January 24). Litwack: He has done more with less than any coach in basketball history. *Philadelphia Daily News.*

Dell, John. (1973, January 26). Rival Big 5 Coaches Saddened by Litwack's Decision to Retire. *Philadelphia Inquirer.*

Entine, Jon. (2001, June 21). Hoop Dream Hebrews. *Jewish World Review.*

Litwack, Harry. Vertical Files, Archives. Naismith Memorial Basketball Hall of Fame. Springfield, MA.

SPHAS, Archives. Philadelphia Jewish Sports Hall of Fame. Philadelphia, PA.

LESSONS FROM THIS LEGEND...

ZONE DEFENSES

By Harry Litwack

A lot of people don't believe in a zone defense. I know for many, many years around the East, there was one team that used a zone defense and couldn't get an invitation to play in a big game in the metropolitan area because the promoters believed zone defenses slowed down the game, and fans wouldn't support it. Later on when the NBA started, they eliminated zones. They wouldn't have a team play a zone because of the same reason. But today, you see zones defenses cropping up all over, and I am sure that in your games, you've been up against a zone, perhaps you've used it, and perhaps it has been good to you.

I have used various zone defenses, and I have been very successful. I'll admit that it wasn't my own. It's one I saw many, many years ago, adopted it, and started to refine it. I have one philosophy about the game, and that is, because of the outstanding shooting and driving that are going on today, if we are going to get beaten, I'd like to get beat from outside shooting. I don't want to lose by a player driving for a 3-point play, or a player going in for an easy lay-up.

ADVANTAGES OF ZONE DEFENSE

1. I believe playing a zone gives you better rebounding position than what you have in a man-to-man defense. In my coaching career, I have not had a lot of tall players.
2. Another reason I believe in using zone defenses is it allows us to keep our players in the game longer. We do not get called for too many fouls. I am a firm believer that although we carry twelve players on our squad, you win games with your first eight. You need to keep those players on the court and out of foul trouble.
3. I also think zone defenses take away from the quickness of a guard. I know if my team had to defend Pete Maravich, we would not be able to stop him man-to-man. I would play zone or some type of a box-and-one or triangle and two. It takes away the driving opportunities for a quick guard.
4. Another advantage of a zone defense is that it enables you to hide a weak defender.

Let me assure you one thing, and that is we teach man-to-man principles. We teach how to defend one-on-one, how to defend against a screen, how to go over the top. We are not naïve enough to think that we can always stay in our zone defense. When we fall behind, we are not just going to sit back and let someone hold the ball. My basic philosophy is that we will play a zone as long as we possibly can.

BOX-AND-ONE DEFENSE

We play the 3-2 zone and, at times, a 2-3 zone. There are also times when you have to do something different. Many years ago, we were preparing our team to face one of the greatest players that I had ever seen. We introduced a different type of defense with four players in a zone and one player playing man-to-man. We were fortunate to beat this great team using the box-and-one.

COMBINATION DEFENSE

Our great teams of 1956, 1957, and 1958 used a different type of defense that was very simple. All we did was tell our star player, Guy Rodgers, that when we yelled "going through," we were in a man-to-man defense and if not, we were to be in a zone defense. Today, I see that defense played, and it is called a combination defense. I didn't have set rules, but I did have two extremely quick guards in Rodgers and Hal Lear and a big player in the middle that was very adept at rebounding and getting the ball out quickly.

Today, when we play teams, I never know when a team is going to use man-to-man, zone, or a combination. You have to be prepared for every type of defense. I think the day is gone when you can strictly play man-to-man defense. Part of the reason is the speed of the game and the number of fouls. With 80, 90, or even 100 points being scored, there are going to be a lot of fouls called, and you will get players in foul trouble. I will use a zone defense as long as I can in order to keep my first eight players on the court as long as possible.

SOURCE

Litwack, Harry. (1970, March). Zone Defenses. *NABC Proceedings.*

LESSONS FROM THIS LEGEND...

THE 3-2 ZONE DEFENSE

By Harry Litwack

I would like to cover the basic principles of the 3-2 zone defense. Some coaches call it a 1-2-2 zone defense. First of all, we don't just stand there and let the offense attack. We want to be the aggressor. We move laterally, forward, and backward as quickly as we can. We do not allow a team to penetrate against us. As shown in **Diagram 1.0**, it is vital to keep the ball out of the middle of the floor. We wave our arms, try to steal the ball, and encourage our opponent to throw a lob pass. Other key points for success are: work with your players, gain their confidence, and get your players to believe in this defense.

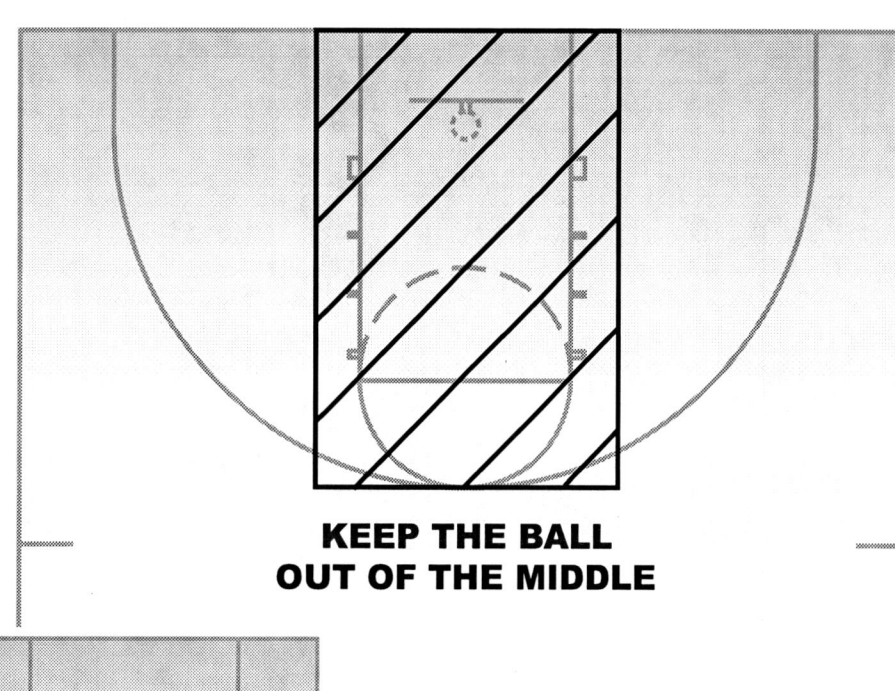

KEEP THE BALL OUT OF THE MIDDLE

Litwack 1.0

INITIAL ALIGNMENT

Diagram 1.1 illustrates the initial alignment of the 3-2 zone.

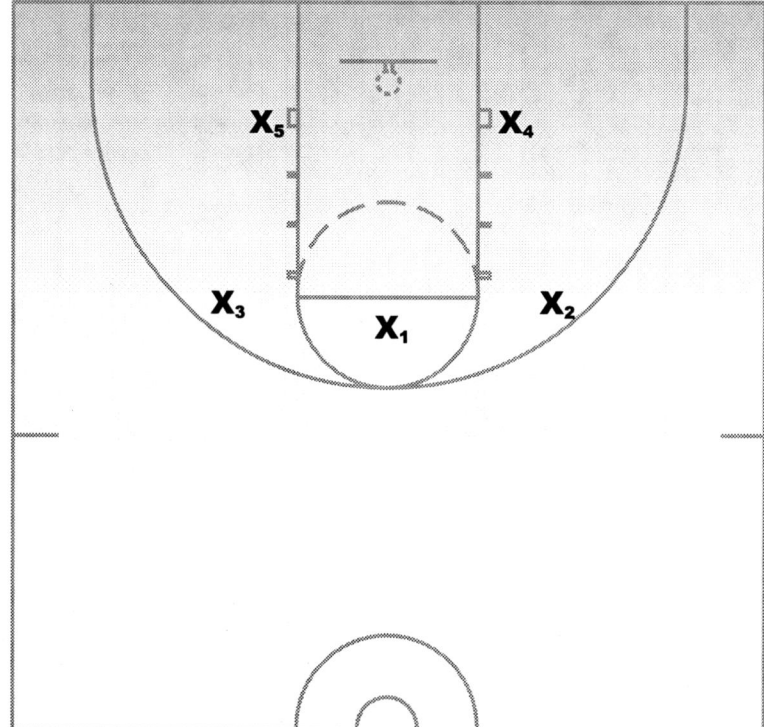

Litwack 1.1

LESSONS FROM THIS LEGEND...

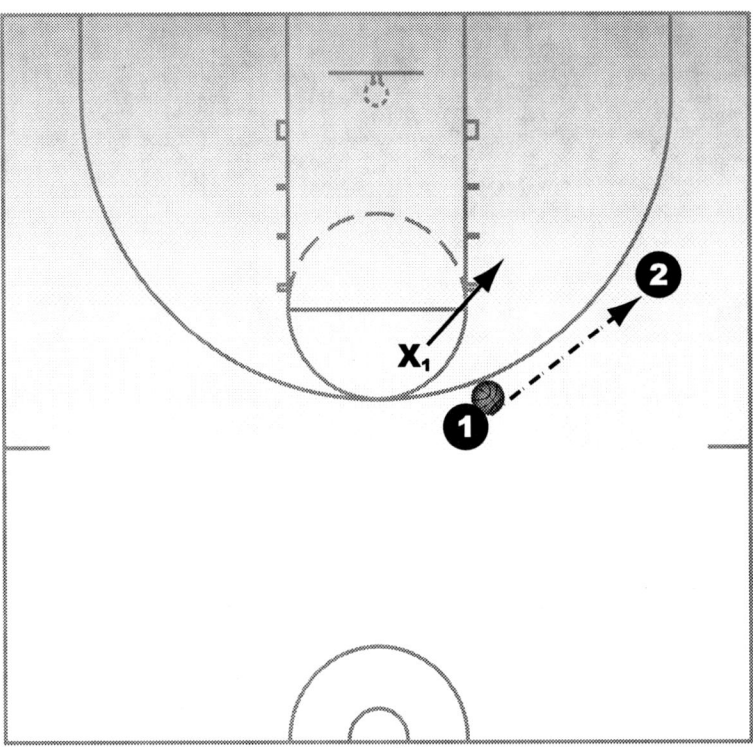

Litwack 1.2

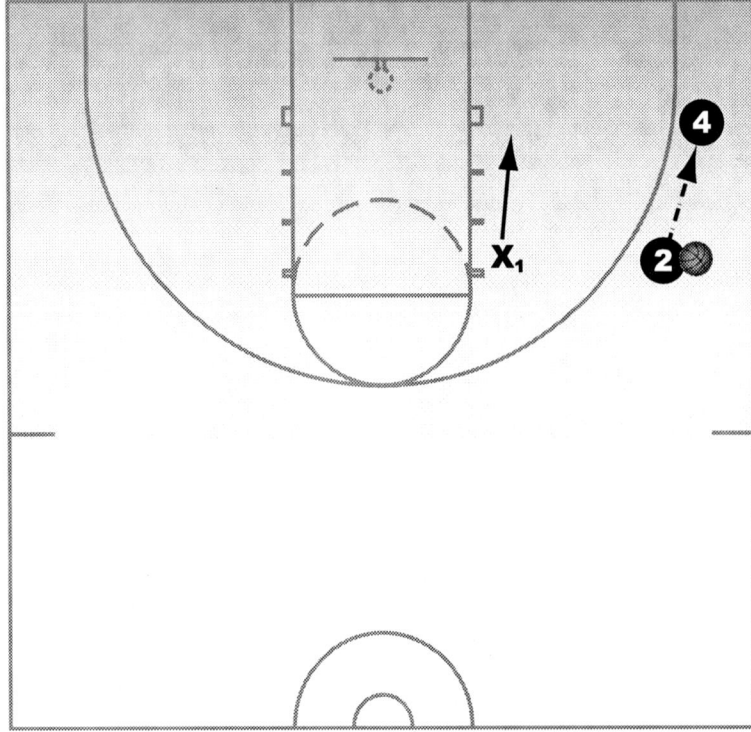

Litwack 1.3

MIDDLE MAN

X1 is the middle man, or may be called the point man by coaches who refer to this defense as a 1-2-2 zone. This player must be quick and is constantly moving. His responsibilities include the following:

1. Attack the ball when it is in his territory.
2. Force the ball out of the middle of the floor toward the wing.
3. Do not allow dribble penetration.
4. If the ball goes over his head into the high post, double-team the ball and make the post player throw it back out.
5. When the ball is passed to the wing, move down and help defend the post area. (See **Diagram 1.2**)
6. When the ball is in the corner, move down and cover the low post area. (See **Diagram 1.3**) When covering the low post, play on the side of the offensive player, rather than fronting.

LESSONS FROM THIS LEGEND...

WING MEN

The wing man's responsibilities include the following:

1. Attack the ball when it is in his area.
2. Do not allow dribble penetration.
3. When the ball is passed over his head, all he does is turn around. We call that blocking the lane. One exception to this is if we know that the offensive wing player is not a good perimeter shooter. In this case, the wing defender will go down and help with post defense.
4. When the ball is in the corner, make it difficult for the corner player to pass back to the wing. The only pass that should be allowed is a lob pass. This gives the defense time to get organized again. (See **Diagram 1.4**)
5. When the corner player begins to dribble, double team with the corner defender. (See **Diagram 1.5**)
6. Against excellent post players, we will instruct our wing defender to help our big player.

Litwack 1.4

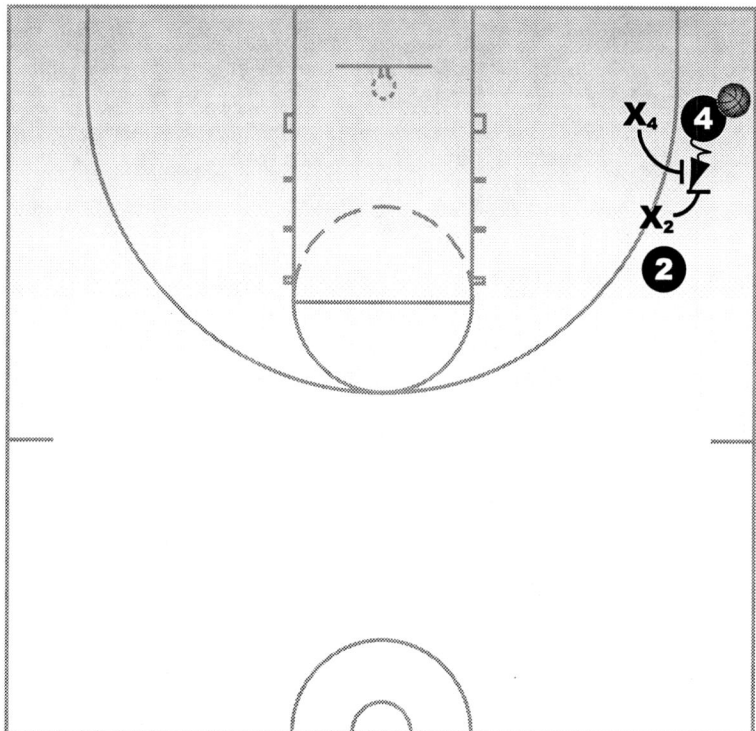

Litwack 1.5

LESSONS FROM THIS LEGEND...

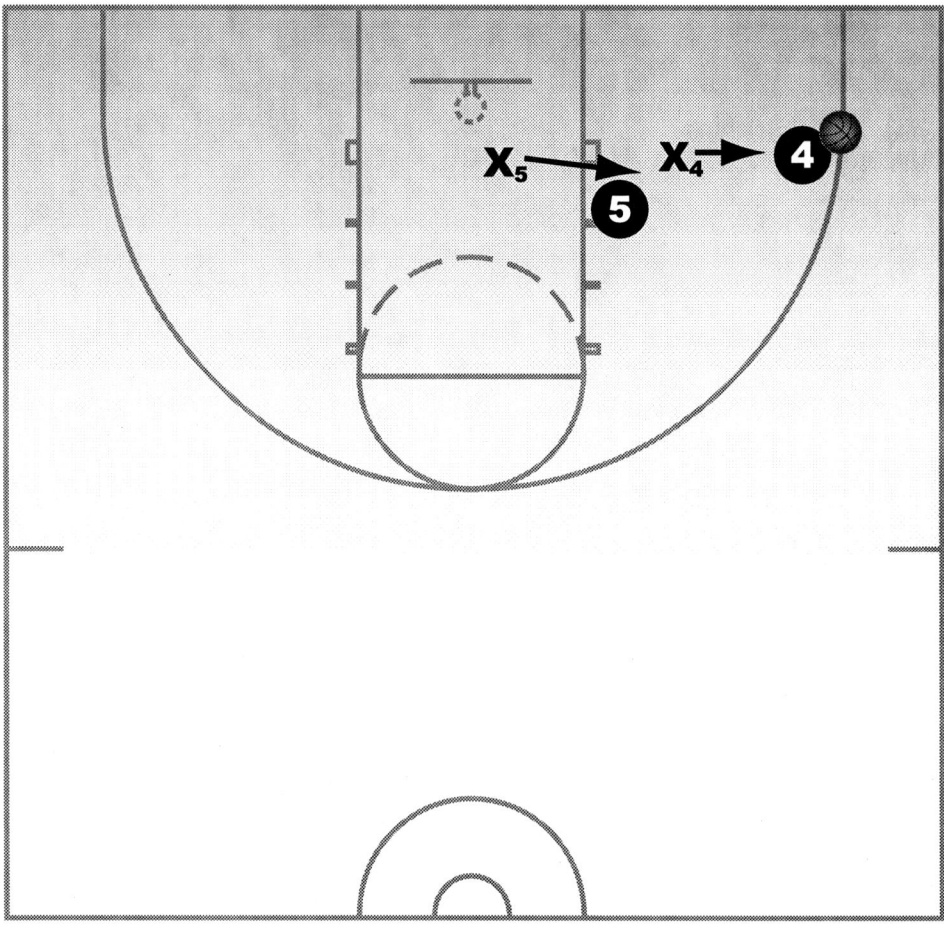

Litwack 1.6

BACK MEN

The most difficult thing that we have found is if we allow dribble penetration down the middle. When this occurs, the two back men do not know who is responsible for the post player. This is why it is so important to keep the ball out of the middle. The back man's responsibilities are as follows:

1. When the ball is passed from the wing into the post, it is the opposite back man's responsibility to come up.
2. The back men must communicate with each other. We use the word "Up." This helps the players quickly know who is responsible for the defensive coverage.
3. We tell the back men that their most important responsibility is to keep the ball out of the low-post area.
4. The weakside back man must come across and defend the low post on the ballside. (See **Diagram 1.6**)
5. The ballside back man will cover the ball in the corner. Our rule is that he must never give up the baseline drive. The ball should be directed back to where there is help.

LESSONS FROM THIS LEGEND...

DEFENSIVE SLIDES IN OUR 3-2 ZONE

I am going to show you the defensive slides when the ball is at the following locations:

1. Ball at the Wing:
   (See **Diagram 1.7**)
   a. X2 defends the ball.
   b. X1 slides down to cover the medium high-post area.
   c. X4 discourages a pass to the low post but has cheated one step toward O4
   d. X5 slides across the lane to help cover O5
   e. X3 moves into the middle of the lane.

2. Ball at the Corner:
   (See **Diagram 1.8**)
   a. X4 defends the ball.
   b. X2 is in the passing lane between O4 and O2.
   c. X5 guards the low post, O5.
   d. X1 slides down to help keep the ball out of the low post.
   e. X3 moves down and protects the basket.

SOURCE

Litwack, Harry. (1970, March). Zone Defenses. *NABC Proceedings*.

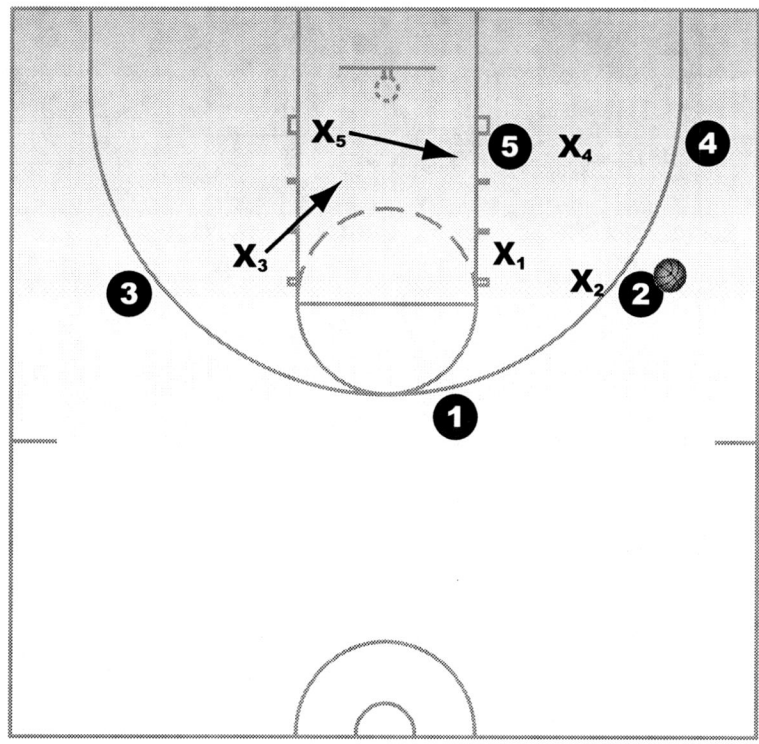

Litwack 1.7

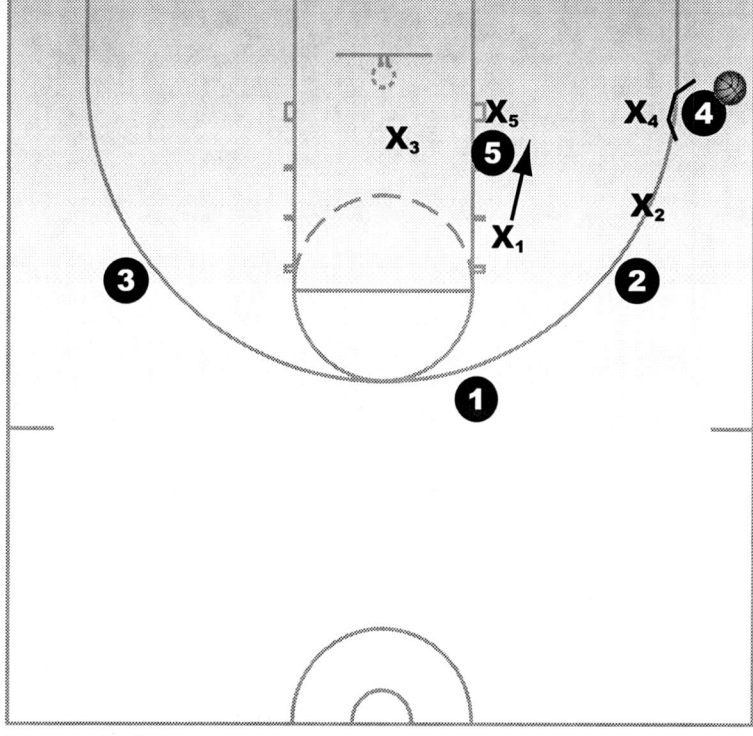

Litwack 1.8

LEGACY OF
Arthur "Dutch" Lonborg

- Led Washburn College (KS) to the AAU national championship in 1925.

- Directed Northwestern to Big Ten championships in 1931 and 1933.

- Instrumental in organizing the first NCAA tournament in 1939.

- Served as athletic director at the University of Kansas and was nationally recognized for his exceptional administrative skills.

- Organized the fund drive to send Dr. James Naismith to the 1936 Olympics, where basketball was being introduced. Enough money was raised to also purchase a home for Naismith in Lawrence, Kansas.

- Served as chairman of the U.S. Olympic Committee from 1956-1960.

- Excelled as a three-sport athlete at the University of Kansas and earned All-American honors in basketball in 1919.

ARTHUR "DUTCH" LONBORG

"The most important point to remember about defense is that an individual player must have balance at all times."
—Arthur "Dutch" Lonborg

BIOGRAPHY

Born: March 16, 1898 in Gardner, Illinois

Died: January 31, 1985

Inducted into the Naismith Basketball Hall of Fame in 1973

Arthur "Dutch" Lonborg was a three-sport letterwinner at the University of Kansas, earning honors in football, basketball, and baseball. He was a three-time all-conference performer in football and twice was named all-conference in basketball. Lonborg received All-American honors in basketball in 1919, while playing for legendary coach "Phog" Allen. After graduating from the Kansas law school, Lonborg began his coaching career at McPherson College and compiled a 23-4 record. He then went to Washburn College and led his teams to an overall record of 63-15. His 1925 Washburn team won the AAU national championship and became the last college team to accomplish that feat. Lonborg left Washburn to begin a 23-year career as coach at Northwestern. He led Northwestern to the Big Ten title in 1931 and 1933. At Northwestern, Lonborg was influential in organizing the first NCAA tournament in 1939. He returned to Kansas as athletic director in 1950 and served in that capacity for 14 years. During his tenure at Kansas, the Jayhawks won 38 conference titles in all sports and captured four NCAA championships, including the 1952 basketball title. He was inducted into the Kansas, Washburn, and Helms Halls of Fame. Lonborg was enshrined in the Naismith Memorial Basketball Hall of Fame in 1973.

...SCOUTING REPORT.....SCOUTING REPORT.....

Arthur "Dutch" Lonborg...

Arthur "Dutch" Lonborg was a farm boy who became a star athlete at Horton (KS) High School and the University of Kansas (1916-20). At Kansas, Lonborg was an all-conference football quarterback and end, a starting infielder on the baseball team, and an All-American in basketball. "Dutch" earned a reputation as a defensive standout under "Phog" Allen's tutelage. He is said to have expended so much energy on defense in a tough road game at Missouri that, late in the game with Kansas ahead and stalling (using the whole court), he just sat down on the floor and watched his four teammates stall the ball. "Phog" Allen went wild.

Following graduation in 1921, Lonborg was an AAU All-American guard with the Kansas City Athletic Club. Lonborg went on to receive a law degree from Kansas, but never practiced law a day in his life. He decided instead to enter the coaching profession.

Lonborg's first job was at McPherson College (1921-23), where his teams were 23-4. He then moved to Washburn College for four years, where his teams compiled a record of 63-14, including two conference championships and the 1925 National AAU Championship. This marked the last time that a collegiate team won an AAU title.

In 1927, Lonborg embarked on a 23-year career as head coach at Northwestern University. He instantly brought respect and credibility to the basketball program at this academically oriented, private institution. He directed Northwestern to their first Big Ten basketball championship in 1931 and a second title in 1933.

Lonborg was an exponent of the short-pass offense, rather than the fast break. His system was based upon teaching his players the fundamentals and utilizing their strengths in a highly organized offense with set plays. He took ordinary material and always made them highly competitive through sound coaching tactics and teamwork. Lonborg's coaching record at Northwestern was 237-198.

Football Hall of Fame player Otto Graham was recruited to Northwestern by Lonborg to play basketball. During an intramural football game at Northwestern, Graham's football talents impressed Lonborg so much that he told the football coach about Graham. Lonborg encouraged Otto to give football a try at Northwestern. The rest is history, as Graham became a legendary football player both at Northwestern and with the Cleveland Browns. Graham earned All-American basketball honors at Northwestern in 1943 and also won a professional basketball championship with the 1946 Rochester Royals. Nobody admired and appreciated Otto Graham more than Lonborg.

Lonborg was selected to coach the College All-Star team that annually competed against the professional champion of that year. During a nine-year period, Lonborg's collegiate all-stars won six games.

Lonborg served as president of the National Association of Basketball Coaches in 1935-36. He and "Phog" Allen led a fund drive to honor the game's founder, Dr. James Naismith. They wanted to send Naismith to the 1936 Games in Berlin, where Olympic basketball was being introduced. Their fund-raising idea included designating a week in which one penny from all gate receipts collected from college and high school games throughout the country would be donated to the Naismith Fund. At some games, tin cans were passed through the crowd. Enough money was collected to not only send Naismith to the Olympic Games, but also purchase a house for him in Lawrence, Kansas.

While at Northwestern, Lonborg helped organize and hosted the first NCAA national basketball championship in 1939. Although the initial championship lost $2,531, Lonborg and "Phog" Allen envisioned that someday the college basketball national tournament would capture the attention of sports fans everywhere. In 1940, they convinced college coaches to have a convention at the same time as the national tournament. This, coupled with moving the game to Kansas City, helped stimulate the growth of the NCAA tournament.

In 1950, Lonborg returned to the University of Kansas as director of athletics. During his 14-year tenure, he guided the Jayhawks to national prominence. Kansas won 38 conference titles and four NCAA national championships. Lonborg was also instrumental in the building of the F.C. Allen Field House, one of the nation's largest campus basketball arenas at the time it was built.

Lonborg served as the chairman of NCAA Basketball Tournament Committee from 1947 through 1960. During this period, the tournament expanded from eight to 25 teams. Lonborg also chaired the U.S. Olympic Basketball Committee from 1956 through 1960. Mandatory retirement forced Lonborg's departure as athletic director in 1964, but he still continued his association with the University of Kansas as director of athletic events.

Besides his enshrinement into the Naismith Memorial Basketball Hall of Fame, Lonborg was inducted into the Helms Foundation Hall of Fame both as a coach and athletic director.

SOURCE

Bjarkman, Peter. (2000). *The Biographical History of Basketball*. Chicago: Masters Press.

Kerkhoff, Blair. (1996). *Phog Allen: The Father of Basketball Coaching*. Indianapolis: Masters Press.

Lonborg, Arthur. Vertical Files, Archives. Naismith Memorial Basketball Hall of Fame. Springfield, MA.

LESSONS FROM THIS LEGEND...

SPECIAL BASKETBALL DEFENSES

By Arthur C. Lonborg

Before dealing with special defenses, I wish to devote some space to individual defense. In this article, man-to-man defense is being discussed.

The most important point to remember about defense is that an individual player must have balance at all times. A good defensive man is one who is able to move swiftly in any direction at all times. This is accomplished by the use of proper footwork.

The proper defensive stance is one in which both feet of the player are fairly close together, with the weight of the body equally distributed on both feet. The body is in a crouched position. The arms are out and bent at the elbows, ready to move in any direction.

Authors' Note: This basic defensive move is today called step-and-slide footwork.

The boxer's step is used by the defensive player in moving over the floor. The step should not be too long. A player shifting to the right first moves his right foot in that direction and then brings his left foot quickly to the side of the right so that he is again in his original starting position. This procedure continues as long as progress is made in that direction.

In guarding a man with the ball, the defensive man should keep one hand up and the other at his side to stop passes or dribbles. A good guard is one who is always between his man and the basket, except in rare cases around the basket. Defensive players must study opposing offensive men, as to speed and other qualifications, and judge how far to play away from them. About three feet is the average distance.

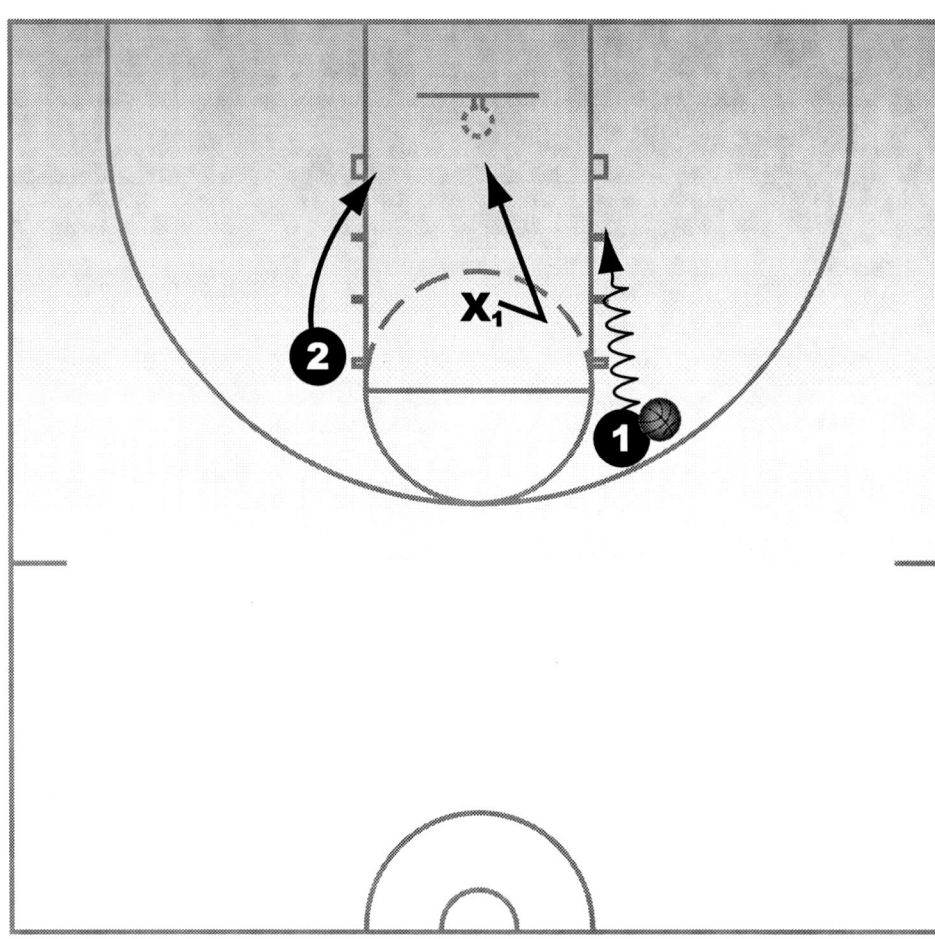

Lonborg 1.0

TWO-ON-ONE SITUATIONS

With the changes in rules during the past few years, the fast-break has come back, and defensive men are sometimes required to guard two men. At other times, two men must guard three.

When a two-on-one situation arises, the defensive man must attempt to stop any short shots and, if possible, by feinting at ballhandler to make the offense shoot from a distance. The defensive man should back up toward the basket, facing both offensive men if possible, always protecting against one or the other and preventing them from slipping behind him for a short shot. He must try to hold them off until help arrives. A guard who is easily pulled out of position will not be able to stop short shots and must therefore be careful to guard the area around the basket.

I like to have the guard who is in a two-on-one situation always know where both

LESSONS FROM THIS LEGEND...

offensive men are, which means that he must not turn his back to either one. You will note in **Diagram 1.0**, that the guard knows where both opponents are located.

THREE-ON-TWO SITUATIONS

In a three-on-two situation, the two guards meet the offense by having one guard try to slow the offense down and the other guard drop back to stop any short shots. As the offense nears the scoring zone, if the ball is in possession of one of the two offensive men on the sides of the court, the back guard covers this man. The front guard drops back a little, forcing the ball and attempting to intercept it in case a pass is made to the man on the other side of the court, as the diagram shows. If the ball is passed back to the center offensive man, the back guard again covers the basket. In this manner, the defense is able to prevent short shots and also hurry shots of medium length. (See **Diagram 1.1**)

FREE THROW LINE SITUATIONS

In modern basketball, there is a great deal of passing to a man cutting to the free-throw line, with the passer cutting in front of the man on the line and perhaps receiving a return pass.

The defense for this maneuver is one of switching men, but care must be taken that the change is not made too quickly. If it is made too soon, the man receiving the ball on the free-throw line may whirl and shoot, or dribble in for a shot. The defensive man involved should call the change, and it should be made quickly. This requires much practice, and the players must be able to work together.

Teamwork is required on defense, as well as on offense. Some teams do not like to change men (switch) on defense. When not changing men, defensive players must short cut behind the screen or break through the screen. Some defensive men have the ability to prevent themselves from being screened and can cover their offensive men effectively. In that case, no change is necessary.

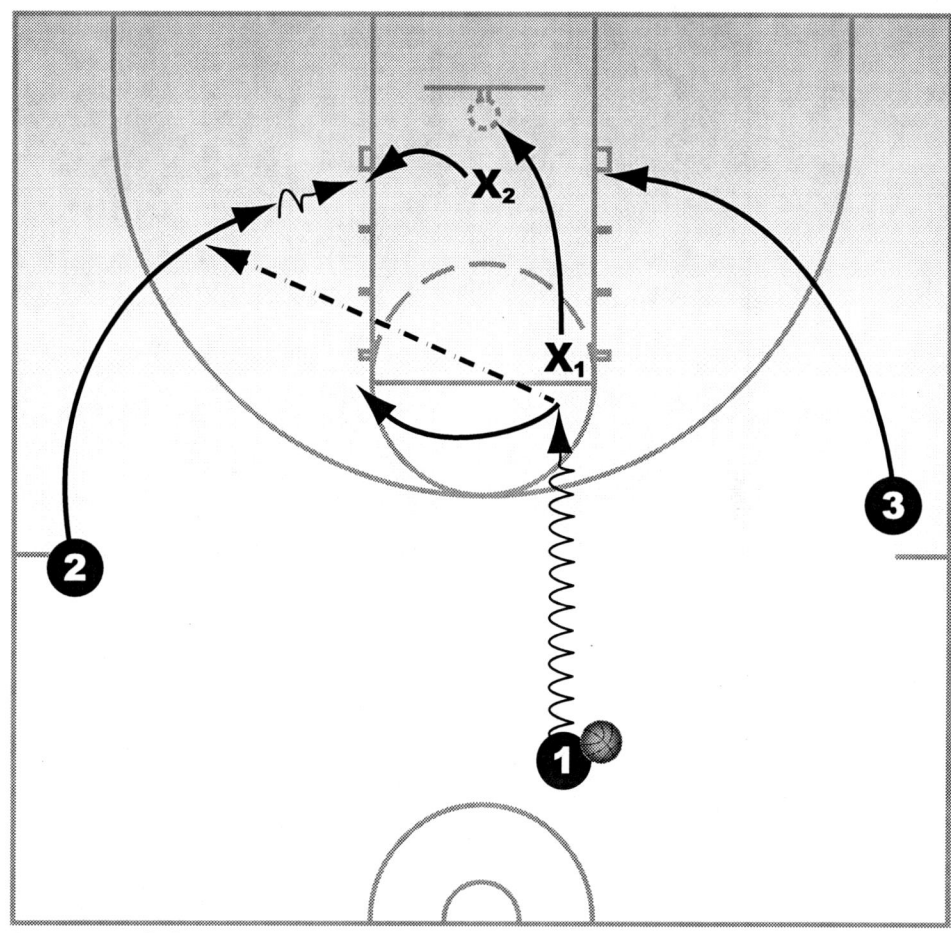

Lonborg 1.1

Another effective way of stopping plays of this kind is to prevent the offensive man from breaking to the free-throw line to receive the ball. An alert, fast defensive man can prevent the pass from being made to the man on the line. This, of course, means that the guard must be careful that the offense does not bluff a break and then cut for the basket to get the pass behind and take a shot. A guard trying to prevent the pass from being made to the man on the line must play rather loosely on his man and beat him to that position.

SOURCE

Lonborg, Arthur C. (1936, January). Special Basketball Defense. *The Athletic Journal*.

LEGACY OF
John "Johnny Mac" McLendon

- Pioneered integrated basketball and heightened awareness of basketball at predominately black institutions.

- Led Tennessee A&I (now Tennessee State) to three consecutive NAIA national championships (1957,58,59).

- Compiled a college-coaching record of 523-165 during his 25-year career.

- Studied under Dr. James Naismith at the University of Kansas.

- Became the first black head coach in the ABL with the Cleveland Pipers in 1961.

- Advocated a fast-break offense, and his teams always featured superior conditioning and pressure defense.

- Possessed exceptional knowledge of the game, and his engaging personality made him one of basketball's leading ambassadors.

- Namesake of the basketball arena at Cleveland State University.

JOHN "JOHNNY MAC" MCLENDON

*"Nils Desparandum, words I always heed;
My inspiration, prayer and creed;
Life's storms cannot my aspirations dim
For these are words I hear from him"*
—John McLendon

BIOGRAPHY

Born: April 5, 1915 in Hiawatha, KS

Died: October 8, 1999

Inducted into Naismith Basketball Hall of Fame in 1979

John McLendon grew up in racially segregated Kansas in the early 1900s. McLendon began his coaching career as an undergraduate student and directed Lawrence Memorial High School to the Kansas-Missouri Athletic Conference championship in 1936. His first head-college coaching job was at North Carolina College, where he compiled a record of 264-60 in 12 years. From 1952 to 1954, McLendon coached at Hampton Institute and led his teams to a 32-14 record. He achieved national prominence at Tennessee A&I from 1954-59 (now Tennessee State University), when he became the first college coach to lead teams to three consecutive NAIA National Championships (1957-59). McLendon pioneered integrated basketball and heightened awareness of basketball at all-black colleges. John was selected National NAIA Coach of the Year in 1958. He compiled a lifetime college coaching record of 523-165. McLendon coached professional basketball with the Cleveland Pipers and the Denver Rockets. Cleveland won the NIBL and AAU championships in 1961. McLendon wrote *Fast Break Basketball,* which is still a primary text for any coach wanting to develop the fast-break attack. He was elected to the Helms Foundation Hall of Fame and the Black Sports Foundation Hall of Fame. McLendon was enshrined in the Naismith Memorial Basketball Hall of Fame in 1979.

...SCOUTING REPORT.....SCOUTING REPORT.....

John "Johnny Mac" McLendon....

Born in Hiawatha (KS), John McLendon was raised in Kansas City, when Kansas was still racially segregated and blacks were not allowed sport opportunities, especially in basketball. Who would have thought that diminutive "Johnny Mac" would become the black pioneer who broke the barriers for persons of color to help make basketball truly "a game for everyone."

"Johnny Mac" graduated from Sumner High School in Kansas City in 1932 and enrolled in Kansas University (KU) as a physical education student. At the time, blacks weren't allowed to play basketball (intramural or intercollegiate) at KU. In fact, he became the first black person in the physical education program. However, good fortune came his way, when his college advisor was none other than the inventor of basketball, Dr. James Naismith. He became a direct link to the legendary Naismith, learning all he could about the game directly from him, even mowing his lawn. McLendon also became a close observer of future Hall of Fame coach Phog Allen, then coaching basketball at Kansas. John had two excellent basketball mentors, but times were still not easy. In a required physical education swimming class, other P.E. majors refused to enter the pool when McLendon swam. Even though humiliated and scorned, Johnny Mac completed all swim-test requirements with special provisions with the instructor and him using the pool. Hardly a crucible of fair play to foster optimism against bias. Yet somehow, McLendon thrived and developed. The determination was strong to become the person who other blacks affectionately called "Coach Mac."

In fact, he eventually became the beacon of hope for black coaches everywhere. It all started at Kansas, when he began his eminent career coaching the Lawrence Memorial High School team his junior and senior years in college. They were 13-3 in 1936 and won the Missouri-Kansas Conference title. John went to the acclaimed physical education master's degree program at the University of Iowa and obtained his degree in 1936-37. He coached from 1937-52 at North Carolina College, becoming head coach in 1940. This is where he began to break down barriers for blacks—originating and organizing the National Basketball Committee in 1949. This group of black coaches and administrators became the change agent for addressing inequities imposed on predominately black colleges, one of which was access to national tournament play. This allowed Tennessee A&I to play in the national NAIA tourney for the first time in 1952-53. He also coached at Hampton Institute from 1952-54. In 1954, Coach Mac moved to Tennessee A&I, and A&I became the first black team to receive an invite to the NAIA Invitational tip-off in Kansas City—he accepted on the condition that his team would be housed in downtown K.C. with seven other teams. A&I won the tournament, and another hotel-restaurant barrier was broken. From 1957-59, Coach Mac's Tennessee A&I team won three straight NAIA National Championships; he became the first coach in history to accomplish that feat and the first coach to win a national-integrated tourney in basketball.

The black barriers continued to come down with Coach John McLendon, Jr. playing the key role:
- First black to coach and win an integrated national tournament
- Coach of first black college team to attain a #1 UPI ranking (Tennessee A&I, 1959)
- First black coach to become head coach of a post-college team (Cleveland-NIBL)
- First black pro-coach—Cleveland Pipers title team (1962) and Denver Rockets of ABA (1968-69)
- First black coach to serve on U.S. Olympic Basketball Staff (1968)
- First black coach to write a basketball coaching book (1965)
- First black head coach at a predominately white university (Cleveland State, 1966-69)

Is there any doubt that "Coach Mac" earned the title as "Father of Black Basketball (and Coaches)" in the United States? He indeed paved the way for all.

.....SCOUTING REPORT.....SCOUTING REPORT...

Mac went on to complete an illustrious 34-year coaching career with the Cleveland Pipers of NIBL (1959-61), Cleveland Pipers of NBL (1961-62), Kentucky State College (1963-66), Cleveland State University (1966-69), and the Denver Rockets of the ABA in 1969. His total career record was 729-240 (.752), which he garnered while also teaching physical education and administering programs in a variety of positions. During his career, his teams won 22 of 29 tournaments they qualified for or entered. Clair Bee, in the twilight of his years in 1972 said, "I have known John for over 35 years. His contributions and accomplishments have been beyond comparison. He is a fine gentleman and an honor to basketball in every respect."

What did "Coach Mac" bring to the game. Neil Isaacs (1975) summed it up best, "to talk about basketball without John McLendon is like talking about the interpretation of dreams without Freud." Mac attributes his legacy to Naismith and Kansas basketball (one-hand shooting, rugged rebounding, and great tradition). His teams always ran and pushed the ball up the floor—one of his North Carolina College teams won the 1947 CIAA tourney, with four players 5 feet 7 inches or under. They were called the "Mighty Mites" and were so balanced none made the all-conference team. Mac pioneered the full-court game; fast breaking, full-court pressure defense (including the early zone press), the revolving pivot/post, multiple offenses, and superb conditioning.

The little known trademark of McLendon teams was exemplary team sportsmanship and bench decorum. He was often characterized as a gentleman and fine sportsman. This almost seems incongruous with the many barriers he must have faced and disadvantages he overcame. But a reality it was; "Coach Mac" became a mentor and model for all. As a symbol of the respect he had earned, his Hall of Fame nomination had the unanimous endorsement of every active black basketball coach and all black institutions in the United States. In the vast network of basketball played in inner cities, most leagues have adopted what is called the "McLendon Rule," which holds that if a coach draws a technical foul, every player on that team roster is accessed a foul. What a tribute to "Coach Mac's" mentorship!!! Leroy Walker, President of North Carolina Central College and former U.S. Olympic Track and Field Coach said of him, "McLendon's impeccable character and great personal traits have permitted his basketball genius to shine through at all levels and among all people."

SOURCE

Isaacs, Neil. (1975). *All the Moves - A History of Basketball.* Philadelphia: J.B. Lippincott.

McLendon, John. Vertical Files, Archives. Naismith Memorial Basketball Hall of Fame. Springfield, MA.

LESSONS FROM THIS LEGEND...

THE FOUR DEGREES OF DEFENSE THEORY

By John McLendon

Players accomplish more in a learning situation when they are aware of the objectives involved. Players are stimulated further when they are given some idea of their position in relation to these outcomes. They learn better when they know where they are in relation to other competitors for the same position. Vague statements and generalized comments in answer to the questions on actual status are not appreciated, nor are they fair. I have emphasized the need and value of objectifying skills and performance for morale, for "psychological conditioning" for determination of personnel for various team assignments, and for the coach's need to be respected. In the theory of "four degrees of defense," there is drawn a definite line between one degree of defensive ability and another, in such a way that the degree of ability achieved will be clear to the player and his coach. Offense has long been measured. Practically every statistic written during a basketball game can assist in an offensive evaluation. By defining the defensive problems and observing how nearly the problems are realized, it is possible to assess objectively the defensive degree to which the player has advanced.

FIRST DEGREE DEFENSE

Defensing (1) an assigned player. First-degree defense is applicable to those game situations in which we find one defensive man assigned to one offensive man (familiarly referred to as the "one-on-one" situation) who must be defensed when he is stationary or moving, with or without the ball. Some offensive maneuvers which are problems for the first-degree, defensive player are:

a. Defensing against the fake during and after passing the ball
b. Defensing against the fake during and after the dribble
c. Defensing movements prior to, and including receiving the ball
d. Defensing faking which occurs before shooting
e. Defensing the offensive moves after the shot (blocking the offensive follow-up)
f. Defensing the field-goal attempt (the mid-air block)
g. Defensing the pivot man (a player who is in position to receive or does receive the ball with his back to the basket)

It is a fact that the first-degree defense (and less) characterizes the limit of most players' ability. To some extent, a demonstration of any degree of defense is influenced by the ability of the offensive player, however, and the proper defensive position, the proper application of sound counter-mechanics in the situation represent the factors which are used to judge the defender in his relationship to the first-degree goal. Can the player play the man assigned man-to-man (nose-to-nose) in the above situations? If so, he can play "first-degree defense."

SECOND-DEGREE DEFENSE

Defensing (1) an assigned player, plus (2) the ball. The ability of a defensive player to keep the optimum defensive advantage each time the ball moves requires second-degree, defensive skill. To be able to play the man assigned in relation to the ever-changing ball position is required defensive play for this degree. The relative position of the defender in relation to the position of his man and in relation to the goal being defended is a fine adjustment natural to few. For most, it requires many tedious hours of practice. Examples of second-degree situations are:

a. Adopting the proper position defensively when the ball is passed from one player (position) to another player (position). The essential skill is that of watching the man assigned and the ball, and being able to play the ball and the man at all times, maintaining optimum position on each in relation to the scoring area.
b. Out-of-bounds plays. The difficult assignment of playing the man and the ball in situations where the ball is behind the defender is a real second-degree defensive problem.
c. Jump-ball situations. Each jump-ball circle requires the defense to assume a different position on the man and the ball. Each circle requires a defense involving playing the man and the ball.
d. Defensing the pivot man. Individual defensive play versus a stationary or moving pivot man must be of the second-degree level or the offense will take over completely. Here is a good example of an area of the game where it is impossible to defend a player (a pivot man) when you have no idea of where the ball is. It is also impossible to play the ball only and still keep a defensible position on the man. Second-degree defense is a must here.
e. Defense against the passer who passes into the pivot man is inadequate defense if both man and ball are not played simultaneously.

LESSONS FROM THIS LEGEND...

    f. Rebounding. Defensive rebounding is best achieved when the defender plays the man first, then the ball. Some may try the reverse, but they fail because players do not play both at the same time. Position play on the backboards is dependent on the second-degree defensive ability.

Players who can manage a second-degree performance are not easily found. Coaching the awareness of and the skills necessary to rising to this level of defense is a worthy challenge for the coach and the player.

THIRD DEGREE DEFENSE

Defensing (1) an assigned player, plus (2) the ball, plus (3) the offensive situation. That degree of defensive play in which the player recognizes and anticipates the offensive maneuver or technique being used, and by skill, ability and "know-how" eliminates the disadvantage to which he is being subjected. A third-degree defensive player must have these abilities:

    a. Ability to slide through, slide under, or "over the top" of his teammates and their respective assigned players
    b. Ability to recognize or anticipate when and when not to slide
    c. Ability to switch
    d. The anticipatory knowledge of when to switch or when not to switch
    e. The cooperative technique involved in switching
    f. The ability to "beat the switch"
    g. The individual and cooperative ability needed to defeat the "blind" screen, the stationary screen inside and outside, and the moving screen inside and outside
    h. The technique of beating the post play (when the pivot man is used as a stationary screen)

All good teams use various stratagems, involving two or more players, to give the offense a temporary advantage. Inasmuch there is already the advantage of prior knowledge on the offense's side, the problem of defeating the maneuver is almost insurmountable unless the defender is equipped with third-degree defensive ability. If he is continually caught in the offensive "traps," he is not in third-degree class. A player knows as well as the coach where he fits in this degree category.

FOURTH-DEGREE DEFENSE

Defensing (1) an assigned player, plus (2) the ball, plus (3) the situation, plus (4) helping a teammate with his assignment. The fourth-degree defensive player is quite rare. He represents the ultimate in defensive ability, and, given rebounding power along with this degree of skill, he is absolutely invaluable. The fourth-degree man not only covers the numerous assignments listed in the three previous degrees, he also assists his teammates with their individual assignments, and he does so in such a way that he sacrifices nothing in terms of carrying out his own defensive responsibilities.

The fourth-degree player is the "double-team" player, the man who helps "sandwich" the pivot man, and the slough-off defender on the away-from-the-ball side of the court. He helps in defensive traps around the court, and he worries the man with the ball or the man about to receive a pass every time he is near him. He is the loose-ball recoverer, the jump-ball causer. This is the type of player who makes a fast-break offense move faster and more frequently. He is the player who makes defensive play a very important part in the offensive plan.

Objective measurement of defensive ability may not be completely feasible using the foregoing "degree" concept, yet it is certainly possible to categorize personnel with reasonable accuracy after applying this formula. The challenge implied is to improve the player's defense as a means of improving him as a well-rounded player. Good defensive play multiplies the opportunities for offensive action. Consequently, it enhances, rather than limits, the offensive-minded players and teams. The player who can add a "degree" or two of defense to his repertoire of skills will, without a doubt, improve his total game. The collective individual improvement will upgrade every phase of team play and add greater possibilities of consistent and rewarding performances.

SOURCE

McLendon, John B. Jr. (1965). *Fast Break Basketball: Fundamentals and Fine Points.* West Nyack, NY: Parker Publishing.

LESSONS FROM THIS LEGEND...

RELATING DEFENSE TO THE FAST BREAK OFFENSE

By John McLendon

The fast-break offense is a full-court offense usually originating from the back-court. The principal source of the launched attack is from the defensive rebound. Furthermore, for years this offense has been channeled from a zone alignment of some kind which waits for the rebound to be secured: No rebound, no fast break; no field-goal attempts, no rebounds; no fast break, no offense. The "forcing" fast break cannot wait. The team must have more opportunities to score than those afforded by a missed field goal. A defense must be devised, developed, and applied which will multiply the scoring chances—one which complements the offensive ideas.

All offenses should have a defensive idea which assists in making the offense more effective. Certain offenses are closely attached to the team defense employed. To couple a full-court, man-to-man, harassing, pressing defense with a slow, ball-control offense would be the height of incongruity. This exaggeration, however, should illustrate the point that offenses and defenses should indicate some degree of coordination and compatibility.

Dr. W. F. Burghardt, whom I assisted in football at one time, successfully taught his linemen that the team without the ball was an offense, even though the opponents had possession. For years, I have used this principle to correlate defense with offense. Even though the opponents have the ball in their possession, the team without the ball uses tactics to get possession, which become part of the offense the moment the ball exchange occurs. In fact, some offensive moves may be in the process of being made in anticipation of possession.

Some of the objectives of attack used by the defense may be listed as follows:
1. Forcing the offense to mishandle the ball or to fumble the ball. The defensive players should attack individually and double-team poor dribblers, poor passers, and poor receivers. They should be attacked:
   a. In the back-court
   b. As they near the ten-second line
   c. As they cross the ten-second line
   d. As they come to a stop after having crossed the ten-second line
   e. In all corners of the front and back-court
   f. In all close-to-the-line areas
   g. When isolated with the ball from their teammates
   h. When their dribble is used up
2. Forcing passes which are interceptable:
   a. Defensing players in such a way and in such positions as to make them throw the ball long and high
   b. Overplaying the passer to force lateral passes
   c. Separating the players to force the cross-court pass
   d. Forcing the player into a back-pivot near the ten-second line so he passes blind
   e. Pressuring the pivot man who receives the incoming pass
   f. Pressuring the player who passes the ball in to the pivot man
   g. Many times, the opponent speeds up his game, including his passing game.
   h. Changing the usual pass patterns to unfamiliar areas and positions
3. Trying for the jump ball situations:
   a. With a double-team on an isolated back-court man
   b. Cornering a man (double-team a player in the corners of the front and back-court)
   c. Quick attack on a "blind" dribble (a player who looks at the ball when dribbling and who turns his back on part of the defense while dribbling across the court, down sidelines, into the corner, along the base line, and down-court after a back-court by-pass of his defense)
   d. Going after all loose balls
4. Forcing the opponents into a position from which the ball may be stolen. Examples: 2b, 2c, 2d, 2h, 3a, 3b, 3c.
5. Forcing a poor field-goal attempt. Every field goal attempt should be contested. Furthermore, the contesting should begin prior to the opponent getting to his shooting area and before he assumes shooting form:
   a. Do not allow the opponent to take his best or favorite shot. This not only refers to form, but to speed also.
   b. Do not allow the opponent to take a shot from his favorite spot.
   c. Change his shot and his spot.
6. Block the close, field-goal attempt. A legal block of the close shot can be made by defensive men who have a good sense of timing, who

LESSONS FROM THIS LEGEND...

can play the man and ball together, and who have good jumping ability. The idea here is to force even the close shot to be altered by the shooter, thus decreasing his percentage, and increasing the possible defensive rebound possibilities.

In reiteration, let me state that any defense which is employed by a fast-break team should originate and force those situations which increase possession and subsequent fast-break thrusts. That defense, when applied, forces the offense to give up the ball.

Stating the theory of the complementing defense another way, the more quickly a defense can place offensive players (those who become offensive players on the ball exchange) in scoring position, the better defense for that offense it is. It is fairly obvious then that the defenses which are best adapted to realizing this objective are those which meet the offense in the back-court, in, and close to, the scoring area itself. When there are interceptions, stolen balls, and loose balls which are retrieved in the back-court area, there is little or no time for defensive adjustment.

This inability of the defense to adjust is not confined to the players involved with the ball; neither can players without the ball adjust to those who are teamed with the defense. The pressure exerted by the offense to go forward against pressing tactics gives the advantage to the defensive team on the exchange of the ball. Before the adjustment can be made, the optimum scoring area is overloaded with offensive players.

Diagram 1.0 shows the areas of the court where defense can give decided advantage to the team taking the ball from the offense. The diagram shows the offensive over-load most likely to occur from various positions on the court when the aforementioned tactics are employed. It is obvious that the defenses most desired would be those designed to gain possession in areas 1, 2, and 3.

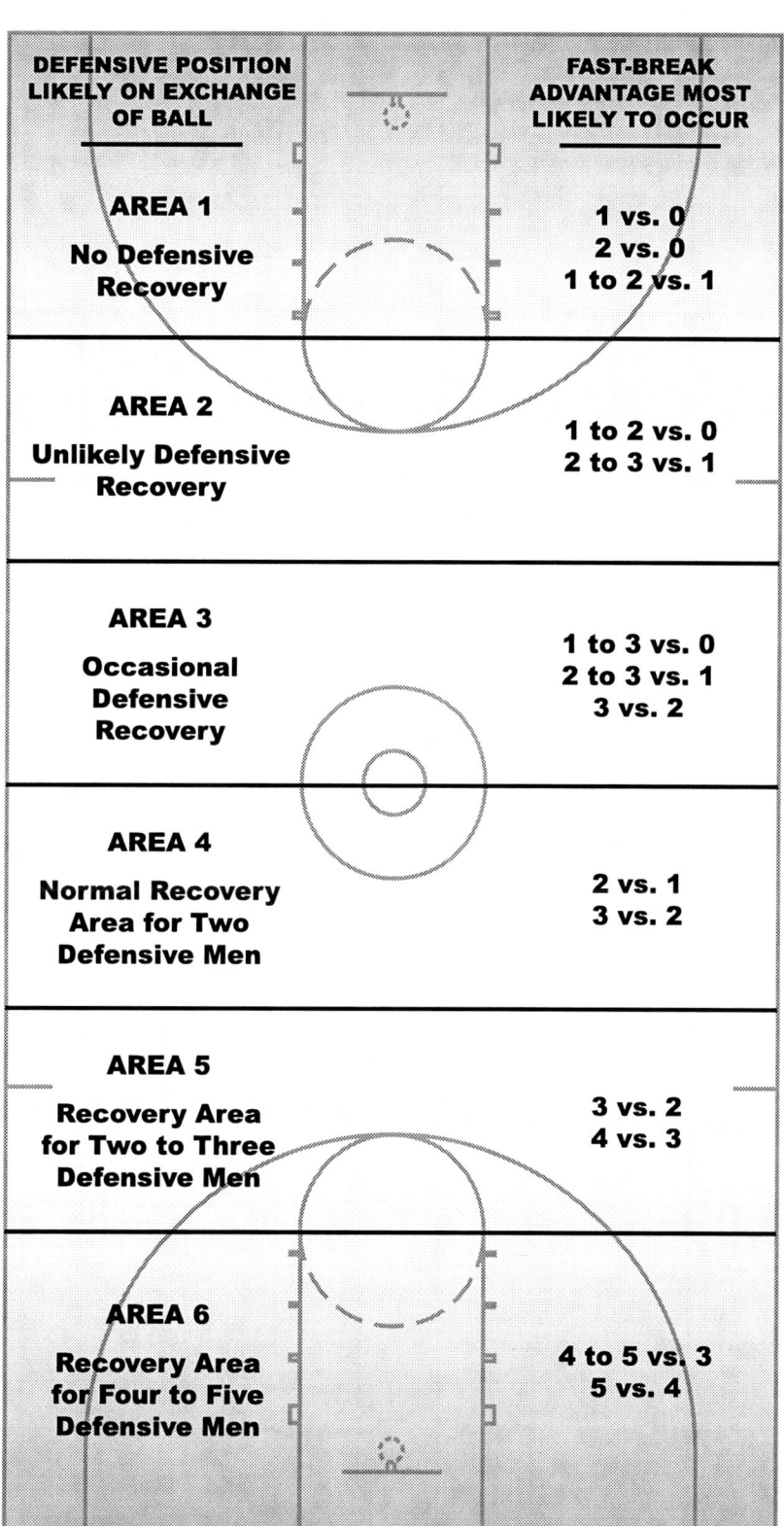

DEFENSIVE POSITION LIKELY ON EXCHANGE OF BALL	FAST-BREAK ADVANTAGE MOST LIKELY TO OCCUR
AREA 1 No Defensive Recovery	1 vs. 0 2 vs. 0 1 to 2 vs. 1
AREA 2 Unlikely Defensive Recovery	1 to 2 vs. 0 2 to 3 vs. 1
AREA 3 Occasional Defensive Recovery	1 to 3 vs. 0 2 to 3 vs. 1 3 vs. 2
AREA 4 Normal Recovery Area for Two Defensive Men	2 vs. 1 3 vs. 2
AREA 5 Recovery Area for Two to Three Defensive Men	3 vs. 2 4 vs. 3
AREA 6 Recovery Area for Four to Five Defensive Men	4 to 5 vs. 3 5 vs. 4

McLendon 1.0

LESSONS FROM THIS LEGEND...

Following is a list of defenses and their relationship to the offensive possibilities employed by a fast-break team. These points are summarized in **Diagram 1.1**.

1. *Full-court press, man-to-man.* Defensive concentration is on areas 1, 2, 3 (See **Diagram 1.1**). It is a primary, full-court defense and should be considered not only as a stratagem but also as basic to the development of effectiveness in other pressing defenses.
2. *Full-court, zone press.* Defensive concentration is on areas 1, 2, 3. The advantage of the zone-press idea used with the fast-break offense is in the automatic, or natural, alignment of players for an offensive advantage. The zone press moves to a position of advantage in numbers with ease, since it is already in that position defensively.
3. *Three-quarter-court press.* Man-to-man and zone defensive concentration is on areas 2 and 3. Ball possession in this area gives consistent advantage to offense.
4. *Half-court press.* Defensive concentration is on area 3 and the ten-second line area of area 4. The defenses which offer pressure at half-court are strong as a complementing defense for the fast-break team. The advantage of such defense is as much with the team gaining possession as with others mentioned, except that the distance from the goal often allows for some defensive recovery. Therefore, defense in this area (3-4) requires that the third lane be filled on offense. The three-lane fast break becomes a necessary preparation, beginning with any defense applied to areas 4, 5.
5. *Normal man-to-man.* The man-to-man defense is basic to all other defenses. A player who learns to play man-to-man defense can play any other defense more effectively. As a fast break complement, it has

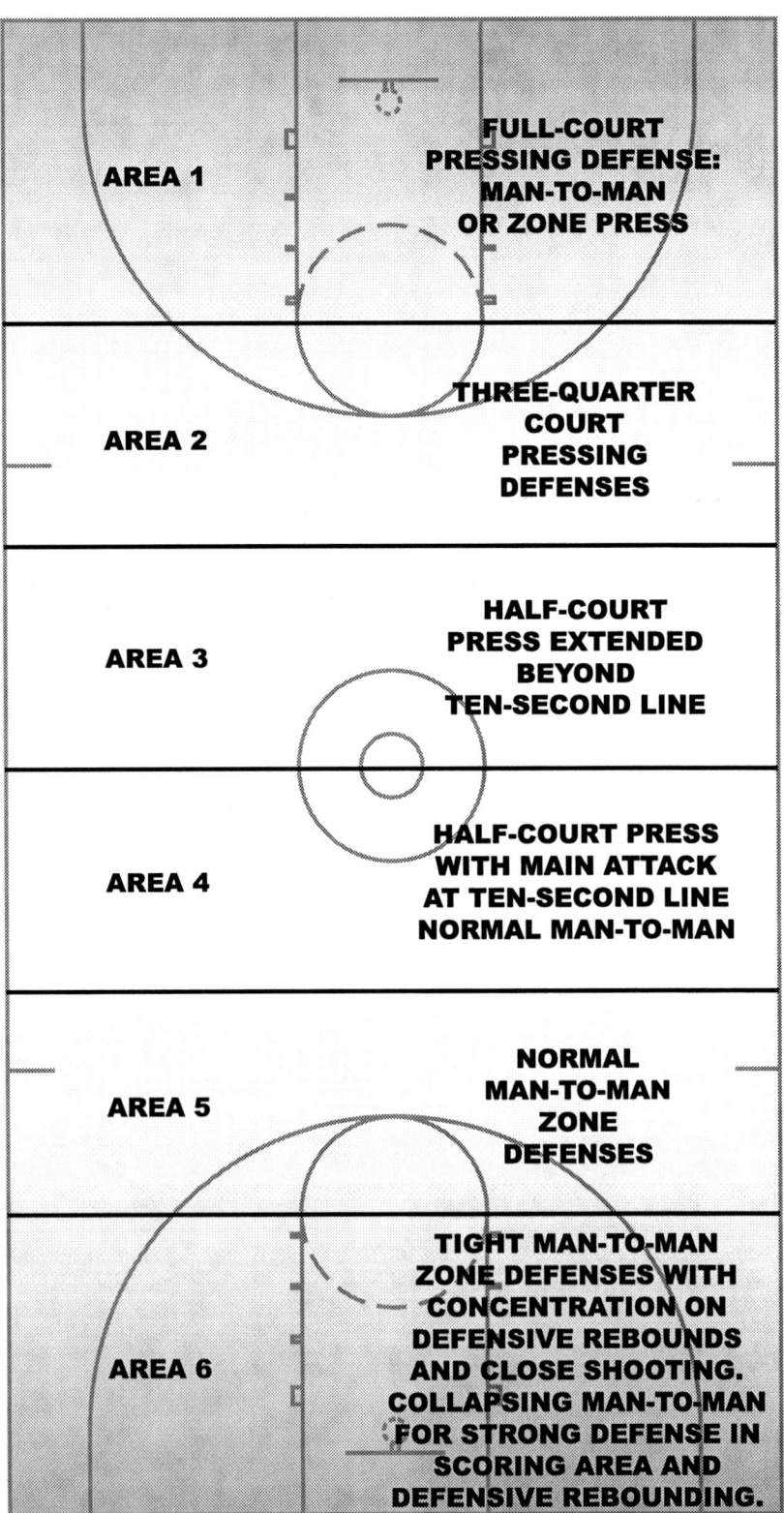

McLendon 1.1

LESSONS FROM THIS LEGEND...

the disadvantage of a poor alignment of personnel for the three-lane idea. It is more difficult to teach the fast break from the man-to-man defense than from defenses with a zone principle. However, once the team learns to fill the lanes, after having established certain responsibilities, it becomes a dangerous threat from areas 4, 5, 6.

6. *Pressing man-to-man.* This defense will do more to gain possession of the ball than the normal man-to-man defense, because it is designed to keep pressure on the offense all over the front-court. It also gives an advantage on the get away, (that down-court, lead step) which makes the fast break go. It is most effective in areas 4, 5, and 6, with particular pressure on the side-line, corners, pivot area, and ten-second line territory.

7. *Zone defense 2-1-2.* Defensive concentration is on areas 5 and 6. Omitting the defensive shortcomings of the 2-1-2 zone, it is the best formation for the fast-break offense. It offers the best position for all assignments, including rebounding and filling the lanes with the desired players, using practically all variations. It offers a strong teaching basis for the assignments and responsibilities of the players and is very good for five-man practice drills. It requires a third lane for most of its success; however, it is one of the best defenses to give a 2-on-1 situation from areas 4 and 5.

8. *Zone defense 2-3.* Defense concentrates on area 6. This defense has most of the good points offensively shown by the 2-1-2 zone, with added strength at the boards.

9. *Zone defense 3-2.* Defense concentration is on areas 4 and 5. The 3-2 zone is very dangerous to any one- or two-out offense, since, when employed, it gives an immediate 3-on-2 fast-break advantage, from which the defense cannot recover. It offers the greatest automatic advantage from the area farthest from the goal and in an area where defensive recovery is usually otherwise possible. It suffers, however, in its inability to defense area 6 and in its two-man rebound responsibility.

10. *Zone defense 1-3-1.* Defensive concentration is on areas 5 and 6. The main purpose of the 1-3-1 defense is not an offensive one. Other zone defenses could just as well be named zone offenses. The possibilities of using the 1-3-1 with the fast break are not as good as with other defenses. With emphasis on stopping the pivot man and the side-court shooter and being perfectly aligned for mass rebounding, the 1-3-1 is not readily adaptable to the fast break because its area of defensive concentration requires a fast-break, involving four to five players moving from the area of the best recovery (area 6) for the most defensive players.

11. *Other zones.* Defensive concentration is usually on area 6. Although most added zones have some fast-break opportunities to consider, their defensive value cannot usually give them a good offensive advantage.

12. *Combination man-to-man and zone defenses.* Defensive concentration is usually assigned. The value of combination defenses to fast-break success is related to how much defensive pressure can be applied to the various areas. Naturally, the defense which uses double-teaming and triple-teaming tactics in areas 3, 4, and 5 will prove most helpful to fast-break objectives.

SOURCE

McLendon, John B. Jr. (1965). *Fast Break Basketball: Fundamentals and Fine Points.* West Nyack, NY: Parker Publishing.

LEGACY OF
Raymond "Ray" Meyer

- Coached at DePaul for 42 years and compiled a record of 724-354.

- Directed the Blue Demons to 21 postseason tournament appearances.

- Led DePaul to two Final Four appearances (1943 and 1979) and one NIT championship (1945).

- Inspirational leader of the highest integrity who gained the respect and affection from players, peers, and media.

- Recognized as a confident, but humble person who spent his entire life helping others.

- Played for future Hall of Fame coach George Keogan at Notre Dame and led the Fighting Irish to the 1936 mythical national championship.

- Led St. Patrick's Academy of Chicago to the National Catholic High School championship in 1932.

RAYMOND "RAY" MEYER

"Individual defense is combat—it is head-to-head, hand-to-hand, and foot-to-foot."
—Ray Meyer

BIOGRAPHY

Born: December 18, 1913 in Chicago, IL

Inducted into Naismith Basketball Hall of Fame in 1979

Raymond "Ray" Meyer was raised on the west side of Chicago, competing in basketball, baseball, football, softball, and wrestling. He was a prep star at St. Patrick's Academy and led the basketball team to the National Catholic High School Championship in 1932. Meyer attended Notre Dame and played for future Hall of Fame coach George Keogan. The Fighting Irish won the mythical national championship in 1936. Meyer entered the coaching profession in 1940 as an assistant at Notre Dame under Keogan. He then accepted the position at DePaul and built the Blue Demons into a national power. Meyer became a coaching institution in his native Chicago, and his DePaul teams compiled a 724-354 record during his 42-year career. He directed DePaul to 21 postseason appearances (13 NCAA and 8 NIT) and 37 winning seasons. Two of his teams reached the Final Four (1943 and 1979), and his 1945 squad captured the NIT championship, the school's only postseason title. Meyer earned National Coach of the Year honors four times. He has been elected into the DePaul and Illinois Halls of Fame. Meyer was enshrined into the Naismith Memorial Basketball Hall of Fame in 1979.

...SCOUTING REPORT.....SCOUTING REPORT.....

Raymond "Ray" Meyer...

Meyer did it all as a player and coach. Starting as a prep player on the west side of Chicago, he became a multi-sport star and, as a high school junior, led St. Patrick's Academy to the 1932 National Catholic High School Championship. Following high school graduation, Meyer enrolled at nearby Northwestern University, with the intent to play football and basketball. That lasted one day. Two days later, he was on his way to Notre Dame to answer a "Moose" call. Future Hall of Famer "Moose" Krause called Meyer and strongly urged him to attend Notre Dame. Meyer again planned to play both sports, until he met basketball coach George Keogan, who told him that the only two games Meyer would play under the Golden Dome were basketball and books.

Meyer was an important cog the next four years for Keogan's Irish teams, going 62-8-1. That's right, during Meyer's sophomore season, Notre Dame tied with future Hall of Fame coach Dutch Lonborg's Northwestern team, one of the few recorded ties in basketball. After the game at Northwestern on December 31, 1935 that ended with a Notre Dame 19-20 loss, an error was discovered in the official scorebook. The scorers had missed recording a made free throw by a Notre Dame player by the name of Ray Meyer—thus a 20-20 tie. Since most players had left, Lonborg and Keogan agreed to the tie. Notre Dame went on to gain the mythical Helms Foundation national title that season (1936). Meyer was elected captain his final two years—becoming known for his leadership, two-hand set shot, and rugged defense.

Ray Meyer, with a degree in sociology, went back to Chicago as a social worker from 1938-40, when he was summoned back to a two-year stint as Keogan's assistant coach. He turned down an offer to coach at Joliet Catholic High School to return to Notre Dame. During his second season, Meyer agreed with Keogan that a tall player from Joliet was just "too awkward" to play big-time basketball at Notre Dame. In 1943, Ray Meyer was named the head basketball coach at Chicago's DePaul University, only to inherit the same player who was not good enough for the big-time. That player was George Mikan, who developed under Meyer to become an All-American and went on to a pro-career with the first professional dynasty—champion Minneapolis Lakers. Mikan was later selected as the best player in the first 50 years of basketball.

In Meyer's 42 years at DePaul, the program rose from the ashes to become a national power and a renowned university. Entering his 42nd year, Meyer was America's winningest active major college coach. He compiled a 724-354 record, as he guided the Blue Demons to 21 postseason appearances (13 NCAA, 8 NIT), with 37 winning seasons (12 with twenty wins or more). Two of his teams (1943 and 1979) reached the Final Four, and his 1945 team captured the NIT title, the school's only postseason title. Ray Meyer was recognized with four National Coach of the Year honors. He also coached the College All-Star's against the Harlem Globetrotters for 11 years in an annual coast-to-coast tour.

.....SCOUTING REPORT.....SCOUTING REPORT...

Coach Meyer was long recognized as a master of the sport, the consummate teacher. In 1967, he wrote, *Basketball as Coached by Ray Meyer*, which is considered an encyclopedia of basketball. Richard "Digger" Phelps, former coach at Notre Dame, called Meyer, "the Godfather of basketball." Meyer became Chicago's best ambassador during his coaching career.

George Mikan said of Coach Meyer—"Ray Meyer is one of the most noble gentleman I have ever known. He is one of the most successful basketball coaches ever. Mr. Meyer fuses these qualities in a bright focus, as one of the truly gifted teachers of the game. He has developed great players, and great teams with his insights and his ingenuity. He molded his teams with his system. There is a tone, a pulse, a color in Ray Meyer's game of basketball. His players have caught the rhythm in the integrity of his personal life." (George Meyer, 1967)

"The greatest satisfaction I got in coaching was in talking to the players, one-on-one, and getting to know them so I'd know how we could help each other. I've been so pleased with the relationship I've enjoyed with so many of these men after they've left school. I've always asked players what ambitions they had in life. With George Mikan it was law; but unfortunately today, most players want to be pro basketball players. It's wonderful to have that dream of being a professional player, but very few achieve it. You tell them they'd better concentrate on their education and develop secondary goals that provide occupation opportunities they can fall back on when the ball stops bouncing for them." (Meyer, 1987)

When asked what advice he would give to young coaches today, Meyer (2003) responded with these recommendations:
1. Be passionate about the game of basketball.
2. Be patient with players.
3. Teach the fundamentals.

Meyer (2003) went on to say, "Today, young players practice what they do well. They don't practice what they don't do well. A coach must be an excellent teacher and motivate players to work on their weaknesses."

"One truth that dawns on you after years of coaching is that winning and losing aren't nearly as important to the players as they are to the coach. It's the coach's livelihood. If he doesn't win enough games, he'll be fired. The player wants to win, but it's not as important to him. He knows his life will go on, whether we win or lose. But, the interesting thing for me as I reflect on my career is the game that seemed all-important at the time is not really that important. I now have a better sense of values. When I started in the coaching profession, I'd walk the streets all night after a loss. I couldn't eat or sleep. As the years went by, I came to realize losing is as much a part of coaching as winning. The game is a slice of life. There is good in every experience, if you learn from it. There were more wins than losses in my career, but you don't measure even a basketball coach's life that way. The good Lord blessed me with more laughs than heartaches, more cheers than boos, a legion of friends, and memories that will entertain me as long as my mind can rerun them." (Meyer, 1987)

Meyer, as a coach, was a man of many qualities: a leader of young men, a kind man with time for charity, a winner in the game of life. But, what set apart the man who came to DePaul in 1942 and spent 42 years coaching there and a lifetime in or near the Windy City? The most important quality is that he was a man of integrity. He was a being complete, a man at peace with himself—a confident, but humble, personality. He has always been forthright, even being said to be too honest. He "told it like it was." And through it all, Meyer always said, "I love to work with youngsters." Ray Meyer demonstrated this passion every day of his coaching career.

SOURCE

Meyer, Ray. Vertical Files, Archives. Naismith Memorial Basketball Hall of Fame. Springfield, MA.

Meyer, Ray. (1987) *Coach*. Chicago: Contemporary Books.

Meyer, Ray. Interview with Ralph Pim. September 5, 2003.

LESSONS FROM THIS LEGEND...

PRINCIPLES OF MAN-TO-MAN DEFENSE

By Ray Meyer

PSYCHOLOGICAL REQUIREMENTS

Individual defense is combat. It is head-to-head, hand-to-hand and foot-to-foot. One must have determination to be a good defensive player. This is a state of mental and physical toughness that can only be developed through intense, all-out effort of every minute of every practice and game. It is a quality that enables you to think and feel you can stop your opponent, even after he has scored on you two or three times.

The good defender must establish a defensive attitude within himself. Defense, more than any other factor, wins games. He must set goals for himself to keep his opponent under his average. Each defender is challenged by being assigned an opponent to stop. Motivation is automatically supplied, if the player is a competitor.

You cannot play good defense without being aggressive. Aggressiveness is characterized by a strong will to dominate your opponent. It is reflected in constant attack and harassment, in denying your man's cutting lanes and passes, and in contesting every dribble, every rebound, and every shot. When applying unrelenting pressure, an aggressive player takes chances and risks in his play. He will take the charge, dive on the floor when necessary, and feel that every free ball is his. He does all the little things that are meaningful, but never appear in the box score.

PHYSICAL REQUIREMENTS

Conditioning is a primary requisite to playing good defense. A player may have great desire and aggressiveness, but it will mean very little if he is in such poor condition that he exhausts himself after several minutes of intense effort. This either reduces his efficiency over long periods of time or results in spending time on the bench. There is no easy road to conditioning. The type of physical and mental toughness necessary in sustaining an intense effort over 40 minutes is acquired only through hours of punishing work.

Pride is an essential in good defense. This is the overall result of determination, aggressiveness, and conditioning. The defender must feel joy or pain, depending on how he handles his opponent. Pride spreads among the individuals and infects the entire team. It is something the players literally can feel. It is shared happiness, thrill, and satisfaction of an all-out individual effort. Pride is never felt by a poorly disciplined individual who plays carelessly without the desire and determination.

POSITION

Defense is played from the hips. Therefore, the defender's body position and stance are very important. He must maintain a staggered boxer's stance, with his strong foot slightly forward (usually the left foot for right handers), and the feet should be about shoulder-width apart.

It should be the widest stance possible, with good balance and mobility. The weight should be evenly distributed over the feet. The defender's head and chest should be up, and his back slightly arched. The knees are flexed, and the tail down, the bending comes from the knees and not from the waist. The hands are held chest high, with palms up. He must keep constant pressure on the ball, with the hand on the side of his front foot. He can't reach with his rear hand, as this will throw him off balance. His body position is between his man and basket. Stance depends a great deal on the individual, for natural ability compensates for errors.

FOOTWORK

In regards to footwork, there are three steps: the retreat, lateral, and advance steps. In the retreat step, the pressure is on the toes of the front foot, and the man pushes the front foot into the floor and shoves off. Simultaneously, he moves the rear foot back, and then he slides the front foot back as far as he moved the rear foot. He can't lift his feet, he slides.

In using the lateral step, the defensive man pushes off the opposite foot in the direction he is going and swings the elbow in the direction of his lead foot. This provides more impetus for the body. In the lateral step, he shuffles and never crosses his legs. Also, the feet shouldn't come together. If they do, it is difficult to change direction.

In the advance step, the defender pushes off the back foot and slides the front foot forward. The knees should be extremely flexed in order to spring forward. The hand corresponding to the lead foot is brought up, and the other hand is held low, anticipating a drive or pass. In advancing, he must be ready to retreat if necessary.

PLAYING MAN WITH BALL

When his opponent has the ball, the defensive man has full command of the fundamentals and employs them in personal strategy to neutralize and eliminate certain moves of the offensive player. Play the man with the ball as tight as possible. If he is a great shooter, the defender must play up on him to pressure the man with the ball. He

LESSONS FROM THIS LEGEND...

can't give the shooter an unmolested shot. If the offensive man is a good driver or cutter, the defender has to give him more room.

The defender not only has the responsibility of keeping his man from scoring, but also keeping his man from throwing a pass that will lead to a basket. He must put pressure on the ball. Play the ballhandler's front foot half-a-man, and you will probably be playing his shooting shoulder also. Thus, you will be making him pass around you or across his body. If he is in front of the basket, overplay to the inside, and if he is on side court, overplay the outside.

POST DEFENSE

In playing post defense, the defender must deny position and the ball; he cannot give both. If the post man is up high on the free-throw line with his back to the basket, the defender is directly between him and the basket, about two-feet back. When the post man turns, the defender closes up and forces him away from the basket. This is his first move, and he must attempt to keep the offensive man from making a direct pass for a score.

Another reason the defender gives him room is that his teammates may pass in between to pickup cutters. Also, when the defender is giving him room, he is in a better position to see cutters and to help out when the ball is passed. If the post man gets the ball in low or close to the basket, the defender takes his position directly behind him. He doesn't lean on him so the defensive man knows where to go. He makes the man with the ball look for him.

If the defender is leaning on the post man, he can't jump to force or block his shot. The defender plays only the ball and no fakes. If he doesn't see the ball, he doesn't react.

In guarding the post man, the defender must keep this rule in mind: "never give a man position and the ball." When he is close to the basket, the defender must not stand behind him and let the ball come in. If the post man is up high to the free-throw line or to the side of the key, the defender comes up a quarter-man on the side the ball is on. The hand nearer the ball should be extended to deflect passes. When the post man moves down the lane, midway between the basket and free-throw line, the defender plays up the ballside, about a half-a-man.

Whenever the post man takes a position close to or under the basket, the defensive man must come up to three-quarters of a man. If the ball is swung to the front or weakside, it will be difficult to go behind the post man to deny the ball. Therefore, the defender will have to gamble and circle in front of him to keep the ball from getting in. When he circles, he circles to the ballside and then plays his three-quarters-of-a-man defense.

The defender can only front a man when he is getting good weakside help. When he fronts, he shouldn't stand still and let the offense get the opportunity to lob over him. If the defender moves from the front to the ballside and back and forth, it is very difficult for the offense to time his movement and lob the ball. I have always found it most difficult to get the ball into the post when the defensive man is very active.

MAKE HIM GO YOUR WAY

The defensive man should make the offensive player go the way he wants him to go... force him to the strongside, to the rear leg.

The move of retreat with the drive or cut can be made best in that direction. He can do this best by overplaying to the side of his forward foot. Thus, the defender eliminates one choice for the offensive man, and he can expect to move toward his strongside or rear foot. He must be prepared to ride the offensive player away from the basket once the initial move has been made. The defender is going to be beaten occasionally.

In practice, you have to work on recoveries and traps so that they work to the defense's advantage. The defender must remember that preventing a drive to the basket is his most important job, since the offensive man has a better chance of scoring close to the basket than he has from 20 feet. He must always be ready to prevent the drive. It is very satisfying for the defender to see his man try several fakes and give up the ball.

HANDS AND ARMS

The hands and arms should be kept moving in order to tip or deflect passes and to cut down on passing lanes. The movement of the hands and arms will assist in leg movement and also aid body balance. In guarding a man out of the scoring area, the arms are extended outward, with the palms up. The tail should be down and ready to move. In guarding a man in scoring range, the defender raises the same hand as the front foot, and other hand is at his waist.

He moves straight in and waves the lead hand in the offensive man's eyes to distract him. Make it tough for him to score, but don't foul him, especially, if he is taking a long, outside shot. The defender should look at his man's midsection. He can fake with his legs, shoulders, and head, but he can't move without moving his midsection.

When a player picks up his dribble, the defender closes in, waving his hands and arms in an attempt to pressure him into turning away from the basket. The hands and arms should be thrust with the movement of the defender. Concentrate on the ball, and attempt to tip each pass with proper arm motion. If the defender can't deflect the pass, make him hurry it or cause a turnover.

ONE PASS AWAY

In guarding a player one pass from the ball, try to maintain a position of "midpoint" vision in which you can point to the ball and see your man at the same time. If you can't maintain a "midpoint" vision, give up the ball, and concentrate on your man. When guarding a man one-pass removed from the ball (other than the post man), maintain a flat-triangle relationship of ball

LESSONS FROM THIS LEGEND...

and man, He must be one step off the passing lane to his man and approximately one-third of the distance from his man in relation to his distance from the ball.

With the ball in the back-court, the defender plays one step off of the passing lane from the ball to his man, and he must play closer to the ball.

At half-court, the guard varies with his defensive position when not guarding the ball. If his team is pressing, the defender who is one pass away from the ball will have his hand nearer the ball extended and will only be one step off the passing lane and one or two steps closer to the ball than his man. He should not be directly in the lane, because he wants the lane to appear to be open and set up his steal. If his team isn't pressing, the guard would open his body toward the ball. He would have an arm point toward his man and the other arm in toward the post area.

If the ball is passed behind him, he must retreat to the line of the ball and be aware of the passing lanes.

GUARDING THE WING

In guarding a man on the wing or corner areas, the defender plays a close, almost fronting position. If the man moves into the post area, the defender applies the post principles for defense. Thus, a defender would be in a fronting position in the area from the goal to 10-feet away, but from that point to about 20-to-22 feet from the basket, the defender plays only his hand ahead of his man. The hand nearer the ball should be right in the passing lane, and the body a step closer to the ball than the offensive man is. His other arm will extend out to act as a feeler to let him know if the offensive man reverses, in case he has lost sight of him. If the man backdoors toward the basket, the defender turns right into him (facing him) and brings his lead arm around in front to prevent the offensive man from getting a return pass. Once the offensive man has moved out of normal scoring range (20 feet or so), the defender will drop off the passing lane, unless he is trying to shut off his man entirely from the ball.

When the offensive forward does receive the ball, the defender goes right to him in an effort to prevent him from doing anything positive with the ball. He tries to prevent any open shot or inside pass. If he drives, the defender overplays the outside to make him go over the middle, where the team defense can pick him up.

TWO PASSES AWAY

In guarding a man two passes from the ball, the defender must be aware that he is in the defensive game. He cannot relax; he must obtain a position to help his mates. This is the sign of a good defender.

When defending a man in the guard area, the defender must open up toward the ball and sag into the free-throw lane to help plug the middle. He should maintain visual contact with both the ball and his man, if possible. If a choice becomes necessary, he will watch his man and then pick up the sight of the ball when he can. Seeing both the man and the ball can only be accomplished by dropping back and opening up, so as to be able to look approximately halfway between the man and the ball to see both by peripheral vision.

In defending a man two passes away in the forward area, the defender has to open up toward the ball and move toward the free-throw lane. He should sag as far in toward the basket as possible. By standing with the body only one step off the passing lane, he can still get in front of his man if he cuts to the ball. The defender must open toward the ball with his hand nearer the point aiming at the ball, while the other hand points toward his man. The defender should able to steal, deflect, or take the charge on any lob passes to the post man. He must be ready and willing to get in front of any drive to the basket, especially the other forward's man who may drive the baseline. He must defend any cut his own man may make to the ball or basket. If the defender is in proper man-ball relationship, there can be no excuse for his man coming to get the ball from a diagonal forward position. On all cross-court passes to his man, the defender must close out hard and fast, as he should arrive simultaneously with the ball. He should run the first half of the distance, then shuffle the final two or three steps closing out slightly on the baseline side. The defender must be prepared to help and recover and, whenever necessary, he has to pick up the free man, stop him, and get back on his own man.

DEFENDING THE SHOOTER

In defending against the shooter, the defender must meet the challenge to stop his opponent. As soon as his man gets the ball, he must close up and prevent him from getting an unmolested shot. He plays him as tight as he can and forces him to put the ball to the floor in the direction he can get help. There must be enough pressure on the offensive man that he can't do whatever he wants.

DEFENDING THE DRIVER

When defending either the driver or the dribbler in the front-court, the defender tries to turn the offense toward the sideline and out of the middle. Basically, it is always good policy to force a driver or dribbler out of the middle. Once a defender is out of position, he should run as fast as he can to regain a good defensive, frontal position on his man. In order to do this, he must run toward the basket ahead of the dribbler where he can cut him off, rather than run alongside him. If someone else picks up his man before he can recover, he will either take that man's opponent or trap, whatever the situation calls for.

In playing the dribbler, the defender must slide and retreat in the same direction with his opponent. He can't cross his feet; he shuffles. While sliding, he plays the ball with his hand closer to the ball—palm up—and he uses his wrist and fingers in an inward movement. He just taps the ball against the dribbler's knees and lets him kick it.

LESSONS FROM THIS LEGEND...

The defender gives the dribbler a little room and forces him to go away from the basket, where he can get help. The defender must be prepared to retreat and protect against penetration. If he is in front of the basket, force him wide, and if he is on the side, force him to the middle.

The defender must play good position defense and be prepared to take a charge. Remember, if the offensive man moves with his head up, he is dangerous as a passer. If his head is down, he is the only threat.

Defending The Passer
When a defender has a passer as his opponent, he wants him to get rid of the ball, but doesn't want him to feel free and confident to make scoring passes. The defender must pressure the ball by closing in on him, with both hands high and moving, especially if he has lost his dribble. Even if a player still has his dribble but is in a particular offense where he is strictly a feeder, the defender crowds right up to him, with both arms up to force him to do something else. The goal is to tip or deflect his pass, but never let him throw without contesting each pass. When the passer does release the ball, the defender jumps back in the direction of the pass on all penetrating passes, looking for a pick or cut.

The man who just passed the ball can be very dangerous in most offenses. The important thing to remember is as soon as a pass is made, the defender jumps back. He must step back and never let his opponent walk into him and break away. The offensive man knows where he is going, and the defensive man reacts. Also, it is more difficult for the offensive man to run his man into picks when there is distance between them. After the offensive man releases the ball, the defender retreats in the direction of the pass, keeping between the ball and his man. He anticipates any cut or screen. If the ball were passed over or behind him, the defender drops back, until he is nearly at the ball and his man. This will allow him to help plug up the middle and also help keep him from being an easy victim to cuts and screens.

Defending The Cutter
In defense against a cutter, the defender takes a position between his man and the basket, only one-step off his direct path to the ball. The defender must be in a position so that he can be in front of any good cut to the ball or to the basket.

In cases where the offensive player is two passes from the ball, the defender should be several steps closer to the ball than he is to his man. He delays the timing of every cutter by being in front and on the ballside. He accomplishes this by sliding over one or two steps as the cutter breaks; then, the defender will hand-check him by placing his hands on the cutter's waist all-the-while trying to stay in front.

Defending The Screen
In guarding against the screen, the man guarding the screener must inform the man likely to be screened of the possible screen as early as possible. The defender should always be anticipating screens by looking and having the hand nearer the direction of his movement out as a feeler, in case his teammate fails to warn him. In general, the switch is made on all screens in the scoring area. The switches may vary with different teams to cover other screens and crosses. With a team that has balanced height, the defense will do a lot of switching. Where there are distinct height variations, the defense will cut down on the number of switches, the rules must fit the team, and the drills must fit the rules. The defender should try to avoid getting screened by playing over the top of the screen. The best way to accomplish this is to throw the leading leg and the hips forward toward his man as he nears the screener.

This will prevent the hips getting hit by the screener and will allow the defender to slide right over the screen unless it is perfectly set. If the defender does get screened in the scoring area, a switch should be made. The defender on the screener must anticipate the switch by being tight on his man and leaning in the direction of the cut, so as to be able to jump in front quickly. The defender on the screener only switches if his man passes the ball. The rule is don't switch off the man with the ball, for he is the only one who can score.

In practicing making the switch, the defender on the screener warns the man being screened by yelling, "left" or "right." Properly warned, the man being screened moves a half-step in the direction of the call, and in this way, he has a good chance of avoiding the screen by going over the top. If the screen is made and a switch is necessary, the defender must jump switch to the ballhandler's outside shoulder. He comes at him high, forcing him to bounce pass or come back and pass across his body. By switching aggressively and forcing a low pass, the defender gives his teammate a chance to come between the screener and the ball, and go for the low pass. If the man guarding the screener doesn't switch aggressively and high, the ball may be lobbed over a smaller defender's head and result may be an easy score. Also while switching, the defender who is two passes away from the ball should be in a ready-help position to deflect the pass or take a charge.

Offense Has Advantage
The offensive man in basketball has a distinct advantage over the defense, for he knows what he wants to do, and the defense must react. The defender must realize this disadvantage and play accordingly.

The defender reacts to all foot fakes toward the basket, in order to maintain proper position ahead of his man and the ball. When the defender reacts to his man's fake toward the basket and then the offensive man pulls his foot back, the defender adjusts his foot position by not picking up his back foot to close on the ballhandler. He moves the forward foot first and slides up, so as not to be caught off balance. If the offensive man fakes forward and pulls his weight back but leaves his foot advanced, the defender shifts his weight a little forward but doesn't move his feet. He

LESSONS FROM THIS LEGEND...

must be prepared to retreat, and he can do this easily, for he has shifted his weight forward, and he can push off the forward foot.

In reacting to lateral foot fakes, the defender moves but doesn't match the ballhandler step-for-step. He reacts halfway, and he must distribute his weight evenly on his feet, so he can go in either direction. He can't overstride in lateral fakes, or he will be caught on cross-over moves. In reacting to all foot fakes, the defender retreats to prevent a drive or cut to the basket.

THE PRESSING DEFENSE

Pressing defenses are good to speed up the tempo of the game. You can use a press if an opponent wants to play slowly against you, and also late in the game, if you're behind. If you cannot press, there's no way you're ever going to catch up if you fall behind late in the game.

A good team should have both a zone and man-to-man press. Quickness and anticipation are the key ingredients in a successful press. Basketball is a game of mistakes, and if you put pressure on the ball, your opponent will make more mistakes. You can expect a forceful man-to-man defense to create more turnovers than a zone defense.

A press is great as a change of pace during a game. In a man-to-man press, a team puts pressure on the ball being inbounded. They let the ball come in when using a zone press, then trap the man who receives it.

SOURCE

Meyer, Ray. (1967). *Basketball as Coached by Ray Meyer.* Englewood Cliff, NJ: Parker Publishing.

LESSONS FROM THIS LEGEND...

OFFSIDE HELP AND RECOVER DRILL

By Ray Meyer

Our defense is built on the principle of stopping ball penetration. It is essential that our players become proficient at helping and recovering. To assist our players in this concept, we designed a drill that we call the Offside Help and Recover Drill. The drill consists of four offensive players and two defenders.

The initial alignment is shown in **Diagram 2.0**. The coach has the ball on the wing, and O3 is standing out-of-bounds. X1 and X2 are in the help position and see both their offensive player and the ball. The drill begins with O2 breaking across the lane. X2 must deny the flash cut.

The following events occur after O2's flash cut: (See **Diagram 2.1**)
1. The coach passes to O4.
2. When O4 catches the ball, O3 steps onto the court.
3. If possible, O4 drives to the basket.
4. X2 stops O4's dribble penetration and recovers to O2.
5. X1 drops down to cut off the pass to O3.
6. If the ball is passed back to the coach, the coach can lob it to O3.
7. X2 must turn and prevent the lob pass to O3.
8. The coach may pass back to O4, and the drill continues until O4 or O3 gets a shot.

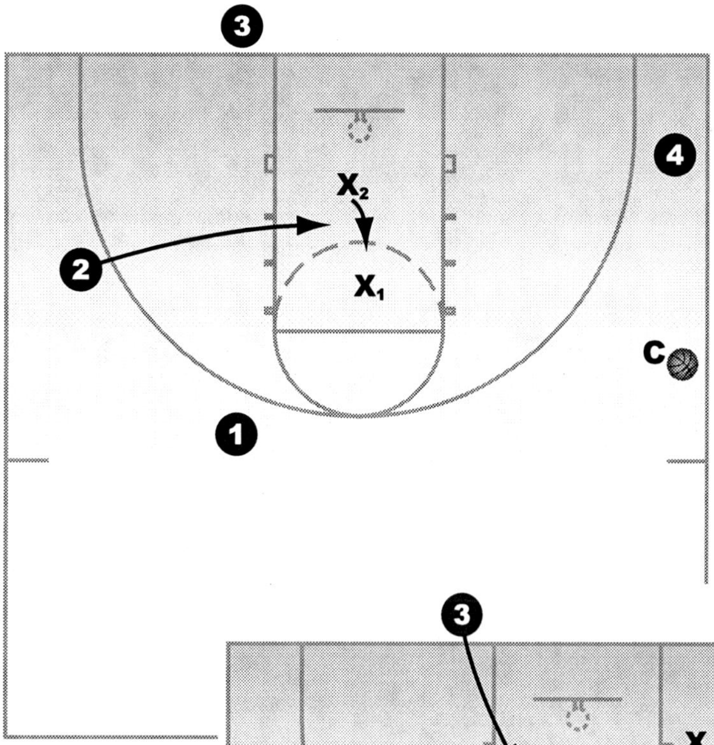

Meyer 2.0

Meyer 2.1

Source

Meyer, Ray (1980) Offside Help and Recover Drill. In *Championship Drills for Basketball (Vol. IV)*. Lake Mills, IA: Graphic Publishing.

LEGACY OF
Ralph "Cappy" Miller

- Played for "Phog" Allen and studied under Dr. James Naismith at the University of Kansas.

- Coached 38 years on the collegiate level and retired as the eighth winningest coach in Division I history.

- Honored twice as Coach of the Year in three major conferences.

- Emphasized pressure defense and an up-tempo offense.

- Considered himself a teacher, first and foremost.

- Believed simplicity and execution were the keys to success.

- Introduced the zone press at Wichita East High School (KS) in 1948.

- Namesake of the Ralph Miller Court at Oregon State University.

RALPH "CAPPY" MILLER

"Games are won or lost on defense and by taking care of the ball. Teach players how not to give the game away."
—Ralph Miller

BIOGRAPHY

Born: March 9, 1919 in Chanute, KS

Died: May 15, 2001

Inducted into the Naismith Basketball Hall of Fame in 1988

Ralph Miller was a legendary player (11 letters) in football, basketball, track, golf and tennis at Chanute (KS) H.S., where he graduated in 1937. He went to Kansas University (1938-41), where he starred in football and played for future Hall of Fame coach Phog Allen. Miller was on the 1940 team that went to the NCAA Finals. He also was a student under Dr. James Naismith in the physical education department at Kansas. Miller led KU in scoring two years and was team captain in 1942. He began his coaching career in 1948 at Wichita East High School (KS). His teams were 63-17 and won the state championship in 1951. Miller is only one of a select few to be honored twice as Coach of the Year in three major conferences—Missouri Valley, Big 10, and PAC 10 Conferences. He coached 38 years on the Division I level. Miller led Wichita State (1951-64) to a 220-133 record and a conference championship. He then went to Iowa (1964-70), where he compiled a 95-51 record and captured the 1970 Big 10 title. Miller's next stop was at Oregon State University (1970-89), where his record was 298-156. Oregon State won three consecutive titles, and Miller was named National Coach of the Year twice. Throughout Miller's career, his teams participated in 14 postseason tournaments (9 NCAA's and 5 NIT's). The playing court at Oregon State is named the Ralph Miller Court. Miller was enshrined in the Naismith Memorial Basketball Hall of Fame in 1988.

...SCOUTING REPORT.....SCOUTING REPORT.....

Ralph "Cappy" Miller...

Ralph "Cappy" Miller's roots ran deep in Chanute, Kansas—his grandfather was a railroad engineer there; his dad, Harold was the high school principal, and his mother played on a state championship Chanute team herself.

He received the nickname "Cappy" from his dad, who had played the role of "Cappy" in a high school play. Ralph eventually blessed one of his sons with that same name.

Ralph wasn't forced into anything, but the opportunities were there. He played the violin and baritone saxophone, as well as sports. At age six, he began golf, and, when his dad went ahead to hit his second shot before Ralph teed off, Ralph plunked him in the back of the head. His dad thought he couldn't hit the ball that far. This was early notice that Ralph would become a great athlete himself.

"Cappy" was captain, all-conference and all-state three years in basketball, all-state in football three years (played four years), four years in track (set the state low hurdle record), and also spent one year in golf and tennis. He won 11 letters in high school, as he became one of the best athletes ever in Kansas, growing up in Chanute, a small farming community in the southeast part of the state. Naturally, he went to Kansas University for college (even though he was recruited by 70 colleges), where he played under future Hall of Fame Coach Forrest "Phog" Allen, one of the most innovative pioneers in the game. Allen's book, *The Basketball Bible*, included almost all aspects of basketball, from strategy to fundamentals. In addition, Miller was exposed directly to the teachings of Dr. James Naismith, the inventor of basketball. This good fortune and timing led Miller to become the last coach in history to have direct ties to both Naismith and Allen. What a coaching foundation! Ralph also found time to quarterback the football team. He had a modicum of success there as well as scoring five touchdowns in one game and garnering all-conference honors in both sports. His 1940 Kansas basketball team lost the national title game to Indiana, his first year of competition as a sophomore. Kansas utilized pressure defenses in 1941 and 1942 to continue Allen's successes in basketball.

Miller considered the 1930s as the Golden Era of basketball. The following significant events occurred during this decade:

1. The center jump was eliminated after a made basket.
2. The 10-second rule was established to stop teams from stalling.
3. Basketball became an international game.
4. The jump shot was introduced.
5. The 2-2-1 zone press was developed. (Coach Miller used the 2-2-1 zone press at Wichita East High School and credits Gene Johnson for teaching him this form of pressure defense.)

Armed with this coaching legacy, Miller still wasn't sure he was going to coach, so he spent three years working and three years serving in the U.S. Air Force. He was then offered a teaching-coaching job at Wichita East H.S. in 1946, and the Hall of Fame coaching journey

began. In three years, his teams compiled a 63-17 record and finished 3rd, 2nd, and 1st in the state (state champions in 1951). There, he first used the 2-2-1 zone press successfully. In 1951, he began a 13-year stay at Wichita State University, where his teams were 220-133, won a conference title, and had four postseason appearances. He went to the University of Iowa in 1964 for a six-year stint in the Big Ten; his teams were 95-51 and were undefeated champions in 1970. Ralph left for Oregon State University in 1970 and finished his career with a 19 year period, coaching the Beavers to four Pac-10 titles, and was honored as National Coach of the Year twice.

.....SCOUTING REPORT.....SCOUTING REPORT...

He was a rarity; achieving Coach of the Year honors in three major conferences. Miller had the charisma of a riverboat gambler and the stage presence of a Barrymore, yet was a devoted family man who only had one other priority—coaching basketball. His stern personality, his relentless chain-smoking of menthol cigarettes, and his fondness for scotch got him tagged with another nickname, "Old Whiskey Sour." Mike Corwin, Associate Athletic Director at OSU, countered by saying of Miller, "all I ever saw of him was a heart of gold." Hall of Fame coach Henry "Hank" Iba said of Miller, "he left every program he coached stronger than when he came to it and provided strong direction and development of character and integrity to countless young men who played for him." He won 657 games during his 38-year collegiate career. The Oregon State Chancellor, William Davis, stated upon Ralph's retirement, "Young people emulate ethical people. That is why they need models of what man at his best might be. Ralph Miller is such a model. Kids need heroes. We all do."

The Miller philosophy, as with most coaches, evolved from his playing and coaching experiences and other contact with the game. Both his father, who was his high school coach, and his junior-high school coach taught him the theory behind the game. He was also the high-school quarterback, who was expected to know the assignments of all 11 players on the team. It helped him grasp the entire concept of the game. He also was fortunate to play college basketball for the legendary Phog Allen at Kansas. He felt the theory, defense, and play patterns hadn't changed since the 1930s, when he was at Kansas.

After gaining coaching experience, he finally came to the hard conclusion that the reason for losing is most often rooted in defense. So he said, "I teach my players how not to give the game away, which is usually with turnovers and on defense." Miller's teams always embodied that philosophy of emphasizing passing, catching, and footwork to reduce turnovers, plus solid pressure defense to create opponent mistakes and prevent easy scores.

Miller earned a reputation for his pressure style of play. He explained his style in these words: "We depend on pressure in our style of play. We use pressure tactics with our offense and defense to eliminate any opportunities for our opponent to rest. Both the offense and defense have to apply pressure to eliminate this rest. This requires instant conversion from offense to defense and vice versa. This is a simple concept to demonstrate. If both teams have the basketball 60 times during a game and neither team used a full-court defense or fast-break offense, at least five seconds would lapse during every exchange of the ball. Multiplication would allow that approximately 10 minutes of every game are available for rest. This is one-quarter of the collegiate game. Our whole premise in our pressure style of play is to eliminate this rest and force our opponent to play for the full 40 minutes in a game." (Miller, 1976)

SOURCE

Miller, Ralph. Vertical Files, Archives. Naismith Memorial Basketball Hall of Fame. Springfield, MA.

Miller, Ralph. (1976) Implementing Pressure Defense. *The Basketball Bulletin.*

LESSONS FROM THIS LEGEND...

PHILOSOPHICAL MUSINGS

By Ralph Miller

Authors' Note: One of the co-authors, Jerry Krause, was fortunate to attend a Miller basketball coaching class at Oregon State in 1982. These beliefs by the coaching philosopher reflect his strong foundation from Naismith-Allen, his clear historical perspective, and his pragmatic philosophy. Miller viewed himself as a teacher first, and always taught a coaching class at the universities where he coached.

His thoughts on teaching and coaching of basketball:

1. Purpose of coaching—teach fundamental skills for competitive purposes.
2. Teach how not to lose; winning will take care of itself.
3. Losing occurs because of mistakes; poor individual and team defense (easy scores), poor defensive rebounding, and turnovers.
4. Players must learn automatic reactions to competitive situations.
5. Coaches must be good teachers; know the subject matter; know what to teach and how to teach it. The mark of a good teacher is the ability to simplify the subject matter for understanding and better comprehension.
6. The #1 fundamental skill is body position and movement (run, stop, pivot).
7. Analyze what the opposition does best and quickest, and then decide how to take advantage of it.
8. Offensive concepts:
   - Attack principles—pass and cut to the basket
   - The pass is a primary weapon (quickest attack).
   - Use mostly air passes for quickness, bounce passes only on a backdoor or in an emergency.
   - When the shot goes up, think defense—you are responsible for the man guarding you (automatic pickup rule).
   - Ballhandler—create a score for a teammate.
   - The jump stop is the most important offensive tool (especially against zones).
9. Pressure defense:
   - Prevent easy scores and gain ball possession.
   - Always see ball.
   - Body position—staggered stance, feet shoulder-width, palms up, unless guarding the shooter.
   - Keep the ball out of the middle.
   - Conserve time and space.
   - Defend with the feet—slide, run when needed, stop, pivot.
   - Every change is initiated with the pivot.
   - No gambles; basketball a percentage game.
10. Teaching tips—basketball is a continuous game:
    - Limit drills; keep them simple; they must fit the system and be competitive; drills are teaching tools
    - Set and require movement goals.
    - All players must do everything.
    - Learn by doing—repetition and use of whole-part.
    - Be patient—give all a chance to learn.
    - Know why you teach what you do.
    - Demonstrate only what you can do well.
    - Criticism must be consistent, constructive, and used for important things.
    - Make changes only to simplify.
11. Be cautious in changing skills:
    - Ages 10-12—guarantee success
    - Ages 13-14—65% success
    - Over 14-35—40% success
12. Eighty percent of possessions from defensive rebounding and made baskets; 20 percent of possessions from opponents' errors, steals, interceptions, etc..
13. A successful program should be interesting and enjoyable for participants and spectators.
14. Conduct a program within the rules, provide equal opportunity, and develop a successful team and individuals (academically, socially, morally).

SOURCE

Krause, Jerry. (1982). Class notes. Corvallis, OR.

LESSONS FROM THIS LEGEND...

A COMPREHENSIVE BASKETBALL DRILL SYSTEM FOR PRESSURE OFFENSE & DEFENSE

By Ralph Miller

The system, developed and used by Ralph Miller of Oregon State University, is a proven method of teaching fundamental skills in an efficient manner. It has been used effectively for over thirty years at many levels of basketball.

RALPH MILLER'S OREGON STATE UNIVERSITY BASKETBALL DRILL SYSTEM

Drills are teaching tools that promote repetition and the theory of learning by doing. Drills develop and improve required skill executions, but unfortunately, they do not always properly integrate skills into the game as a whole. Therefore, in practice, organization drills should be limited in number and duration.

Skill execution during games relies primarily upon conditioned, automatic-reflex responses. It is a coach's responsibility to develop correct reactions. Responses are developed through game experience, scrimmage, and drills. Therefore, most drills should employ actions that closely resemble game conditions whenever possible. Drills and pressure tactics should utilize the entire floor in order to develop appropriate game reactions.

Individual skill executions should be developed to function within the team concept of organization, and this factor should be emphasized at all times, regardless of the number of individuals involved in a particular drill. The rules for team execution must apply to each drill activity to develop automatic-reflex responses.

Our program involves seven drills. Three do not involve competition. Four utilize the full-court, since full-court competitive drills best develop correct team responses and reactions, and as many fundamental acts as possible have been combined in these single drill activities.

Drills should involve approximately 50-to-60 percent of the available time for a practice session during the first two weeks of a season. Subsequently, approximately 25 percent of practice time should be devoted to drills through the remainder of a season. Of the drills used, competitive and full court activity should take 75-to-80 percent of the available drill time. Sample practice sessions explain drill and time-usage during various stages of a season's practice.

PRACTICE SCHEDULES

First Day:
    2:00-2:10 Body position
    2:10-2:20 Set-up drills (2)
    2:20-2:30 Speed drills (2)
    2:30-2:35 Free throws
    2:35-2:50 3-on-3
    2:50-3:05 4-on-4 half court only
    3:05-3:10 Free throws
    3:10-3:30 Fast break (FT Line)
    3:30-3:55 Fast break (missed FG)
    3:55-4:00 Free yhrows

Fifth Day:
    2:00-2:15 Body position
    2:00-2:20 Free throw
    2:20-2:25 Set-up drill (1)
    2:25-2:35 Speed drills (2)
    2:35-2:40 Free throws
    2:40-2:55 3-on-3
    2:55-3:15 4-on-4 (full court)
    3:15-3:20 Free throws
    3:20-4:00 Half-court offense

Tenth Day:
    2:00-2:25 Body position
    2:25-2:30 Free throw
    2:30-2:45 Speed drills (2) (with D)
    2:45-2:50 Free throws
    2:50-3:05 3-on-3
    3:05-3:20 4-on-4 (full-court)
    3:20-4:00 5-on-5 (full-court scrimmage)

Eleventh Day or More:
    2:00-2:15 Body position & set-ups
    2:15-2:30 Speed drills
    2:30-2:35 Free throws
    2:35-2:50 4-on-4 and 3-on-3
    2:50-2:55 Free throws
    2:55-4:00 5-on-5

DRILL DESCRIPTION

Body position and movement is often used for quick warmups throughout the season, because it emphasizes position and foot executions and is an effective conditioner. The correct position and the description for teaching involve the following: place your feet shoulder-width apart with a toe-to-heel stagger, stand straight, take a deep breath and then exhale. As you exhale, your body relaxes and sags, and your knees bend, allowing your buttocks to drop straight to the floor. Your neck, head, and eyes remain straight (level) throughout the drill. Continue the process until your hands rest just above your knees. Raising your arms to waist level with your palms upward completes the stance. Your body and extremities should be relaxed, and your body weight should rest lightly on your front foot.

LESSONS FROM THIS LEGEND...

Pivoting, which is learned from this position, has proven to be the most essential act required for good defensive coverage. Quarter- half- and full spins are executed, and should be practiced until full pivots can be performed without a loss of body balance. A reverse-type of spin is used in defense. In this instance, your front foot moves first and to the rear (See **Diagram 1.0**). Your head, shoulders, and arms remain level during execution, so that your original body position is maintained throughout the action. Pivoting is used in all assignments and phases of defensive coverage.

Miller 1.0

Your remaining footwork includes forward, lateral, and backward (recovery) steps. Lateral and forward moves utilize sliding, toe-to-heel action, so that your feet never cross. These movements can involve running, when necessary, and can cease with a jump shot being taken. Recovery acts originate by pivoting prior to the sliding or running action. This procedure can be utilized in extended periods of drill activity. Continual movement, while maintaining a proper position, begins with five-minute periods and can increase to twenty within ten days. Extended drill periods condition the athlete and prove that good position can be maintained for any length of time.

LESSONS FROM THIS LEGEND...

Two-ball handling and shooting drills for the half-court are simply called "lay-up" and "split-post" drills. The lay-up rarely utilizes defense, but it is included with split-post work. Close supervision promotes good executions and furthers the development of discipline.

The lay-up drill (See **Diagram 1.1**) is a standard two-line operation to improve shooting and ballhandling skills. Lines are formed at the junctions of half-court and the sidelines. The shooter moves at top speed and enters the shooting area at a 45-degree angle from the free-throw line extended. After shooting, the player runs to the rear of the feed line at a relatively high rate of speed. The feeder moves to the free-throw line, executes a pivot, and passes to the shooter. He then rebounds the shot, moves behind the baseline opposite the shooting lane, returns the ball to the next feeder, and goes to the rear of the shooting line, but remains off the floor. Line assignments reverse, so that players can shoot with their opposite hand. Two balls are used in the exercise. Shooting is done after a full-speed runup, the takeoff is outside the free-throw lane, and the leap is to the top of the square painted above the basket. Feeders should execute the pivot whenever possible, and passes should be crisp—never lobbed or bounced. The shooter presents a passing target with both hands at chest level, and his eyes should remain on the ball until it is secured.

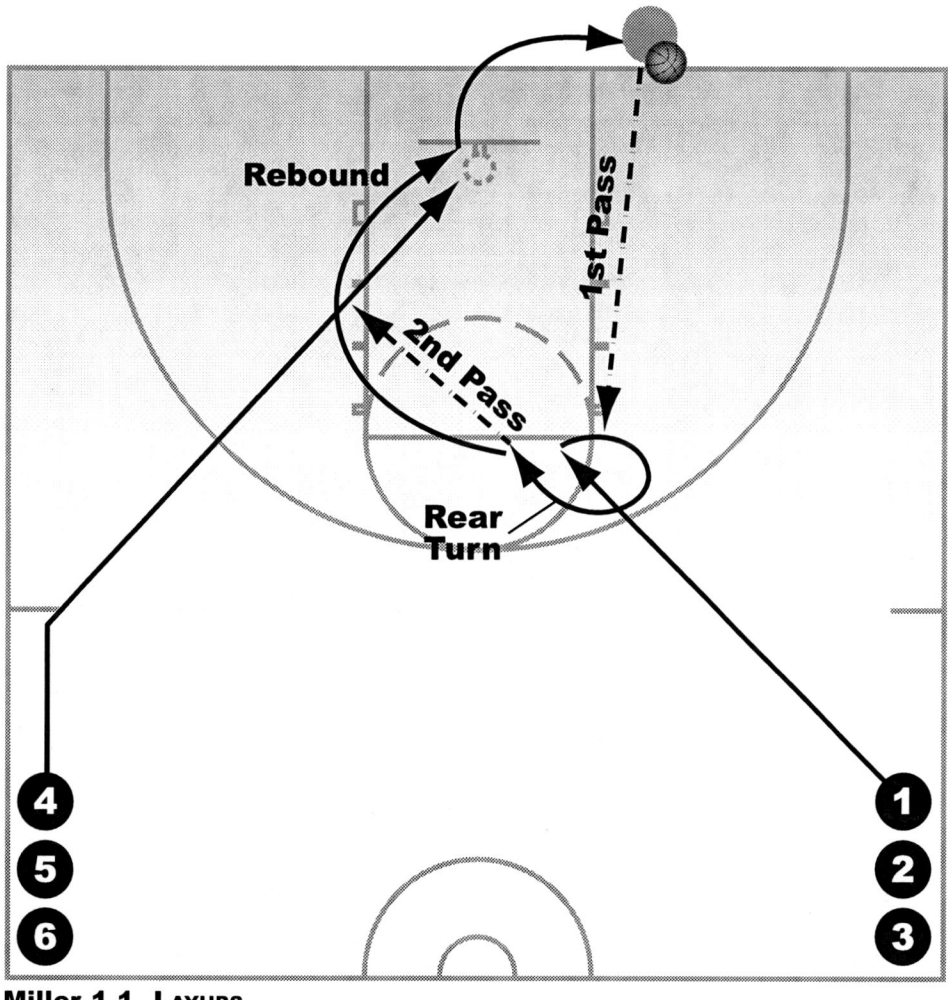

Miller 1.1 LAYUPS

LESSONS FROM THIS LEGEND...

The split-post drill (See **Diagram 1.2**) utilizes three lines, two located at each junction of half-court and a sideline. The post men form out of bounds and outside the lane. In post play, increased passing, new shooting angles, jump shots, pass-offs, and high feeds are integral skills. A guard-to-guard pass starts the sequence. The receiver then dribbles cross-court to the other cutter, who moved into position by going behind the dribbler, executed a jump stop and a pivot prior to receiving the ball. During the second pass, the post man positions at the free-throw line to await the third pass. The first cutter is the passer, the scissors occurs outside the free-throw lane, the lay-up angle is 90-degree to the backboard, and the path is outside the lane. Normally, the second cutter receives the post feed, but either man may be used to shoot the lay-up shot with or without defense. Post defense of the action produces a shot or pass off to the partner. Instead of the lay-up, jump shots may be used, and if defense is used, the shot or pass occurs. Lastly, a fake jumper is used, and a return high feed is given to the post for a dunk or follow-type shot. Coaches denote which action will be used in the drill. Often, all of them are used.

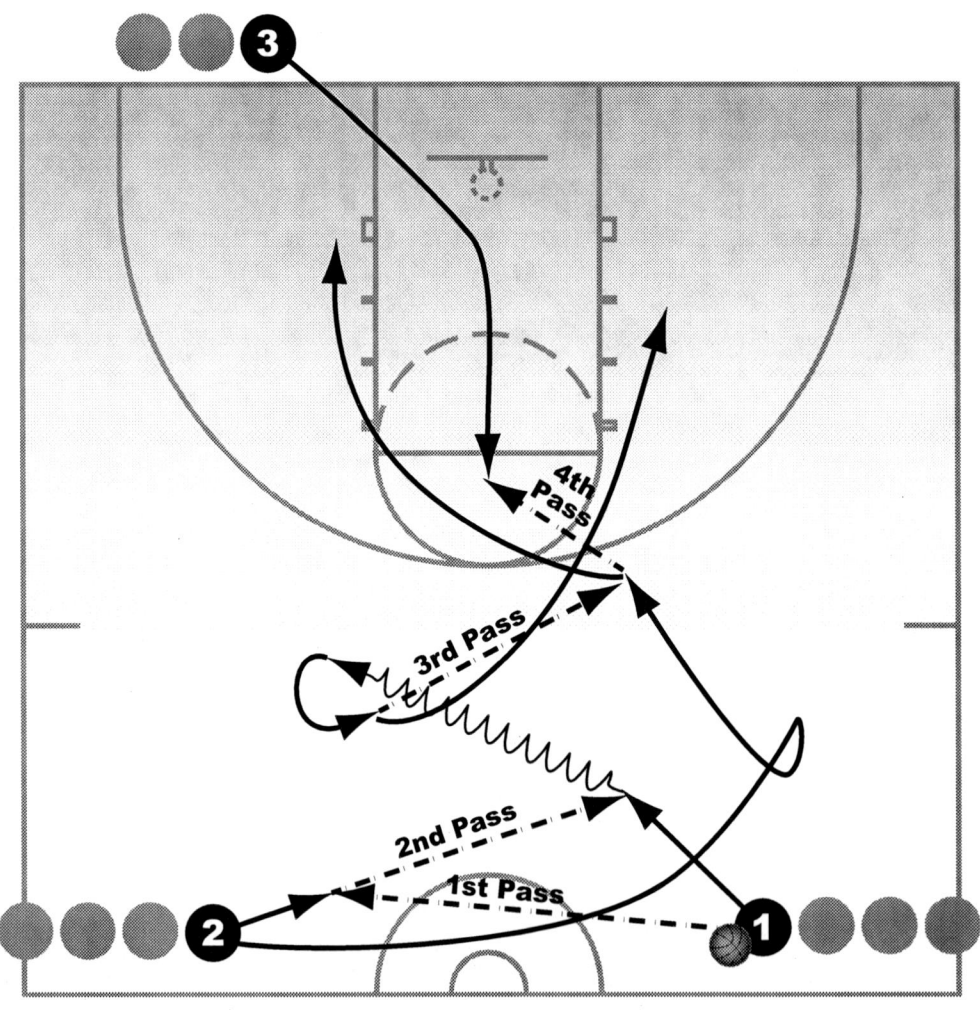

Miller 1.2 SPLIT POST

LESSONS FROM THIS LEGEND...

Speed game drills include a three-lane rush and a wide figure 8. Both operate on the full-court, with or without a defense. All ballhandling is done at top speeds without dribbling. Fast-break rules, as well as assignments, are emphasized. Three lanes, one located under the basket and the others within three feet of the sidelines, form behind the base line for both exercises. Two balls are used in this drill that starts with an inbound pass to either wing. In both drills, one or two defensive players may be stationed in the scoring areas for coverage purposes.

Three-lane rush movements are in straight lines at top speed (See **Diagram 1.3**). The wings remain within three feet of the sidelines and five feet ahead of the middle man, until reaching the free-throw line extended, where a 45-degree angle cut to the hoop occurs. The ball is passed continually between participants without ever dribbling the ball. Lay-ups taken by the wings are rebounded by the middle position and the wings under the basket and behind the baseline to within three feet of the sidelines, before turning up-court on the return trip. The return sequence initiates with a pass to a wing. Shots taken by the middle man are rebounded by the feeder who fills the middle spot, and the shooter moves to the sideline opposite the feeder to assume the wing position. The other wing follows the normal procedure in positioning for the return trip. One or two defensive men may be stationed in basket areas for competitive purposes. Two balls are used in the activity.

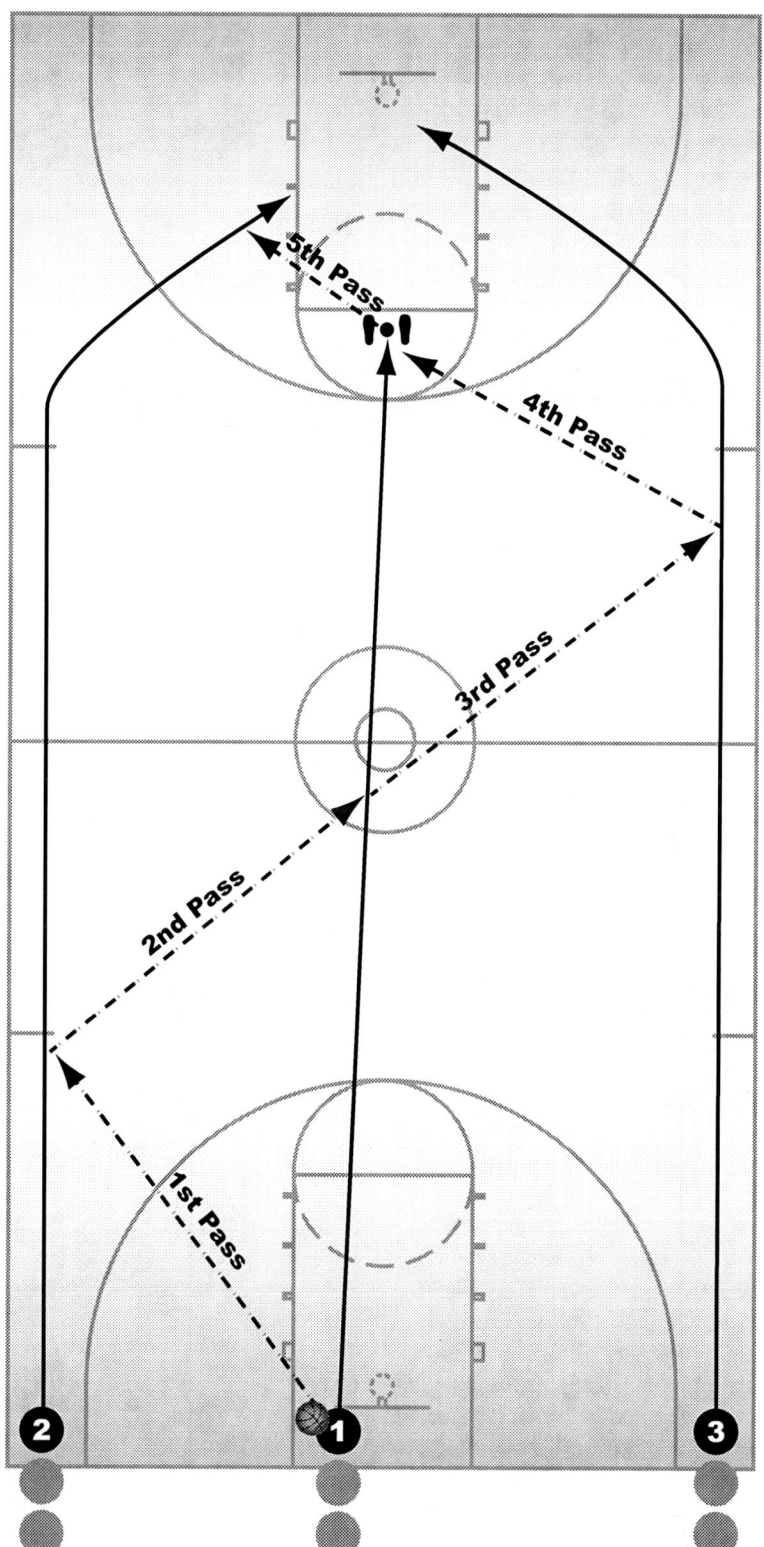

Miller 1.3 Three Lane Rush

LESSONS FROM THIS LEGEND...

The wide figure 8 utilizes the same procedures used in three-lane rush operation, but floor movements change, and passes are elongated. Basic rules: the passer always cuts behind the receiver and sprints until reaching a new position within three feet of the opposite sideline and five feet ahead of the ball. A pass must always move ahead of its floor position, and only one bounce is allowed. However, one such pass should seldom be necessary. The wings use 45-degree angle cuts to the hoop from the free-throw line extended. The rebounder is always the wing opposite the shooter at the time of execution, and the return trip is initiated by a pass to either wing spot. Basic rules apply for return action, and one or two defensive players are at one or both free-throw areas for competitive purposes (See **Diagram 1.4**).

Competitive drills include the full-court three-on-three and four-on-four. This drill combination provides full exposure to offensive and defensive pressure executions, but the training cycle is incomplete without adequate five-on-five full court scrimmage activities. These drills build the foundation for pressure-style basketball. They should involve approximately 75 percent of the allotted drill time in practice sessions.

Three-on-three utilizes all skill executions, except free throwing. Similar to the speed drills, three lines are formed. The first man in each line steps on the court to assume offensive purposes, and the ball is maintained by the middle man standing out-of-bounds. The defensive unit pressures all offensive personnel. The sequence originates by an inbounds pass. Full-scrimmage conditions exist until the offense scores or the defense gains ball possession. A made basket stops play. The ball is then taken out of bounds, and group assignments are reversed, unless the basket was scored from a second shot attempt. In this case, the defense is penalized by remaining on defense for the return trip against the original offensive group. The return sequence begins with an inbounds pass, and the scrimmage action is initiated. Possessions gained by defense or by other means does not stop action, but immediately reverses assignments and evokes a speed attack. Offensive personnel, when reversing assignments, automatically pick up the man defending them at the time a score occurred, or ball possession is lost.

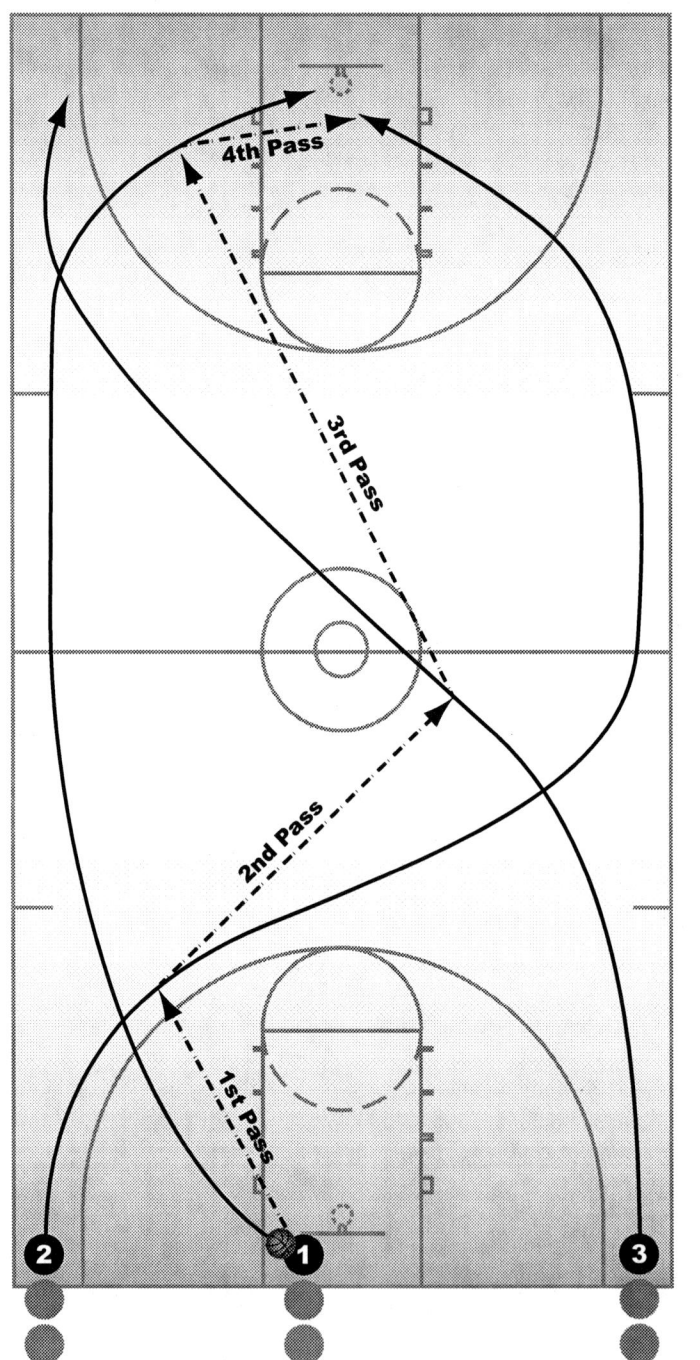

Miller 1.4 WIDE FIGURE 8

Normally, a six-man group makes only one round trip before moving off the floor, however, additional round trips may be used if desired.

LESSONS FROM THIS LEGEND...

Early usage evokes a hockey-type rule, namely, "a ball may not be passed across the mid-court line." This limitation slows the offensive attack and activates more dribbling and screening maneuvers to force switches in one-on-one coverage. However, the long pass or "bomb" is an offensive weapon against pressure, so in general, the hockey rule is used only in the early weeks of practice.

Four-on-four was originally designed for only half-court work, but now, has been expanded to involve the coordination of immediate conversions in assignments and responsibilities on the half-court to full-court attacks. In either case, sequences originate in a similar manner. **Diagram 1.5** shows the basic starting positions in this drill. Floor positions include a post at the high or low positions, a point guard, two wings operating on the sidelines, and corresponding defensive personnel. All rules for defensive coverage and offensive executions are operable except during free throws, and no restrictions govern play. The point guard initiates action by passing or executing a one-on-one maneuver. Scrimmage conditions exist until a basket is made or ball possession is gained by the defense, if usage is limited to half-court activities. The offense then assumes defensive positions, a new offensive group is formed, and the defense moves off the floor, except when a score is made off an offensive rebound. In this case, the defense is penalized by retaining their assignments for another tour against the same offensive group.

Expanding the drill to include full-court activity merely continues scrimmage conditions through a defensive recovery and allows one speed attack and shots to be taken. The original offensive group scoring moves the ball out-of-bounds to be put into play by the defensive group with an inbound pass. Offensive personnel immediately pick up the man defending them at the time scoring occurred and apply full-court pressure to all positions. Other defensive-ball recoveries automatically reverse assignments and require an automatic pick

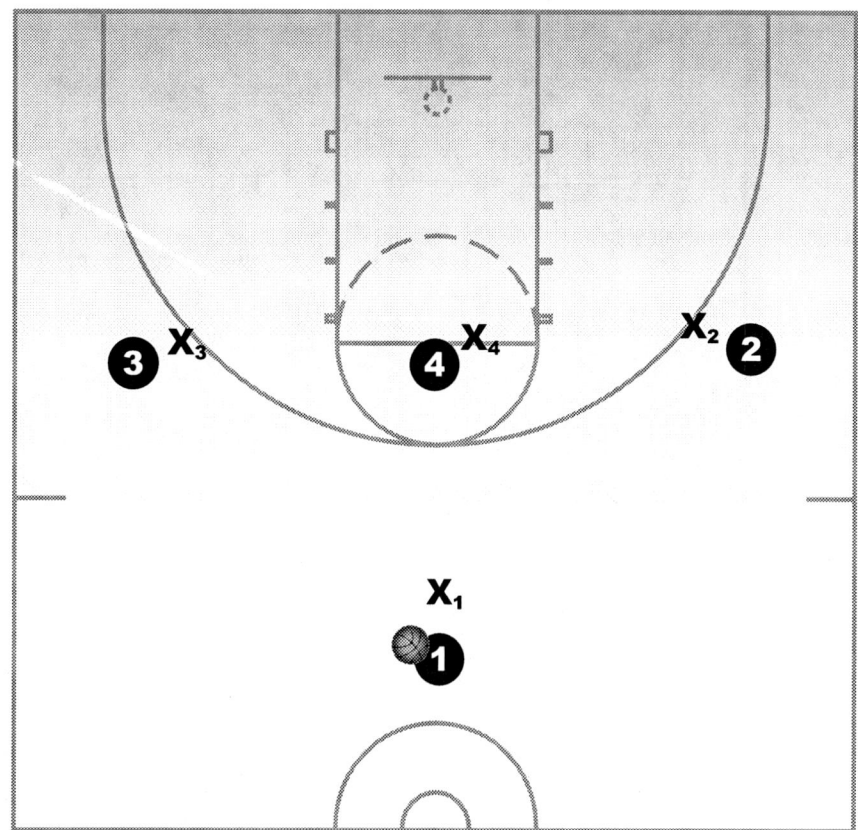

Miller 1.5

up to slow the forthcoming breaking attack. Action ceases with a shot from the speed attack in each case. The original defensive group maintains possession, establishes offensive positions on the half-court, and initiates the sequence under similar conditions. Normally, each group makes only one round on the floor, but better exposure from truer game conditions is gained by continuing scrimmage conditions throughout more than one complete circuit per group.

The seven drills described are the only drills used throughout an entire year's practice sessions. With the exception of expanding four-on-four usage, there have been no drills added since teaching pressure tactics began in 1948. Strangely enough, these were exactly the same drills used in teaching basketball skills prior to adopting pressure tactics in 1948. Today, usage varies only by an additional concentration upon full-court activities.

This drill system for individual players is an all-inclusive approach to learning fundamental skills. It is especially effective if it is used on a consistent basis and when it is used in the off-season. You must remember at all times that "practice makes permanent."

SOURCE

Krause, Jerry. (1984). *Better Basketball Basics: Before the X's and O's*. New York: Leisure Press.

LEGACY OF
Robert "Lute" Olson

- Master builder of basketball programs.

- Dignified coach who has always conducted himself with class.

- One of only eight coaches in basketball history to coach in five or more Final Fours.

- Has nation's best winning percentage over the last 16 seasons (429-101, .809).

- Led Arizona to 19 consecutive NCAA Tournament appearances, which is the longest current streak in college basketball and is the second longest in NCAA history (behind North Carolina's 27).

- Named National Coach of the Year in 1988 and 1990.

ROBERT "LUTE" OLSON

"I've always said that the best evaluation of the program and the effect that the program had on the players is five to 10 years after they leave. Our job as coaches is to push them to be the best that they can become."
—Robert "Lute" Olson

BIOGRAPHY

Born: September 22, 1934 in Mayville, ND

Inducted into the Naismith Memorial Basketball Hall of Fame in 2002

Robert "Lute" Olson has compiled a 795-259 record coaching at Long Beach City College, Long Beach State, Iowa, and Arizona. He is one of eight coaches in collegiate history to coach in five or more Final Fours. Olson led Arizona to the Final Four in 1988, 1994, 1997, and 2001. He took Iowa to the Final Four in 1980. Arizona won the NCAA championship in 1997. Under Olson, Arizona's 19 consecutive NCAA tournament appearances is the longest current streak in college basketball and is the second longest in NCAA history. Olson became coach at Arizona in 1984 and in 20 seasons has compiled a 499-147 record. Over the last 16 years, he has compiled the nation's best winning percentage (.809). Olson was named National Coach of the Year in 1988 and 1990. He earned Gold Medals as coach of the R. Williams Jones Cup team (1984) and World Championship Team (1986). Olson spent 11 years coaching high school basketball and compiled a 180-76 record. As an undergraduate at Augsburg College (MN), Olson was a three-sport standout and selected the top male student-athlete. Olson was enshrined into the Naismith Memorial Basketball Hall of Fame in 2002.

...SCOUTING REPORT.....SCOUTING REPORT.....

Robert "Lute" Olson...

Robert Luther Olson, or Lute as he is affectionately known, grew up in Mayville, ND, a town with a population of 1,800. When Olson was five-years old, his father passed away from a stroke. Nine months later, his 21-year old brother, who had come home to run the family's farm, died in a tractor accident. To help his mother, Lute knocked on neighbors' doors, asking to shovel snow or mow lawns. When Olson was in the sixth grade, he got a job as a flagger for crop-dusting planes dispensing DDT. At age 11, Lute was driving without a license to transport his blind grandfather.

His humble beginnings helped Olson understand the importance of hard work and persistence. He started playing basketball in grade school, and when he was just 13 years old, he knew that he wanted to become a basketball coach.

As a senior, Olson led Grand Forks Central High School to the state basketball championship in 1952. "I had moved to Grand Forks in 1951," said Olson. "It was the largest school in the state, and they had good basketball teams. The group I joined had played together for a number of years, and the team was already very good. At 6-foot 4-inches, I was the post-up guy on a pretty quick, small team. We weren't favored to win anything, but we beat a couple of good schools to win the championship." (Weber, 2002)

Olson selected Augsburg College (MN) as the place to further his education, because he felt more comfortable at a smaller school, plus it allowed him the opportunity to play three sports (basketball, football, and baseball). As a senior, Olson was recognized with the Augsburg Honors Athlete Award, which is given annually to the top male student-athlete.

Olson spent 11 years in the high-school coaching ranks, before becoming the head coach at Long Beach City College. "The biggest change I had to make in going from high school to college," said Olson, "was the recruiting part of it. As far as my style of play was concerned, I didn't change anything. My philosophy has always been to play up-tempo and to pressure defensively, at least to half-court. By that time, those principles were pretty well imbedded in me. John Wooden was at UCLA and having his great run. Jerry Tarkanian was at Long Beach State, and Bob Boyd was having great success at Southern California, so I'd say that most of my philosophies were coming from those coaches." (Weber, 2002)

Olson led Long Beach City College to four state championships and then spent one season at Long Beach State, going 24-2. Olson then accepted the challenge of rebuilding the basketball fortunes at the University of Iowa. The Hawkeyes were last in the Big Ten and were looking for a change. In nine years at Iowa, Olson compiled a record of 167-91 and took the Hawkeyes to the Final Four in 1980. In 1983, Olson took over an Arizona team that went 4-24 the previous season, raised it to 11-17 in his first season and then 21-10 the following season. In 20 seasons at Arizona, Olson compiled a 499-147 record and led the Wildcats to 17 consecutive 20-win seasons.

"I have long said that Lute's the Frank Lloyd Wright of coaching," said college basketball analyst Dick Vitale. "He's a builder of programs. If you look at his long-term record and what he's done with the programs he's been at, how can you not appreciate him?" (Rivera, 2002)

In 1997, Arizona stunned the basketball world by becoming the first NCAA title team to knock off three number one seeds (Kansas, North Carolina, and Kentucky) in the process.

"As a coach, he gets the most out of the talent that he has," said former Arizona player Craig McMillan. "And he does as good a job as anyone at adjusting his style to what talent he has. He's always looking at new ways to have success in the program." (Rivera, 2002)

Olson has always believed that you win with people of high character. "Jerks draw jerks," said Olson. "Great kids attract great kids." (Moredich, 1996)

"If you start with good people, you are going to have a good product," said Olson. "It's true in everything."

"I've always said that the best evaluation of the program and the effect that the program had on the players is five to 10 years after they leave," Olson said. Our job as coaches is to push them to be the best that they can become."

Olson emphasized to his players that there was more in life than just basketball. "Basketball is a means to an end," stated Olson. "We discuss our players' academic and career goals. We insist that our players are competitive in the classroom. We have required study sessions Sunday through Thursday."

"We have a player evaluation card," said Olson. "We ask the player to list some of his goals, both personal and

.....SCOUTING REPORT.....SCOUTING REPORT...

team. We also want them to evaluate each other by having them answer specific questions:"
1. Rate the players by position and overall team rating.
2. List the three best team players.
3. List the three best defensive players.
4. List the three best rebounders.
5. List the three best passers.
6. List the three who have the best team attitudes.
7. List the three who need to improve on defense.
8. List the three who need to improve their rebounding.
9. List the three who need to improve their passing.
10. List the three who need to improve their team attitude.

"The last one is the most important," said Olson. "We have a meeting with the various members of the squad, one at a time. If their name appeared on several of the last categories, then we ask them about it, because in my opinion, if their name reappears on the last category, there is a problem." (Murrey, 1987)

Nearly every player who has ever played for Olson reaps praise on his former coach. Ronnie Lester, star guard on Iowa's Final Four team in 1980, said that Olson always carried himself with class and dignity. Four-time NBA title winner Steve Kerr said that he wouldn't have had a chance at a pro career without the experience that he gained under Olson. "He really helped my whole life," said Kerr. "I grew up while I was at Arizona, and Lute was a major part of that. Not only learning the game, but the work ethic and the people. It was an amazing experience."

Jon Darsee, former Iowa player, said, "Coach Olson taught us the value of hard work by outworking all of us. He demonstrated an enormous capacity for organization. A half-hour before we began practice each day, the minute-by-minute schedule of every detail was printed and posted in the lockerroom. The two-plus hour practice was outlined to the second, so that each of us knew where and when and with whom we would do each task during the duration of every drill, scrimmage, or shoot-around. We practiced every conceivable game situation over and over. Not a moment was wasted. To this day, nothing in my life has rivaled the intensity of those practices."

All-American Sean Elliott, who surpassed Lew Alcindor's Pac-10 scoring mark with 2,555 points, said, "I think the work ethic is the biggest thing that Coach Olson instilled in me. Even when you played a great game, he was never satisfied. He was always making your work harder the next day. There's no better teacher in the game than him." (Moredich, 1996)

Steve Rivera (2003) of the Tucson Citizen described Olson's actions on the basketball court in these words, "He's as serious as serious gets and as stoic as ever. Lute Olson is the poker face of college hoops."

Olson prides himself on his lack of public emotion on the court. "My philosophy has always been that if players are going to maintain their poise and composure on the court, then they shouldn't see a raving maniac on the sidelines. I feel our job as a staff is to make sure that we are there providing the adjustments that need to be done."

Olson's most tragic moment came when his wife of 47 years, Bobbi, died after a two-year battle with ovarian cancer in 2001. Bobbi was a perfect compliment to Lute and was an important part of Olson's program. "The big thing from a player's standpoint was that she could be a friend, a mother, the comforter," said Olson. "She could soften the blows and had a remarkable feel for what needed to be done and said."

During the 2000 season, Arizona officials named the McKale Center's court "Bobbi & Lute Olson Court."

At the time of the announcement stating Olson's induction into the Naismith Basketball Hall of Fame in 2002, Lute said, "Being elected is the crowning achievement of a career. It would have been great for Bobbi to be here with me, but then again I know that she will have a front-row seat."

SOURCE

Moredich, John. (1996). *Arizona Wildcats Handbook*. The Wichita Eagle and Beacon Publishing.

Olson, Lute. (1987). Motivation. In Murrey, Bob (ed.), *Motivating Your Athletes*. Waukesha, WI: MacGregor Sports Education.

Olson, Lute. Vertical Files, Archives. Naismith Memorial Basketball Hall of Fame. Springfield, MA.

Rivera, Steve. (2002). Master Builder. *Naismith Memorial Hall of Fame Enshrinement Program*.

Rivera, Steve. (2003, March 25). Lute Olson is the Poker Face of College Hoops. *Tuscon Citizen*.

Weber, Ben. (2002, April). Winningly on the Lute: From the Mountains to the Prairies, Lute Olson Wins Everywhere. *Coach and Athletic Director*.

LESSONS FROM THIS LEGEND...

DEVELOPING DEFENSE THROUGH DRILLS

By Lute Olson

PHILOSOPHY

Any discussion of developing a sound defensive basketball team must begin with one basic premise: the defense, regardless of how technically sound, will only be as good as the effort expended by the individuals within the defense. The old adage, "defense is 10 percent inspiration and 90 percent perspiration" is as true today as it was 30 years ago. Possibly, you may not agree with the percentages, but the fact remains that a great defensive player is one who gives it every ounce of effort available to him.

BASIC CONCEPTS

Pressure basketball is considered to be the most critical phase of University of Arizona Basketball. The defense is used to supplement our offense, and in many games, more than half of our points come about as a result of forcing opponents into turnovers.

Arizona's pressure defense is based on maintaining constant pressure on the basketball, denying all penetrating passes, affording immediate help if a teammate has been beaten by his opponent, and limiting the number of second shots afforded the opponent.

A combination of full, three-quarter, and half-court pressures are incorporated into the man and zone being employed as a change of pace to the primary defense.

INDIVIDUAL FUNDAMENTALS

Any defense, whether zone or man-to-man, must be built on sound individual fundamentals. Our beliefs in this regard are not unique. One will be as effective as one's fundamentals will allow, assuming that we understand that maximum effort will be demanded at all times.

The first step in developing a player's skills begins with the basic stance. We break the stance into five basic parts. The five are: head, back, legs, feet, and arms and hands.

1. HEAD

The first point that we attempt to establish with our players is the importance of the head in body balance. To emphasize this, we will get the entire squad in a normal defensive stance. We will then direct them to move their head forward until such time as they lose their balance and fall forward. We do the same thing moving the head backward and then sideward with similar results.

At this time, we establish the fact that if the head is allowed to bob up and down, we will not be in good balance. We also point out that if a player reaches with his hand and arm, he will bring the head along, thereby disrupting basic body balance. Our purpose in the above demonstration is to implant in the player's mind why we do not reach or bob. It has proved a valuable tool for us in teaching and is worthy of your consideration if you have difficulties in this area.

2. BACK

The back is to be kept relatively straight while in the defensive stance. Because of our thoughts on hand and arm position, which I will explain later, we may keep the back straighter than some whose hands are carried lower.

3. LEGS

The knees are bent enough to allow the player to be within four or five inches of being in a seated position. We indicate for the player to drop the butt down to where he would be sitting down on an imaginary chair and then to come back up the four or five inches alluded to earlier.

4. FEET

The feet are to be kept considerably wider than the shoulders. The body weight is to be kept primarily on the ball and toes of the foot, with no appreciable pressure on the heels. In an effort to teach the players how to keep the feet apart throughout the defensive slide, we emphasize what we refer to as the "broomstick" and "power leg."

The "broomstick" is nothing more than providing a mental picture of foot position to our players. After getting them into a good, solid defensive stance, we ask them to look down at their feet and imagine that we had cut a broomstick the width of their stance. We indicate under no circumstances are they to bring their feet any closer together while in a defensive stance.

The "power-leg" approach has been a great teaching aid to our staff in helping our players maintain a wide stance. We will get our players in the defensive stance and indicate we are going to have them slide to their right. At that time we tell them that their left (or trail) leg is to provide the power for the move and that they are to simply lift the right foot slightly and push with the left or power leg in this situation. We will have them make a three-step slide at half-speed and require that they yell, "push, push, push" to better establish the technique we want used with the feet and

LESSONS FROM THIS LEGEND...

legs. The power-leg theory is very simple—the trail leg in any slide should be the power source, rather than being dragged.

5. Arms and Hands

We have made some recent changes in our philosophy of utilization of the hands and arms in playing defense. Most of the changes have come about because of the improved dribbling skills of today's players. It is our opinion that the player has enough dribbling skills that for our defender to carry his hands low to play for steals or to discourage changes of direction is no longer a sound-percentage play.

Our philosophy is to keep the hands and arms at waist level or higher. We do this for three reasons. The first is that the main threat to our defense is the pass, and we believe we have a better chance to deflect or intercept the ball if the hands are up and out. The second is that we can provide a wider obstacle to the dribbler in an attempt to control his penetration by the dribble. The third reason is that we feel we can cut down on costly fouls by not encouraging the player to reach as much as he would if his hands were carried lower.

Regardless of whether you agree or disagree with our hand and arm position, it is vital that players understand one basic rule. That rule is, the primary tools in playing defense are the feet; the secondary tools are the hands and arms.

Developing Defense Through Drills

Our defense will be developed through a series of defensive drills. These drills will be divided into on-ball and off-ball skills, and will be taught by the whole-part-whole method. We will explain the basic defensive theory to our players, work on individual techniques without an offensive player, and then go one-on-one, to two-on-two, etc. until we have reached the desired five-on-five.

During the course of teaching the defensive skills, we demand the following:
1. An all-out effort
2. The feet must be kept apart.
3. The legs must be bent.
4. The hands are to be kept above the waist.
5. The head must be kept in a balanced position, directly above the center of the feet.
6. The player must learn to communicate with his teammates.

Eight Drills to Develop Individual On-Ball and Off-Ball Skills

Drill #1 - Lead Pass Drill

In this drill, we have our players off the court in the endline area. We have the players work in pairs, with one on defense and the other on offense. We start by having the first pair step out to a position halfway between the sideline and the free-throw lane and just above the endline. The coach who is in a normal guard position will slap the ball to indicate the start of the drill. With the slap of the ball, the offensive player will make a "V" cut to try to get open in the normal forward position. (See **Diagram 1.0**)

Olson 1.0

In attempting to deny the ball to the offensive player, the defender is to use the following fundamentals:

a. The defender is to have the hand and arm nearest the passer fully extended into the passing lane. We also require that the palm on that hand is facing the passer (thumb down).

b. The arm nearest his opponent is to be placed in a flexed position, with the arm bent at the elbow in a 90-degree angle. We refer to this position as the "arm-bar" position. The purpose of the "arm bar" is to keep the opponent from getting to the defender's feet, thereby limiting his foot movement.

c. The defender is to keep a gap between himself and his opponent until the offensive player reaches the free-throw line extended. At that time, the defender is to make contact with his opponent with the "arm bar." Our thinking here is that the possibility of a backdoor cut becomes greater if there is no contact with the offensive player.

d. The defender is to keep his vision focused at the midpoint between the ball and the potential receiver. He should look neither at the ball nor at the defender.

e. The defender is to stay in a low stance, with a wide base. He is to avoid reaching or lunging for the ball. We constantly remind our players of the importance of the head in maintaining balance.

f. The back leg is the "power leg."

g. If the offensive player receives the ball, the defender is to immediately readjust his position so that his inside foot is pointing to the offensive player's crotch, thereby overplaying a "half-man" toward the baseline.

LESSONS FROM THIS LEGEND...

DRILL #2 - CUTTING OFF THE BASELINE DRIVE AND "BELLYING UP"

a. The offensive player who received the ball is to immediately "face-up" and attempt to drive the baseline.

b. The defender takes an angle of retreat toward the baseline to cut off the offensive player.

c. The defender is to cut the offensive player off by placing his baseline foot directly on the endline. His hands are to be up and his chest out in anticipation of any contact initiated by the offensive player. (See **Diagram 1.1**)

d. Once the offensive player has picked up the dribble, we want the defender to adjust his foot position, so his back is "squared" to the high-post area. We feel this cuts off the potential pass to the area of the court that creates the largest number of problems to our defense.

e. At the same time the offensive player stopped his dribble, we will make a "dribble-kill" call indicating the dribble has been used and signaling all four teammates are to get into the passing lanes and go for a five-second count.

f. The offensive player in this drill is told to hold the ball for a two-count before throwing the ball back to the coach. This enables us to check the defender's foot position, belly-up position, and "dribble-kill" call.

g. The defensive player is to "mirror" the ball with his hands and try to get a deflection of the pass as it is made back out to the coach. Once the ball passes over the defender's hands, he is to immediately jump toward the ball and resume his denial position. (See **Diagram 1.2**)

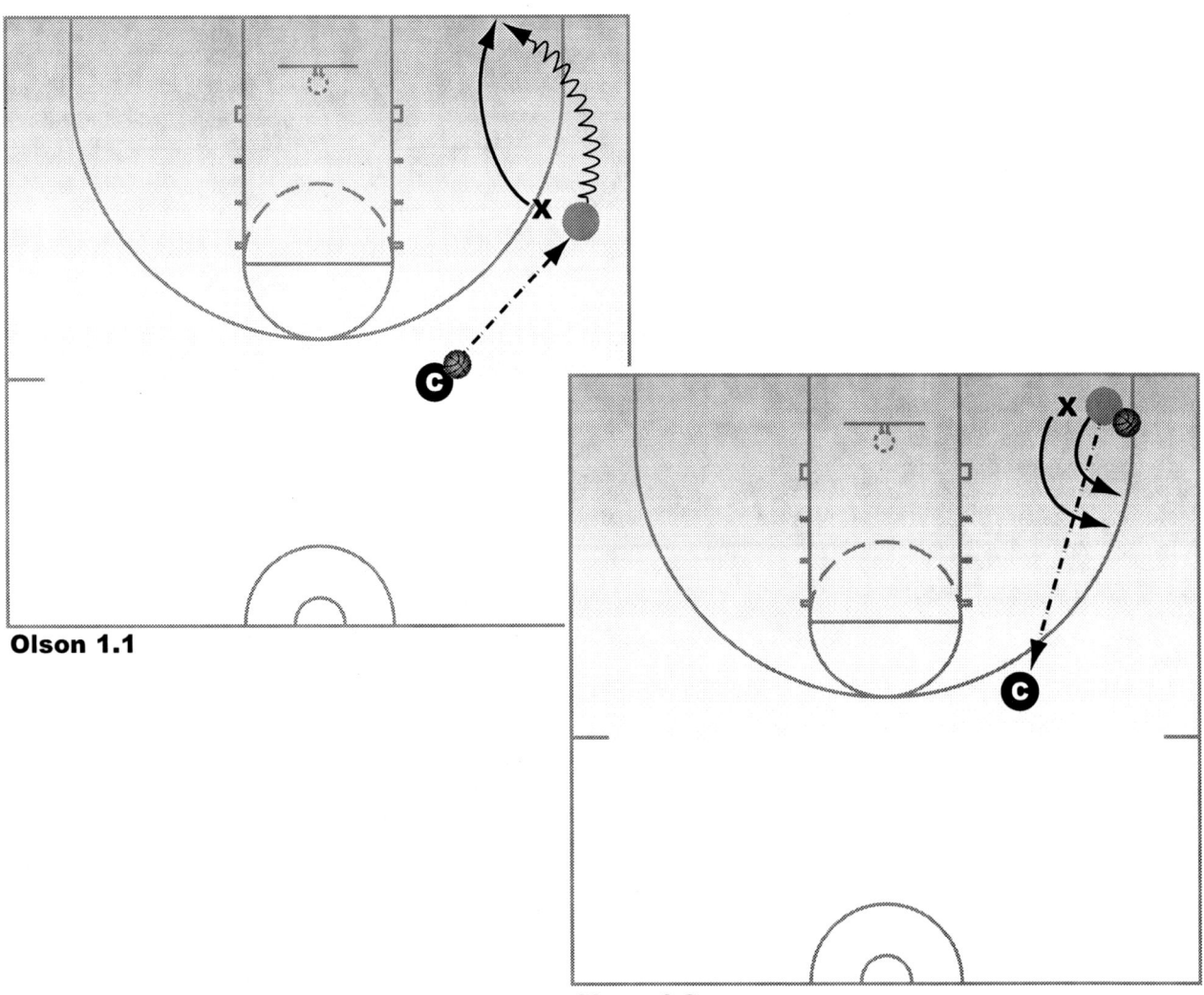

Olson 1.1

Olson 1.2

LESSONS FROM THIS LEGEND...

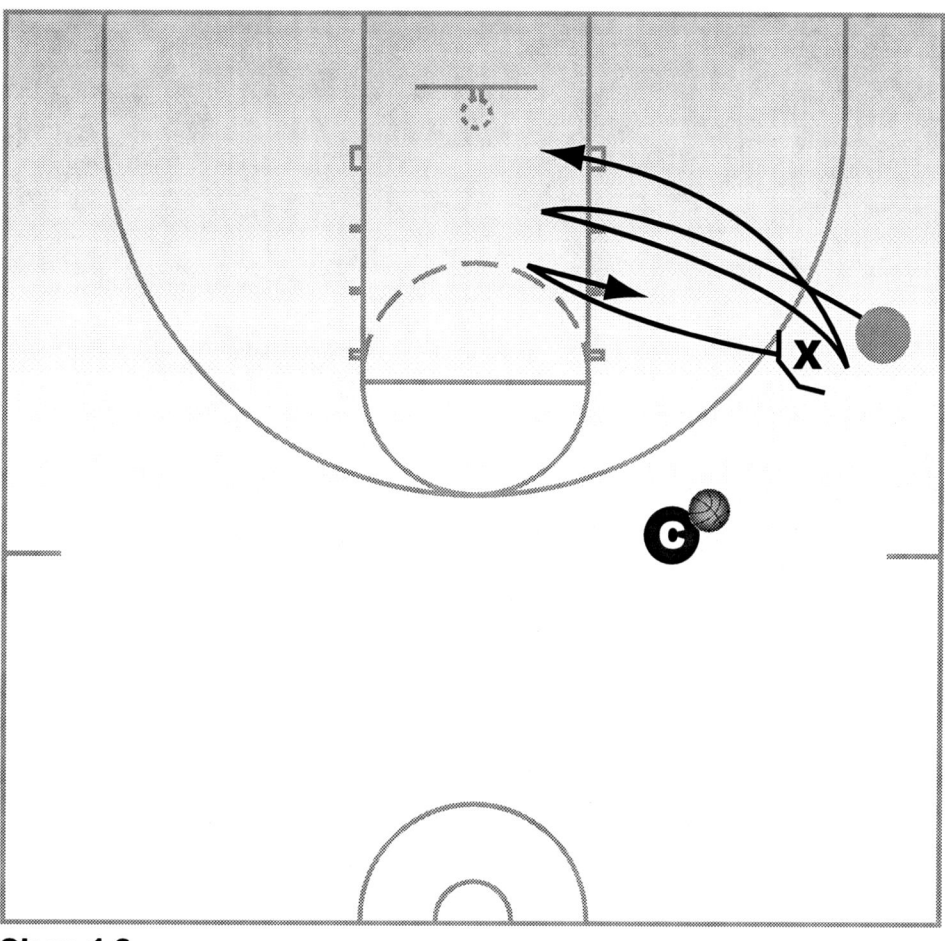

Olson 1.3

DRILL #3 - BACKDOOR COVERAGE

a. The offensive player follows normal procedure for creating a lead pass (V-cut, thrust step, and target hand).

b. Once the offensive player has reached the free-throw line extended, the coach fakes a pass, keying the backdoor cut by the offensive player.

c. The defender is to retreat with the offensive player until vision is lost, at which time, the defender is to snap his head over the shoulder closest to the basket in an effort to pick up vision on the ball. The hand and arm positions are switched quickly with the "head turn." The arm and hand nearest the basket are thrown into the passing lane, while the other hand and arm will be placed in the "arm-bar" position. (See **Diagram 1.3**)

d. If the offensive player does not receive the pass, he is to break back out to the lead position, with the defender reacting quickly to a lead-pass defensive position.

LESSONS FROM THIS LEGEND...

DRILL #4 - DEFENDING THE POST

Two feeders are used with an offensive and defensive post man. One feeder is in the normal forward position, with the other one at the guard position. (See **Diagram 1.4**) Our basic rules on defending the post areas are as follows:

a. If the ball is above the free-throw line extended, the defender is to be on the high side of the post in a three-quarter front with his denial hand and arm into the passing lane. His other hand and arm are in the arm-bar position. The arm bar is to be used to keep the offensive post man from getting to the defender's legs and body.

b. If the ball is below the free-throw line extended, the defender is to be on the low side of the post in a 3/4 front position. The normal lead-hand and arm-bar positions are used. (See **Diagram 1.5**)

c. The exception to the above positions is if the post is below the block position. The defensive post should then be on the high side, regardless of the ball position. The reason for this is that if the ball is thrown to the post in that position, we feel we can contain him behind the backboard and force him to "charge" the defender if he goes to the basket, or be forced to pass the ball back out.

d. In changing positions from high-to-low side and vice-versa, we use a basic "half-moon" slide. This slide involves moving around the post by a direct face-to-face movement of the other position. The arm-bar and lead-hand position changes as one goes from high-to-low and vice-versa.

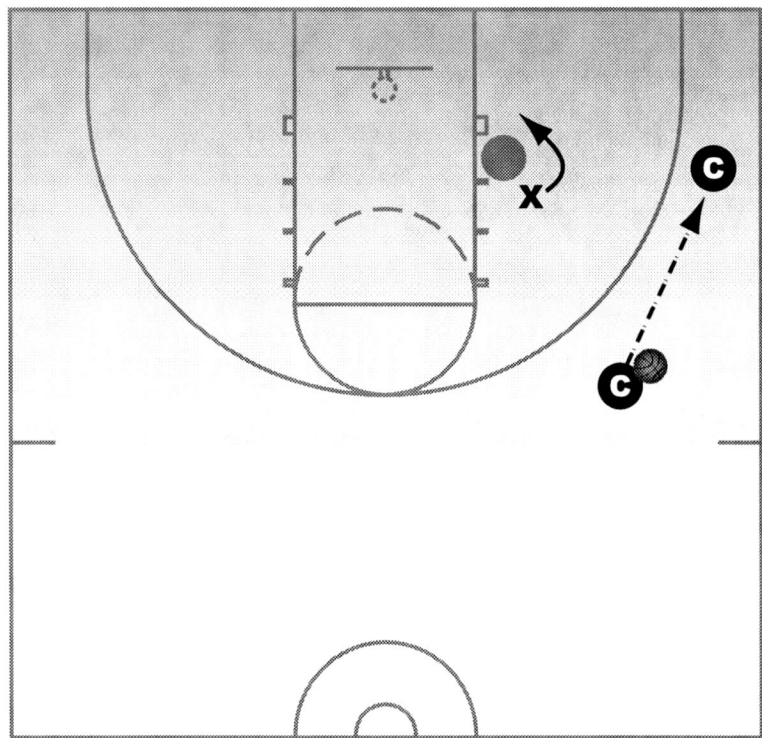

Olson 1.4

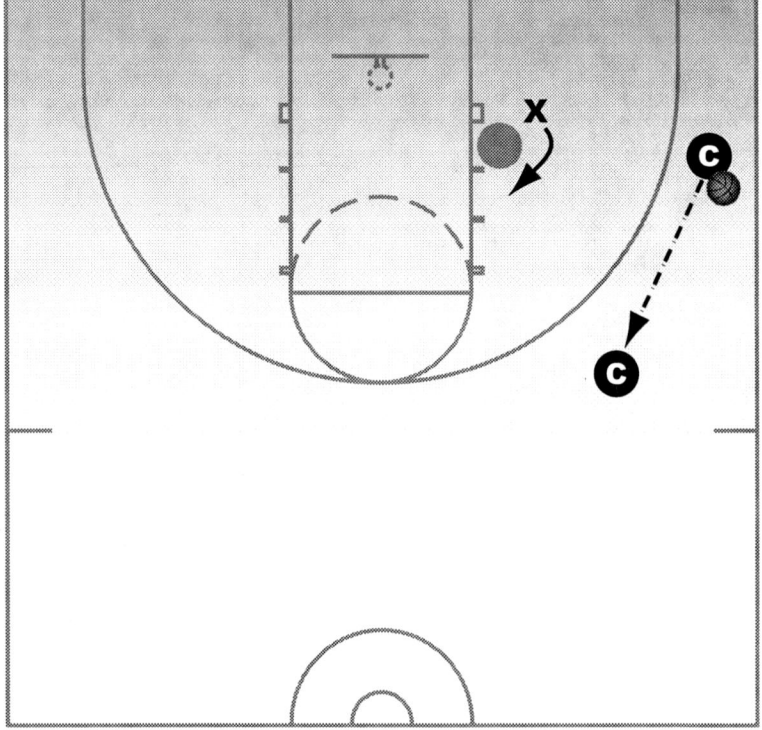

Olson 1.5

LESSONS FROM THIS LEGEND...

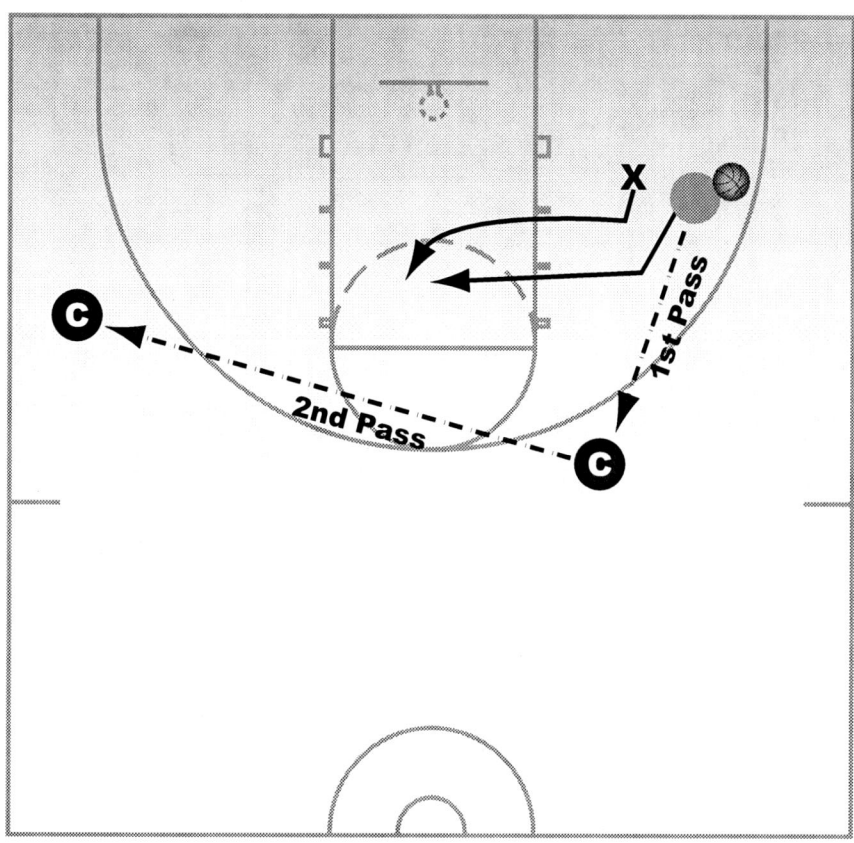

Olson 1.6

DRILL #5 - DENYING THE LATERAL CUT (FLASH POST)

Two feeders are used in this drill, with one located at the guard position and the other located at the forward position. (See **Diagram 1.6**)

    a. We start the drill with the ball in the offensive right-forward position, with the defender on him. The offensive player passes to the guard position.

    b. The guard then throws the ball cross-court to the feeder at the left-forward position.

    c. The offensive player makes a "flash-cut" to the ball.

    d. The defender "jumps" to the ball with each pass. As the offensive player breaks through the lane, the defender is to make contact with him as he reaches the middle of the lane. This contact is made with the arm bar, again trying to keep the offensive player from getting to his feet or body.

    e. We prefer that the defender try to force ("funnel") the cutter above the third free-throw lane position into the back of where the defensive guard would be playing. We try to avoid allowing the man to back-cut our defender, thereby getting an opportunity to get open at the block.

LESSONS FROM THIS LEGEND...

DRILL #6 - DEFENDING THE DIAGONAL CUT

Two feeders are used in this drill, with one at a guard position and the other at the forward position on the opposite side of the floor. We start the ball at the forward position, with the offensive player in the block position on the ballside. With the pass being thrown to the off-guard position, the offensive player takes two steps out toward the corner and then cuts hard toward the ball. The offensive player will attempt to get the ball in the high post area. (See **Diagram 1.7**) The defender is to follow these basic principles:

    a. Establish contact with the offensive player as he enters the lane. This body contact should be made with the arm bar.

    b. "Funnel" the offensive player away from the high-post area. Force him outside of the circle by "riding" him up the lane. Defending this cut is critical to stopping the back-door play, which is often used versus a pressure-type defense.

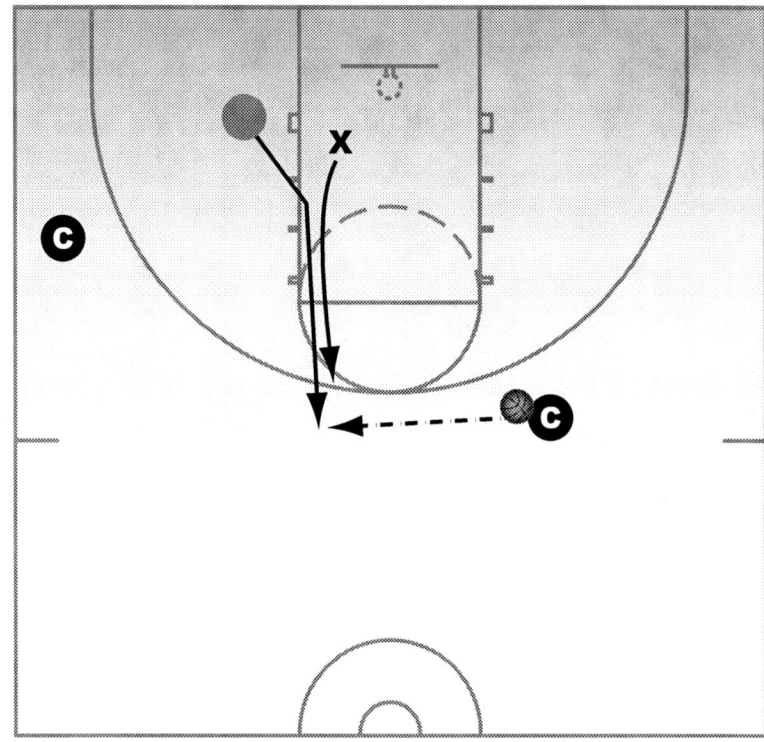

Olson 1.7

DRILL #7 - ONE-ON-ONE OPERATIONAL

This drill is one of the most important drills we use. It is used on a daily basis, and if properly taught and supervised, this drill is key to our on-the-ball defense. The squad is again divided into pairs. Each pair is assigned a basket (if possible). If there are not enough baskets, we will assign one pair to each side of the basket and have them stagger their play.

    a. The defensive player, after assuming the defensive stance, will hand the ball to the offensive player, who has assumed a "ready" stance, anywhere from 15 feet to 18 feet from the basket.

    b. Once the offensive player has received the ball, he has only two seconds in which to make his move.

    c. Once the offensive player takes the shot, the defensive player is required to pressure the shot by attempting to: 1) block the shot; 2) change the shot; 3) change the rhythm of the shooter; or 4) affect the shooter's vision.

    d. Once the defender has pressured the shot, he must yell "shot" to try to break the shooter's concentration, screen out, and then rebound the ball if missed.

    e. If the shot is made, the defensive player will take the ball and walk back to another position 15 feet to 18 feet from the basket and repeat the procedure.

    f. If the shot did not go in and the offensive player gets the rebound inside the lane, he is to make a quick power move to the basket.

    g. If the offensive player gets the rebound outside the lane, he is to hand the ball to the defensive player and then take a position 15 feet to 18 feet from the basket for another attempt.

    h. If the defender rebounds the ball, he hands it to the offensive player and walks out to 15 feet to 18 feet from the basket and assumes the offensive position.

    i. We will set certain restrictions on the offensive player and change them on a daily basis. For example, one day we may allow one dribble, the next day two dribbles.

    j. The games are usually played to seven or ten baskets.

DRILL #8 - SEVEN-IN-ONE DRILL

Once we have taught the seven drills described above, we go to a drill called seven-in-one to give us constant review of the basic fundamentals. This drill has proved to be a great timesaving drill. We combine the individual seven drills into one continuous drill covering the fundamentals in the following order: 1) lead pass; 2) baseline drive and belly-up; 3) back-door; 4) post; 5) lateral cut (flash-post); 6) diagonal cut (back-door play); and 7) one-on-one operational (defending the ball).

    a. We start this drill in the same position as described in the lead-

LESSONS FROM THIS LEGEND...

pass drill. The only difference is that we will add two feeders to the one already described. This will give us one feeder, for example, at the right-guard position, one feeder who is off the court near the right-forward position, and a third feeder at the left-forward position. (See **Diagram 1.8**)

b. The offensive player breaks out to receive the ball and continues to move until he catches the ball at the forward position. On reception of the ball, he "faces-up" and immediately drives the baseline, trying to "turn the corner." The defender must retreat and cut the man off as previously taught.

c. Once the defender cuts the driver off, he follows basic fundamentals taught in the belly-up and "kill" portion of the baseline drill. After the two-second count, the offensive player passes the ball out to the original feeder and tries to create another lead pass. If he is open, the feeder passes him the ball, and the offensive player again drives the baseline. He will continue to do this until he is denied the ball.

d. Once the offensive player has been denied the ball, the feeder gives a "ball fake," which keys the back-door cut. The passer then tries to hit the cutter with a pass. The pass cannot be thrown into the lane, however, because that coverage is the offside defender's responsibility.

e. The back-door cut continues into the lane, and if he has not received the ball, he cuts back to the ball-side and takes a post position above the block. At this point, the second feeder at the right-forward position steps onto the court.

f. The first feeder at the guard position tries to feed the post. If the defender is denying the ball, it is then passed to the right-forward feeder, who tries to get the ball into the post. The ball is passed back and forth from the forward to the guard positions. The defender is working on his "half-moon slides."

g. Once feeder #1 decides that the post coverage is acceptable, he will make a cross-court pass to the left-forward position. With that pass, the postman flashes across the lane, trying to get the ball. The defender follows his flash-post fundamentals in denying the ball. The cutter is restricted to receiving the ball from the third free-throw position along the lane down to the baseline.

h. If the defender has denied the ball to the cutter, the forward feeder will return the ball to the original feeder position. With that pass, the cutter will attempt to make a diagonal cut into the top half of the free-throw circle to receive the ball. The defender denies the ball, as described in the "diagonal cut drill."

i. If the cutter is forced out of the circle, the feeder passes the ball to the offensive player at the top of the key. At that time, the two players go one-on-one under the regulations described in the "one-on-one operational drill." The drill is complete once the shot has been taken and made, or the miss is rebounded by the defender.

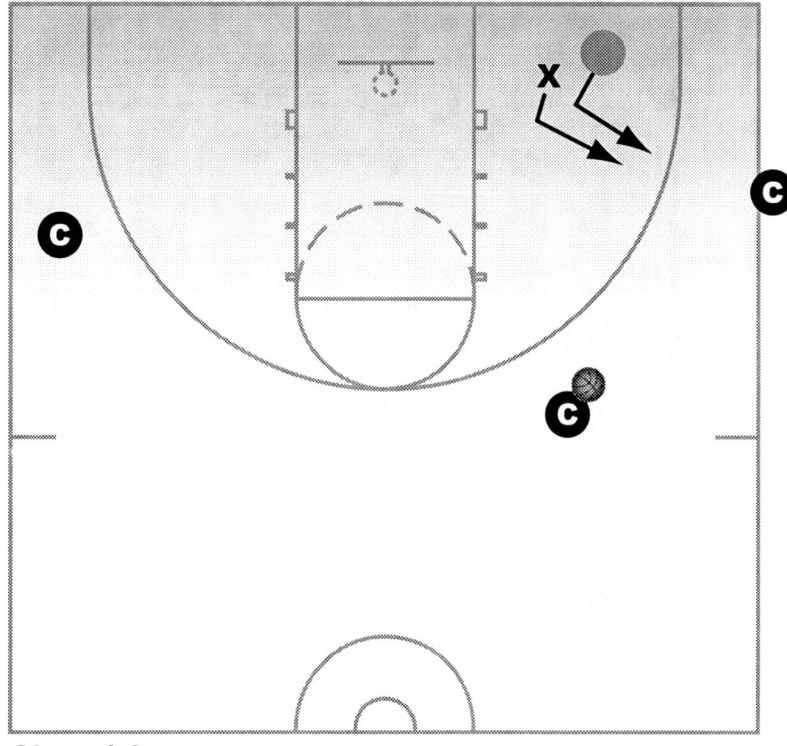

Olson 1.8

SOURCE

Olson, Lute. (1983). *Arizona Pressure Defense*. Tucson: University of Arizona.

LEGACY OF
Jack Ramsay

- Coached in the NBA for 20 years and compiled 864 victories.

- Led Portland to the NBA championship in 1977.

- Highly recognized for his extraordinary attention to detail, conditioning regimes, and knowledge of the game.

- Inspired greatness in his teams through his teaching and motivation.

- Earned doctorate degree; called "Dr. Jack" of Basketball.

- Viewed the game of basketball as an art form; compared basketball to ballet.

- Led St. Joseph's (PA) to 10 postseason appearances and a third place finish in the NCAA tournament in 1961.

JACK RAMSAY

*"Well-coached teams are never surprised;
they can adapt to anything they see."*
—Jack Ramsay

BIOGRAPHY

Born: February 21, 1925 in Philadelphia, PA

Inducted into the Naismith Basketball Hall of Fame in 1992

Jack Ramsay was a head coach at the professional, college, and high school levels for almost 50 years, and his overall coaching record includes 1,164 wins. He coached Philadelphia, Buffalo, Portland, and Indiana in the NBA and guided the Trailblazers to the 1977 NBA championship. Ramsay was general manager of the Philadelphia 76ers in 1976, when the 76ers won the NBA championship and set a league record for most victories in one season. He coached at St. Joseph's (PA) from 1955 to 1966 and compiled a 234-72 record, including ten post season tournament appearances. Ramsay led St. Joseph's to the Final Four in 1961. The Hawks were defeated by defending champion Ohio State in the semi-finals but came back to win the third-place trophy by beating Utah 127-120 in four overtimes. He played basketball and baseball at St. Joseph's and captained the Hawk's basketball team his senior year. He also played professional basketball for six seasons in the Eastern Basketball League. Ramsay received a Ph.D. in education in 1963 from the University of Pennsylvania. Ramsay was enshrined in the Naismith Memorial Basketball Hall of Fame in 1992.

...SCOUTING REPORT.....SCOUTING REPORT.....

Jack Ramsay...

Jack Ramsay was born in Philadelphia but soon moved to Milford, Connecticut, where he grew up shooting baskets at a goal nailed to the side of a barn. His family moved to Upper Darby, Pennsylvania, a suburb of Philadelphia, when Jack was in high school, and he starred in basketball, baseball, and soccer. He then entered St. Joseph's University and earned a starting position on the basketball team. Ramsay left school after his first year and joined the Navy. He was commissioned an Ensign in 1944 and served with underwater demolition teams in the Pacific. After his discharge, Ramsay returned to St. Joseph's and made the All-Philadelphia team during his junior and senior years.

After graduation from St. Joseph's, Ramsay coached six years on the high-school level and played in the Eastern Basketball League. In 1955, he was named head coach at his alma mater, St. Joseph's. In his first year, Ramsay led the Hawks to a 23-6 record, the school's first Big Five championship and a trip to the NIT tournament. During his 11 years at St. Joseph's, his teams compiled a record of 234-72 with ten postseason appearances.

In 1966, Ramsay accepted the position of general manager of the Philadelphia 76ers. In his initial campaign, the 76ers set an NBA record for victories and won the world championship. He stayed in the front office one more year, before returning to the sidelines. During his NBA career, Ramsay coached in Philadelphia, Buffalo, Portland, and Indiana.

When he became head coach of the Portland Trail Blazers in 1976-77, Ramsay inherited a team that in its six years of existence had never had a winning record or made the NBA playoffs. In Ramsay's first year, the Trail Blazers shocked the basketball world by winning the NBA championship. Ramsay transformed his players into a smooth functioning, confident team. His positive approach made all the difference in the world. Ramsay (2003) recalled stopping a training camp scrimmage following a brilliant segment of play to tell his players, "We can win if we play like that! I mean the whole thing ...the NBA championship." Ramsay believed that in coaching, a positive approach makes all the difference.

In the championship series, Portland lost the first two games to the Julius Erving-led Philadelphia 76ers. The Trail Blazers had not played well, and Ramsay detected a bit of nervousness among his players. He knew that it was crucial that he portray confidence in his players. Instead of changing his line-up or altering his offense and defense, Ramsay reminded his team about how they had blown out the 76ers in a regular-season game. He told them that he was confident that they could duplicate that kind of performance, if they played their game. The players responded to his message, and Portland stormed back to win four straight games.

Ramsay's coaching genius was instrumental in creating the phenomenon, Blazermania. In 1993, Portland retired jersey number 77 in Ramsay's honor, symbolically recognizing the 1977 Championship.

Ramsay continually talked to his players about the will to win. He believed that everyone has the will to win, but that some individuals have a greater desire than others. Ramsay (2003) listed the following players as the most determined that he had seen throughout his years in the NBA—in chronological order—George Mikan, Bill Russell, Jerry West, Dave Cowans, Larry Bird, Magic Johnson, Michael Jordan, Hakeem Olajuwon, Shaquille O'Neal, and Kobe Bryant.

When asked to describe the game of basketball, Ramsay (1978) stated, "The game is unified action up and down the floor. It is quickness; it is strength; it is skill, it is stamina; it is five men playing as one. It is tenacity on defense; it is quick penetration on offense. It is taking advantage of every offensive opportunity. It is stifling the opponent; it is jamming up the one-on-one player. But most of all, it is the spirit of winning as a team. It is the solidarity of a single unifying purpose, the will to overcome adversity, the determination never to give in."

Ramsay often compared the movements in basketball to those in ballet. "Basketball is a graceful sweep and flow of patterned movement, counter-pointed by daring and imaginative flights of solitary brilliance," said Ramsay (1978).

Ramsay believed coaching was a means of self-expression. Ramsay (2003) said, "A foundational principle of success—in any endeavor—is to be yourself. Trying to be someone else, no matter how admirable we may think that person is, just doesn't work."

To become a successful coach, Ramsay (2002) believed there were five key factors:
1. Know the game, and have your team play their best within the rules of the game.
2. Develop an effective game plan that gives your team its best chance to win.
3. Teach the game to your staff and players. Use the whole-part-whole method. Give the players an overall view of what the end-product looks like, break it down into its essential parts, and then put all the parts together.
4. Coach the game. Go over the game plan with your players, and simulate at practice the game that you expect them to play. At the same time, you must prepare them to meet the unexpected.
5. Obtain quality personnel. A good coach makes maximum use of the talent that he has, but if he has less than standard quality players, he can't win. Talent is the coach's lifeblood, and good talent has to be well-coached.

Ramsay has always been highly respected by his peers. Jim Calhoun, head coach at Connecticut, said, "There are only a few 'teachers' we all learn from, and Dr. Jack is one of them."

Hall of Fame coach Harry Litwack (1992) described Ramsay in these words, "Jack is an outstanding competitor and motivator, and his knowledge of the game is incredible. He's an outstanding individual, a wonderful family man, and regarded by everyone as a genuine human being."

SOURCES

Ramsay, Jack. Vertical Files, Archives. Naismith Basketball Hall of Fame. Springfield, MA.

Ramsay, Jack. (1978). *The Coach's Art.* Forest Grove, OR: Timber Press.

Ramsay, Jack. (2002, September 19). *My Secrets to NBA Head Coaching Success.* Website: http://www.espn.com.

Ramsay, Jack. (2003). *Dr. Jack's Leadership Lessons Learned From a Lifetime in Basketball.* Hoboken, NJ: John Wiley and Sons Publishers.

LESSONS FROM THIS LEGEND...

THE ROLE OF DEFENSE

By Jack Ramsay

RELATIONSHIP OF DEFENSE TO PHILOSOPHY

A basketball team's style of play must be predicated upon the defensive system that it employs. It has always seemed incongruous to me that a coach would adopt a particular style of offensive play before full consideration was given to the defense to be used. However, it seems that many coaches spend most of their time planning their offense and attach only incidental significance to the vital defensive phase of the game.

PROMOTING "DEFENSIVE THINKING"

At St. Joseph's, we feel that defense is the foundation and heart of our game. It is primarily through the medium of defense that we manifest the hustle and aggressiveness expressed in our philosophy. We try to promote a positive defensive attitude among our players. We want them to feel that our kind of defense will win games for us. We want our players to take pride in their ability to accomplish our defensive objectives. In order to accomplish them, we strive to develop players that are basically sound, aggressive, challenging, and daring in their defensive play.

THE OFFENSIVE ASPECT OF DEFENSE

We strive to make our offense a natural outgrowth of our defense. We must be alert to shift quickly from defense to offense in order to take advantage of steals and deflected and intercepted passes. We try to obtain as many such easy field goals as possible. Since this success depends upon defensive skill, we devote the greatest amount of pre-season practice time (about 65 percent) to the fundamental individual and team tactics demanded by our defensive principles.

TYPES OF DEFENSES

The defense referred to is fundamentally a pressing man-to-man. It is an aggressive attack on the opponent. It demands an adamant defensive attitude and a tremendous all-out effort by each player. It requires careful attention to the defensive fundamentals of stance and movement. The pressure defense makes use of ball denial, jump switches, double-ups, and an element of risk in order to obtain possession of the ball.

We will frequently resort to the zone press to realize our objectives. This variation blends well with the man-to-man style in the "pressure cooker" and produces a savory type of game that whets the basketball appetites of player, coach, and spectator.

A third ingredient in our defensive recipe is the standard zone defense. We turn to this formation occasionally in order to keep our opponent off balance.

With these defensive forces prepared, we feel we are ready to begin each new season.

GENERAL OBJECTIVES

We have two general objectives in the pressing defenses we employ:
1. Prevent the opponent from playing the kind of game he wants to play
2. Maintain constant pressure on the opponent to force him into ill-timed maneuvers on which we might capitalize

Let us briefly examine each of these objectives. We attempt to force our opponent into a different style of play, because we feel that he will operate less efficiently in a style less familiar to him. Therefore, if our opponent uses a set-play offense, we try to prevent him from getting his plays started. If our opponent runs a pattern style of offense, our objective is to disrupt the pattern so that it is never completed. If he concentrates on working off a post (high, low, or side), we attempt to keep the ball away from that objective. If the opponent is a slow and deliberate team, we try to speed up the tempo of play by forcing action through defensive pressure. If it is a fast-breaking team, we want to slow him down by pressuring the rebounders and overplaying the outlet pass receivers.

The second objective helps us to attain the first. In a sense, it implements the first because, by exerting pressure on our opponent, we force him to play a different kind of game than he planned. Beyond this factor is, of course, the desire to capitalize on the results of pressuring (steals, interceptions, opponent's violations) to stimulate our offensive attack.

Our general defensive objectives, therefore, touch both the defensive and offensive phases of the game. The pressure may be applied over the full-court, three-quarter court, or half-court. It may even take place at the conventional defensive position at the top of the circle. It may be a man-to-man or zone press.

Regardless of the type press to be utilized, or at what point on the court it is applied, we strive to force our opponent from his predetermined plan of attack and, at the same time, get our own offense off to an explosive start.

LESSONS FROM THIS LEGEND...

10 Principles of Man-to-Man Defensive Team Play

1. Maintain a defensive stance: knees flexed; head up; foot nearer the vertical court division forward; hands in close while moving; forward hand up on man with ball; eyes on the midsection of the opponent with ball.
2. Overplay the next potential pass receiver.
3. Use peripheral vision to see both man and ball—but especially the ball.
4. Never turn your back on the ball. Face the ball; keep the lanes jammed by backing through, as the offensive player moves without the ball.
5. Use a defensive shuffle in defensive movements; rely on the position of the body to impede offensive moves. Don't cross feet in movements.
6. Slough off players without the ball (except the next potential pass receivers), look for pass interceptions, pick up the driver or pass receivers, or draw the charge from the offensive player; keep a position between the man and the ball.
7. "Jump switch" on all lateral backcourt offensive movements involving the ball; "hedge" on vertical moves involving the ball, using defensive fakes.
8. The defensive man playing screener has the option of doubling-up on the ball when it seems a sound risk.
9. If the defender has given up his man in an attempt to steal and has failed, he must be quick to pick up the open player in recovering.
10. Concentrate individual defensive efforts around the position of the ball; strive to get possession at every opportunity.

Pressure Man-to-Man Coaching Tips

1. Sell players on the group benefits and responsibilities of pressure defense.
2. Emphasize the "watch-the-ball" defense.
3. Encourage the "go-for-the-ball" defense.
4. Emphasize sloughing off weakside players.
5. Praise the drawing of the offensive charge.
6. Encourage the attempt to steal, but demand the move to recover if the attempt fails.
7. Overplay the opponent, but demand the vital block-out in order to keep him off the backboard.
8. Stress the immediate burst from defense to offense when possession of the ball is obtained.

Zone Press Coaching Tips

1. Stress careful compliance with press shifts at all times.
2. Drill players in all zone-press positions they may be required to play in the game.
3. Practice "double-teaming" situations from all areas of the court to improve their effectiveness.
4. Encourage players to take good risks to deflect or intercept pass.
5. Stress exaggerated movements and shouting by pressing defenders to fluster opponents.

Strategic Use of Pressure Defense

1. Discover during practice and scrimmage sessions the strength of your press and use it accordingly during the games.
2. Try some form of the zone press during the first half of the game. It will give you an idea of the opponent's attack at a time when possible damage may be overcome.
3. Use the zone if you are having trouble penetrating the opponent's defense.
4. Use the zone press if your opponent wants to hold the ball for one shot before the end of the half or the end of the game.
5. Be ready to adjust the press if the opponent finds consistent scoring openings.
6. Counteract an opponent's press with one of your own.
7. Never assume defeat. Use every defensive tactic at your disposal to help your team win the game.
8. Zone press the team that relies on one or even two good ballhandlers to advance the ball. By forcing the other players to handle the ball, the pressing team may be able to benefit from many ballhandling errors.
9. Full-court press the team that is poorly conditioned or shallow in bench strength. Use of the press for extended periods of time will eventually pay dividends.
10. Zone press the inexperienced team.
11. Zone press to spark your offense when it seems to be lagging.
12. Press the team that is rallying against your second-half lead.
13. Apply moderate, no-foul court pressure to the opponent when your team is leading by one or two points with only seconds remaining.
14. Zone press the team with an overwhelming height advantage.

SOURCE

Ramsay, Jack. (1963). *Pressure Basketball.* Englewood Cliffs, NJ: Prentice-Hall.

LEGACY OF Adolph Rupp

- Nicknamed the "Baron of the Bluegrass."

- Retired as the all-time winningest coach in college basketball history.

- Feisty, controversial coach whose basic tenet was "Play to Win."

- Produced fundamentally sound, fast-breaking teams.

- Namesake of Rupp Arena on the University of Kentucky campus.

- Led Kentucky to four NCAA championships (1948, 1949, 1951, 1958).

- Compiled a record of 876-190 (.822) at Kentucky.

- Was a master at developing local talent. He took more than 80 percent of his players from the hills of Kentucky and turned them into champions.

ADOLPH RUPP

"I know I have plenty of enemies, but I'd rather be the most hated coach in the country than the most popular one. Show me a popular coach, and I'll show you a loser."
—Adolph Rupp

BIOGRAPHY

Born: September 2, 1901 in Halstead, KS

Died: December 10, 1977

Inducted into the Naismith Memorial Basketball Hall of Fame in 1969

Adolph Rupp coached 42 years at the University of Kentucky and made Kentucky basketball synonymous with greatness. His teams won 876 games, including NCAA championships in 1948, 1949, 1951, and 1958. Rupp also led Kentucky to the NIT title in 1946. Nicknamed the "Baron of the Bluegrass," Rupp was a master of developing homegrown talent. Over 80 percent of his players came from the state of Kentucky. Rupp's teams appeared in 20 NCAA tournaments and won 27 SEC titles. Rupp retired as the all-time winningest coach in college basketball. He was regarded as one of the fiercest competitors in the game of basketball. As a college player, Rupp played for future Hall of Fame coach "Phog" Allen on the 1922 and 1923 Kansas team that was named national champions. Rupp co-coached the 1948 Olympic team to a gold medal. Rupp was enshrined in the Naismith Memorial Basketball Hall of Fame in 1969.

...SCOUTING REPORT.....SCOUTING REPORT.....

Adolph Rupp...

Adolph Rupp was raised on a farm in Halstead, KS and, at a young age, began playing basketball, using a homemade ball and a barrel nailed to a barn door. He attended the University of Kansas and formulated much of his basketball philosophy from future Hall of Fame coach "Phog" Allen and the game's inventor, Dr. James Naismith.

Rupp received his degree in business from the University of Kansas and had no intention of entering the coaching profession. He discovered quickly, during this period before our country's depression, that jobs were scarce in the banking business. Rupp returned to the University of Kansas as an assistant instructor. He then accepted a position at Burr Oak, KS, teaching history and coaching all sports. Rupp soon discovered that there was no place to play basketball. The only facility was a renovated barn that had been converted into a skating rink. Basketball was only played when no skating was scheduled. Rupp knew that this was not the place for him and eagerly accepted a position at Marshalltown High School in Iowa. He was disappointed again when he arrived, only to find out that he was to coach wrestling, not basketball, as he had anticipated. Totally unfamiliar with the sport of wrestling, Rupp purchased a wrestling book and then coached his team to the state championship.

Rupp moved the following year to Freeport High School in Illinois and led his basketball teams to a 67-16 record. While coaching at Freeport, Rupp attended summer school at Columbia University and received his master of arts degree. Rupp learned that John Mauer was leaving the University of Kentucky for the head-coaching position at Miami of Ohio. He applied for the job at Kentucky and was named head coach in May of 1930. He was given a two-year contract for $2,800 a year. Rupp was 28-years old and had no college coaching experience. When asked why he should get the Kentucky job, Rupp responded, "Because, I'm the best damned basketball coach in the nation."

One of Rupp's first moves after arriving on campus was to call Carey Spicer, the team's captain, and tell him of the fast break and man-to-man defense that the Wildcats would use. Rupp made an instant impact in the South, when his Kentucky team won their first ten games and advanced to the finals of the Southern Conference, before losing to Maryland on a last-second shot.

At Kentucky, Adolph Rupp became one of the all-time most powerful men in sports. Rupp ruled with an iron fist and was basketball's version of General MacArthur and General Patton rolled into one. When he issued a compliment, it was worth something. When he talked, people listened, for he was a man of authoritative expression. Critics accused Rupp of taking the fun out of the game, but he countered by saying that "his boys" get their fun by playing for national championships. "We do not wish merely to participate in sports," stated Rupp. "We wish to be successful in sports. In order to be successful, we must create within these boys the competitive spirit that will bring success. Defeat and failure to me are enemies. Without victory, basketball has little meaning." (Padwe, 1970)

In opponents' gymnasiums, Rupp was the hated enemy. Auburn fans threw tomatoes at him. During World War II, Tennessee fans gave him the ultimate insult by linking his name with Adolph Hitler. Rupp's strength, dedication, and confidence prevailed against all those who attacked him. "To sit by and worry about criticism, which too often comes from the misinformed or from those incapable of passing judgment on an individual or a problem, is a waste of time," Rupp said. "I've gotten a lot of publicity for being a mean man. But, it's not true."

"I have always thought that an excerpt from Parkenham Beatty's *Self Reliance* contained a good philosophy for every coach," said Rupp:
> By your own soul learn to live,
> And if men thwart you, take no heed,
> If men hate you, have no care,
> Sing your song and dream your dream,
> Hope your hope and pray your prayer.

"I am sure if a coach will follow this philosophy of life, he will be successful," stated Rupp. (Rupp, 1958)

Rupp was rough on his players, and they often didn't understand their coach until after their playing days were over. "He wanted everybody to hate him—and he succeeded," said former Wildcat star Bill Spivey. "He called us names some of us had never heard before."

All-American guard Louie Dampier said, "Coach Rupp was a very strict disciplinarian. He was tough to play for, and a lot of guys left because they didn't like it. I never crossed paths with him when I was playing, but I never developed much of a relationship with him then either. It wasn't until after I graduated that I got to meet him on different grounds, as a man, and I grew to love him then."

.....SCOUTING REPORT......SCOUTING REPORT...

Practices under Rupp were long and hard, and above all they were silent. "It is generally understood out there," Rupp explained, "that no one is to speak unless he can improve on the silence...Why should boys constantly chatter in a class in basketball any more than they do in a class in English?"

Hall of Fame player Cliff Hagan (2003) described practices as extremely demanding. "It wasn't a whole lot of fun," Hagan said. "It was work, work, work, and more work. Scrimmaging and playing the games were about the only thing that were fun when playing for Coach Rupp. But, it was worth it, because Coach Rupp was something special."

When asked what were Rupp's greatest qualities, Hagan quickly listed six that stood out above the others:
1. "He was a perfectionist and never settled for anything less."
2. "He was exceedingly demanding of his players and himself."
3. "He was exacting in the drills. Our plays were part of our practice drills. It became second nature to go right from the drills into our plays."
4. "Conditioning. We believed that we were in better condition than any team we played against."
5. "He was very bright. He was probably brighter than most people he was coaching against."
6. "He was a good recruiter. He could recognize talent."

Rupp pushed his players to great levels of success. Twenty-four players earned All-American honors, seven captured Olympic gold medals, and 28 played professional basketball. Legendary coach "Red" Auerbach said, "Rupp-trained players are better grounded in the fundamentals than any others."

Rupp stated, "It's the work we give them in the fundamentals, there's no other way. The first thing you have to do is curtail the individual desire of the boy in the interest of team play. Then, you have to correct two deficiencies every boy has—in playing defense and in recognizing the value of ball possession."

Rupp was a colorful collection of rituals and superstitions. He always wore a brown suit to games and attended every practice dressed in khaki pants. On game days, Rupp would not step on the court without a buckeye, a rabbit's foot, and a four-leaf clover in his pocket.

Rupp declared his biggest thrills in basketball came when he and his five Kentucky players won Olympic gold medals and when he occupied a front row seat at a U.S. Armed Forces track meet in Frankfort, Germany in 1945, along with George S. Patton and 20 other World War II generals.

Rupp was a strong advocate of the fast break and a tough man-to-man defense. From an offensive standpoint, Rupp believed the greatest offense was the pivot-post offense. Rupp said, "We employed the pivot-post at Kentucky the entire time I coached there. The Original Celtics made the offense perfect. I studied that play with them many nights, talking and talking into the wee hours. I discovered that if you don't have a good pivot man, you're not going to get anywhere with it. We had ten basic plays with the pivot-post offense that we worked on and worked on....not only hours, but hundreds of thousands of hours in order to perfect them." (Rupp, 1976)

Hall of Fame coach Ray Meyer (2003) said, "I played and coached against Mr. Rupp, and I consider him one of the fiercest competitors in the game of basketball. I always liked to play his team early in the season, because he would always tell me what was wrong with my team."

The "Baron of the Bluegrass" established a legacy that few can match. His teams won 876 games while losing only 190 for a winning percentage of .822. He retired as the winningest coach in college basketball. Adolph Rupp made Kentucky Basketball synonymous with winning.

SOURCE

Hagan, Cliff. Interview with Ralph Pim. September 5, 2003.

Meyer, Ray. Interview with Ralph Pim. September 5, 2003.

Padwe, Sandy. (1970). *Basketball's Hall of Fame.* Englewood Cliffs, NJ: Prentice-Hall.

Rupp, Adolph. Vertical Files, Archives. Naismith Memorial Basketball Hall of Fame. Springfield, MA.

Rupp, Adolph. (1958, December 8). Defeat and Failure To Me Are Enemies. *Sports Illustrated.*

Rupp, Adolph. (1976). Reflections. *The Basketball Bulletin (Winter Edition).*

LESSONS FROM THIS LEGEND...

THE SEVEN CARDINAL RULES OF DEFENSE

By Adolph Rupp

Many—you might even say most—basketball experts contend that defense is being shamefully neglected. They point to the astronomical scores and shake their heads. "Defense," they say, "is being thrown out the window. It isn't like the old days when a coach worked just as hard on defense as he did on offense."

I don't believe this is true. On the contrary, I believe we're working harder on it today than we ever have in the past. We've got to. The modern offensive player is tremendously better equipped than the player of 30 or even 20 years ago, and coaches must work twice as hard to stop him.

To anyone who believes that modern defensive basketball is being neglected, I'd like to pose these questions:
1. How do you defend the quick, running, one-handed shot?
2. How do you instruct your players to guard against the hook shot?
3. How do you teach your players to guard the pivot man on the step-in-step-out hook shot?
4. How do you teach your players to guard the running jump shot?
5. How do you teach a player to stop the dribble-stop jump shot?

After thinking about these things for a while, I believe you'll come to the same conclusion that I have: offensive techniques have simply outrun defensive techniques.

Even today, a low-scoring game doesn't necessarily indicate that good defense was employed. What I'd want to know is:
1. How many shots were taken?
2. How long did it take a team to set-up a play?
3. Was ball control permitted?
4. Was any attempt made to deliberately withhold the ball from play?

The answers to these questions may be the key to the low scores.

Many spectators and coaches don't appreciate defensive play. Being unspectacular, good defense is often disregarded. But, I believe that a check of the outstanding teams year after year will reveal that good defense has contributed greatly to their success.

Their coaches know that defense is less ephemeral than offense; that on an evening when the offense isn't clicking, the game can be salvaged by that steady, consistently good defense. A team without a good defense hasn't anything to fall back on when its shooting is "off."

At Kentucky, we're convinced that our defense will save us on the nights when our offense isn't working. Our players are taught to realize the importance of defense—individual as well as team play and we spend one-third of our time on it.

I believe that good defense embodies seven cardinal principles, as follows:

1. **Reduce the number of your opponent's shots.**
   You've all heard the saying, "Take enough shots and the percentage will take care of itself." That may be true, so the first thing to do is cut down the number of shots you give the other team.

   In going back over our shot charts for a period of five years, we've found a very reliable trend on the number of shots taken—that is to give the opponents as few shots as possible. They still must shoot to score, and if you can reduce their scoring opportunities by aggressive defense, you will eliminate the danger of a high score.

2. **Force your opponent into low-percentage shots.**
   We tell our players to be aggressive at all times. It's hard, tough work, but a lot of players like to play that kind of ball. It's a good feeling to have one of your players come up and ask to be assigned to the outstanding player on the opposing team.

   Several years ago, we had such a player. He wasn't interested in how many points he scored, but he liked to take an opponent with a 20-point average and whittle him down to seven or eight. Before he left the dressing room, he'd come up and ask, "Have I got Smith Saturday night?"— Smith being the star of the opposing team.

   If you can force a team to take hurried, off-balance, inaccurate shots, you'll destroy their shooting percentage. And that's the difference between aggressive defense and defense that permits a team to get good shots. When a coach comes up after a game and says, "We couldn't hit tonight," maybe there was a reason.

LESSONS FROM THIS LEGEND...

3. Control everything inside 18 feet of the basket.
I like to put this in, because it fits in well with the philosophy of collapsing or floating defenses. It certainly is in their favor. If you'll draw a circle 18 feet out from the basket and attempt to cut down everything in that area and get all the rebounds, you'll have a foolproof defense. I realize this is impossible, but the fact still remains—don't give them a shot close in to the basket! If you can imprint this upon the minds of your players, they will get the idea and work toward this goal.

4. Eliminate second shots.
A good defense shouldn't permit a team to get the second and third shots at the basket. While it's often difficult to get the rebound, the first thing to do after a shot has been taken is to see that your man doesn't get the rebound.

You should block out your man, and then, after you have him out of play, go for the rebound yourself. If you permit a second and possibly a third shot, one of these is apt to fall in. A good, tough rebounding team won't permit these additional shots after the initial attempt has been taken.

5. Allow no easy baskets.
How many times have you seen a good, well-played game broken up by a cheap interception, with the defender going all the way and scoring? Ever have an opponent on your own free-throw line slap a jump ball over the head of your defensive players and go all the way in to score? How many times have you had a pass-in under your defensive basket intercepted and laid in for an easy basket? How many times have you seen a ball fall aimlessly to the floor and have it picked up by an opponent and thrown up for an easy basket? How many times have you seen an opponent get an easy basket on a rebound after a missed free throw?

These are examples of easy baskets. Some are due to carelessness, some are due to bad judgment, but in a game between teams of equal ability, an easy basket at a critical time often proves the deciding factor.

6. "Point" the ball on all long shots.
As the ball is maneuvered on the outside, the defensive man on the ball should always play tight. Two of the cardinal principles are to cut down on the number of shots and the number of the good shots. If you'll allow good long shooters to get set unmolested, they'll ruin you.

Therefore, the man with the ball should always be "pointed." This is true even in floating defenses. In strict tight man-to-man defensive play, this should always be true.

(*Authors' Note:* Rupp's use of the term "point" the ball is now more commonly called "pressuring the shot" or closely guarding the shooter and putting a hand up on the shot.)

7. Prevent the ball from going to the pivot.
I believe that most teams feel exactly as we do—that the ball should never be allowed to go in to the pivot man. If you let the opponents do this, they can set their screens without worrying about ballhandling. We permit the ball to go to the side of the floor, but always try to prevent it from going to the pivot man.

As soon as the pivot man has the ball, you have a dangerous offensive center. He can take a hook shot, jump shot, or jump-flip shot. He can fake on one side and go to the other. He can pass to a cutting teammate who has been freed by a screen.

The ball is in an extremely dangerous position when a player in the pivot area has possession of it. The highest field-goal shooting percentage is from this position.

My objective has been to give you the benefits of our experience down through the years. On those long nights that are sure to come during the season, it might be well to check on these seven cardinal principles and see if any of them are being abused. Maybe, somewhere along the way you may find your source of difficulty.

Even if your team is doing well, you can still check. The star of your team offensively may not be a star at all. His defensive inability may be losing ball games.

Bear this in mind: I repeat it to my players thousands of times every year—your defense will save you on the nights that your offense isn't working.

SOURCE

Rupp, Adolph. (1955, November). My Seven Cardinal Defensive Principles. *Scholastic Coach*.

LEGACY OF
Dean Smith

- Recorded 879 wins during his 36-year coaching career and is the all-time winningest college coach in the history of the game.

- One of only three coaches to win the "Triple Crown" of coaching.

- Holds the NCAA Tournament record for most appearances, most consecutive appearances, and most tournament victories.

- His teams were known for their unselfish play, outstanding teamwork, and a tenacious man-to-man defense.

- Popularized the four-corner offense and the run-and-jump defense.

- Created a basketball program based on integrity, honor, and respect.

DEAN SMITH

"What to do with a mistake—recognize it, admit it, learn from it, and forget it."
—Dean Smith

BIOGRAPHY

Born: February 28, 1931 in Emporia, KS

Inducted into the Naismith Basketball Hall of Fame in 1983

In thirty-six years at the University of North Carolina, Dean Smith compiled a record of 879-254, a winning percentage of .776. The 879 victories are the most by any coach in college basketball history. He led North Carolina to the NCAA championship in 1982 and 1993. Under Smith, the Tar Heels made twenty-three consecutive NCAA appearances. His Carolina teams also won or shared a record seventeen ACC regular-season titles and won a record thirteen ACC tournament championships. Smith was head coach of the 1976 U.S. Olympic basketball team, which won the gold medal. He was highly regarded as an innovator and developed the four-corner offense and run-and-jump defense. Smith played for Hall of Fame coach "Phog" Allen and was a member of the 1952 University of Kansas NCAA championship team. ABC and ESPN named him one of the seven greatest coaches of the twentieth century in any sport. Smith was enshrined in the Naismith Memorial Basketball Hall of Fame in 1983.

...SCOUTING REPORT.....SCOUTING REPORT.....

Dean Smith...

"We Are Family," the 1978 hit by Sister Sledge, aptly describes Dean Smith's North Carolina teams during his illustrious 36-year coaching career. The lyrics depict the togetherness and camaraderie of the North Carolina basketball family. If you were tuned into the radio during that era, the words will come back with comfortable familiarity:

> "Everyone can see we're together
> As we walk on by
> (Fly!) and we fly just like birds of a feather
> I won't tell no lie
> (All!) all of the people around us they say
> Can they be that close
> Just let me state for the record
> We're giving love in a family dose
> We are family!"

Smith's Tar Heels flew "like birds of a feather" past their opponents with amazing consistency. Under Smith, North Carolina had an all-time record of 879-254, and his teams won more games than those of any other college coach in history. The Tar Heels won at least 20 games for 27 straight years. North Carolina was the dominant force in the Atlantic Coast Conference and finished in the top three for 33 successive seasons. In that span, the Tar Heels won the ACC 17 times and finished second 11 times.

Despite such success, victories were secondary in North Carolina's "We Are Family" environment. Smith's number one priority was developing people of high character. He placed this above everything else, including winning. "Coach Smith was concerned about preparing players for life after college, and the game of basketball was a platform for him to do that," said James Worthy, a member of the 2003 Basketball Hall of Fame enshrinement class.

Smith structured the North Carolina basketball program on the tenets of respect and loyalty and created a fraternity like no other in the basketball world. "His program was very much a different style than most college basketball programs," stated former Tar Heel and NBA coach George Karl. "He built his program around team and family and togetherness and camaraderie and helping each other. There was always a family kind of unity that I don't think existed anywhere else."

Smith's emphasis on family values developed during his childhood in Emporia, Kansas. His parents, both public school teachers, reinforced the important life lessons of integrity, compassion, industriousness, humility, and love. "I was raised in a relatively strict home, and I learned most of my values from a very loving mother and father," said Smith.

"Value each human being" was a central theme in Smith's household, and he was taught to treat every person with respect and dignity. Smith had been in Chapel Hill just one year, when he and his pastor escorted a black student into a restaurant where blacks were not served. It was not a popular move in the segregation-inflicted South of the 1960s, but that did not concern Smith because he would not tolerate racial injustice.

Smith transferred the lessons he learned as a young man into his basketball philosophy. He created a basketball program based on integrity, honor, and respect. Players learned how to live with people from different backgrounds and different cultures. They gained an appreciation for working hard and playing according to the rules. They learned the importance of teamwork and unselfishness. They were provided daily opportunities to experience success in an arena much larger than basketball.

Smith's players received a daily practice plan with a "Thought for the Day" at the top of the page, and they were expected to memorize it. It usually had nothing to do with basketball, but rather was a philosophical statement that put basketball into a larger context. Smith used the Serenity Prayer on occasion or a statement, such as "don't let one day pass without doing something for a person who cannot repay you." Smith started each practice with a few comments and then asked a player to recite the "Thought for the Day." If for any reason a player failed to give the correct response, the entire team had to run. Players made sure they learned the "Thought for the Day," because they didn't want their teammates to run for their mistake.

The basketball program at North Carolina was built on three goals: 1) play together, 2) play hard, and 3) play smart. The goals were clear and concise, and Smith seldom discussed winning with his players. He believed that winning was merely a by-product of players demonstrating unselfishness, hard work, and proper execution.

Smith promoted rituals that encouraged togetherness and teamwork. One ritual was pointing to the passer to acknowledge the unselfish act of passing the ball to an open teammate. Coach John Wooden told Smith that he always wanted the receiver of a pass to say a quick thank-you to the passer or wink at him. Smith decided that he wanted a more obvious gesture and asked his players to point to the passer. He hoped this gesture would alert fans and members of the media to the importance of passing. It became a ritual not

.....SCOUTING REPORT.....SCOUTING REPORT...

only with the players on the floor, but also with the coaches and players on the bench. It wasn't long until Tar Heel fans adopted the ritual and were showing their appreciation for unselfish play.

Another North Carolina ritual was to have everyone on the bench stand and applaud when a player was taken out of the game. "We told our players that if the president of the United States entered the room, we'd stand out of respect," said Smith. "To our way of thinking, a teammate was more important than anybody. So, when a player came out of the game, his teammates showed their appreciation by standing and applauding. The coaches also stood to applaud, even if the player hadn't played well. That did wonders to promote unselfishness."

Smith treated every player as an important member of the team. He did not differentiate between the lesser-skilled and higher-skilled athletes. "Whether you were a starter or a twelfth man, he made us all feel like we were the most important player who ever played for him," remembered former player and future Hall of Fame coach Larry Brown.

Smith created a practice environment that was conducive to learning and was recognized by his coaching peers as a master teacher. "Dean Smith is a better teacher of basketball than anyone else," said legendary UCLA coach John Wooden.

Each session was carefully planned and meticulously organized. Players sprinted from one drill to the next. As they moved, they were reminded of the specifics of the North Carolina philosophy. Virtually everything during practice was graded, based on execution.

"Practice was the foundation of everything that we did," explained Smith. "We used practice and repetition to teach our players what we wanted. Our players always felt that our practices were harder than games, and that's the way it should have been. The teaching I did in our practices was what I really missed the most when I retired."

Smith's goal in coaching was not to become the all-time winningest coach. He does not talk about the 879 wins. He talks about the people behind the victories...their successes and their accomplishments. Like a proud father, he smiles when reflecting on the fact that 97 percent of his players graduated and almost forty percent later attained post-graduate degrees. His greatest desire is that his players succeed as people and find happiness in life.

Smith has always been there for his players. When Michael Jordan's father was murdered in the summer of 1993, it was Smith who met Jordan at the Wilmington, North Carolina Airport. "The two most important men in my life have been my father and Dean Smith," said Jordan.

David Chadwick, a forward on the great North Carolina teams in the late 1960s and early '70s, wrote a book entitled *The 12 Leadership Principles of Dean Smith*, based on what he considered were Smith's guiding principles. During one of his conversations with Coach Smith, the phone rang in Smith's office, and Smith looked puzzled. "I don't understand," said Smith. "I gave explicit instructions not to be interrupted." The phone stopped ringing and Chadwick continued his conversation with his mentor. The phone started ringing again, but this time, Smith wasn't puzzled.

"Excuse me for a moment," said Smith. "That must be my private line. It's either one of my children or another former player. They're the only ones who have my private number. They are the only ones who can get to me any time they want."

All-American Phil Ford may have described it best when he said, "I always tell Coach that he's the only father in the world with three hundred children, and only five of them are his own."

Bill Bradley said, "Dean Smith epitomizes what a coach can be—teacher, counselor, mentor, example, friend." During his stellar career, Smith has received numerous awards, including *Sports Illustrated's* 1997 Sportsman of the Year and the 1998 University Award, the highest honor given by the Board of Governors of the 16-campus University of North Carolina.

Smith is more than the all-time winningest coach in the history of college basketball. He is a man of unyielding integrity whose "North Carolina basketball family" is an internationally recognized symbol of what intercollegiate sports should represent.

SOURCE

Chadwick, David. (1999) *The 12 Leadership Principles of Dean Smith.* New York: Total/Sports Illustrated.

Pim, Ralph. (2003). Family Style. *Naismith Memorial Hall of Fame Enshrinement Program.*

Smith, Dean. Vertical Files, Archives. Naismith Memorial Basketball Hall of Fame. Springfield, MA.

Smith, Dean. Interview with Ralph Pim. June 18, 2003.

Smith. Dean. (2002) *A Coach's Life.* New York: Random House.

LESSONS FROM THIS LEGEND...

THE RUN-AND-JUMP DEFENSE

By Dean Smith

The run-and-jump is a rotating man-to-man defense. While it is more conservative than a zone press, it still affords many of the same opportunities for interceptions. It is very much a man-to-man defense. However, there is no set assignment after the first run-and-jump occurs, and any one defensive man may be guarding another offensive man.

HISTORY OF THE RUN-AND-JUMP DEFENSE

It all began, as far as I am concerned, back in the 1952-53 season at the University of Kansas. We were in true pressure defense, as outlined by Dr. "Phog" Allen, our head coach, and Dick Harp, his assistant. We had won the NCAA Championship in 1952 because of excellent play by our center, Clyde Lovellette, and a pressure defense which placed the defensive man between the ball and his man, rather than the man and the basket, which was typical in those days.

One of our players during those years was an extremely competitive athlete by the name of Al Kelley. Al did not play regularly as a sophomore in 1952, but I do remember that none of our players wanted Al guarding them during practice. Al was very aggressive. In fact, to the best of my knowledge, he led the nation in personal fouls as a junior in 1953.

It was in practice that I remember Al guarding a defensive man one pass away from the ball. A guard began dribbling in his direction. Instead of supporting to help out on the dribbler, Al left his man completely to take the ball away from the dribbler about ten feet away. Of course, the man guarding the dribbler automatically reacted by picking up Al's man, although he was probably upset with Al for not doing what he was supposed to do. However, Dick Harp, the assistant coach, actually congratulated Al for making things happen, even though he fouled the ballhandler when he surprised him.

Many times, from that point on, Al would make the dribbler charge him, or the dribbler would pick up the ball and throw it out of bounds. Al was the only player who could do this, although several of us decided it would be fun to surprise the dribbler. It was all part of our basic man-to-man pressure, and was not used as a separate defense at that time. This is how the run-and-jump came into being, as far as I can remember.

If we had stopped to think about it back then, we would have labeled the play the run-and-surprise. That is probably an even more appropriate description of its intended effect.

We used the run-and-jump sparingly at the University of Kansas. However, in 1953, when most of the team was lost to graduation and we were very small, our coaches felt we might be able to make this defense our true defense. We would take the action defensively and make the offense react to us by doing so-called stunting, as football teams do. Keep in mind that this was during the early 1950's, when teams either zone pressed or played a straight man-to-man press. Our relatively short team, with 6'2" and 6'1" forwards, managed to win the Big Eight Conference (after being picked to finish low in the Conference), and we lost to Indiana by only one point in the NCAA Finals.

Coach Bob Spear had seen the 1953 finals and was impressed with the Kansas pressure defense. He wanted to know more about it when I joined him as his assistant at the Air Force Academy. Our Air Force Academy team was extremely small, and we needed to do things defensively, instead of sitting back and letting the offense handle us. The man-to-man pressure defense, incorporating the run-and-jump, became one of our primary defenses at the Academy in the years that followed. It was during this period that we first used the run-and-jump as a full-court defense occasionally. Prior to that time at Kansas, it had been used strictly at half-court out of our basic pressure defense.

When I first assumed the head coaching position at the University of North Carolina, we again were very small, but did have three very quick guards in Larry Brown, Donnie Walsh, and Yogi Poteet. All three picked up the run-and-jump quickly and executed it well. Their success with it encouraged the forwards to enter into it any time a dribbler approached them.

In fact, our players enjoyed it so much during those early days at North Carolina, it eventually created a problem for us. Up to that point, the run-and-jump was not a separate defense, but part of our basic pressure defense. Our players were given the freedom to use it any point on the court they felt they could surprise an approaching dribbler. However, since surprise is important to the run-and-jump, its effectiveness tends to diminish when it is used too often. When our players become too keyed up over the play, we finally had to do something to cut down on its frequency. We did this in 1965 by making it a separate signaled defense.

LESSONS FROM THIS LEGEND...

Morgan Wootten, the highly successful basketball coach at DeMatha High School in Washington, D.C., liked our run-and-jump defense and instituted it at DeMatha. He called the defense "the blitz," which is perhaps better terminology.

Another example of success with the run-and-jump could be found in Barberton, Ohio, where high school coach Jack Greynolds has been teaching pressure defense for some time. Coach Greynolds has told me he would let the players run-and-jump as soon as the dribble occurred without even waiting for the surprise element. He had watched several of our practices and came upon this idea on his own. Of course, Coach Greynolds does a great job of teaching, as does Morgan Wootten, in running our defense. DeMatha has an outstanding record and, much to Coach Greynold's credit, Barberton won the 1976 Ohio State Championship with some very small but active players.

Run-and-Jump in the Full-Court

To begin our diagramming of the run-and-jump, let us assume that we will be picking up the offense at three-quarters court. The quarterback signals the run-and-jump. We are now in our 33 defense: run-and-jump at three-quarters court. Keep in mind, however, that the run-and-jump can be used at any point on the court, and at times other than following our field goals.

If we call for 33 defense, we continue to use the run-and-jump throughout that particular possession of the opponent. Even if the opponent shoots and gets the rebound, we stay in our 30 defense. The same would hold true if we begin in 32 defense, which means that we would be picking up the offense at half-court.

Diagram Smith 1.0 picks up the action after the in-bounds pass has been made to O1. Except for X1, we want our players staying as far from their offensive men downcourt as possible without jeopardizing their ability to recover if O1 were to throw long. Each defensive player guarding his man without the ball plays between the ball and his man as in our 20 defense (straight man-to-man).

X1 plays O1 very tight. Good pressure here is important so that O1 doesn't have the opportunity to find the open man. We want the ballhandler putting the ball on the floor. X1 then has the job of making O1 move downcourt at a forty-five degree angle. We are less concerned with the direction O1 takes than we are with preventing him from beating our defensive man handily. As shown in **Diagram 1.0**, O1 dribbles left-handed in the direction of O2, who begins to clear out. X2 follows O2 part of the way, but then realizes he has a good chance of surprising O1. X2, therefore, runs-and-jumps on the outside shoulder of the dribbler.

The Rotation

As X2 returns to jump the dribbler, O2 is left unguarded and must be picked up quickly. There are no ironclad rules to determine who will pick up the open man during the rotation. For that matter, it is not required, nor even preferable most of the time, that every player join in the rotation. Proximity and judgment will usually determine these factors. The direction of the rotation, however, is determined by the direction taken by the dribbler. If, as shown in **Diagram 1.0**, X1 moves downcourt to his right, players rotating on the perimeter will do so in a counterclockwise direction. The initial defender of the dribbler, however, (X1 in **Diagram 1.0**) sprints back, looking for the open man in a clockwise direction. The reverse patterns are in effect if the dribbler comes downcourt to his right.

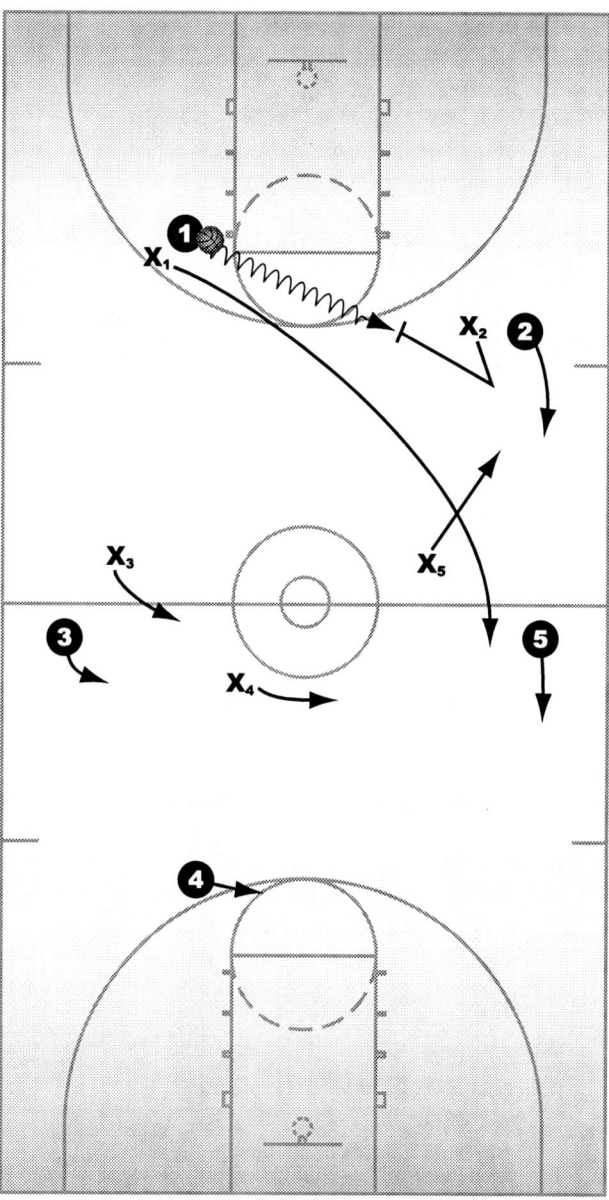

Smith 1.0

X5, anticipating and then observing X2's run-and-jump move, leaves his man to pick up O2. X4 could choose to pick up O5. However, in this case, he remains guarding O4, and X3 stays on O3. X1 never breaks his stride. Playing with his back to his teammates, he doesn't know at the outset

LESSONS FROM THIS LEGEND...

when his help is coming. Therefore, he plays O1 tight until in his periphery, he spots X2 leaving and surprising his man. X1 then heads downcourt around the perimeter in a clockwise direction to pick up the open man. In this case, it happens to be O5. However, it could have been O2, if X5 chose to stay on O5. It also could have been O4, if X4 moved to O5 on X5's move to O2, and so on.

We usually end up in what really amounts to a three-man switch. Very seldom would there be as many as four different men changing their defensive assignments. The most typical situation is the one with X1 picking up O5, X2 picking up O1, and X5 taking O2. The other most prevalent move is a simple switch between X1 and X2. (See **Diagram 1.1**)

INDIVIDUAL RESPONSIBILITIES
Let's review the responsibilities of each player using **Diagram Smith 1.0** as the example.

Player Guarding Initial Ballhandler (X1)
1. Plays man tight—applies pressure in an effort to prevent the ballhandler from finding an open man. Tries to get ballhandler to put the ball on the floor.
2. Avoids letting the ballhandler slice quickly to the middle of the court. The job of the man guarding the dribbler is to encourage him to place the ball on the court with a dribble at a 45-degree angle, while keeping pressure on the ball.
3. Stays with his man until he sees in his periphery the run-and-jump man attacking the dribbler—then enters rotation looking for an open man.

Players Guarding Men One Pass Away (X2 and X3)
1. First responsibility is to prevent pass from ballhandler to their man.
2. When the ballhandler starts dribbling away from them, they start

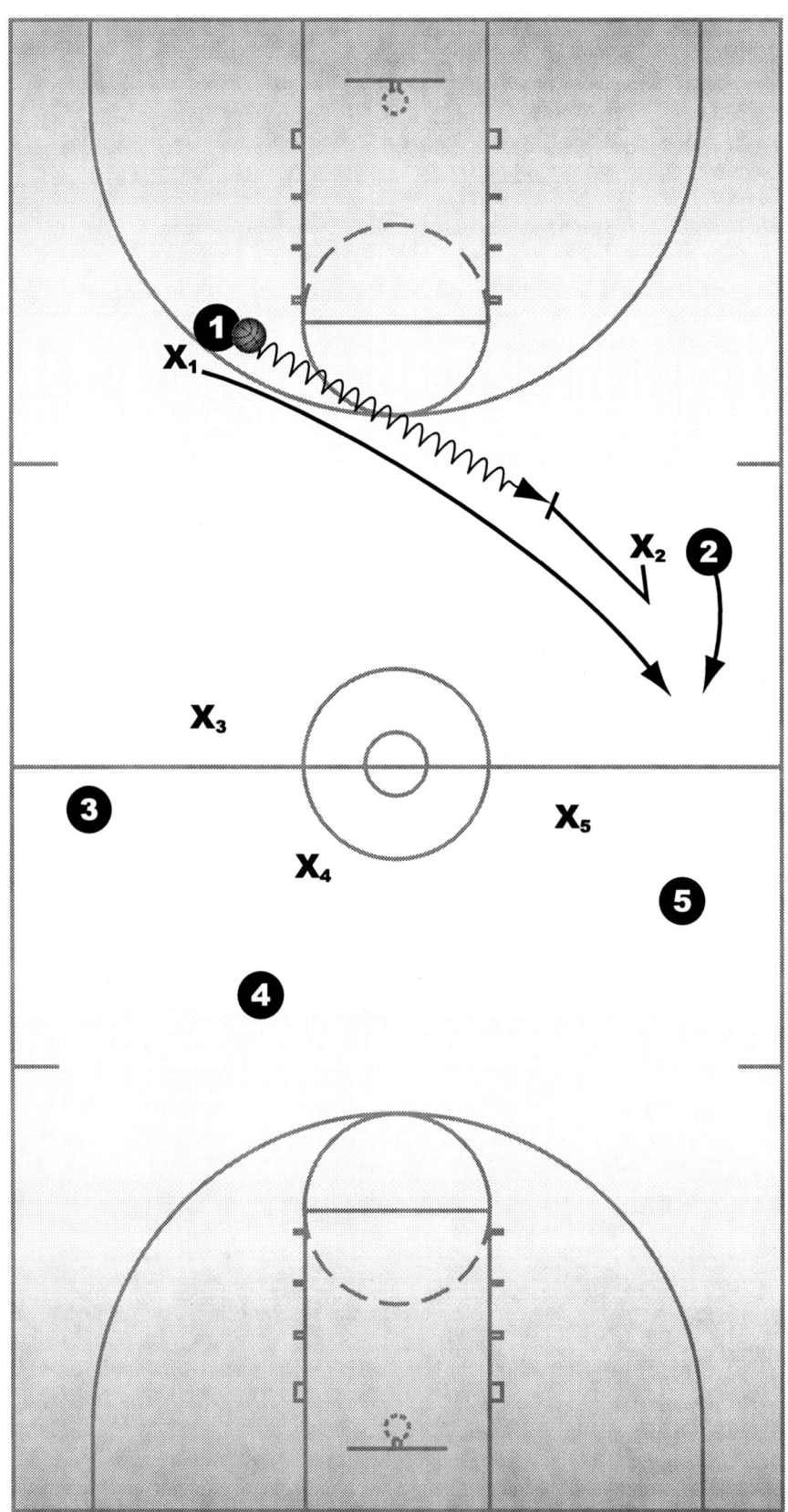

Smith 1.1

LESSONS FROM THIS LEGEND...

giving ground in the direction of the dribble. They are still playing man-to-man, however, and must always be able to get back to prevent a pass.

3. When the ballhandler starts dribbling toward them, they start thinking about the proper surprise point to initiate the run-and-jump. The correct point to surprise the dribbler would vary. It would be dependent upon the distance from the dribbler and the speed with which he dribbles. For example, if O1 were dribbling very fast, X2 could surprise him from 10-15 feet away. If the dribbler was coming slowly, X2 should not leave until he was approximately six feet away.

Players Guarding Men Two or More Passes Away (X4 and X5)

1. First responsibility is to prevent pass from ballhandler to their man.
2. When the ballhandler starts dribbling away from them, they start giving ground in the direction of the dribble. They are still playing man-to-man, however, and must always be able to get back to prevent a pass.
3. When the ballhandler starts dribbling toward them, they begin to prepare for rotation. For example X5 in **Diagram Smith 1.0**, must decide whether to come up and play the possible pass to O2 on X2's run-and-jump. The other option is to stay where he is and let X1 pick up O2, as shown in **Diagram Smith 1.1**. The decision depends on whether or not he feels he can get the ball, as well as the jump on O2. If O2 decides to break, X5 should go for him.
4. If X5 is 6'10" and not very active, he probably should not make a decision to enter the rotation, unless O2 was going all the way to the basket. X5 probably would not want to play O2 whom, we may assume, is a 6'0" guard.

Diagram 1.2 is a continuation of the play and illustrates that the run-and-jump defense does not necessarily conclude after one run-and-jump play. The run-and-jump option remains in effect throughout the entire possession.

O1, after being surprised by X2, attempts to get the pass to O2. X5 tries to intercept the pass but is unsuccessful. X5 then stays tough on O2, who dribbles the ball toward the sideline in the direction of O5, who is now covered by X1. Admittedly, we have quite a mismatch here with X1 on O5. However, we have always felt that the temporary mismatch is overrated. A mismatch like this could be brutal under the board, but more often than not, it doesn't get that far. I am convinced the mismatch is overrated from an offensive standpoint and often fails when the offense stops everything to exploit it.

In **Diagram Smith 1.2**, X1 chooses to run-and-jump the new ballhandler, O2. The rotation begins again. This time, X4 picks up O5, who is the offensive player initially left uncovered as a result of the run-and-jump. X3 picks up O4, and X5 comes around the perimeter to take O3.

As a coach, you can decide whether to make the run-and-jump a separate, signaled defense or simply tell the team in basic man-to-man pressure that they may jump a dribbler when they think he can be surprised. It really makes little difference. However, I still like the idea of controlling when we play our run-and-jump defense 30 by making it a separate call.

The additional advantage is that knowing ahead of time perhaps puts us in a better position to rotate.

SOURCE

Smith, Dean. (1981). *Basketball: Multiple Offense and Defense*. Englewood Cliffs, NJ: Prentice-Hall.

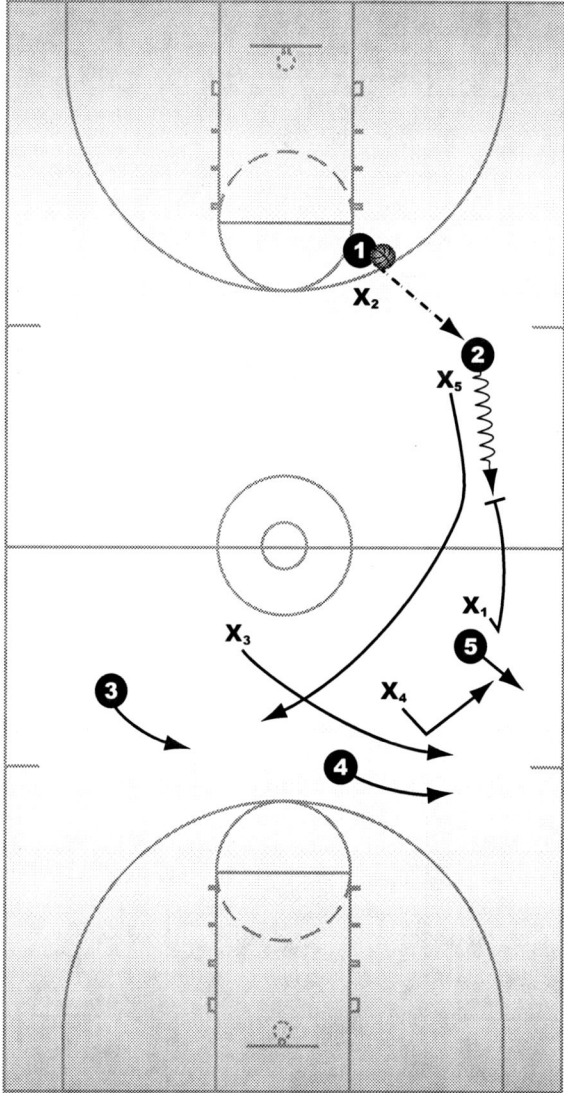

Smith 1.2

LESSONS FROM THIS LEGEND...

THE NORTH CAROLINA FOUR-ON-FOUR COMBINATION DRILL

By Dean Smih

This drill is my favorite drill of all, offensively or defensively. We tried for years to come up with a defensive drill that would encompass all of the defensive techniques we want to teach. This drill does it all.

We also like this drill because we can work with eight players at a time, and the others can be shooting on the other end. We teach all of our techniques in this drill. Once a player learns what to do in this drill, it makes it easier to pick up the techniques we require in our defenses.

SWING DRILL

We start out with a shell to teach position. (See **Diagram 2.0**) In this situation, we make the offense stand and pass the ball. The emphasis in this drill is put upon the idea that you must move and adjust to the ball as it is moved. The rule we teach here is to retreat in the direction of the ball. When O1 passes to O3, all players adjust to the ball. X3 puts immediate pressure on the ball. X1 drops back and in the direction of the ball. X2 and X4 drop back into the lane and protect the offside.

We tell our team that our defensive principles will prepare them to handle any situation. We don't like to change our techniques, so we emphasize what we do best. It is essential that our players believe in our defensive system. The swing drill teaches our players how to adjust to the ball and how to stop the ball from being passed to a spot where it will hurt our team defense. One thing that we allow the offense to do is stand. We don't want this in our offense, but we tell the offensive players that it is a passing drill and an opportunity to improve their ability to move the ball.

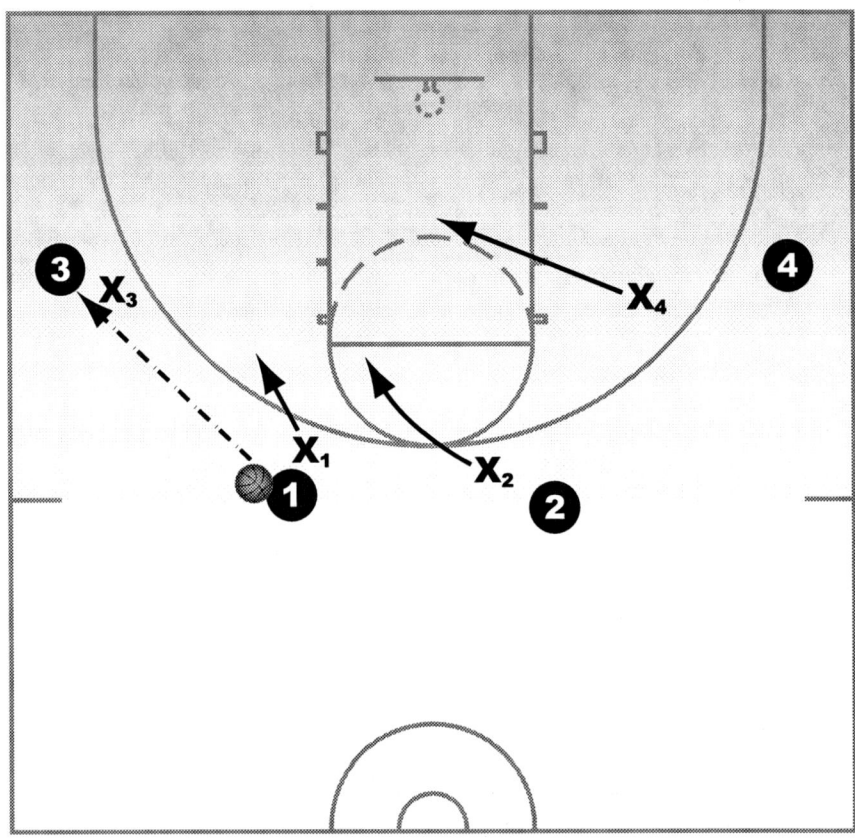

Smith 2.0

LESSONS FROM THIS LEGEND...

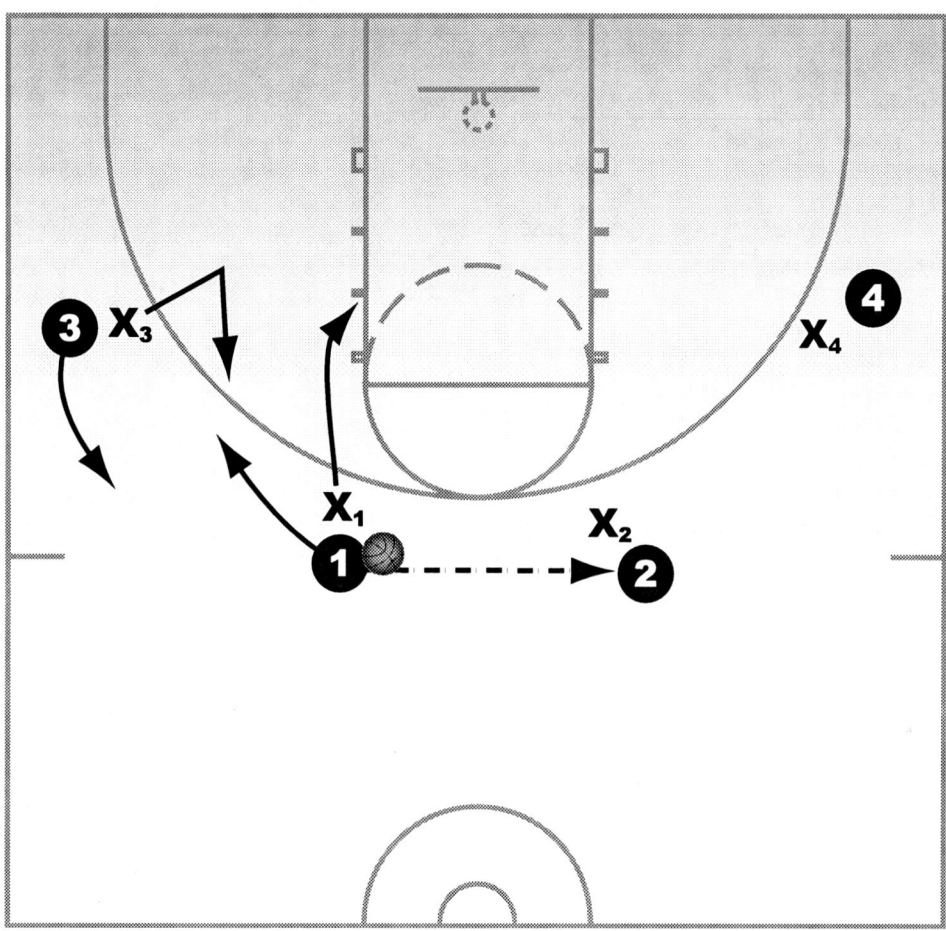

Smith 2.1

TRANSITION DRILL

After the swing drill, we run a transition drill. (See **Diagram 2.1**) The purpose of this drill is to teach transition. It is called transition, because it teaches adjustment and movement. In this drill, O1 passes to O2 and exchanges with O3. We have specific rules for this drill:

1. Retreat toward the ball
2. X1 must plant and open up in the lane. We believe that X3 should retreat off of the ball and then beat his offensive player to the pass. If O3 reverses on X3 who is fronting and pressuring, X1 can pick him up deep.
3. X2 pressures the ballhandler.
4. X4 overplays O4. If O4 goes backdoor, it is the responsibility of X1 to pick up the backdoor cut on the baseline.

On the screen on X3 by O1, our route must be to drop toward the ball and then beat the player to the ball. X3 has retreated, opened up in the lane, and there is a gap for him to shoot through to get his man. Sometimes, he may go over the top of the pick; at other times, he will have to slide through.

LESSONS FROM THIS LEGEND...

SUPPORT DRILL

The third situation we teach is our support drill. (See **Diagram 2.2**) In this drill, we tell O1 to penetrate with the dribble. X2 drops back and must make O1 go wide. We encourage our offensive players to penetrate and pitch. To penetrate and pitch is a good offensive technique, so we are again learning moves on offense.

If O1 penetrates and pitches to O4 and O4 drives the baseline. X3 will cross the lane and stop the ball with straight man-to-man pressure. (See **Diagram 2.3**) There is a temporary double team by X3 and X4. X1 drops back into the lane. In case of a shot, we need rebound position, and we can also cut off a weakside pass under the basket. In a drill situation, O4 will find O1 at the edge of the foul lane, but not in a game. This drill starts to teach rotation by the players, coverage on the offside, and support on stopping the ball and picking up the loose player.

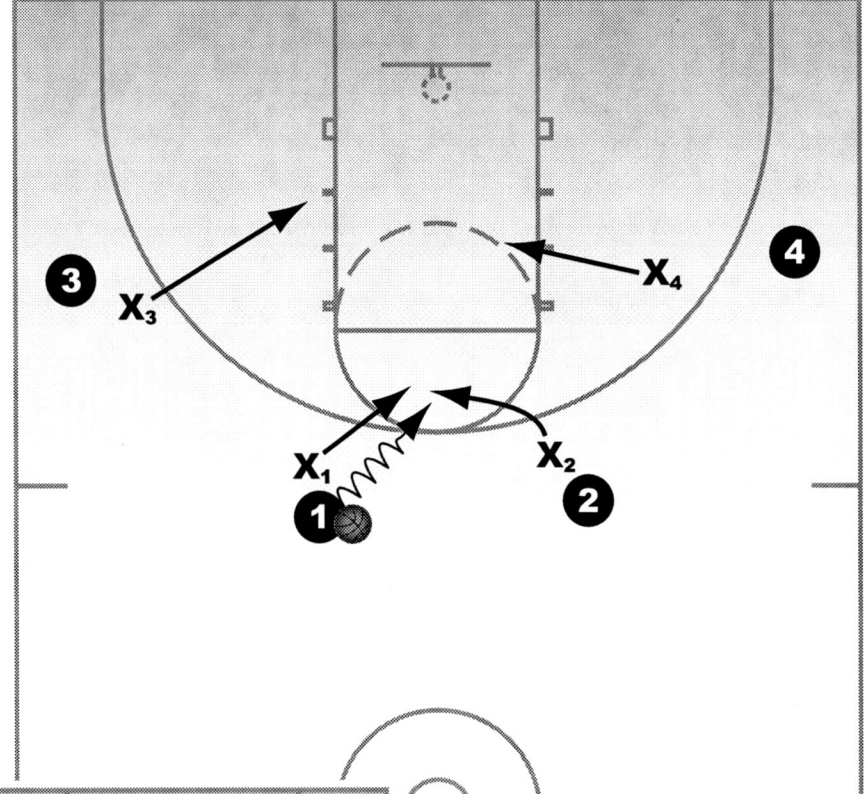

Smith 2.2

Smith 2.3

GUARD-FORWARD ACTION

This drill has more movement in it. A pass from O1 to O3 creates this situation (See **Diagram 2.4**). This attempts to teach X1 to retreat in the direction of the ball and prevent the cutter from getting the ball back. On the clearout, X1 opens up when he gets to the lane and looks to see what is coming his way. If O1 comes back out, X1 comes back up the middle to pick him up. We tell our players that if the offensive player they are guarding clears out, forget him as long as he has cleared away from the ball and is clear across court from the ball. This situation teaches X1 to prevent the cutter from getting the ball, and when he gets to the lane, he must be ready to support.

X3 must put pressure on the ball quickly as O3 receives the pass. X2 retreats in the direction of the ball into the lane and gets ball high. X4 drops into the lane. X4 is very important because he is the offside player.

LESSONS FROM THIS LEGEND...

Many times teams will flash the offside forward to the foul line for the ball. The second move in this drill is to teach X4 to cut off O4 on a flash move. (See **Diagram 2.5**) On this move, X4 must give ground toward the ball. X4 must check the cutter by beating his man to a spot, turning his back, and making contact with O4. He must force O4 to go away from the ball or force him high. We used to check with the closed stance. We may go back to the closed stance. I think either way is good.

CLOSING COMMENTS

Our four-on-four combination has been an excellent drill for us. During our initial teaching, all situations are controlled. After the defenders understand our rules, we allow the offense to do any of these things. We reward our players in competitive drills. We, of course, know that people will have someone inside, and we do teach our players how we want the post man played. We play clearly in front of the post. Many coaches don't like to front, because when the shot is taken, you are clearly at a rebounding disadvantage. Our philosophy in all situations is to have extreme pressure on the ball and make it very difficult for the offense to get the ball where they want it. Sometimes, we cannot cover every occurrence in our fundamentals of defense, but you have to decide what is most important to you and teach your players to play it the way that you want.

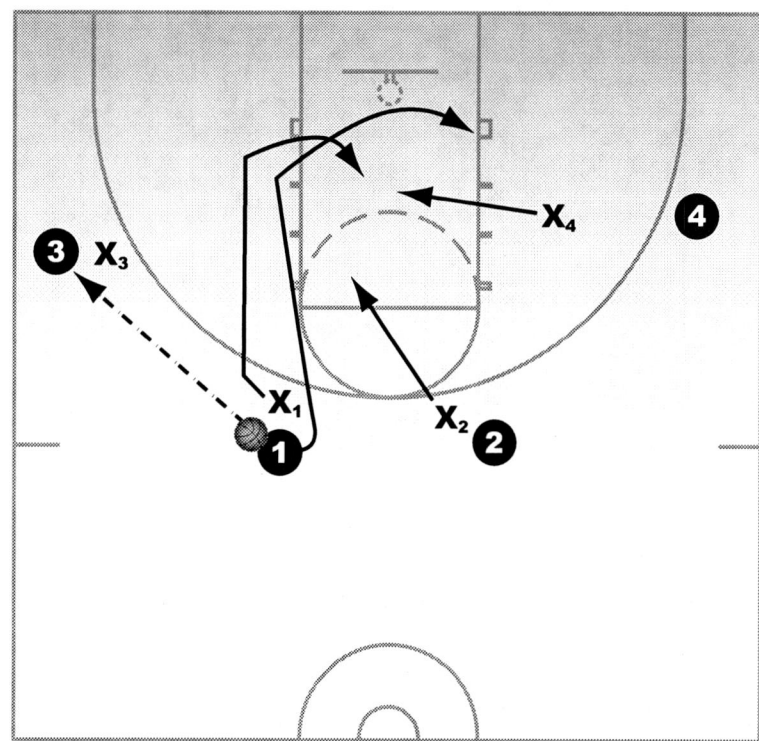

Smith 2.4

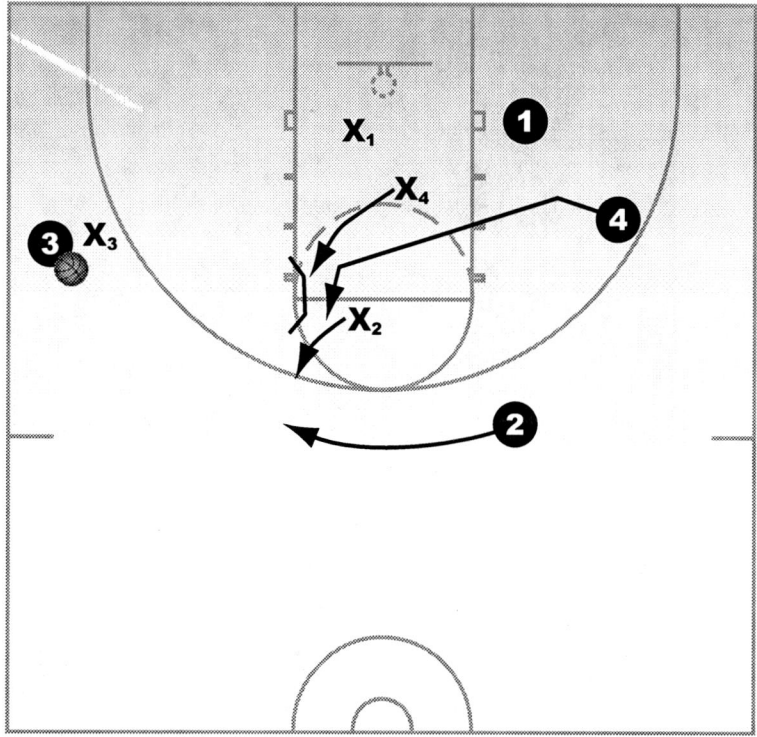

Smith 2.5

SOURCE

Smith, Dean. (1974, June). The North Carolina Four-on-Four Combination Drill. *The Basketball Bulletin.*

LEGACY OF
Pat Head Summitt

- Became the all-time winningest Division I basketball coach on March 22, 2005.

- Selected the Naismith Coach of the Century.

- Became the first woman to reach the 800-win plateau.

- Has led the University of Tennessee to six national championships.

- Coached the 1984 U.S. Women's team to their first gold medal in Olympic competition.

- Builds her teams on the premise that defense wins games, and rebounds win championships.

- Teaches life skills through the game of basketball.

PAT HEAD SUMMITT

"Sometimes, basketball is the least of what I teach."
—Pat Head Summitt

BIOGRAPHY

Born: June 14, 1952 in Henrietta, TN

Inducted into the Naismith Basketball Hall of Fame in 2000

Pat Head Summitt became the all-time winningest Division I basketball coach on March 22, 2005, breaking the record held by legendary Dean Smith. To commemorate her incredible achievement, the University of Tennessee named its basketball court at the Thompson-Boling Arena, "The Summitt." Pat, who took over the reins of the University of Tennessee program at the age of 22, has led the Lady Vols to six national championships and 16 Final Four appearances. During her 31-year tenure, Summitt's teams have an incredible 15 seasons of 30-plus wins. She has been named the NCAA Coach of the Year on seven occasions. In 2000, she was named the Naismith Coach of the Century. In 1999, Summitt was the first woman to receive the Naismith Basketball Hall of Fame's John Bunn Award. In 1984, Summitt coached the U.S. Women's team to their first gold medal in Olympic competition. As a player, Summitt was co-captain of the 1976 U.S. Olympic Team that won a silver medal. She was enshrined in the Women's Basketball Hall of Fame in 1999 and the Naismith Memorial Basketball Hall of Fame in 2000.

...SCOUTING REPORT.....SCOUTING REPORT.....

Pat Head Summitt...

Pat Head Summitt was the fourth of five children of Richard and Hazel Head and the first girl. Her father was a strong disciplinarian, and "Tricia," as she was known as a youth, grew up competing with three older brothers and working hard on the family farm. She learned that laziness was not tolerated, and that excuses weren't accepted. When she wasn't working in the fields or attending school, Summitt was playing basketball in the hayloft with her brothers. She was a four-year starter at Cheatham County (Ashland, TN) High School and was an All-District 20 Tournament selection in 1970.

Summitt attended the University of Tennessee at Martin and received her degree in physical education. She led the Lady Pacers to a 64-29 record and two appearances in the national championship tournament. Summitt scored 1,045 points during her career and graduated as UT-Martin's all-time leading scorer.

Summitt was a member of the 1973 U.S. World Games team and co-captain of the 1976 U.S. Olympic team. She earned two silver medals and had the opportunity to play for coaches such as Cathy Rush, Billie Moore, Sue Gunter, and Alberta Cox, some of the greatest coaching minds in women's basketball.

Summitt was only 22 years old when she took over the program at the University of Tennessee. In her first year, she led the team to a 16-8 record, attended graduate school, taught physical education classes, and earned a playing spot on the U.S. Women's World Championship team.

No coach in women's college basketball history has been to more NCAA tournaments, coached in more Final Fours, or won more national championships than Pat Summitt.

To win championships, it takes talented players. Summitt believes two key ingredients of a championship team are a go-to player in the paint and a point guard who is the quarterback of the team. Her system is built on great defense and rebounding. Summitt said, "Offense sells tickets, defense wins games, and rebounds wins championships."

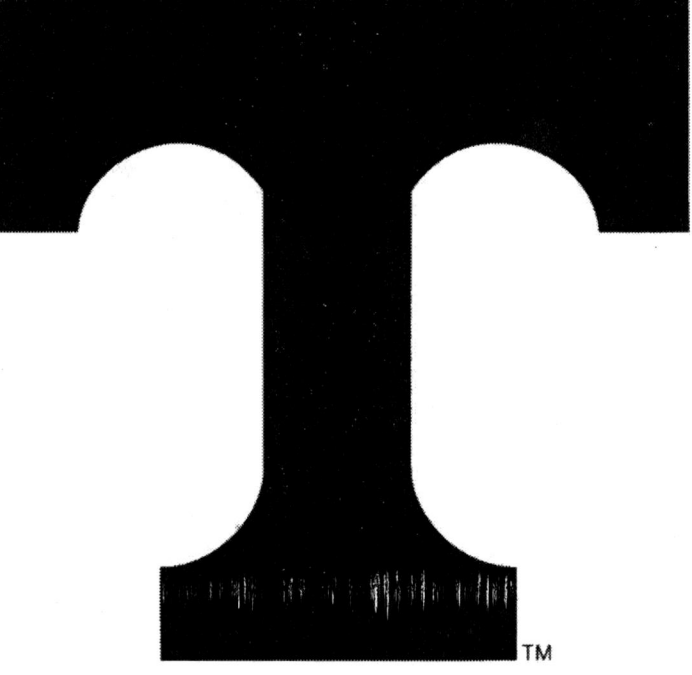

Summitt preaches the team concept, and every player is expected to understand and play her role. "I've always felt that you had to go out and play great defense every night and board with people," said Summitt.

Summitt is an intense, demanding, and focused competitor. She instills a pattern of success in her players and constantly challenges them to reach their maximum potential. "I'm someone who will push you beyond all reasonable limits," said Summitt (1998). "Someone who will ask you not to just fulfill your potential but to exceed it. Someone who will expect more from you than you may believe you are capable of."

Player Semeka Randall said, "Having Pat is like having a second mom—tough love." Teammate Kristen Clement added, "Yeah, Coach will get on you and she'll make you feel really bad at times, but I think she brings out the best in you, and you really grow to love her."

To her athletes, she is "Pat" from the minute she meets them on a recruiting trip to the day they receive their diploma.

.....SCOUTING REPORT.....SCOUTING REPORT...

Summitt believes her primary mission is to prepare players to win at the most important game of all—life. "We're teaching life skills," said Summitt. "I don't want average people. Average people cut corners. Winners know there are no shortcuts."

If a player does not go to class, she cannot play. Players are expected to sit in the first three rows in class and pay attention. They are to complete all assignments on time and treat everyone with respect. Every Lady Vol who has completed her eligibility at Tennessee has received her degree or is in the process of completing her degree requirements.

To Summitt, a coach assumes many different roles such as a teacher, a parent-figure, a friend, a counselor, or a psychologist. Her program is concerned with three dimensions: the person, the player, and the student. "It's more than X's and O's," said Summit. "It's about caring about individuals. Basketball is a way in which we teach life skills." (Packer, 1999)

Summitt said that some of the best advice on how to develop championship teams came from Hall of Fame coach Billie Moore. "She's the most professional person I've ever known. Her advice to me was to always do things the right way and be a professional. There's a right way and a wrong way to do things. Things are black and white. Do not live in the gray. Do not move into the gray for any decision. Keep things as they should be, and do them the right way." (Packer, 1999)

On March 22, 2005, Summitt led her Lady Vols past Purdue, 75-54, in the second round of the NCAA Tournament. The victory was the 880th of her coaching career, which moved her past the legendary Dean Smith of North Carolina (879) as the all-time winningest coach in NCAA basketball history, men or women.

Assistant coach Dean Lockwood (2005) said, "If you had been in our staff meetings on a daily basis, you would not have known that record was imminent or on the horizon. It was not brought up or discussed by Pat. Her only focus was that of our basketball team. All the other things were peripheral to Pat. I think that speaks so much to Pat's genuine and true humility. She is so unconcerned about personal glory and personal recognition. Pat is probably the most humble person I have ever been around."

"Even as great a coach as Pat is," continued Lockwood, "she is even a better human being in terms of how she cares about our players and how seriously she takes her responsibility as a leader and a role model. It is sacred to her. She is totally committed to preparing young people for success in life. As much as she has accomplished as a coach, and as many Hall of Fames as she is in, there is nothing that means more to Pat than acting with character and integrity."

SOURCE

Lockwood, Dean. Interview with Ralph Pim. March 26, 2005.

Packer, Billy and Roland Lazenby. (1999). *Why We Win*. Chicago: Masters Press.

Summitt, Pat. Vertical Files, Archives. Naismith Memorial Basketball Hall of Fame. Springfield, MA.

Summitt, Pat and Sally Jenkins. (1998). *Reach for the Summit*. New York: Broadway Books.

LESSONS FROM THIS LEGEND...

TENNESSEE LADY VOLS MAN DEFENSE PHILOSOPHY

By Pat Summitt

Authors' Note: The key points in Pat Summitt's man-to-man defensive philosophy are presented in the following outline taken from The Lady Vols Basketball Notebook.

❏ **DEFENSIVE PHILOSOPHY:**
No easy passes; no easy shots; and no second shots).

- Point of Pick up:
  ✓ Early pick up on the ballhandler
  ✓ Force the dribbler to use weak hand
  ✓ Get the ball out of the middle (establish ballside)

- On the Ball:
  ✓ No stance, no chance;
    - slightly staggered stance (back foot in position to influence to the corner)
    - arm length away
    - head lower than shoulder
  ✓ Constant ball pressure; get fingers on every pass
  ✓ Force the dribbler to the corner (no direct drives to the paint):
    - first step is a pull step; second step is a cut-off step
    - can use closed arm bar (1-2 second count)
  ✓ Contest all shots – make the shooter shoot over your fingertips:
    - call "shot"
    - all five players box out and pursue the ball
  ✓ Dead ball (mirror the ball; hard denial everywhere else)

- Wing Defense:
  ✓ One pass away:
    - deny one pass away (up the line, on the line)
    - deny out of comfort zone
    - defending cuts:
      a. back door – deny until you can't deny anymore; open up and close back down, or turn head and close down
  ✓ Two passes away:
    - sprint to the help line to show early help (go on the pass)
    - point your guns in an athletic stance
    - play ball-man defense (be very unselfish)
    - defending cuts (don't let the cutter cut across your face):
      a. give and go – jump to the ballside; send the cutter behind; arm bar if need be
      b. cuts to the ball – from the helpside, as the player gets closer to you or the helpline bump the cutter (arm bar) and end either high and wide (out of comfort zone) or behind you

- Post Defense:
  ✓ One pass away:
    - deny one pass away (up the line; on the line)
    - deny out of comfort zone
    - defending cuts:
      a. high post cut – from the helpside, bump the cutter and send either high and wide (out of the comfort zone) or behind you
  ✓ Low block:
    - high-shoulder denial – have the up hand and up foot in the passing lane when the ball is above the free-throw line
    - step in front – face guard when the ball goes below the free- throw line
    - play behind – arm bar; keep off the block when you want the post to catch the ball
    - red – doubleteam the post from the helpside

- Helpside Defense:
  ✓ Sprint to the helpline to show early help (go on the pass)
  ✓ Point your guns in an athletic stance
  ✓ Play ball-man defense (be very unselfish)
  ✓ Be active and recover playing the passing lanes
  ✓ If someone gets beat, quickly help and rotate (scramble); always help the helper

❏ **FOUR WAYS TO DEFEND SCREENS ON THE BALL:**

- Keep the ball to one side
- Show numbers as the guard steps over the top; the post player lets the guard through; force the ball to the screen; "call it, touch it, show it"

LESSONS FROM THIS LEGEND...

- Trap – show numbers and force the ball to the screen and trap; "call it, touch it, trap it, close it"
- Switch – switch is called by the player whose person is going to set the screen; "call it, touch it, switch it"; attack the ball

❑ **SITUATIONS WE MUST PREPARE TO DEFEND:**
  - Give and go – no one crosses your face; jump to the ball
  - Screens on the ball – "call it, touch it, show it"
  - Screens off the ball – back screens, down screens, cross screens, flare screens
  - Hand-offs – help and recover; switch and slide through
  - Hand-offs into ball screens
  - Flash – duck in – "play uphill"
  - Split post and shuffle – cut off high post
  - 1-4 low
  - Wing isolation
  - Lob – pursue as though it's a rebound

❑ **TRANSITION DEFENSE:**
  - Designate a full back and a half back
  - The player who picks up the ball, calls "ball"
  - Maintain constant pressure on the ball
  - All teammates provide early help; "sprint to help" and help the helper
  - Eliminate lay-ups and open shots; "contest every shot":
    - ✓ 2 on 1 – hedge; don't fully commit; give up the jumper, don't allow lay-ups, make them make the extra pass
    - ✓ 3 on 2 – defense in a tandem; back has the first pass, front drops back
  - Eliminate second shots and "box out" (hit and get, or check and go); pursue the ball

❑ **HALF COURT MAN DEFENSES—MAKE THEM PLAY IN A BOX:**
  - "0" – deny one pass away; no easy passes to the wing
  - "1" – open denial; let the ball go to the wing; keep on one side
  - "1 OUT" – let the ball go to the wing; trap on the pass

❑ **NINE "MUSTS" FOR THE DEFENSIVE PLAYER:**
  - Play in a stance – "high hands, low hips, quick feet"
  - Deny one pass away when we are in our "0" defense
  - Take away both passes to the middle (thrown over your fingers) and drives to the middle; keep the opponent out of the lane
  - Jump to the ball; show early help; point your guns; keep the ball and your man in front of you (have double vision)
  - Sprint to help; help the helper; show numbers on help and rotate
  - Communicate
  - Contest every shot
  - Box out
  - Pursue the missed shot

❑ **BE A SMART DEFENDER:**
  - Avoid overrunning the ball; don't put your teammates in a scramble five-against-four
  - Avoid running into screens
  - Eliminate fouling – do not foul on help; don't bail out the defense
  - Play smart position, on and off the ball; see the ball and the man; "point your guns"
  - Talk to your teammates
  - See what is happening; anticipate
  - Have an attitude
  - Finish the play – box and pursue

❑ **DEFENSIVE STATISTICS:**
  - Steals
  - Deflections
  - Contested shots
  - Box outs
  - Rebounds
  - Charges

SOURCE

Summitt, Pat. (2005). *Defensive Philosophy.* Tennessee Lady Vols Basketball Notebook. Unpublished.

LEGACY OF
John Wooden

- Led UCLA to 10 national titles, including 7 in a row.

- Philosopher-coach who developed the "Pyramid of Success."

- Emphasized character development and taught life-enhancing skills.

- Inducted into the Naismith Basketball Hall of Fame as both a player and a coach.

- Selected NCAA College Basketball Coach of the Year six times (1964, 1967, 1969, 1970, 1972, 1973).

- Compiled a record of 885-203 (.813) during his 40-year coaching career.

- Led UCLA to 88 consecutive victories.

- Considered one of the finest teachers the game has ever seen.

JOHN WOODEN

"Success is peace of mind which is a direct result of self-satisfaction in knowing you did your best to become the best you are capable of becoming."
—John Wooden

BIOGRAPHY

Born: October 14, 1910 in Martinsville, IN

Inducted into the Naismith Memorial Basketball Hall of Fame as a player in 1960 and as a coach in 1973

The John Wooden-coached UCLA teams reach unprecedented heights that will be difficult for any team to match. The Bruins set all-time records with four perfect 30-0 seasons, eighty-eight consecutive victories, thirty-eight straight NCAA tournament victories, twenty conference championships, and ten NCAA national championships, including seven in a row. Wooden is considered one of the finest teachers in the history of the game. He is one of only two people enshrined in the Naismith Memorial Basketball Hall of Fame as both a player and a coach. Wooden was a three-time All-American at Purdue University and was selected the College Player of the Year in 1932. He played for legendary Hall of Fame coach Ward "Piggy" Lambert and helped lead the Boilermakers to the 1932 National Championship. Wooden coached at Dayton (KY) H.S., South Bend (IN) Central High School, and Indiana State University prior to his arrival at UCLA. In 2003, Wooden received two special honors. He was awarded the Presidential Medal of Honor, and UCLA named the court at Pauley Pavilion the Nell and John Wooden Court. Wooden was enshrined in the Naismith Memorial Basketball Hall of Fame as a player in 1960 and as a coach in 1973.

...SCOUTING REPORT.....SCOUTING REPORT.....

John Wooden...

John Wooden was a philosopher-coach, who believed our stature as a nation depended fundamentally on the strength and character of our people. He instructed his players with life-enhancing lessons. Wooden believed that athletics, when properly coached, provided an environment where individuals learned about themselves and about life. The skills he taught on the court are the same that are needed in the real world.

Wooden's remarkable success came primarily from his values and his consistency in living up to these values. He was selfless in example and was committed to helping others reach success and find inner peace.

It was Wooden's belief that participation in athletics should be a character-building experience. He emphasized to his players that they should be more concerned with their character than their reputation, and explained to them the difference between the two. Character is what you really are, while reputation is only what people say you are. A person of high character is trustworthy and honest.

Wooden believed that dishonesty was unacceptable. His father provided him with simple and direct rules for life. These were called "Two Sets of Three" and served as a compass for trying to do the right thing. The first set dealt with honesty: 1) never lie; 2) never cheat; and 3) never steal. The second set dealt with how to handle adversity: 1) don't whine; 2) don't complain; and 3) don't make excuses. Everyone encounters adversity, and people must discipline themselves to do the best that they can under the circumstances. An important key to success is how individuals respond to their perceived setbacks or disappointments. Unfortunately, many individuals blame others for their mistakes in an attempt to excuse themselves. Wooden acknowledged that he made many mistakes, but he had no failures because he did the best that he was capable of doing.

Winning was a word that Wooden rarely used. He preferred the word success, and success did not always mean scoring more points than your opponent. His emphasis was on doing your best. Wooden considered success a personal matter, because only you, as an individual, can tell if you did everything within your power to give your best effort. His focus was not on beating his opponent, but rather on developing the individuals on his team, so they grew both individually and collectively. Wooden strove for his players to attain a peace of mind that came only from giving their best effort. The goal that he believed was most important was the goal of making the most of one's ability.

EIGHT SUGGESTIONS FOR SUCCEEDING

1. Fear no opponent. Respect every opponent.
2. Remember, it's the perfection of the smallest details that make the big things happen.
3. Keep in mind that hustle makes up for many mistakes.
4. Be more interested in character than reputation.
5. Be quick, but don't hurry.
6. Understand the harder you work, the more luck you will have.
7. Know that valid self-analysis is crucial for improvement.
8. Remember that there is no substitute for hard work and careful planning. Failing to prepare is preparing to fail.

It was Coach Wooden's observations that the primary cause of unhappiness was people wanting too much materially. They overemphasized money and the material things that went with it. When it didn't come quickly or when it didn't come at all, people became discontent and unhappy. Peace of mind and inner happiness should not be dependent on material things.

NINE PROMISES THAT CAN BRING HAPPINESS

1. Promise yourself that you will talk health, happiness, and prosperity as often as possible.
2. Promise yourself to make all your friends know there is something in them that is special and that you value.
3. Promise to think only of the best, to work only for the best, and to expect only the best in yourself and others.
4. Promise to be just as enthusiastic about the success of others as you are about your own.
5. Promise yourself to be strong, so that nothing can disturb your peace of mind.

·····SCOUTING REPORT·····SCOUTING REPORT···

6. Promise to forget the mistakes of the past and press on to greater achievements in the future.
7. Promise to wear a cheerful appearance at all times and give every person you meet a smile.
8. Promise to give so much time to improving yourself that you have no time to criticize others.
9. Promise to be too large for worry, too noble for anger, too strong for fear, and too happy to permit trouble to press on you.

Wooden valued the principles of teaching and coaching as a sacred trust. The powerful influence of a teacher and coach must never be taken lightly. A coach helps mold character and instill productive principles. Wooden believed that coaches should be role models and provide positive examples to those with whom they come in contact. He lived and coached by his credo of industriousness and selflessness. His teams reflected his passion for hard work and teamwork. Wooden urged his players to try their hardest to improve and to make their work on that particular day a masterpiece. He explained to players that once they came to practice, they ceased to exist as an individual. They were part of a team. Every player and team manager had a role, and there were no subordinates. Wooden said, "It is remarkable how much can be accomplished when players think beyond themselves."

Wooden utilized the pedagogical principles of the whole-part method during practice sessions. He showed the desired outcome and then divided it into teachable parts. Wooden said that he believed the laws of learning should be increased from four to eight because of the importance of repetition. His eight laws were: 1) explanation; 2) demonstration; 3) imitation; 4) repetition; 5) repetition; 6) repetition; 7) repetition; and 8) repetition. His goal was to create a correct habit that could be produced without conscious thought under great pressure. Wooden believed the best teacher was repetition of the fundamentals, performed correctly day after day, throughout the season.

When asked why he taught, Wooden responded, "There is no better place to find finer company." He warned people about taking themselves too seriously. Wooden said, "Talent is God-given, be humble; fame is man-given, be thankful; conceit is self-given, be careful."

Wooden's philosophy can be summarized in the creed given to him as he entered high school from his father:
1. Be true to yourself.
2. Help others.
3. Make each day your masterpiece.
4. Drink deeply from good books, especially the Bible.
5. Make friendship a fine art.
6. Build a shelter against a rainy day.
7. Pray for guidance and count and give thanks for your blessings every day.

In pursuing success and living every day to its fullest, Wooden identified the following as some of his favorite maxims:
1. Happiness begins where selfishness ends.
2. Big things are accomplished only through the perfection of minor details.
3. Discipline yourself, and others won't need to.
4. Ability may get you to the top, but it takes character to keep you there.
5. If you do not have the time to do it right, when will you find the time to do it over?
6. Don't let yesterday take up too much of today.
7. It is what you learn after you know it all that counts.
8. Do not permit what you cannot do to interfere with what you can do.
9. Love is the greatest of all words in our language.
10. Never make excuses. Your friends don't need them, and your foes won't believe them.
11. The more concerned we become over the things we can't control, the less we will do with the things we can control.
12. Do not mistake activity for achievement.
13. Treat all people with dignity and respect.
14. You cannot live a perfect day without doing something for another without thought of something in return.
15. Acquire peace of mind by making the effort to become the best of which you are capable.

SOURCE

Hill, A. with J. Wooden. (2001) *Be Quick - But Don't Hurry.* New York: Simon & Schuster.

Krause, Jerry and Ralph Pim. (2002) *Coaching Basketball.* New York: McGraw-Hill.

Wooden, John. Vertical Files, Archives. Naismith Memorial Basketball Hall of Fame. Springfield, MA.

Wooden J. and S. Jamison. (1997) *Wooden: A Lifetime of Observations and Reflections On and Off the Court.* Chicago: Contemporary Books.

LESSONS FROM THIS LEGEND...

THE 2-2-1 ZONE PRESS

By John Wooden

Authors' Note: The 2-2-1 zone press, commonly attributed to Coach Wooden, was developed much earlier but was certainly popularized by his early UCLA teams, and was key in winning their first national championship in 1964.

Our unusual success the last few seasons with the zone press was due to the tremendous personnel that we had for this type of defense. The player material that we had fit into this extremely well. The press we used took advantage of our own peculiar abilities. The theory behind this zone press is far more important than any particular set-up we happened to use.

We never permit our freshmen to use a zone press. They use a man-to-man press, so that they become adept at the man-to-man principles. In our zone press, we actually play a man-to-man defense in a zone area when the man comes in that area. So, there is a tie-in, and it is hard to have one without the other. You must have pressure on the ball. We are playing high and trying to close the outlets. That's the zone principle. Actually, our man-to-man defense is with a zone principle.

Defenses are peculiar things. To say that a team leads the nation in defense because it has had the fewest number of points scored against it is as much of a fallacy as it is to say the best offense is a good defense. Teams that break and give up the ball a lot are going to have more points scored against them. Yet, they may play very fine defense. I'm not trying to say that ball-control teams don't play good defense. I want an aggressive defense and an aggressive offense, and a zone defense is not an aggressive defense.

When I talk about the individual fundamentals in defense, these are some of the mental requirements:
1. **Desire or determination**—If a player does not have the desire to become a good defensive player and is not willing and determined to accomplish this goal, he will never become one.
2. **Alertness**—Be ready for any eventuality and react instantly. "Read" what the player with the ball will do.
3. **Poise**—Don't get upset or rattled.
4. **Initiative and aggressiveness**—These two qualities are combined and make up one of the most important mental traits of a player.
5. **Pride**—Defensive players can be very proud of their defensive accomplishments on the floor.
6. **Concentration**—Give basketball your undivided attention when playing.
7. **Confidence**—Dominate your opponent.
8. **Judgment**—Know your own ability, how to use it, and when to use it.

Now, the physical requirements:
1. **Quickness**—Quickness is the most important physical asset any athlete can have. A player doesn't have to have great speed to be quick. Quickness pays off.
2. **Body balance**—Footwork and body balance very important.
3. **Hustle, size, and speed**—These three attributes are other important physical requirements.

LESSONS FROM THIS LEGEND...

Your defense before your man has the ball is as important as your offense without the ball. A player should realize he can make his job much easier if he will play aggressive, alert, thinking defense before his man gets the ball. Too many players continue to permit their man to receive the ball, and then they start playing defense. Think in terms of how far you should play away from your man. You must constantly be "reading" the man with the ball.

This is what we try to teach our men, particularly back men and weakside men. This will tell men where they can cheat a little. If they can get a step advantage, it may be the difference. They must learn to anticipate and know what to expect from certain individuals. Encourage opponents to throw long passes down the sidelines.

When we line up in our zone, we are either going to contest the pass in, or we aren't. If we are going to contest it, we try bottling up the inbounder. We have one man on the inbounder and behind him we may have a 2-2, a 3-1, or a 2-1-1. We adjust to the situation. **Diagram 1.0** shows how we line up when the ball is inbounded where we want it to be. We line up this way to get them to throw the ball into a certain area. Height is important to basketball, but it should not be measured by height to the top of the head, but by reach of your arms, plus ability to get up there and get the ball. Quickness and jumping ability enters in too. I may play a 6-foot 3-inch boy before a 6-foot 8-inch guy, because he can get the ball better. I just think that it is a fair criticism when I say that most coaches go overboard in trying to recruit size. I am excluding Bill Walton, since he is truly a great player. However, few of us ever have a boy such as Walton. Our team would do many things differently if Walton had not been on the team.

Additional facts to keep in mind when using a zone-press defense are:

1. Gambling type of defense—requires continued effort and limitless patience if it is to pay dividends.
2. Value will come from demoralizing opposition and upsetting their game.
3. Can speed up game—force the opponent out of their normal style.
4. Can cause disharmony and disunity.
5. Do not reach in to attempt to take the ball away from opponents; play position and force errors when opponents "hurry." Cuts down fouling and helps to establish proper philosophy. I don't want my defensive men to get their hands out in front of their body. I want team balance, physical balance, mental balance, emotional balance, and floor balance.
6. Permit only lob or bounce passes forward. Passes back toward your offensive basket will not hurt you, but crisp passes forward cause trouble.
7. When the ball passes your individual line of defense, turn and sprint toward your defensive basket—pick up the most dangerous man open. Strongside men should be alive to "two-time" as they go back, weakside men should be alert to intercept.
8. All players must be well-grounded in individual fundamentals. I use only a man-to-man pressing defense for our freshmen, but employ zone principles.
9. If no opponent is in your zone, close in toward the zone that is being attacked.
10. Use tight man-to-man principles if the man in your zone has the ball, and floating man-to-man principles, depending upon how far from the ball your man is in the other areas.
11. Results come often in spurts, so apply immediate pressure after acquiring the ball through an error. Often, they will make more errors. Our 1964 team had at least one "spurt" in a period of approximately two minutes in all thirty games in which we outscored our opponents from ten to twenty points. Sometimes, it did not come until the middle of the second half, but we would usually have at least one spurt before the end of the first half.
12. Players must realize the necessity and value of and be willing to make necessary sacrifices to attain and maintain top condition.
13. Players must be unselfish in regard to scoring. I like players who can pass, and will pass, if passed to. Walt Hazzard was that type of player. The rest of the boys liked to pass to him, because they knew he would pass it back to them.
14. An outstanding player for the important #5 position is essential. Must be quick, alert, courageous, unselfish, able to "read" the man with the ball, very good at handling deep defense when outnumbered, a fine rebounder, one who can get the ball out quickly, very aggressive, with the judgment that prevents committing himself too soon, and a player who really loves a challenge.

LESSONS FROM THIS LEGEND...

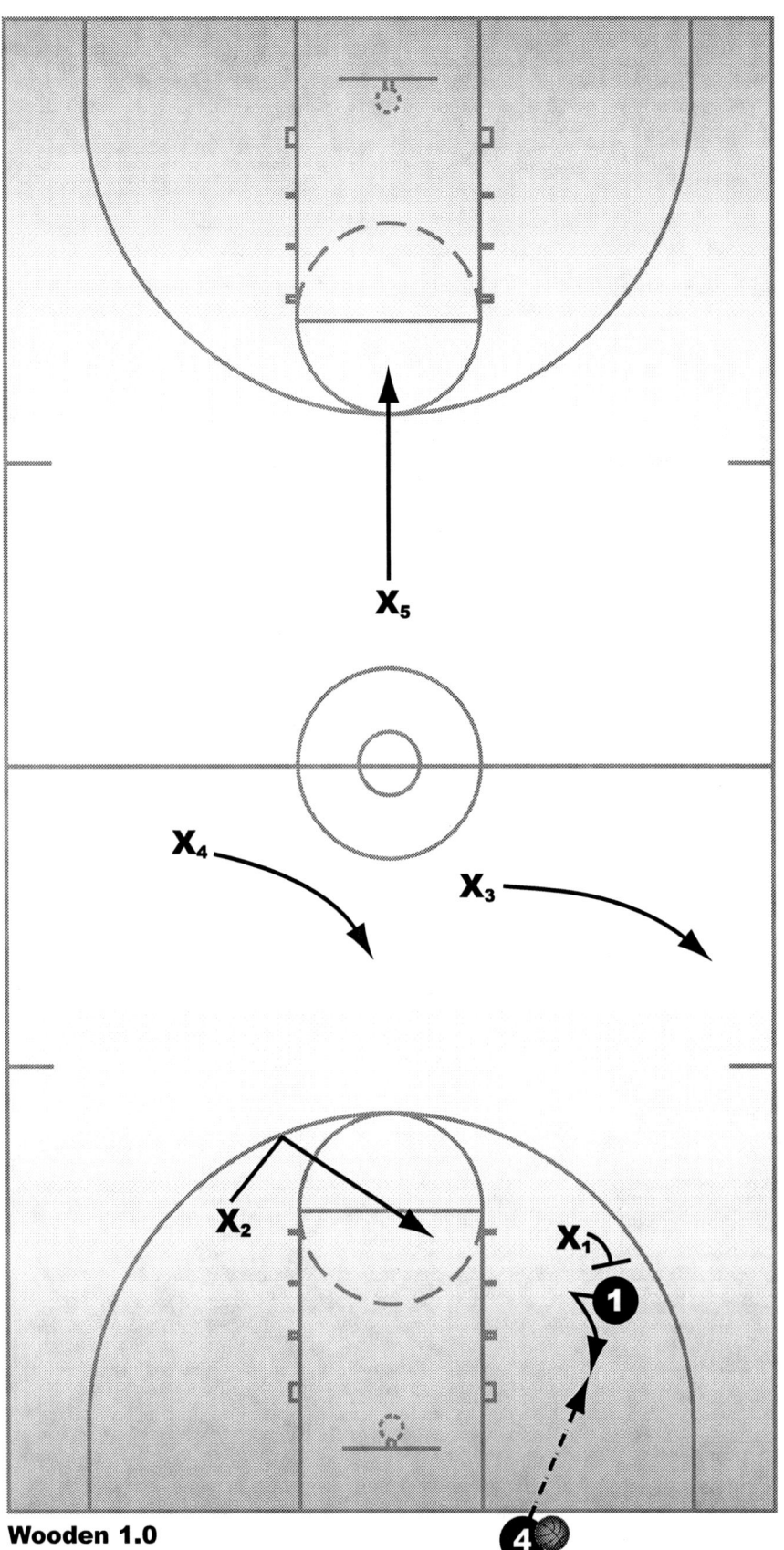

Wooden 1.0

ASSIGNMENTS FOR PRESS

X1's responsibility is to invite the other team to pass the ball to a man in the area indicated. He advances on the receiver, and keeps him from driving on by the sideline. If he starts to dribble, try to make him stop and turn away, where he will be "double-teamed" by X2. If he does not dribble, X1 advances on him and tries to force him to throw a lob or bounce pass without too much time to the locate receivers. X2 discourages the pass to his side and moves out quickly to prevent a return pass to the inbounder in the middle of the floor. X2 should be alert for a double-team with X1 in case the receiver of the inbounded pass would start to dribble.

X3 is responsible for the area behind from the center line to the foul line and to stop the driver that might get by X1 on that side of the floor and prevent a receiver from getting the pass either from the man inbounding the ball or from the man who did receive the short pass from him. He should intercept any lob pass thrown to a receiver in this area.

X4 is responsible for covering the middle of the floor to his left, as he faces the inbounder. He is responsible for the area on his side from the center line to the foul line, or even deeper when X2 moves over. As soon as the ball is inbounded into X1's area, this becomes an important responsibility.

X5 gets to the center circle as fast as possible and directs the defense from there. He is responsible for any man who went down the floor and is expected to intercept any pass thrown to any spot on the offensive end, if it was thrown from any position as far back as the foul-line extended. He should challenge anyone to throw the ball over and past him.

Some important details: The backboard with the net hanging down helps to discourage opponents from passing the ball in on the opposite side. If they did happen to do this, the roles were just reversed.

LESSONS FROM THIS LEGEND...

Our ability to change quickly from offense to defense often enables us to capitalize on errors of our opponents. We often catch them going the wrong way, or with their "heads down."

Players were taught not to grab, but to pressure just enough to prevent the straight pass and encourage the lob or bounce pass. We try to keep them from dribbling. If they dribble, we want them moved into the double-team situation.

Running back quickly whenever the ball gets past you toward your defensive basket and sizing up the situation as you sprint back are important and should be stressed.

Players should be drilled in chasing the man from behind and knocking the ball toward a teammate who is back further. Stress the "no-contact" aspect and the fact that he is not trying to get the ball himself.

If a team is hurting our press too much by quick, clever passing, we may go out of the zone press and try a man-to-man press for a while, or change it to a 1-3-1, 2-1-2, or 1-2-1-1 zone, and operate with the same principles.

Never worry if the opposition passes backward toward your offensive goal. We like that. Try to stop short, crisp passes forward. Encourage the long lobs, and then go after them.

The first man back takes the most dangerous man. Never worry about the outside shooter being dangerous at the end of the press. But, don't give them easy shots. Get back and protect the basket, then come out and challenge them.

SOURCE

Wooden, John. (1975). The 2-2-1 Zone Press. *Medalist Flashback Notebook.*

LEGACY OF
Phil Woolpert

- Leader in human relations and civil rights.

- Sensitive and caring coach who was committed to helping others.

- Highly intelligent coach who was called "Socrates" by his peers because he exhibited deep philosophical beliefs focused upon ethics and selfless service.

- Dedicated to preserving the integrity of the coaching profession.

- One of only six coaches to win back-to-back NCAA I championships and the youngest coach to win it at the age of 40.

- Favored pressure defense with the ultimate shot blocker, future Hall of Fame player Bill Russell.

- Believed strongly in mentoring younger coaches.

PHIL WOOLPERT

"It's a cardinal sin for a player, once the ball goes by him, to waste any time getting back to the defensive end of the court."
—Phil Woolpert

BIOGRAPHY

Born: December 19, 1915 in Danville, KY

Died: May 5, 1987

Inducted into the Naismith Basketball Hall of Fame in 1992

Phil Woolpert directed San Francisco to back-to-back NCAA national championships in 1955 and 1956 and a third-place finish in 1957. His teams won 60 consecutive games from 1955 to 1957, an NCAA record until UCLA's eighty-eight game winning streak. San Francisco led the nation in defense on three occasions. During the 60-game winning streak, the Dons held opponents below 60 points 47 times. Woolpert was named National Coach of the Year in 1955 and 1956. Two of his former players, Bill Russell and K.C. Jones, were inducted into the Naismith Hall of Fame. He coached the San Francisco Saints in the ABA, before finishing his career as athletic director and basketball coach at the University of San Diego. Woolpert played for legendary coach Jim Needles at Loyola Marymount University, along with future Hall of Fame coach Pete Newell. Woolpert began his coaching career at St. Ignatius High School (CA) and then joined Newell's staff at San Francisco. He succeeded Newell as head coach at San Francisco in 1951. Woolpert was enshrined in the Naismith Memorial Basketball Hall of Fame in 1992.

...SCOUTING REPORT.....SCOUTING REPORT.....

Phil Woolpert...

Phil Woolpert played college basketball at Loyola Marymount University in Los Angeles under the legendary coach Jim Needles. One of Woolpert's teammates was Pete Newell, and they both incorporated many of Needles' principles in their coaching philosophies. Woolpert began his coaching career in 1946 at St. Ignatius High School in San Francisco. At the same time, he also was Newell's assistant and freshman coach at the University of San Francisco. Newell credits him with being very instrumental in USF winning the NIT championship in 1949.

Woolpert succeeded Newell as head coach at San Francisco in 1951. At the time, USF was so small that it lacked a campus gymnasium. Woolpert had to beg practice times at places such as the boy's club, the local parish hall, or nearby St. Ignatius High School. Left with only one veteran player and a tough schedule, Woolpert compiled losing records in his first three seasons. His fortunes began to change when he offered a scholarship to Bill Russell, who played at Oakland's McClymonds H.S., where he had scored more than ten points in a game only once.

San Francisco opened the 1955 season with two victories, but then lost at UCLA. At this point, Woolpert inserted three black starting players. During this period in our country, many coaches adhered to an unwritten quota that limited the number of black players that could be in the starting line-up. Woolpert would have nothing to do with that type of thinking. At the All-College Tournament in Oklahoma City, Woolpert chose to have his entire team stay in a dorm, rather than having the white players check into a whites-only hotel.

"As great as Phil's achievements were as a coach, they did not equal his achievements in human relations," stated Pete Newell (1985). "Phil was so far ahead of the rest of us in recognizing human and civil rights that we couldn't discern what he meant."

Hall of Fame player K.C. Jones played for Woolpert at San Francisco and described him in these words (1992), "Phil was his own person and an innovator, starting five black players when advised otherwise. He was honest and cared about all of his players, both on and off the court. Phil had a great sensitivity to what we were like as individuals, what our strengths were, how we best worked together, and he capitalized on this. He listened to our personal problems and showed concern for racial issues at the time. He was an extremely bright person and recognized the same high intellectual level in Bill Russell. Bill and Phil had a special appreciation for one another, and Bill, like the rest of us, gave Phil his best effort. He treated us all like we were members of his own family. Phil was truly an exceptional person. He was like a father to all of us."

At a time when the country's best teams were averaging 80 or more points per game, the 1955 Dons topped the nation by allowing only 52 points per game. They played suffocating defense. The guards pressed, the forwards fought through screens to contest shots, and their center, Bill Russell, blocked shots like no one had ever seen before. Woolpert reasoned that, "If your opponent can't shoot, they can't score." (Giethschier, 1996).

Woolpert led San Francisco to back-to-back national championships in 1955 and 1956, with future Hall of Famers K.C. Jones and Bill Russell leading the way. In 1955, Woolpert, then 40, became the youngest coach in NCAA history to win the title. He was named National Coach of the Year in 1955 and 1956 and led the Dons to a then record 60 straight victories. The year after Jones and Russell graduated, San Francisco advanced to the Final Four, where it lost to Kansas and Wilt Chamberlain in the semi-finals, before beating Michigan State for third place.

Woolpert coached the San Francisco Saints in the American Basketball League for one year and then became the athletic director and basketball coach at the University of San Diego. Woolpert coached basketball for seven seasons at San Diego and compiled a record of 90-90. He was inducted into the University of San Diego Hall of Fame in 2000. Woolpert's son, Phil, said, "I think he enjoyed his coaching career at San Diego more than anywhere else because he had enjoyed fame earlier. He was happier building character than worrying about wins and losses."

.....SCOUTING REPORT.....SCOUTING REPORT...

Bernie Bickerstaff, the coach and general manager of the NBA expansion Charlotte Bobcats, played for Woolpert at San Diego. Bickerstaff vividly remembers the impact that Woolpert had on his life. "I had an athletic game," said Bickerstaff. (Scott, 2003) "Coach Woolpert was into fundamentals, and he said to me, 'this is our system; you have to do it.' There was a guy who played in front of me, and there was no comparison in our skills. But, it had to be done a certain way. I made the transition, because I wanted to play. And the man was fair about it. I understand it all a lot better now."

Eugenia Bickerstaff said, "It took an exceptional person to make Bernie understand he was part of the team, and that he wasn't the show. And Bernie came to really love and respect Coach Woolpert for it." (Scott, 2003) (*Authors' Note:* Woolpert hired Bickerstaff as an assistant coach at San Diego, and Bickerstaff was promoted to head coach when Woolpert resigned)

At home, Woolpert fostered a family attitude that stressed competitive success. On some nights, he wouldn't let his oldest daughter, Lorrie, go to bed until he managed to beat her in Yahtzee. Lorrie later became an outstanding basketball player and was one of the final cuts from the 1976 U.S. Olympic women's basketball team. Three of his five children went on to become basketball coaches.

Woolpert's youngest son, Paul, was a highly successful professional coach in the CBA and coached the Yakima Sun Kings and the Sioux Falls Skyforce. He led Yakima to the 2000 CBA championship. Paul credits his father for his competitive spirit and winning attitude. Paul worked as a ballboy during his father's coaching days in San Diego and remembers his father as being kind of nervous and always fidgeting. "I was too young to appreciate what he was doing. But looking back and talking with his former players and assistants, it's easy to see that he was a very intense and passionate man," said Paul.

Woolpert always made himself available to help other coaches. Stu Inman (1985) said, "Young players and young coaches are always so impressed when someone they admire and respect has time to visit with them and encourage them. I remember this so vividly about Phil, both when I was a player and also when I was a young coach. Phil was always available and never gave you the feeling that you were imposing on him. Rather, he gave the impression that this was one of his primary responsibilities."

Many opposing coaches referred to Woolpert as "Socrates," because they considered him a basketball philosopher and strategist. He was a man consumed with improving the game not only from a technical point of view, but also from an ethical point. Woolpert felt deeply about protecting and encouraging the integrity of the coaching profession. His thoughts in these areas greatly influenced the coaching fraternity.

Newell (1985) said, "To say Phil Woolpert is a principled man is an understatement. Throughout his life, he has been guided by strong and fair principles. He left the arena of big-time college basketball. Personal fame ran a poor second to his principles of what was right and wrong. It was because of this that he went to the University of San Diego and established a sound athletic program and built a basketball team that performed far beyond its normal expectancy. Phil is and has been happy driving a school bus the past ten years or more in Sequim, Washington. He is supremely happy. I guess this possibly explains Phil Woolpert more than anything I could say. He is still doing things for other people, not a bit concerned with personal glory or fame and certainly not apologetic about a position that many would call menial. Personally, I would feel very safe if he was the driver that picked up my children and what is more important than that in life."

SOURCES

Giethschier, Steve. (1996, January 15). San Francisco Dons Win 60 Consecutive Games. *The Sporting News.*

Inman, Stu. (1985, January 17). Letter to the Naismith Basketball Hall of Fame.

Newell, Pete. (1985, February 28). Letter to the Naismith Basketball Hall of Fame.

Scott, David. (2003, October 19). *Bickerstaff Carves Out Solid Basketball Career.* Website: http://www.Charlotte.com.

Three for the Record Book, Voices - News and Events from the University of San Diego. Website: http://www.sandiego.edu/publications/voices/oct-nov00/athletics2.htm.

Woolpert Phil. Vertical Files, Archives. Naismith Memorial Basketball Hall of Fame. Springfield, MA.

LESSONS FROM THIS LEGEND...

SAN FRANCISCO'S THREE-QUARTER COURT PRESS

By Phil Woolpert

The three-quarter court press employed so successfully by San Francisco in recent years is nothing new. Many coaches have used the same defense or variations of it over the years. Dr. Phog Allen was probably one of the originators of this and other pressure defenses, and in recent years Pete Newell of California and Ralph Miller of Wichita, among others, have exploited the three-quarter press with substantial effect.

At San Francisco, we use this defense more consistently whenever we are blessed with two or more quick, agile, alert, and heady guards. The past two years, K.C. Jones and Hal Perry, along with sophomore Gene Brown, filled the bill excellently. Each of these players was able to recover from a mistake as quickly as anybody I've ever seen.

A fourth guard, Warren Baxter, was used to spell any of the above, and he did a wonderful job. This depth is important, as the pressing defense is a tiring one and requires a great deal of stamina.

In general, we initiate our three-quarter press in the areas shown in **Diagram 1.0**. Guards X1 and X2 are stationed 10-15 feet beyond the center line, and generate the pressure from here.

There are two methods of playing the three-quarter court press. In one method, the defense attempts to force the offense to bring the ball down the middle of the court, where a double-team can be applied just before the mid-line. In the other method, the defense tries to force the dribbler to the outside of the court.

We use both systems and will alternate them during a game, except when we haven't any choice—since it isn't always possible to force the dribbler to the middle or to the side. It's difficult to force a good dribbler to take a specific route. The defensive man may want to force him to the outside, and bingo! There he is on the inside or down the middle. The defensive aim is either to play the dribbler from the inside or the outside, and it's important for each defensive man to know which plan is being used.

As in the full-court press, our defensive men automatically switch on any lateral movement of the ball. Each front-line man plays half the court, switching whenever the offensive men shuttle laterally back and forth across the imaginary longitudinal mid-line of the court. (See **Diagram 1.1**)

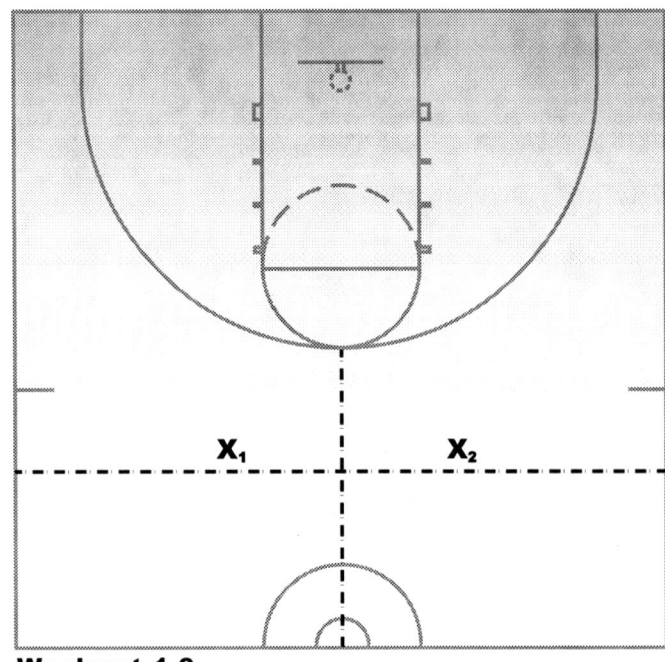

Woolpert 1.0

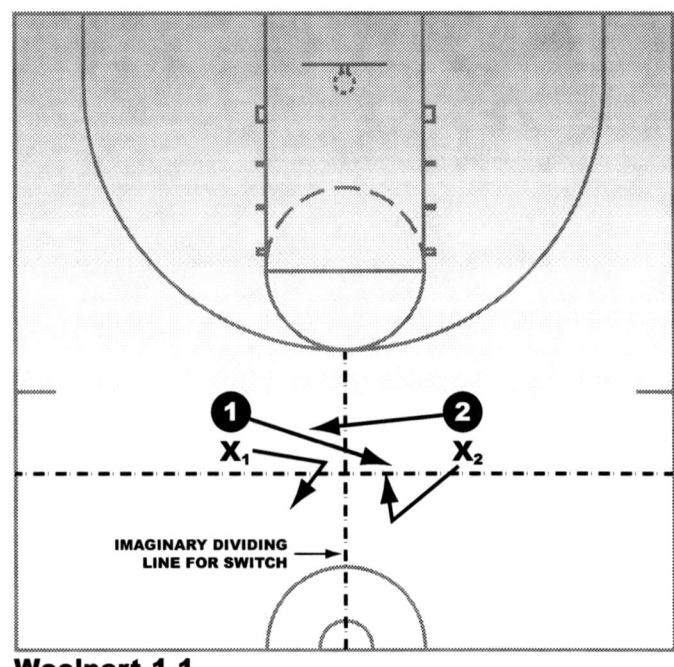

Woolpert 1.1

LESSONS FROM THIS LEGEND...

If the guard forces the dribbler to the middle, an attempt will be made to two-time him, either before he dribbles past the midline or after he crosses it. **Diagram 1.2** shows how the dribbler may be double-teamed before crossing the mid-court line.

As X1 forces O1 to the middle, X2 moves in for the one-two pinch. This responsibility for covering O2 now falls to our weak-side forward, X5, the forward away from the ball.

The other defensive forward, X3, and the center, X4, will normally play their men tight. However, when X5 switches to O2, both X3 and X4 start playing zone in the backcourt, as indicated.

The purpose of putting the two-time pinch on the dribbler is to make it difficult for him to see all the openings off the different leads he may have—which may be O2, O3, O4, and possibly O5. We try to choke him with the one-two pinch before he has time to spot a lead.

The first objective in two-timing the dribbler is to get the ball. If we cannot take the ball away from him, we must try to force him to stop. If we succeed in this, we must try to make it impossible for him to complete a pass to his lead or make it so difficult to get the pass off that he'll make a bad pass.

The defensive men are instructed to go for any ball they think they have a 60-40 chance of intercepting. The initial lead by the offense in this situation is O2. Since the dribbler will look for his lead first, we'll direct our first effort toward trying to prevent the ball from being passed to him.

If we can prevent the pass from going in to this first lead, by the time the dribbler finds any other lead the pressure on him will be so intense that he may make a bad pass.

One of the main disadvantages of this defensive system is that the players have a tendency to foul. They get over-eager, they grab, they hold, they hook, and the "man" with the whistle calls a foul or causes you to lose the effectiveness of the press.

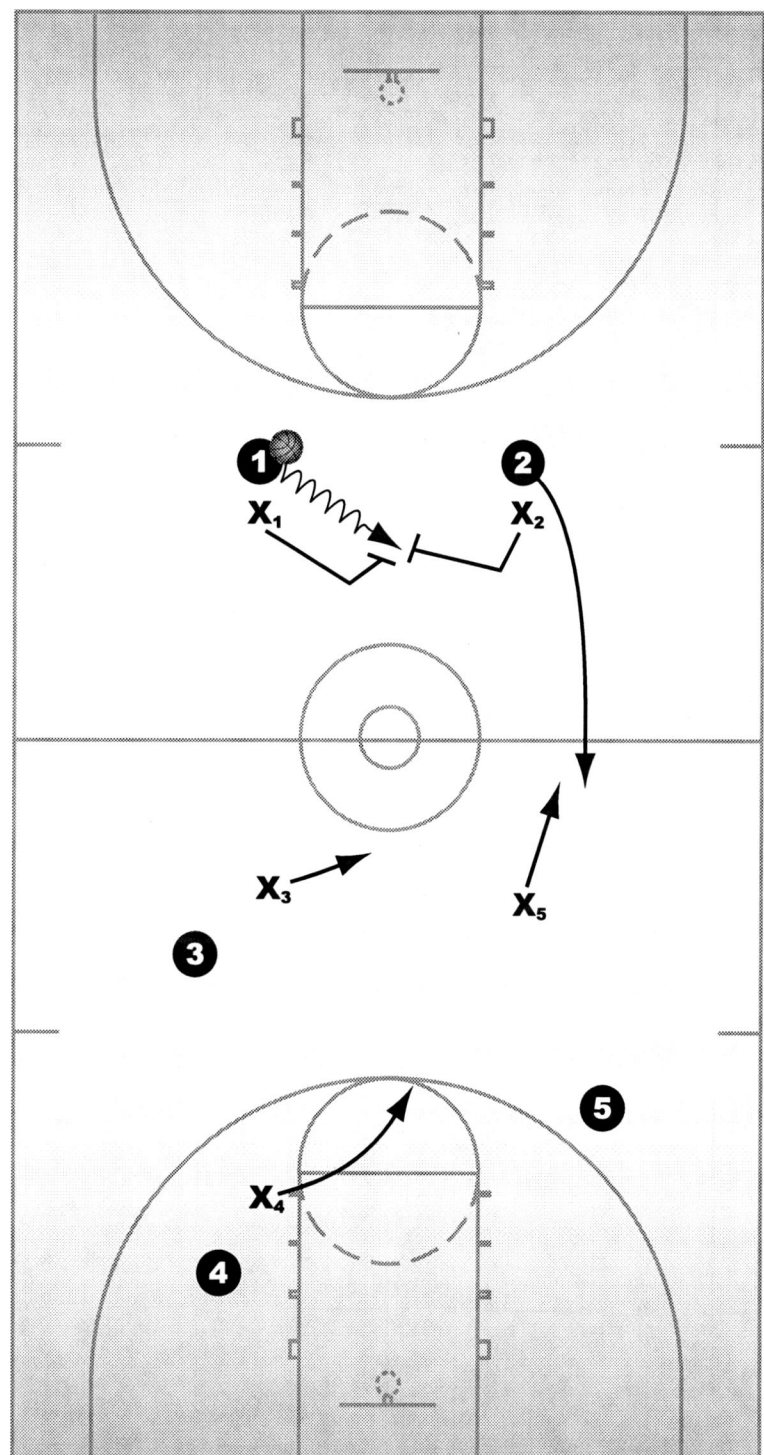

Woolpert 1.2

If the two-time pinch forces the dribbler into a rear turn, the defensive team is in good shape.

LESSONS FROM THIS LEGEND...

Let's assume now that the guard has forced the dribbler to the outside instead of down the middle. (See **Diagram 1.3**) As soon as X1 forces the dribbler to stop, X2, who has been convoying O2 down the court, moves in to two-time the dribbler just past the mid-line—this is, if he's in position to do this. In some instances, especially on a wide court, X2 will be too far removed to come over and help X1 two-time O1. In this contingency, we want X2 to stay with his man.

When X2 does move in for the two-time pinch, as shown in **Diagram 1.3**, the weakside forward, X4, moves up to choke the initial lead, O2. It's now X4's responsibility to prevent a pass from reaching O2.

Of course, we must recognize the fact that whenever a guard tries to drive his man to the side by playing tight and somewhat ahead of him, he'll be vulnerable to a quick cut back to the middle. However, if the guard remains alert and plays a half-step ahead of the dribbler, in position to prevent him from cutting back to the middle, his chances of stopping the dribbler are excellent.

Our strongside forward, X3, must be alert to choke off the dribbler, if X2 is unable to do it. This method of stopping the dribbler is illustrated in **Diagram 1.4**. When X3 releases to help X1 two-time O1, our center, X5, must be extremely alert to prevent a pass to O3. X5 must also start zoning and be ready to intercept any long pass.

As in all good defenses, the three-quarter court press requires a great amount of teamwork, practice, coordination, and talking among the players. As soon as penetration is effected, the backcourt men must immediately yell for help.

Unless the defensive men in the frontcourt—once the ball has gone by them—immediately hustle back to the defensive end of the court, the defense is going to be very vulnerable to a quick basket. It's a cardinal sin for a player, once the ball goes by him, to waste any time getting back to the

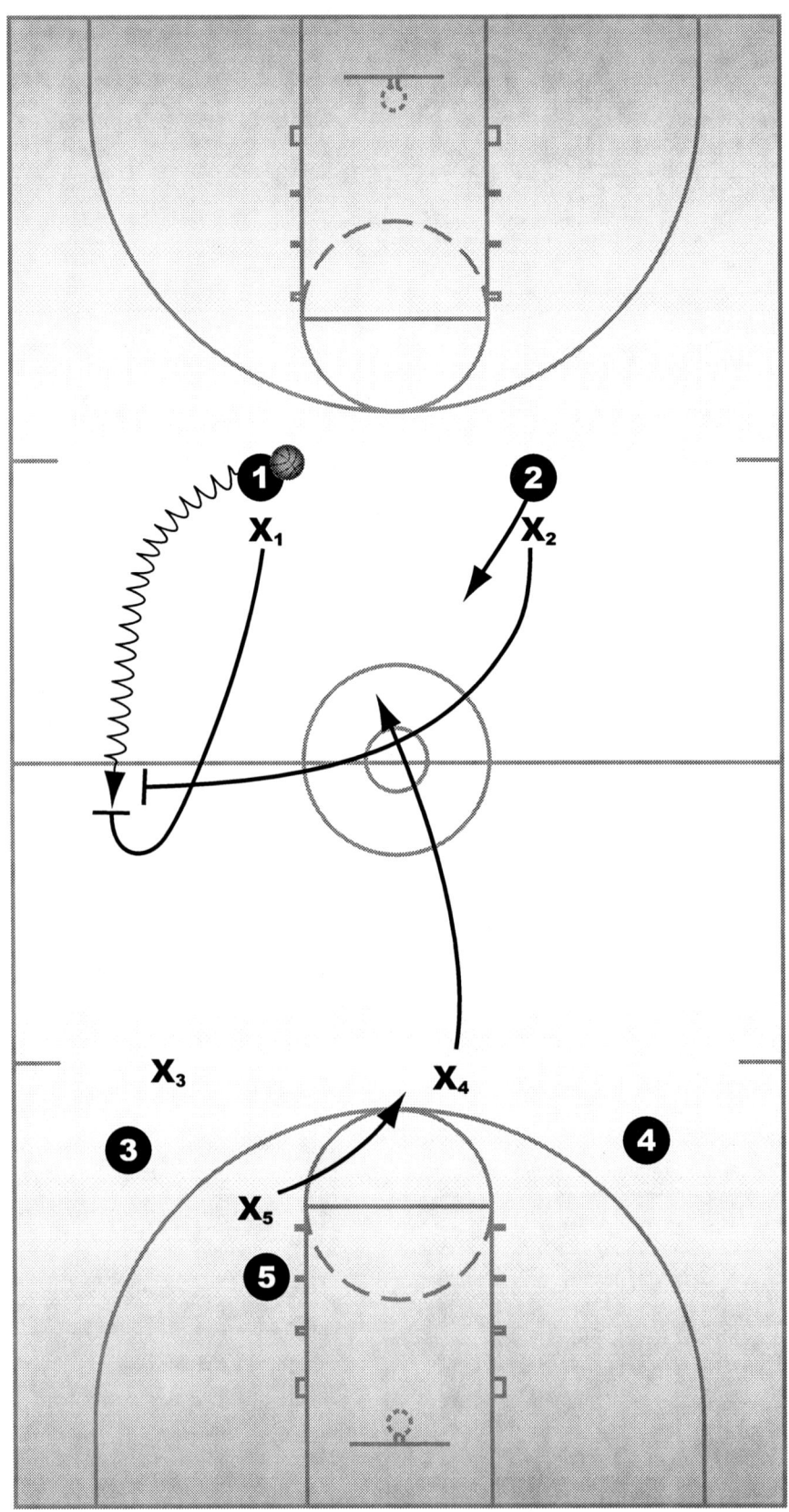

Woolpert 1.3

LESSONS FROM THIS LEGEND...

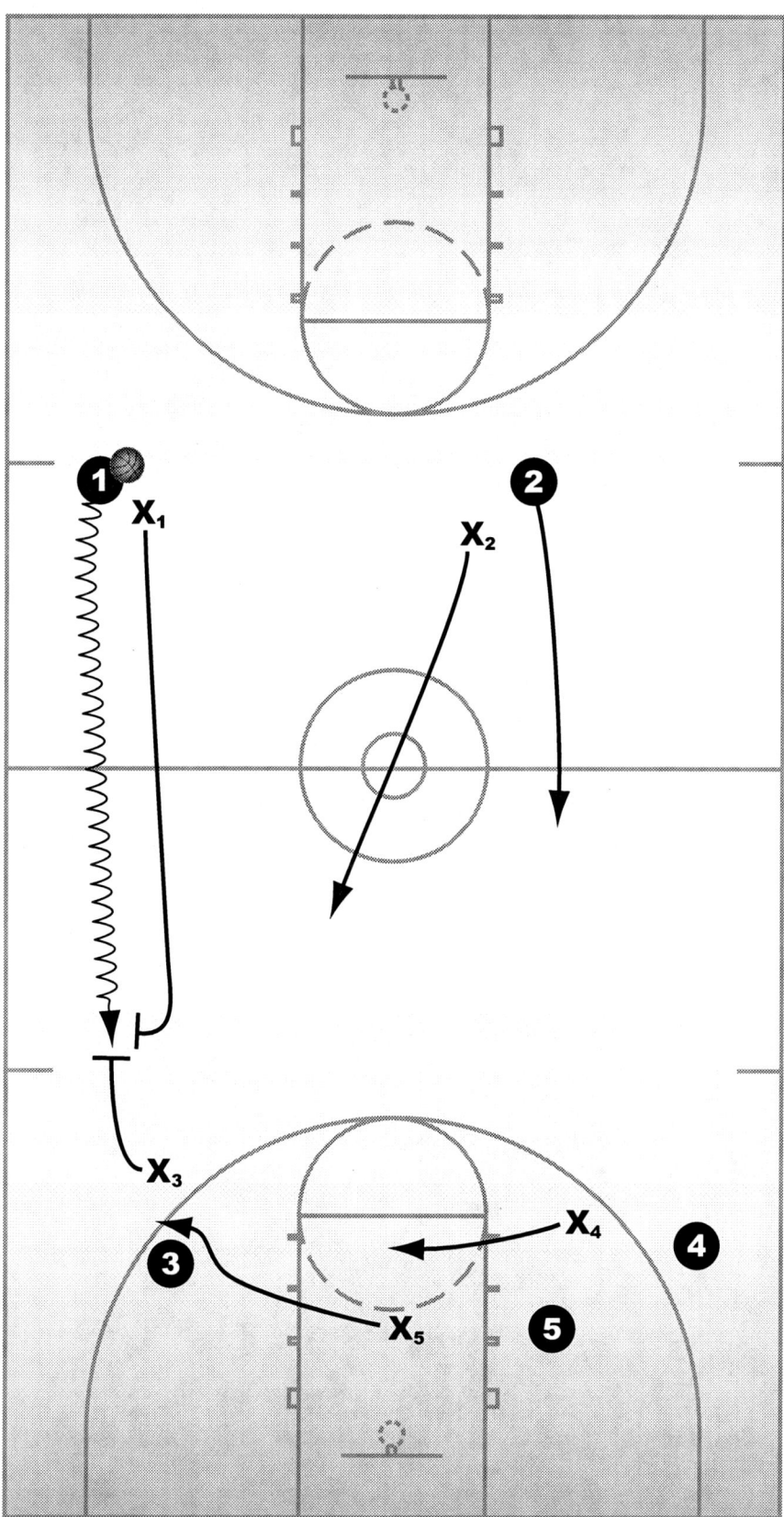

defensive end of the court. His first and immediate reaction should be to get back.

If any one of the three offensive players in the defensive area comes up to the middle of the court, his opponent must move up with him and attempt to prevent any pass from coming in to him.

The advantage of the three-quarter press over the full-court press is that it reduces the gravity of any error, since the area in which the players operate has been lessened. When the players operate over the entire floor in a press situation, an error is more costly than when they operate over only a portion of it.

The susceptibility of the players to error is also less. In using the mid-court press, the mid-line serves as an ally. Once the dribbler goes beyond the mid-line, he no longer can come back or pass back to the backcourt. On the other hand, if the dribbler is stopped behind this line, he'll be forced to throw the ball within 10 seconds.

One disadvantage of the three-quarter press, as in every press defense, is that a player is more prone to foul than when in any other type of defense. Another disadvantage is that at the instant the offensive team gets penetration, the press is vulnerable to an easy basket—and if every member of the three-quarter press isn't hustling like the dickens, the offense will probably get penetration.

As in all basketball situations, the success of this defense will be directly proportionate to the ability, desire, and determination of the players employing it.

SOURCE

Woolpert, Phil. (1956, November). San Francisco's Three-Quarter Press. *Scholastic Coach*.

Woolpert 1.4

LEGACY OF
Morgan Wootten

- Compiled the all-time best record (1,274-192) among high school coaches and the highest winning percentage (.868).

- Recorded 44 consecutive seasons with at least 20 wins.

- Led DeMatha to five mythical national high school championships.

- Advocated the three D's - defense, desire, and DeMatha.

- Emphasized the importance of education, and during a 30-year period, every player earned a full college scholarship.

- Urged players to set their priorities in the following order: God, family, school, and then basketball.

- Emphasized the development of character and integrity.

- Selected as the top high school coach of the 20th century by the Naismith Foundation.

MORGAN WOOTTEN

*"Inch by inch, life's a cinch.
Yard by yard, it's really hard."*
—Morgan Wootten

BIOGRAPHY

Born: April 21, 1931 in Durham, NC

Inducted into the Naismith Basketball Hall of Fame in 2000

Morgan Wootten began his coaching career in 1951 at the St. Joseph's Home for Boys in Washington D.C. He then coached at St. John's High School and compiled a 60-9 record. Wootten was appointed coach at DeMatha High School (MD) in 1956, and he stayed as a teacher and coach for 46 years. During that time, DeMatha won five mythical national championships (1962, 1965, 1968, 1978, and 1984). Wootten compiled the all-time best record (1,274-192) among high school coaches and the highest winning percentage (.868). With DeMatha's win on January 15, 2000, Wootten became the first basketball coach at any level (high school, college, or pro) to reach 1,200 wins. *USA Today* chose him the 1984 National Coach of the Year. Wootten's 1965 team broke the 71-game winning streak of Lew Alcindor's (now Kareem Abul-Jabbar) Power Memorial team. In 1991, Wootten was the first recipient of the Walt Disney Award, presented to the top sports coach in the United States. He also received the John Bunn Award in 1991 for his extraordinary contributions to the game of basketball. Wootten was enshrined into the Naismith Memorial Basketball Hall of Fame in 2000.

...SCOUTING REPORT.....SCOUTING REPORT.....

Morgan Wootten...

Morgan Wootten credits his mother for his intense drive and love of competition, and his father for teaching him to tell the truth and be himself. He was strongly influenced by his parents, teachers, and coaches, and this is readily observed in his philosophy. One of Wootten's favorite sayings is, "I am me, and I want to be the best me that I can be."

Wootten's high school coach, Tony Creme, influenced him by stressing fundamentals, player communication, and the importance of being a gentleman and a father figure to his players. Other people who helped Wootten formulate his philosophy are: Ken Loeffler of LaSalle, in the area of offensive strategy; "Red" Auerbach of the Boston Celtics, with regard to having a feel for the game and developing roles for each player; and Jim Kehoe of Maryland, for stressing the value of discipline, organization, and thoroughness. The heart of Wootten's philosophy seemed to come from Knute Rockne of Notre Dame who said, "We can only measure our success after 10 or 15 years when we see how our players turn out. After all, the real game is the game of life. And it's the one that we cannot afford to lose."

Morgan intended to become a lawyer after college, but was persuaded to coach the St. Joseph's Orphanage sports' teams in 1950 at the age of 19. Something happened there that forever changed Wootten's career plans. Under his direction, the teams had mixed success, but he arranged a visit and motivational talk at the orphanage from Rocky Marciano, the new heavyweight champion of the world. One of the orphans asked Rocky if he thought he could beat Coach Wootten. Marciano said he thought he could, but it would be a terrific fight. The questioning boy countered, "I don't think you can. I think Morgan would kill you." That incident deeply affected Wootten, when he saw the affect and impact a coach could have on a boy. From that time on, Morgan Wootten knew his mission in life—to teach and coach young people about life using the vehicle of sports.

And he became a master of it—starting in 1956 at DeMatha High School and carving out a legendary Hall of Fame career, spanning over 46 years. It was a marriage made in heaven; the school and the coach put each other on the map.

A legendary game between DeMatha and Power Memorial Academy in New York is still talked about long after that night of January 30, 1965. Over 12,000 fans jammed Maryland University's Cole Field House to see the long-awaited high school duel between DeMatha's Stags and the Power Panthers, led by its 7' superstar, Lew Alcindor (now Hall of Famer Kareem Abdul-Jabbar). Power had carved out a 71-game winning streak of its own. The game created a local and national media frenzy. DeMatha shocked the basketball world by defeating Power Memorial by five points, holding Alcindor to 16 points (he averaged 30). This came in Wootten's ninth year at DeMatha. He had his team prepare for the game by holding tennis rackets above their head to simulate shooting over Alcindor.

With all of his success, Wootten achieved his biggest win in July, 1996, when he collapsed while coaching in summer camp and was diagnosed with primary billiary cirrhosis of the liver, a rare disease that is usually fatal. With only hours left to live, a liver donor was found that was a perfect match for him, and the transplant was carried out to save his life. Wootten returned to coach the next season. During that season, he passed on to his players some of the lessons learned from the experience:

- My illness confirms the priorities needed for success: God, family, and education—in that order. Anything else, including basketball, can be no higher than fourth.
- Appreciate every day—sunrise and sunset, spring and autumn.
- Be thankful for families and friends.
- Enjoy each day, one day at a time.
- Inch by inch, life's a cinch. Yard by yard, it's really hard.

Morgan reminisced about his lengthy stay at DeMatha; we opened with 18 boys shortly after World War II, and now we have over 900. But, we have always emphasized "character over credentials." "We stress men of integrity and character. If you don't embrace those qualities, you're out of here. We still have the coat-and-tie dress code, our students still study religion every day of their four years here and, at the start of each day, they stand to recite the Lord's Prayer and the Pledge of Allegiance. We have won championships in every sport—more than 50 in basketball, football, and baseball alone. But, we have also won national high school Blue Ribbon awards from the Department of Education for excellence in education. After my transplant and the remarkable 1996-97 season, I often asked why my life was spared. The answer was clear—God was telling me, he wants me to stay here so I can continue to do what he wants all of us to do—to touch peoples' lives.

.....SCOUTING REPORT.....SCOUTING REPORT...

Coach Wootten explained his defensive philosophy in these words. "The name of the game is defense. We are going to make something happen. We want to get the ball. We want to get the ball almost any way we can. We are going to trap, rotate, and not foul. We have practiced it over and over. We put our player through every imaginable situation. We score points off our opponents' mistakes."

Wootten concluded by stating, "We are very lucky to be working with young people. And the rule of thumb that we have with our coaching staff is that we feel we should be the kind of coaches that our own son or our own daughter could play for. We are lucky because players keep us young and enthusiastic. Young people today are better than ever. Obviously, they are the future of America."

Wootten has been called the "Wizard of Washington." Mike Brey, head coach at Notre Dame and former DeMatha player, said, "All great high school coaches are local heroes. Morgan is a national one. You think about him, and you think about John Wooden and Dean Smith, and you stop there."

James Brown of Fox Sports played for Wootten at DeMatha and then chose Harvard over North Carolina to further his education and basketball career. Brown had this to say about his mentor: "Morgan absolutely abides in his own life by the principles he instructs his pupils. He is the best teacher, psychologist, and motivator at any level of basketball, professional or amateur."

Wootten is often asked why he hasn't gone to the so-called "next level" of college coaching. He has turned down offers from Georgetown, Maryland, and North Carolina State, among others. On March 8, 1980, he turned down an offer from North Caroline State for $700,000, plus free college education for his five children.

Jim Valvano took the job, and those players to an NCAA National Championship. When asked why he declined a college job for that much money, he replied that "money has never been in the top three priorities in life (God, family and education) and will never be the primary factor in my definition of happiness for me and my family." He also added, as for climbing mountains, they are where you find them. Any time I help a student in one of my classes get a better start during his formative years or touch the life of one of my basketball players, I feel I have climbed another mountain. That's the kind I prefer to keep on climbing." And so he did for over a half century of teaching and coaching excellence.

Hall of Fame coach John Wooden said it best with the following statement. "Morgan Wootten has been called the finest high school coach in the country. I disagree. He is the finest coach, at any level, I have ever seen."

SOURCE

Wootten, Morgan. Vertical Files, Archives. Naismith Memorial Basketball Hall of Fame. Springfield, MA.

Wootten, Morgan and Bill Gilbert. (1997). *A Coach for all Seasons*. Indianapolis: Masters Press.

LESSONS FROM THIS LEGEND...

BLITZ DEFENSE

By Morgan Wootten and Hank Galotta

At DeMatha, we feel that one of the keys to our success over the years has been defense. It has been the factor which led us to many big wins. Some of the more notable ones were the victory over the 1965 Power Memorial team led by Lew Alcindor. Lew's team had won 71 in a row before that string was snapped by a DeMatha defense, which held the high-scoring Power team to only 43 points and Alcindor, perhaps the best to ever play the game, to a mere 16 points. In 1968, a strong Lutheran High of Long Island led by Bill Chamberlain, now a star performer at the University of North Carolina, had DeMatha down 23 points at the beginning of the fourth quarter. Our DeMatha Blitz defense was then put into play, and at the end of the game, we were holding the ball to protect our lead. This same defense which can so drastically turn the tide in a basketball game is what will be presented here.

DEFENSIVE PSYCHOLOGY

Before a coach can install a workable defense, he must sell his team on the value of defense. The offensive star gets the publicity, but there is little outside praise given to the outstanding defensive player. This is where the coach's responsibility begins. We feel that there is a great deal of psychology involved in getting players to play good defense. It is essential for a coach not only to concentrate on teaching this phase of the game, but he must also make his squad aware of how important defense is to the success of the team. He must constantly emphasize that it is generally defense that wins the tough games. The best defensive plays should constantly be praised during practice. Throughout the years, we have placed so much emphasis upon defense that our teams react more enthusiastically over a player taking a great offensive charge than they do over a great scoring play. The coach should make a point of announcing excellent defensive play at the team meeting after games. Often, this important aspect of team statistics is overlooked. Also, when phoning in results to the news media, use the name of a boy who played an outstanding defensive game. His name might not get into the paper every time, but when it does, watch the defensive hustle improve at your next practice. This is the attitude that a coach must instill in his team if he is to build a successful defense.

One of the greatest incentives which a coach can use on his team is to tell them that the best defensive player on the squad will always be in the starting line-up. We make this statement during the first week of practice and repeat it often during the season. This is no idle promise. Our best defensive player will always start, and because we place such an emphasis upon this phase of the game, we usually find that the second and third-best defensive players are also in the starting line-up.

PHILOSOPHY

The basic foundation of a defense must be the defensive philosophy, in other words, what you are trying to accomplish through your defense. Without a philosophy, a coach would not be able to evaluate the success or failure of his defense. Long before we decided what defense would be appropriate for our team, we decided what we wanted to accomplish through our defense. The philosophy which we chose was "to get the ball." This sounds very simple, but it encompasses a great deal. We want to get the ball almost any way we can, through the steal, the charge, the walk, bad passes, etc. The only way that we do not want to get the ball is after our opponent scores. We feel that these mistakes are caused by our tenacious defense; they don't just happen. We also feel that our blitz defenses are the most effective in accomplishing our philosophy, because nothing we have found causes turnovers at a greater rate.

TERMINOLOGY

It is very important to find a convenient method of identifying your defenses in a way to make it clear to every team member what you are doing defensively. We have found that a numerical system best suits our purposes. We apply a single number to identify a particular half-court defense, for example #3. Then, if we want to extend the defense full-court, we double the number, #33. In addition to the numbers, we add words, for example #33 blue, #22 run and jump, etc., to show variations of that particular defense.

Our standard defense is our #2. This is our half-court, man-to-man, full over-play defense. By full overplay, we mean that our players are in a denial position, and they will not allow their men to catch the basketball. In this defense, we want to make the offensive player move without the ball to be a receiver. Only a poor defensive player will allow his man to catch the ball without making him work very hard to do it. It is also one of our objectives in our #2 to invite the long pass. Because our players position themselves in the passing lane and off of their man, the lob pass appears easy to complete. We feel, however, that the lob pass is one of the most dangerous ones in basketball, and we should be able to pick off most of them by using proper techniques. If we want to extend this overplay

LESSONS FROM THIS LEGEND...

defense full-court, we will call for the #22 tough. The same principles apply here as they did in the #2, except now we deny all over the court. The basic difference between the #22 and the #22 tough is that in the #22, we will let the primary receiver catch the ball in front of us and then apply intelligent pressure on the ball. In the #22 tough, no one is allowed to catch the ball.

The #1 is a half-court, man-to-man defense which positions the defensive player between his man and the basket, instead of between his man and the ball as is done in the #2. In the #1 defense, the offensive man can catch the ball any time he wants. If this defense is extended over the full court, it becomes a #11.

Between the #1 and #2, we use fractions to show the different degrees of pressure which will be applied to the pass. For example, the #2 1/2 defense would not be a true overplay defense, but there would be a light degree of pressure on the pass. The #1 3/4 defense puts more pressure on the pass, but it is not a true overplay as seen in the #2. If we want to refer to a full-court #1-1/2, we simply call it #11-1/2.

It should be pointed out, however, that we seldom use anything less than a #2 man-to-man defense at DeMatha. We find these terms very helpful at practice, though, when we simulate our opponent's defense or when scouting.

Our #3 series is our zone-press series. We generally use colors after the numbers here to indicate different alignments. Following along with what was previously stated, to extend the zone press over the full-court simply refer to it as #33.

Our #4 series is our straight zone series, and again we use colors to differentiate different zone alignments. In addition to the four series that were mentioned, we can also use combinations which change the defense. For example, our #43 combines the principles of a straight zone with the principles of the zone press. The #43 would be a half-court, trapping zone defense.

We have found this system to be the most efficient one, because it covers not only everything that we use defensively, but also everything we are likely to encounter in games throughout the season.

DEFENSIVE STANCE

We know that it would be impossible to attempt to teach a student an entire textbook at one time. It is necessary to break the book down into chapters and teach one chapter at a time. In the same way, it would be impossible to teach an entire defense at one time. At DeMatha, we attempt to break down our blitz defenses into different teaching steps. We begin teaching our blitz defenses by concentrating on individual defensive techniques. Obviously, a team defense can only be as good as the defensive ability of the individuals on the team. Because we sincerely believe in this principle, we constantly work on individual defensive fundamentals.

We begin our defensive instruction by teaching the correct stance. The stance that we teach requires the players to have one foot forward—we have no adamant rule as to which foot is forward—and the feet must be at least shoulder-width apart. We use the following method of teaching to facilitate having uniformity among our players in the defensive stance:

1) Using half the floor, the players line up in tandem in five lines, an arm's-length apart, facing the sideline to their right.
2) The feet are shoulder-width apart, with the toes pointing straight ahead toward the sideline; the feet are now parallel.
3) The players stand up straight and place their hands on their knees, the right hand on the right knee and the left hand on the left knee; the elbows are not flexed.
4) The players keep their head up, with the eyes looking straight ahead; the head must be the midpoint of the shoulders, dividing the body into two equal parts.
5) The players drop their weight slightly by lowering the buttocks; the back is kept straight and is at a 45-degree angle to the floor.
6) The players plant the heel of their left foot and the toes of their right foot into the floor and pivot ninety degrees to their left, keeping their hands on their knees.

Now, they should be in a position facing the baseline of the nearest basket, with their left foot forward and their feet shoulder-width apart. From this position, we tell the players to adjust the feet slightly, until they are comfortable, and to remove the hands from the knees, placing them with the fingers cupped in front of their chest, thus imitating a karate expert. We reiterate keeping the buttocks low and the head straight, directly between the shoulders for good balance.

The following points should be stressed:
1. **Head**—up and directly in the middle of the shoulders. If a straight line were drawn from the forehead over the nose and down to the floor between the feet, the body should be divided into two equal parts.
2. **Eyes**—looking straight ahead.
3. **Shoulders**—parallel to the floor.
4. **Back**—fairly straight, no more than 45-degree angle to the floor.
5. **Waist**—not flexed.
6. **Buttocks**—low to the floor in a squat position.
7. **Thighs**—fairly tight and at a 45-degree angle to the floor.
8. **Knees**—flexed; the body is bent at the knees and not at the waist; the player gets lower by bending his knees and lowering his buttocks.
9. **Feet**—slightly wider than the shoulders; weight equally distributed on the balls of both feet; one foot forward—left foot—pointing straight ahead. One foot back—the right foot—pointing straight ahead, parallel with the left foot. The heel of the front foot is slightly in front of the toes of the back or rear foot.

LESSONS FROM THIS LEGEND...

RETREAT STEP

The next phase of defense that we stress is footwork. The first skill we teach in defensive footwork is the "retreat step." The player already has one foot in front of the other in the good stance. Now, if the player he is guarding makes a move toward the basket to his right or left, the defensive player's first reaction is to take a step backwards with his rear foot, or to retreat. The following is an analysis of the "retreat step," assuming the left foot is the front foot.

POINTS TO STRESS

1. The defensive player is low, in a good defensive stance.
2. Exaggerate getting low by having players touch the floor between their feet with the palms of their hands.
3. Put pressure on the toes of the front foot—the left foot.
4. Push the front foot into the floor and shove against the floor, simultaneously taking a step backwards with the rear foot.
5. Never bring the feet any closer than shoulder width.
6. Do not lift the front foot off the floor—slide it back.
7. Keep the shoulders level and parallel to the floor.

SWING STEP

The next skill in teaching defensive footwork in progression is the "swing step." The swing step is a defensive maneuver to counter the offensive player's changing direction usually through the use of the cross-over step or the reverse dribble. Moreover, most offensive players are coached to drive in the direction of the defensive player's front foot. The defensive swing step is a reaction to protect the defensive player.

POINTS TO STRESS

1. The defensive player is low, in a good defensive stance.
2. The first step is back by pushing with the front foot and sliding the rear foot—a retreat step.
3. Lock the shoulder of the arm corresponding with the front foot—the direction the offensive player chooses to go.
4. The elbow of the locked shoulder is in front of the chest and at a 45-degree angle to the chest.
5. The forearm of the locked shoulder is parallel to the floor.
6. Literally throw or swing the elbow of the locked shoulder in the direction you want to go; the impetus created by the whipping action of the elbow, and its momentum automatically forces the entire body around in the direction of the front foot and in the path of the offensive player.
7. From this position, the defensive player has regained his advantage and continues to shuffle or "scoot" with the offensive player, staying between the offensive player and the basket.

ADVANCE STEP

The next skill that we include in teaching defensive footwork is the "advance step". The advance step or defensive thrust is the maneuver essential to our concept of dominating the offensive player. In our defensive thinking, we want to be the actor and the offender the reactor. We must make the offensive player react to what the defensive player does. Subsequently, the actor always wins. Thus, the advance step is the main vehicle for enabling the defensive player to be the actor. We use the terms "challenging", "snaking", and "bluffing" in an attempt to make the offense react to the defense. The terms are useful in making the offense do what the defense wants it to do.

POINTS TO STRESS

1. Take a good defensive stance.
2. Hands up, the chest high.
3. Push with the back foot.
4. Slide the front foot forward toward player with the ball.
5. Extreme flexion of the knees to help get the body lower.
6. Exaggerate lowering of the weight by dropping the buttocks.
7. Bring the hand that corresponds with the front foot up toward offensive player's face, faking at the ball as the hand is being brought up.
8. Yell "HEY."
9. The other hand is low, palm up, fingers pointing down, to defend against the bounce pass or dribble.
10. Be prepared to push off the front foot and step backward with the rear foot in executing the retreat step.

LESSONS FROM THIS LEGEND...

SLIDE DRILL

Stresses: Footwork and conditioning

Procedure: The coach stands under the basket facing the squad, which is spread across the floor in several lines. The coach gives the verbal command "step-slide," and the squad reacts by performing the retreat step. After the squad has become adroit at this drill, the coach will use the whistle as a signal for performing the retreat step. We use the term "slide," because the retreat step requires two basic moves. First, upon pushing with the front foot, the rear foot takes a step backwards; second, the front foot slides toward the back foot in returning to the original stance. Everybody has the same foot forward.

POINTS TO EMPHASIZE

1. Maintain a proper defensive stance.
2. Put pressure on the front foot.
3. Push with the front foot and step backwards with the rear foot.
4. Drag the front foot backwards in returning to initial position.
5. Do not bring feet together.
6. The feet are always at least shoulder-width apart.
7. Keep the head straight for balance.
8. Stay low; do not become higher as drill progresses.
9. Keep the shoulders parallel to the floor.
10. Do not bob the head or shoulders.

"HEY DRILL"

Stresses: Defense and conditioning

The next drill is one of our favorites, and one the squad really enjoys. We call it the "hey drill." We like to think it is a unique drill which originated at DeMatha. In general, the "hey drill" is a counter to the crossover step, dribble, stop-and-shoot-the-jump-shot move. The components of the "hey drill" are as follows: advance step, retreat step, swing step, and defensive shuffle.

Procedure: The squad forms three lines across the floor facing the coach, who is standing on the baseline under the basket. The players assume the defensive stance position; everybody has the same foot forward. When the coach blows his whistle, the squad will respond quickly by executing the advance step, simultaneously yelling "hey," taking a retreat step back, then a swing step, and then taking two shuffle steps, pointing the toes of the lead foot. Now, they will be in their good defensive stance, with their opposite foot their front foot. The drill is repeated the length of the floor.

Let's analyze the "hey drill," using the left foot as the front foot:

POINTS TO STRESS:
LOW AND IN GOOD STANCE

Advance Step:
1. Push with the back foot and slide the front foot forward.
2. Rock up over the knee of the front foot.
3. Yell "HEY."
4. Exaggerate dropping the weight low.

Retreat Step:
1. Push off the floor with the front foot.
2. Step with the back foot.
3. Slide the front foot back.
4. Do not bring feet together.
5. Take only one step backwards.
6. Stay low.
7. Keep the head straight for balance.

Swing Step:
1. Lock the shoulder, throw the elbow, and pivot the body in the direction of the ball.
2. Do not turn back on the ball.
3. Keep your eyes on the ball.
4. Stay low as the body swings toward the ball.

Shuffle:
1. Take two shuffle steps, pointing the toes of the lead (left) foot, stay low, keeping hands moving.
2. Bend the knees.
3. Maintain the head in the midpoint of the shoulders for balance.
4. Do not bring feet together.
5. After two shuffle steps, the player stops and is in position to repeat the drill, this time with the opposite foot as the front foot.

Needless to say, we love this drill, because it incorporates all of the basic skills involved in our defensive footwork. We usually repeat the drill up the court and back two times. One of the seniors determines which foot will be forward each time the players reach the baseline. In addition, we sometimes have the players bring the feet up and down on the floor quickly, much like a machine gun or typewriter; then, we blow the whistle, and they react by performing the "hey drill."

LESSONS FROM THIS LEGEND...

ONE-ON-ONE

Perhaps our most effective drill in developing skill in individual defense is our full-court, one-on-one drill. This drill combines good stance with movement of the ball and dominating the dribbler. Our defensive objective is to harass and contain the dribbler, stealing the ball if possible, but not allowing him to advance the ball up the court without being contested. We want the defensive man to turn the dribbler, and force him to change directions as many times as he possibly can on the trip up the court. In essence, we want the trip up the court to be long and hard for the dribbler, one he won't likely forget the next time his team gets the ball. (See **Diagram 1.0**)

Procedure: All squad members get behind the baseline. The players get into pairs, and each pair has a ball. We like all our men to get the opportunity to play defense against our quicker men. One player gets behind the baseline and dribbles up the court against constant pressure. The next pair does not begin until the previous group has passed the opposite foul line. When the entire squad has reached the opposite baseline, the men switch assignments, offense to defense and defense to offense, and repeat the drill going back.

POINTS TO EMPHASIZE

1. The defensive player should be close enough to the offensive player to be able to put the palm of his hand on the offensive player's chest.
2. The defensive player should keep his eyes and head on the ball.
3. The hands are constantly putting pressure on the ball, and the feet are moving in the defensive shuffle.
4. Play the ball from the floor up, the palms are up, and the fingers are jabbing at the ball.
5. Pressure the ball with the hand nearest the direction the dribbler is going; for example, if the dribbler is going left (to the defensive man's right), he pressures the ball with his right hand, the outside hand.
6. Turn the dribbler by shuffling in front of his intended path.
7. Do not cross the feet or bring them together.
8. Do not turn the head or back on the ball.
9. Turn the dribbler, forcing him to change or reverse his direction, a basic rule in our trapping defenses.
10. If getting beat, take a short cut by running to the middle of the foul line and then picking up the dribbler.

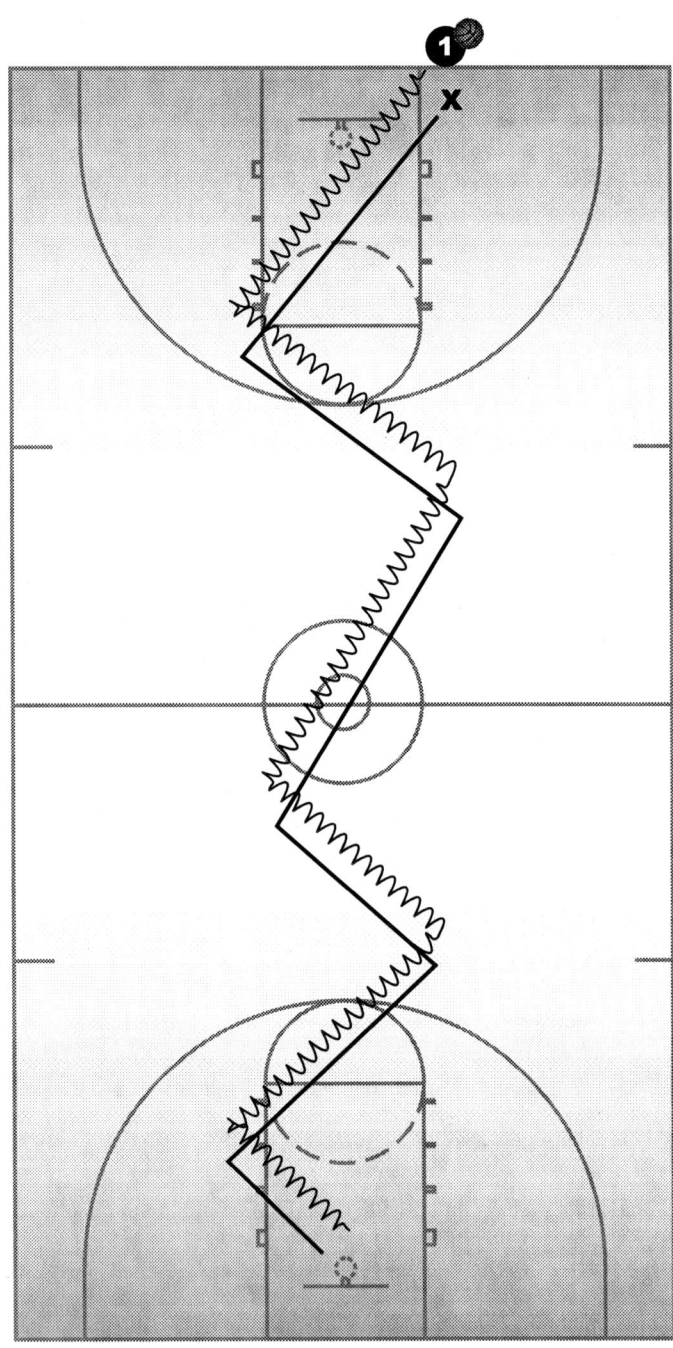

Wootten 1.0

Essentially, in teaching the full-court, one-on-one, we are beginning to build on our full-court defense, because every player must be able to contain his man full-court if our blitzing defense is to be effective.

After we have taught the fundamentals of individual defense, we begin building our team defense. When teaching team defense, we always break our instruction up into special drills, designed to place emphasis on a special phase of the defense. As was mentioned before, we do not want to concentrate on too much at a time, so we use the "break-down" method, in order to emphasize the techniques which we feel are so important to accomplishing our defense philosophy.

LESSONS FROM THIS LEGEND...

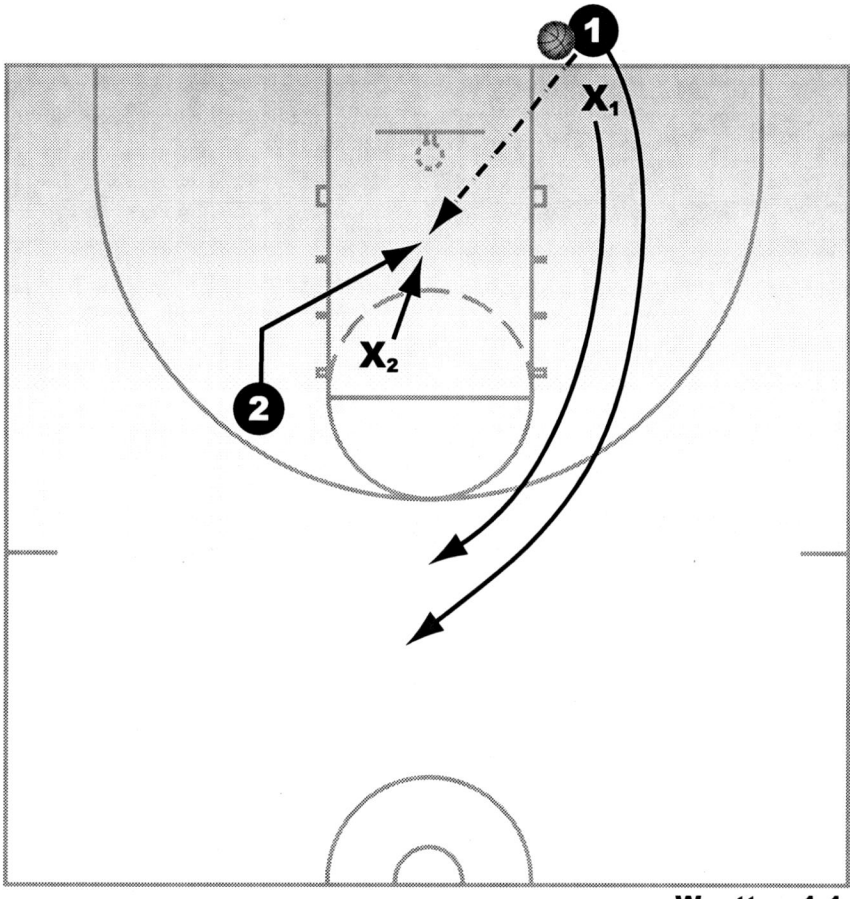

Wootten 1.1

FULL COURT TWO-ON-TWO

The next phase in building our full-court defense is our two-on-two, full-court drill. This drill combines full-court pressure defensive tactics and adds the element of contesting the inbounds pass. (See **Diagram 1.1**)

Procedure: We use three groups of players in this drill, four players in each group, two defensive players and two offensive players. We use only one ball throughout the entire drill. When the first two offensive players have completed their trip up the court (play stops after a score or a defensive rebound), they will play defense against the first two defensive players in an immediate return trip down the court. Each group must be ready to go as soon as the group in front of them is finished.

We line up in this drill, with O1 the left side and O2 at least as far back as the foul-line extended on the opposite side of O1. We feel this alignment gives the offensive players the maximum amount of room to maneuver to get the ball inbounds, thus putting great pressure on the defensive players to keep the ball from getting inbounds. X1 lines up just off the baseline, and it is his responsibility to make the in bounds pass as difficult as possible by yelling, jumping up and down, flashing his arms, etc. X2 positions himself away from his man toward the ball. He must keep one hand in the passing lane; that is the path the ball must take from O1 to O2. Positioning himself in this manner will allow X2 to see both the ball and his man, which is a necessity in our defensive picture. When O1 slaps the ball, O2 begins to make his move in an attempt to receive the pass, but this cannot be beyond the foul-line extended. X2 will attempt to deny the pass to O2. If O2 does receive the pass, O1 clears the area, as shown on the diagram, in a maneuver which we call "guard in front". X2 then plays O2 one-on-one up the court to the scoring area at the opposite side. The play continues as two-man basketball, until a defensive rebound or a score.

POINTS TO EMPHASIZE

We want great pressure on the inbounds pass. Once the ball is in play, we want the same principles applied as the one-on-one drill. We want pressure on the ball by keeping the head on the ball; we want the dribbler turned as many times as possible, and ultimately, we want the dribbler stopped and the defensive man to close up on him; meanwhile, the other defensive player is not allowing his man to catch the basketball.

LESSONS FROM THIS LEGEND...

FULL COURT THREE-ON-THREE

The three-on-three drill is another device for building our full-court defense, since many teams attack full-court pressure with two immediate receivers. (See **Diagram 1.2**)

Procedure: Similar to two-on-two, but this time we use groups of six, three offensive players and three defensive players. We use one ball, and when one group reaches the end of the court, the groups exchange positions and return down court.

O1 takes the ball out. O2 and O3 line up in tandem, in the middle of the foul line. X2 and X3 position themselves away from their men and toward the ball. O3 breaks first, using O2 as a screener if possible. If O3 cannot receive the ball, then O2 is the second cutter, going in the opposite direction from where O3 made his cut. X1 has the same responsibility as in the two-on-two drill. X2 and X3 must keep their men from catching the ball. If the pass is completed, the two offensive players without the ball "guard in front," with the defensive men keeping themselves between their man and the ball. The defensive player guarding the ball puts aggressive pressure on the ball, while turning the offensive player as often as possible. If the ball gets across half-court, they play three-on-three basketball. There is no switching at any time during this drill. If there is a screen, the defensive man must fight over the top, while staying with his man. This is essential to all our defenses, because we never want anything coming between our defensive man and the ball. To make this drill most effective, work against as many different alignments as possible.

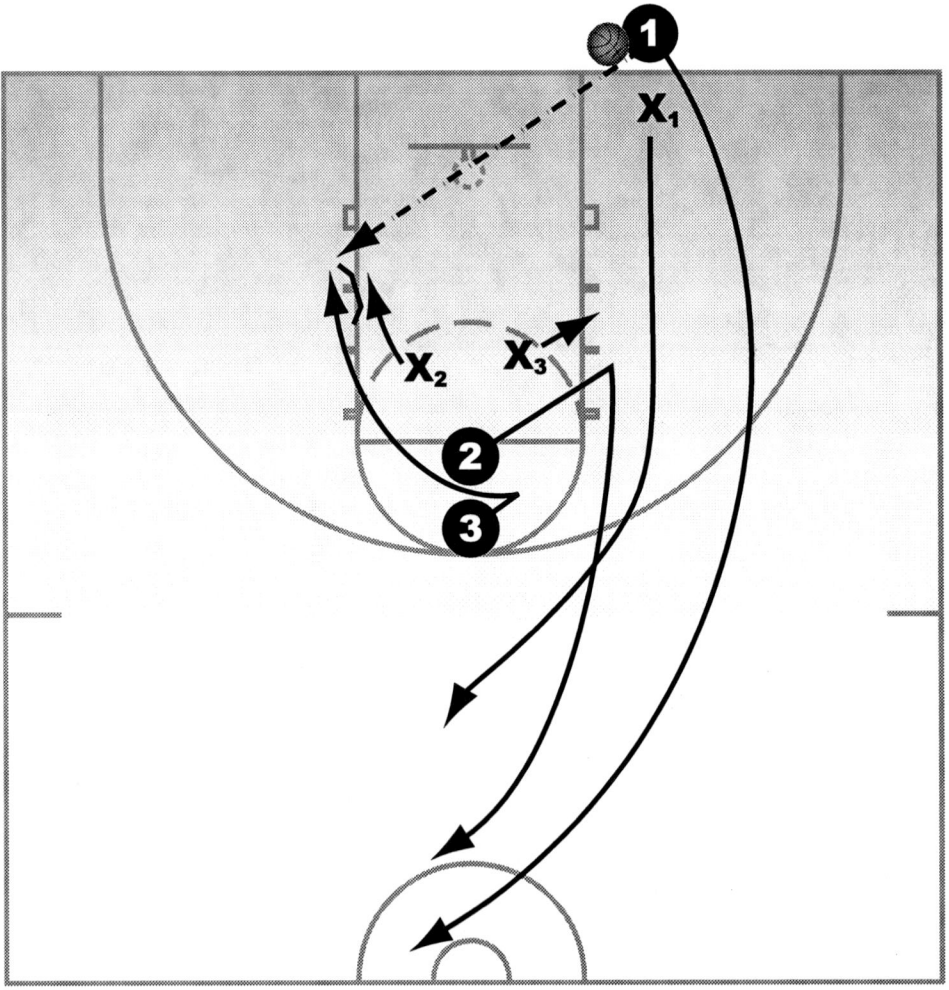

Wootten 1.2

LESSONS FROM THIS LEGEND...

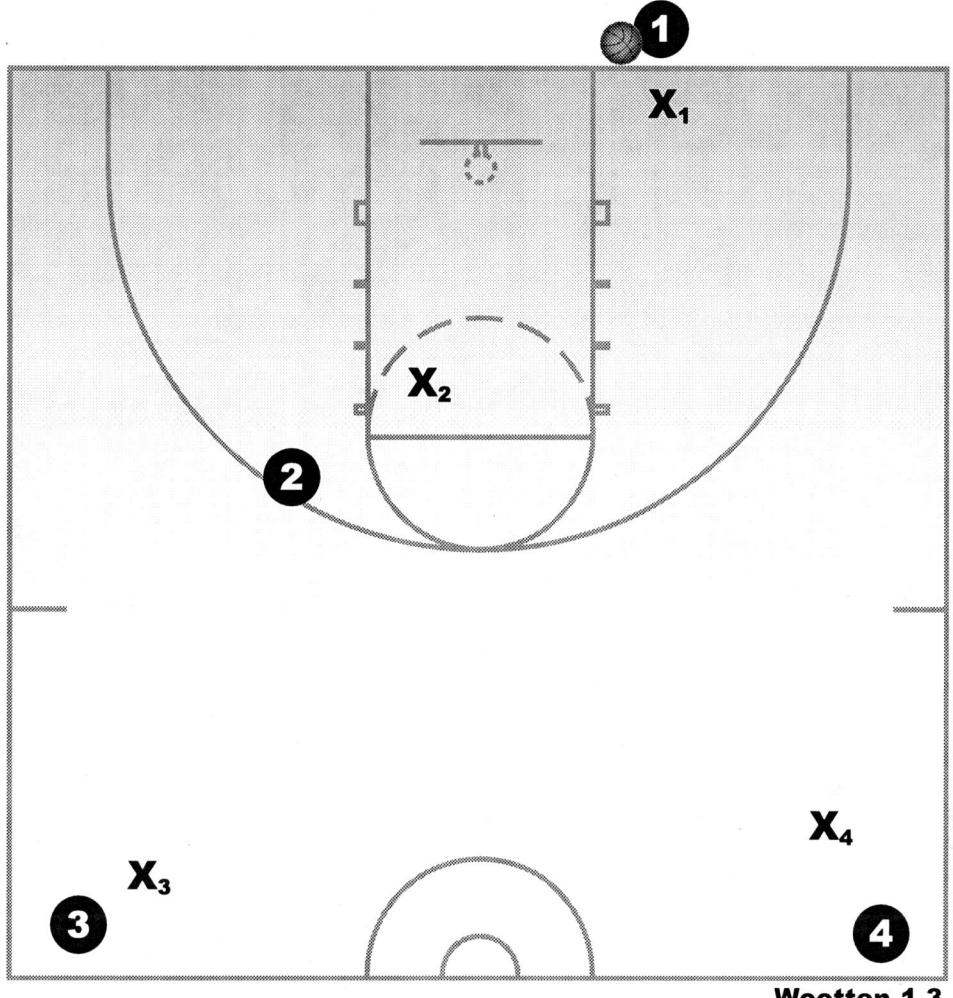

Wootten 1.3

FULL COURT FOUR-ON-FOUR

Procedure: This drill involves four offensive players and four defensive players. We use three groups alternating their assignments frequently. (See **Diagram 1.3**)

Offensive players O1 and O2 line up, using the same rules as the full-court, two-on-two. Offensive players O3 and O4 line up behind the ten second line as mid-court receivers, ready to help bring the ball up. In this drill, O2 is the primary receiver, and it is X2's responsibility to deny him the ball. O3 and O4 will act as secondary receivers, and they can move to receive the pass if O2 needs help. We will allow O1 to attempt the long lob in this drill to see how X3 and X4 react to the pass. There is more pressure on them here than in the regular five-on-five defense, because there is no defensive post man to help on the long pass. If the pass is completed short to O2, we again want O1 to "guard in front," and X2 must put good aggressive pressure on O2 on the trip up the court. When the ball crosses the mid-court line, it becomes a game of four-man basketball. We like the drill very much, because it puts so much pressure on X3 and X4. They must be able to react up or back in order to keep the ball away from their men. This drill is very helpful when we begin working on our #22 blitz defenses. By eliminating the offensive post man, nothing changes, because in our trapping defenses, the defensive player guarding the post area is not involved in the rotation caused by the trapping tactic.

LESSONS FROM THIS LEGEND...

FULL COURT FIVE-ON-FIVE

The five-on-five drill is in essence our #22 tough defense. We set the offense up in many different alignments, depending on what type of front our opponent presents when breaking full-court, man-to-man pressure, but the alignment that we use most often is the one-man front. (See **Diagram 1.4**)

We line up in the same manner as we did in the four-on-four drill, except we add the post men, O5 and X5, down-court. The responsibilities for X1, X2, X3, and X4 are the same as in the four-on-four drill. X5 must play well off O5 to insure that O5 does not break up-court to release the pressure, but he must be close enough to his man to be able to intercept the lob pass that might be thrown.

POINTS TO EMPHASIZE

Everybody has a man, and it is his responsibility to keep his man from catching the ball.
1. X1 puts aggressive pressure on the man taking the ball out.
2. X2 overplays his man, forcing the lob pass.
3. X3 and X4 do not let their men receive the inbounds pass and are in position to intercept the lob pass forced by X2.
4. X5 is far enough away from his man to prevent him from breaking up-court to release the pressure, and he is in position to intercept the lob pass forced by the defensive play of his teammates, X2, X3 and X4.
5. Every defensive man must completely overplay his man, because we want the offensive players to go without the ball, and we want the offense to lob the ball.

In summary, the basic rules for both the #2 and the #22 tough defenses are as follows:
1. We cannot let the offensive players catch the ball; if they should catch the ball, however, we must put aggressive, but intelligent, pressure on the ball. Get the dribbler to pick up his dribble and close up on him.
2. We want a complete overplay of the first receiver. Be off the man and toward the ball. Have one hand in the passing lane.
3. When the offensive player is not an immediate receiver, (i.e., two passes away from the ball), the defensive man should be well off his man and in position to help if help is needed.

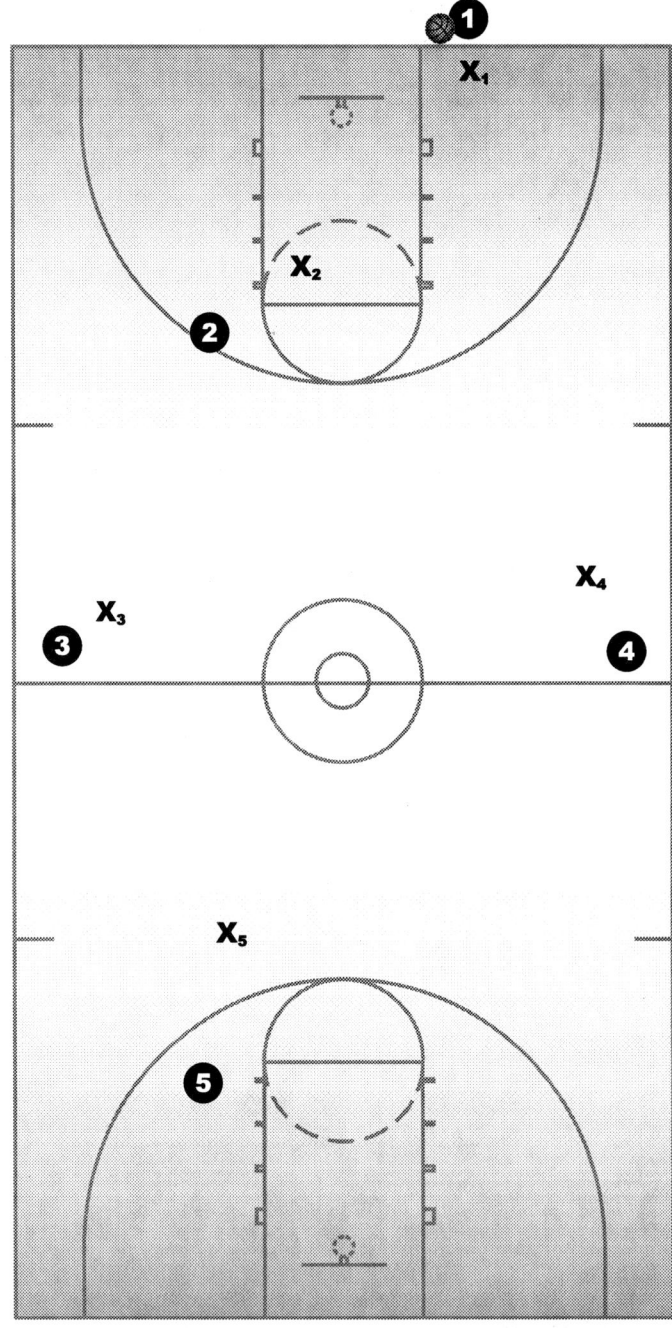

Wootten 1.4

Our objectives are as follows:
1. To get the ball
2. To make the offensive player go without the ball
3. If he should catch the ball, to get the offensive player to put the ball on the floor
4. To get the dribble stopped

LESSONS FROM THIS LEGEND...

VARIATIONS OF THE #22

We have three basic variations of the #22 (blitz), which we adapt to the style of play of our opponents. The first of these is the shortstop.

SHORTSTOP
(See **Diagram 1.5**)

In the shortstop, X1, who normally guards the man taking the ball out-of-bounds, plays between the ball and the receiver. X2 moves behind O2, creating what is, in effect, a double-team. If the ball should get inbounds, X1 would react back to O1, and we would play it as a normal #22. This defense is particularly effective against a team with only one good ballhandler or a team with an exceptional guard from whom the ball should be kept away. This simple tactic is also very successful against a well-patterned ball club that depends upon a single point to initiate the offense. By shortstopping the primary receiver, this type of team has a tendency to forego their patterned style and play a more haphazard style. In effect, their strength offensively is neutralized.

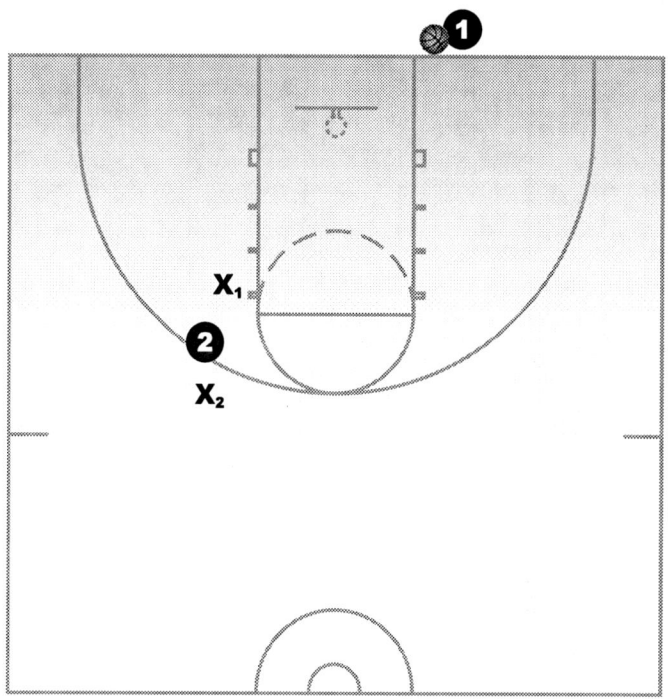
Wootten 1.5

CENTER FIELD
(See **Diagram 1.6**)

The center field is a tactic in which the defensive man guarding the player taking the ball out-of-bounds plays around the top of the circle. It is particularly effective when a team uses back-court screens to break full-court pressure. In this case, the center fielder would cheat toward the screen and pick up the open receiver. This also gives our #22 a zone "look," which often causes the offensive team to make needless and dangerous adjustments to break the press. X2 and X3 can now put on an even more determined overplay, because the lob is covered.

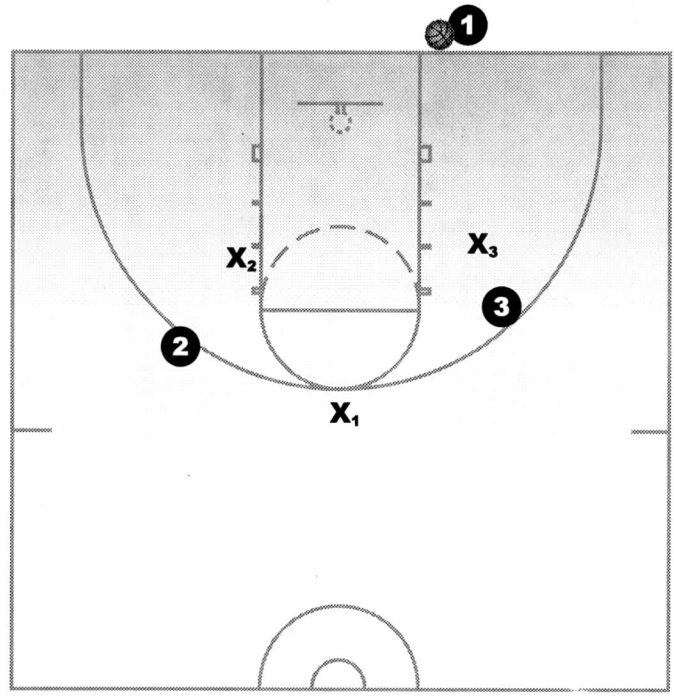
Wootten 1.6

LESSONS FROM THIS LEGEND...

LEFT FIELD
(See **Diagram 1.7**)

The purpose of this defensive alignment is obvious. The man guarding the ball will play at the opposite foul line, in an effort to stop the offensive team from throwing the "bomb," the full-court pass. This puts added pressure on the other four defensive men, because if the pass is completed to one of their men, the press is broken by a simple throw-back to the open man, O1. They have the assurance, however, that they can fully overplay their men without having to worry about their men breaking down court for a long lob.

Each of these variations is simple, but, collectively, they help give our standard #22 many useful options without drastically changing the assignments of the majority of the defensive players. Also, the concept of giving your defense a "new look" is very helpful in keeping your opponents off-guard.

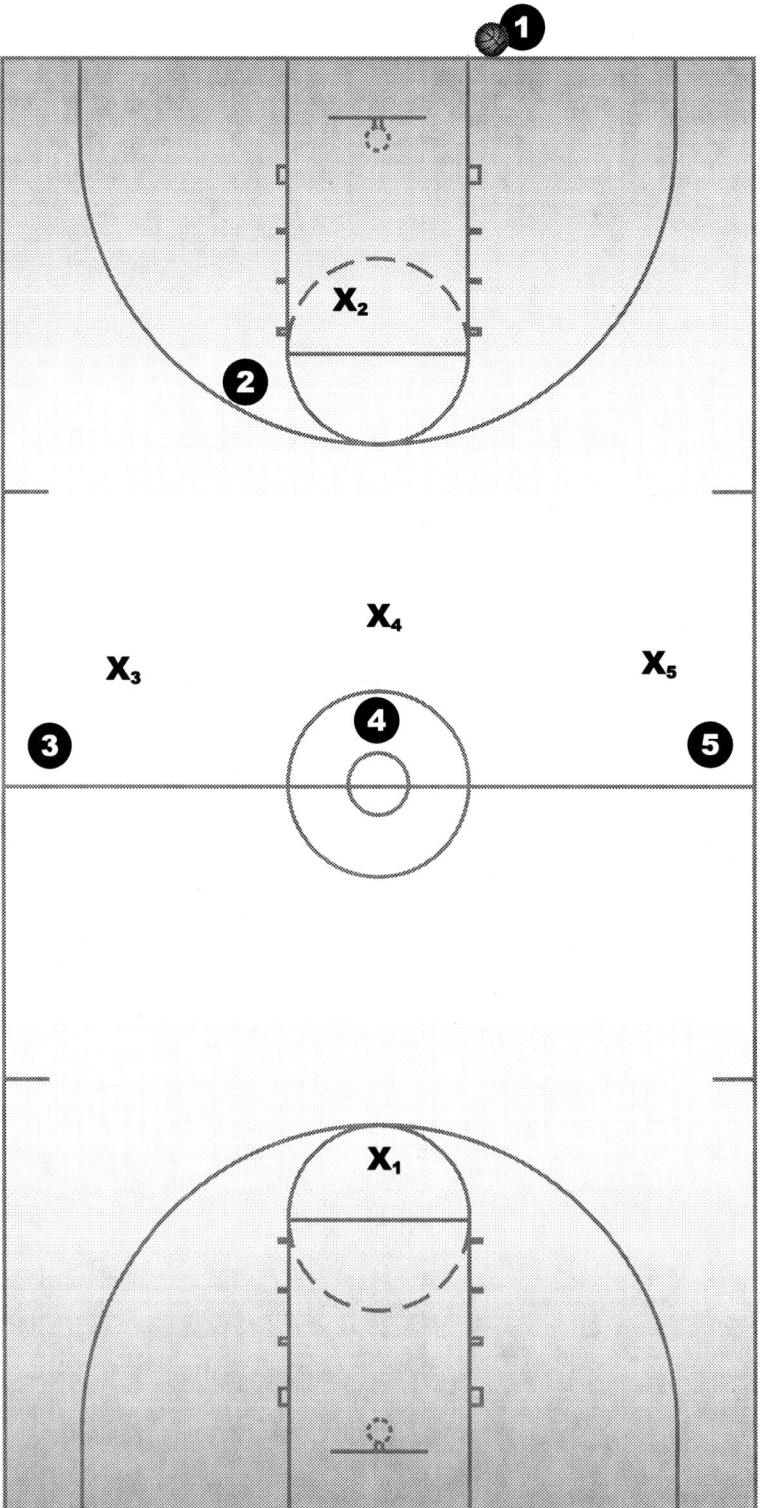

Wootten 1.7

LESSONS FROM THIS LEGEND...

#2 Defense

Our #2 defense is our standard half-court defense. It is a full overplay defense, with a helping rotation.

Our basic rules for the positioning of our players are:

1. The defensive player on the ball will put intelligent pressure on the ball in an effort to get the dribble stopped. He will attempt to make his man put the ball on the floor, then he will make him pick it up.
2. When guarding a man who is one pass away from the ball, the defensive man must position himself off his man and toward the ball. He must have one hand in the passing lane. For example, if X1 in **Diagram 1.8** is guarding O1, he would have his left foot back toward the basket. He would be in a good defensive stance, with his right hand in the passing lane. X3, however, would have his right foot back, and he would have his left hand in the passing lane. This position, we feel, puts the defender in a good position to be able to stop the pass, either with his extended hand or with a simple pivot move on the up foot. He is also in position to contest the back-door move. We feel that an offensive wing could take two to three full steps toward the basket, and the defensive wing could still be in position to contest the pass without moving. We do not advocate a stationary defensive wing, of course, but this gives the defensive player a great deal of security when denying the pass.
3. When guarding a man who is two passes away from the ball, as X4 is in **Diagram 1.8**, the defensive man should have one foot in the foul lane. He should position himself so he can see both his man and the ball. This should put him in position to either stop a driver on the ballside of the court or react to the lob pass to his man.
4. When guarding a man who is three passes away from the ball, as X4 is in **Diagram 1.9**, the defensive man should position himself completely in the lane. This puts him in the best possible spot to stop the ballside drive.

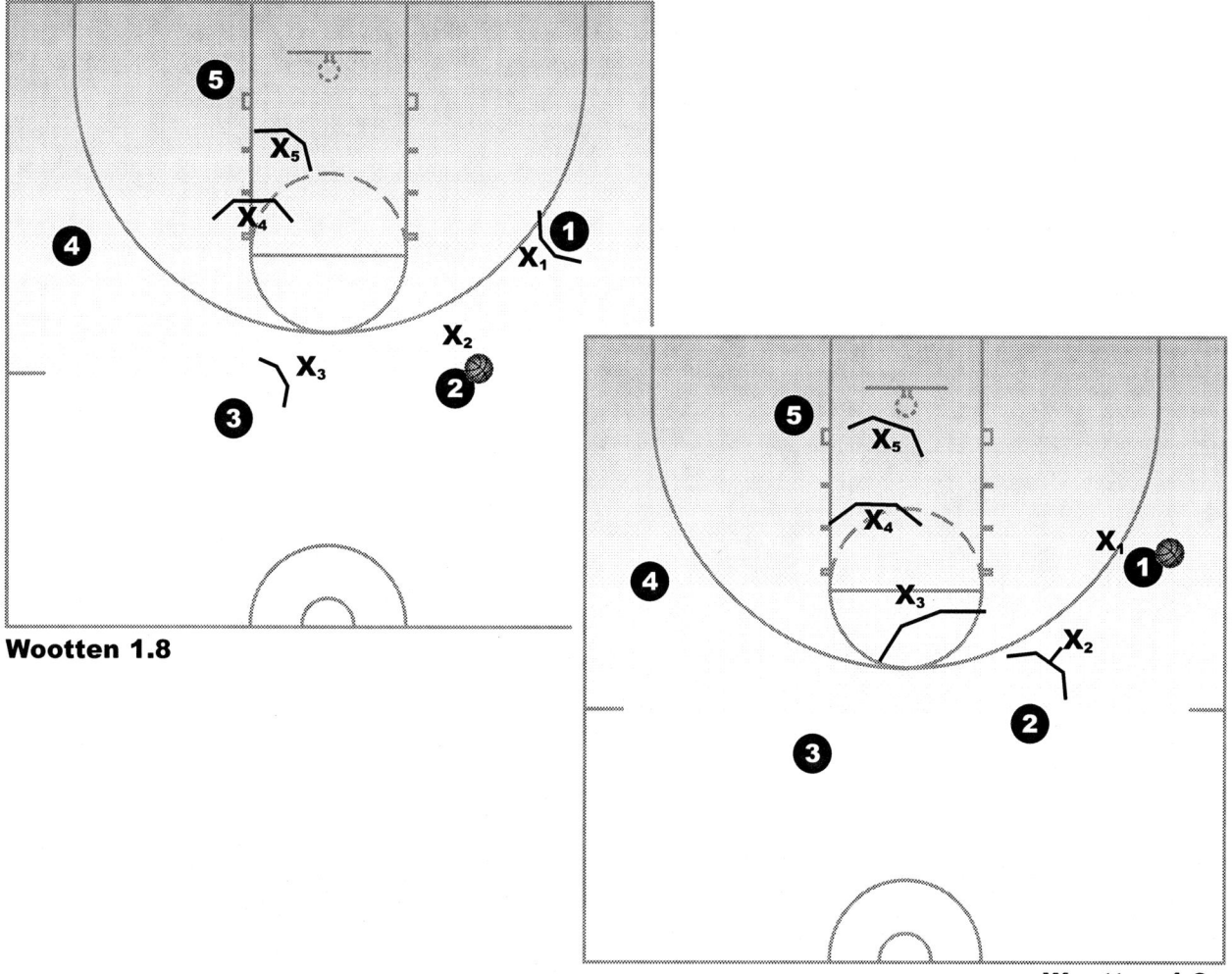

Wootten 1.8

Wootten 1.9

LESSONS FROM THIS LEGEND...

THE HORSESHOE DRILL

To teach the basic responsibilities of the #2 defense, we use a drill called the "horseshoe drill." When initiating the team defense, we use the drill with only eight men. Usually, they are two offensive guards, two defensive guards, two offensive wings, and two defensive wings. We eliminate the post men, because in our #2 defense, the defensive post man, either the high or medium post, will never become involved in the rotation. In the early stages of practice, we feel that the players get a better picture of the defensive rotation if the post men are missing. It should be noted, however, that we make all of our players participate in the drill, because in some situations, it might become necessary for our post man to guard a wing, and, thus, he would become part of the rotation.

Diagram 1.10: The four defensive men will line up according to the position of the ball. The rules, of course, are the same as those previously stated for our #2 defense. We then tell the offensive team to pass the ball around the perimeter. For example, if O4 has the ball, he would pass to O3. O3 would hold the ball, and the coaching staff would examine the defense to make certain that each defensive player has adjusted his position with respect to the position of the ball. On a signal, O2 would pass to either O3 or O1, and, again, the positions would be checked. Since we use this drill to teach only defensive position and responsibility, we will tell the defense to let the passes be completed. Under game conditions, however, each pass would be contested.

After we are assured that each player on the squad knows the position he should be in with respect to the ball, we begin to show the rotation of the defense. There are two basic times when we rotate our defense. We rotate to save, in other words, to stop a driver or to help on a successful back-door play, and we rotate to steal the ball.

Diagram 1.11: On a given signal, the wing will drive to the basket. X1 will allow O1 to drive. The off-wing, X4, will sprint across the lane to stop the driver. We prefer to have X4 yelling as loud as he can as he approaches O1. This serves a two-fold purpose. First, it serves to distract the driver, which may cause him to pick up his dribble or even commit a turnover. Secondly, it alerts the other defensive players that the rotation is on. As X4 proceeds to challenge the driver, X3 must retreat down the lane. It is his responsibility to seal off the off-wing position. He also has a great opportunity to steal a pass across the lane. X2 will move toward the foul line to protect against an open man in this dangerous scoring area.

If the shot goes up, the block-out assignments would correspond with the position of the players after rotation. X4 blocks out O1. X3 blocks out O4. X2 blocks out the nearest guard, O3 or O2. After correcting any errors, we would re-set and again begin passing the ball around the perimeter.

The rotation from the guard position is slightly different.

Diagram 1.12: If O2 drives to the outside of X2, it is X1's responsibility to stop the driver. If X1 is not in position to stop the driver, then X4 must come across the lane to stop him. X3 must then seal off the wing area. X1 would then seal off the on-wing, O1.

Diagram 1.13: If O2 takes an inside route, X3 should make an effort to stop him before he penetrates the scoring area. If X3 cannot stop the driver, he will proceed to seal off the wing area, and X4 will stop the driver.

As the season progresses, we run the same drill with a post man. We will run the drill

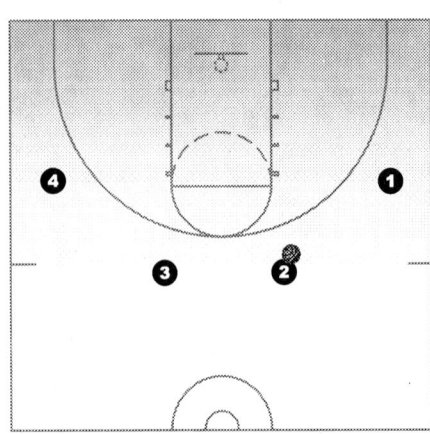

Wootten 1.10

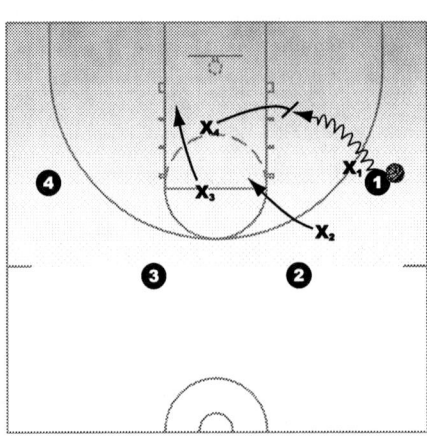

Wootten 1.11

Wootten 1.12

LESSONS FROM THIS LEGEND...

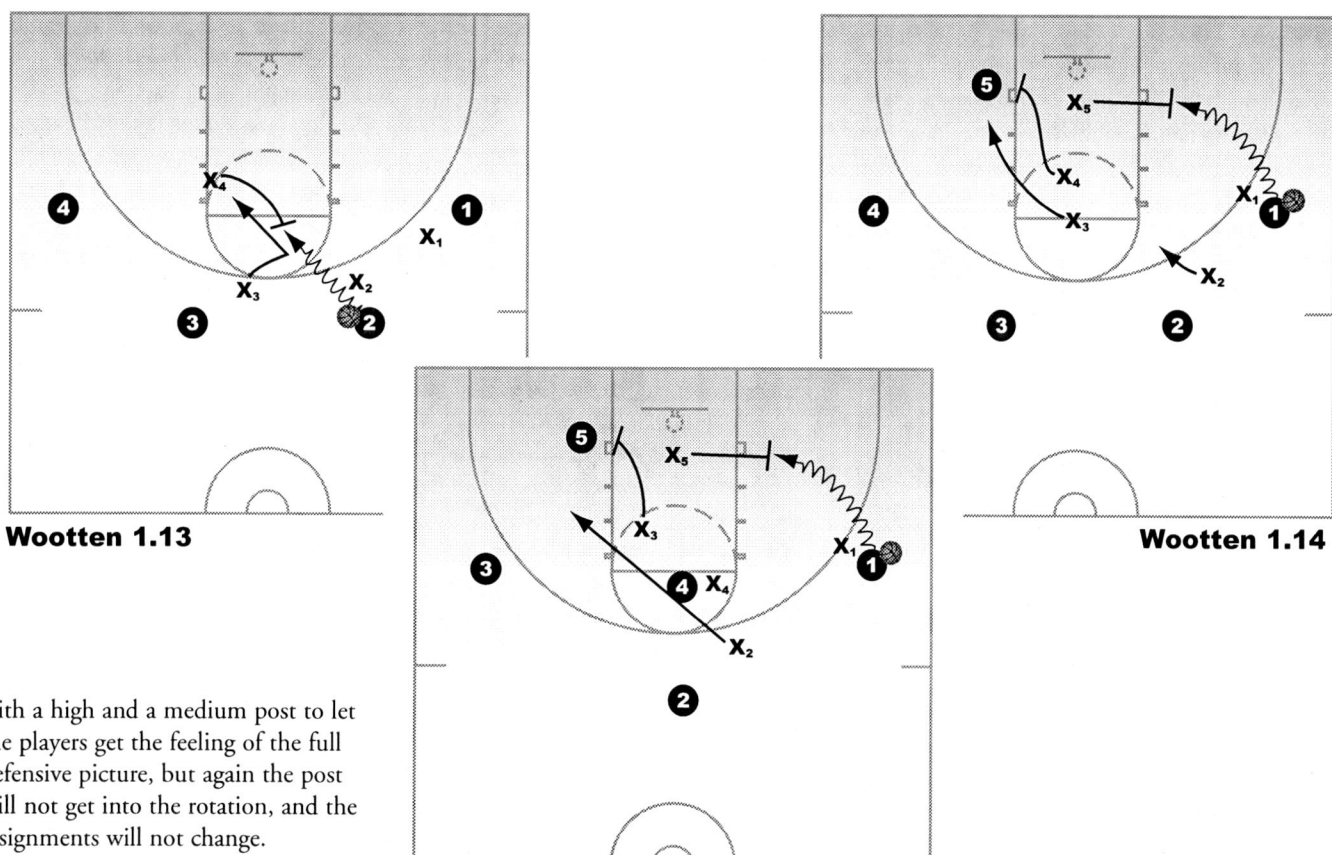

Wootten 1.13

Wootten 1.14

Wootten 1.15

with a high and a medium post to let the players get the feeling of the full defensive picture, but again the post will not get into the rotation, and the assignments will not change.

With a low post, however, the assignments change slightly, but the principles remain the same. The off-forward and guard rotate one man toward the ball.

Diagram 1.14: The defensive low post will rotate to pick up the driver, O1. X4 will seal down on the offensive low post, O5. The off-guard, X3, seals off the off-wing, O4. The on-guard, X3, will slide toward the foul line, keeping alert for the pass.

The horseshoe against the one-man front applies the same rules.

Diagram 1.15: Again the low post, X5, rotates, but the high post will not.

We run this drill against any type of offensive set, and the rules will remain the same.
1. The high post never gets involved in the rotation.
2. The low post, off-forward and off-guard will rotate one man toward the ball.

DRIBBLE-USED DRILL

When we are in our #2 defense, there are two primary objectives which we want to accomplish with respect to the man with the ball. The first thing we want to do is to make the offensive player put the ball on the floor. Secondly, we want to make him pick up his dribble. This in effect will neutralize him as a scoring threat, because we will immediately make the defensive man close up on him. This will, of course, take away his outside shot and make his pass difficult to complete.

The drill which we use to teach this tactic is the dribble-used drill. We have found it convenient to run this drill after the completion of the horseshoe drill, because we use the same alignments, and it gives continuity to our defensive instruction.

The drill is run with five offensive and five defensive players. One of the offensive players will be told to dribble the ball. After about two or three dribbles, he will pick up the ball, and the defensive player guarding the ball will close up on him. The other four defensive players will put on an even more determined overplay. Every other offensive player will work as hard as he can to be a receiver. Since the player with the ball is now in effect frozen as an offensive threat, we can take this opportunity to cash in on his weakness. If every defensive man makes his man go without the ball, the result should be a five-second call, a walk, or a frustration pass that usually results in a turnover. Each one of the offensive players will have an opportunity to start the drill, thus enabling us to check the overplay with the ball in every position on the court. In our full #2 defense, whenever a dribble is picked up, the player on the ball will yell, "dribble used," and we will go into what in effect is our dribble-used drill.

LESSONS FROM THIS LEGEND...

OVERPLAY DRILL

Every player on the squad works on overplaying the receiver. First, the offensive player O1 starts at the wing position, anticipating a pass from the coach nearest him in the guard position. X1 assumes the defensive overplay position. In teaching the overplay, we put two offensive players on the floor, about ten feet apart. One offensive player has a basketball. He rolls the ball on the floor to the other offensive player. The line in which the ball rolls from one player to the other is the passing lane. In the overplay position, we want the defensive player to be in a position about halfway between the ball and his man, with the hand closest to the ball in the passing lane. We want his palm to be facing toward the ball, and he should be able to see both his man and the ball. He is low and in a good defensive stance, with the foot closest to the ball forward, a stride away from the passing lane. He must prevent his man from catching the ball.

The drill begins with O1 jockeying for position, and X1 staying between his man and the ball in the overplay position, contesting the pass. O1, not being able to receive the ball in the wing area or farther back near midcourt, will make a back-cut for the basket. X1 will go with him by pushing off the front foot and stepping with the back foot and then shuffling, closing the gap between himself and the path of O1. When O1 comes into contact with X1, X1 will open toward the ball and front O1 across the free-throw lane, underneath O1's basket. If O1 cannot receive the ball from the coach, he continues to the opposite wing, looking for a pass from the other coach as the ball is swung to his side of the court. X1 continues with O1, getting further away from O1 as they go further from the basket; X1 remains in the deny or overplay position this time, with his opposite hand in the passing lane, and his corresponding foot forward. When in the overplay position, the defensive player looks straight ahead, splitting the distance between his man and the ball, but able to see them both.

This same drill should be run from guard-to-guard to give the defense the feeling of the overplay from this position. The principles will remain the same.

POINTS TO EMPHASIZE

1. The defensive man must learn to ignore the offensive man's first step forward. The defensive man must not react to the first step. If he does react, the offensive player can take a quick step back and receive the ball. The defensive man must not open to the ball too soon or too late, but open as soon as he feels contact (as illustrated in the **Diagram 1.16**), or as soon as he sees the pass being attempted.
2. The defensive man must front through the post area.
3. The coach must encourage the offensive man to go hard for the basket without the ball. When we want the offensive man to back-cut, we call his name; this is the signal that the offensive player must cut for the basket.

We constantly remind the defense that in a game, there would be pressure on the ball; therefore, the back-door pass would be extremely difficult to complete. The six points of emphasis are:

1. Contesting—overplay position
2. Making contact with the cutter
3. Opening to the ball
4. Fronting through the post area
5. Contesting on the other side
6. One-on-one, if the pass is completed on other side

In the early season, we use the same drill, except we don't swing the ball to the other side. Instead, we have one coach working with a group at each end of the floor. The offensive player breaks out to be a receiver. If he is contested properly, he then back-cuts. If the pass is not completed, the drill ends, and two more players go. We intentionally allow the defense to be successful in intercepting or deflecting our pass to the offensive receiver; this helps to build confidence in the defensive player's ability to make his man go without the ball. In addition, we keep a statistical chart that tells how many times each of our players' men were allowed to catch the ball. The rule of our #2 defense is not to let your man have the basketball; he must be made to play without it. No player has ever scored without the basketball. Furthermore, not many high school players do a good job of playing without the ball.

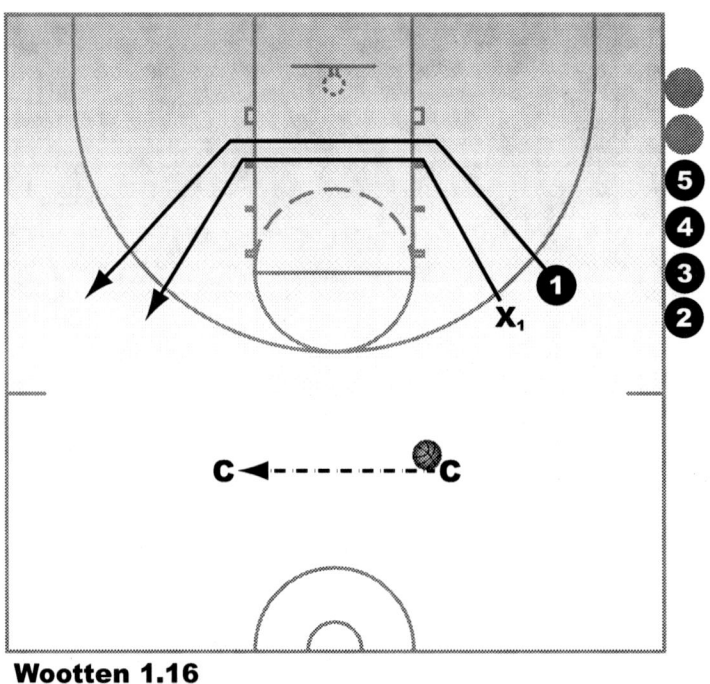

Wootten 1.16

276 JUMP

LESSONS FROM THIS LEGEND...

To complete our team-defensive picture, we begin to install our trapping and switching tactics. There are four basic defensive plays that we add to our regular #2, #22 series: jump trap, jump switch, blitz trap, and blitz switch. We will first introduce these defensive tactics, and then we will show how they fit into our team defense.

Jump Trap

The jump trap is used when the offensive team will cross a man with the ball. It is also effective against a team which employs the dribble screen, a tactic in which the dribbler actually sets the screen for another offensive player.

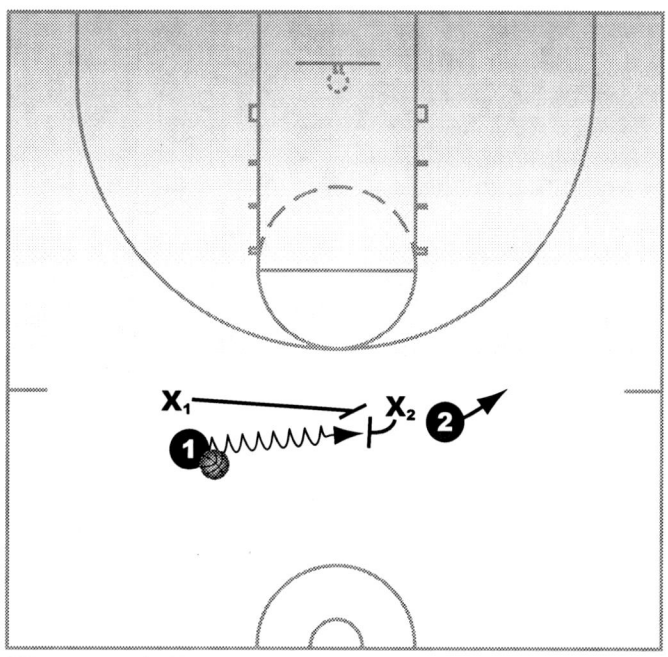

Wootten 1.17

Diagram 1.17: The dribbler, O1, will be allowed to move the ball toward O2. Before the cross can be completed, X2 will leave his man and jump into the path of the dribbler. He will have his body fairly low, the knees bent slightly, and the arms extended upward. The feet should be held wide apart, but the base should not be so wide as to hinder movement. X1, who has moved with the dribbler so as to direct him into the trap, will form the other half of the trap. The trap should form a "V," with the wide side away from the scoring area. For example, if the cross would be attempted from guard-to-guard, we would want the open side of the "V" to be directed away from the offense's goal. If the cross would be a guard-to-wing cross, the open end of the "V" would face the near sideline. The trap should be accomplished with the feet and the body. With these, we will pinch the offensive player, and our arms will be flashing to make the pass more difficult. Since the "V" trap presents an easy escape if the dribbler is not picked up, we would like to divert the attention of the dribbler away from the open side of the trap. In order to do this, we want to make the dribbler attempt to break through the trap. Breaking through the double-team should be impossible if the correct principles of trapping are employed; so, we ask the defensive men to be good actors and make the double-team "appear breakable." We do not want to steal the ball. An overanxious defensive player who attempts to steal the ball will probably accomplish little more than to send the offensive team to the foul line. What we are looking for out of the jump trap would be:

A. A charge
B. A violation, walk, double dribble, etc.
C. A bad pass
D. A jump ball

The jump trap would bring about a rotation which would be a rotation to steal.

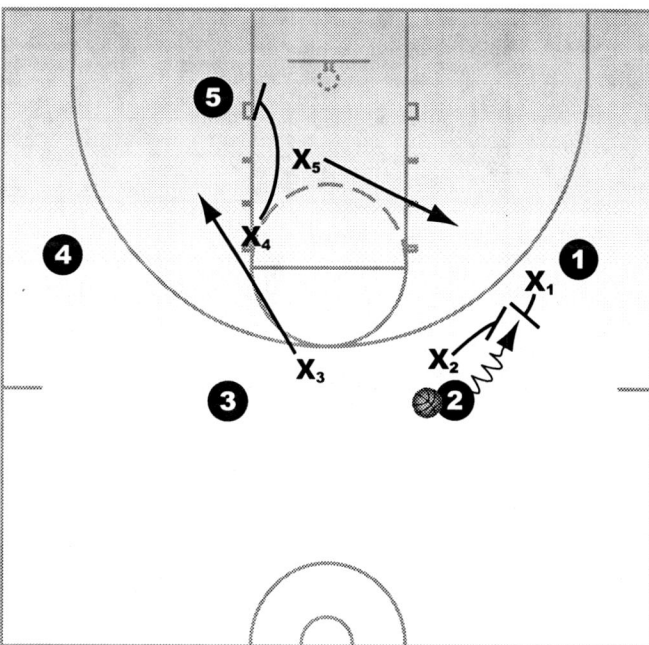

Wootten 1.18

Diagram 1.18: This rotation is the same as was demonstrated in the horseshoe drill. Since every defensive player should be able to see both their man and the ball, the men not involved in the actual trap will be able to see the trap coming and rotate accordingly.

LESSONS FROM THIS LEGEND...

JUMP SWITCH

Diagram 1.19: The jump switch will employ the same principle as the jump trap. X1 will allow O1 to move toward O2. X2 will wait until O1 approaches O2 and jump into his path. X1, however, instead of forming a trap with X2, will continue on through and pick up O2. Because there will not be an offensive player left unguarded, there is no need for any rotation, and the other three defensive players will continue to play a normal #2 defense.

Wootten 1.19

BLITZ TRAP

Many teams will not cross the ball and man in their offensive patterns. In this situation, if we want to trap, we will use our blitz series.

When the blitz is in effect, the defensive man on the ball, X1, must fully direct the dribbler. We want to force him into the trap. This is different from the jump series, where the dribbler will put himself in jeopardy. As shown in the **Diagram 1.20**, X1 would play on O1's left side, thus taking away his left-side drive. O1 is then directed toward X2. When O2 is three strides away from X2, X2 begins the blitz maneuver. He runs directly at O1 at full speed. We want him to be hollering as soon as he makes his move. This should aid in making O1 pick up his dribble. When the trap is made, X1 and X2 will follow the rules for trapping that were explained in the jump trap. As is the case in the jump trap, this tactic requires a full rotation toward the ball.

Diagram 1.21: Again, the only man that we are leaving open is the one who we feel can hurt us the least. If the blitz trap is broken by a pass back to O3, we should have enough time to rotate back before we get burned. Of course, like the jump trap, this is a gambling defense, and the offense is bound to score occasionally. But, we feel that we can force enough turnovers to make it worth our while.

Wootten 1.20

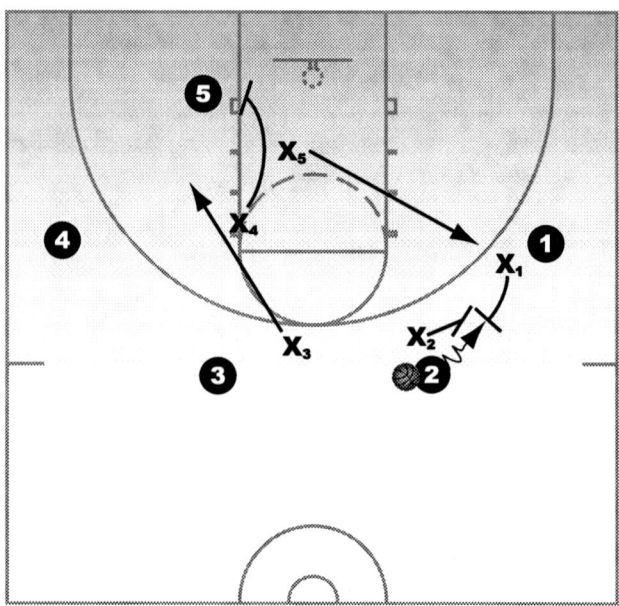

Wootten 1.21

LESSONS FROM THIS LEGEND...

BLITZ SWITCH

The blitz switch, **Diagram 1.22**, utilizes the same principle as the blitz trap. O1 is directed to the defensive man, X2. When he is three strides away, X2 will run at him, yelling all the way. When X2 reaches O1, X1 will continue on through to pick up O2. This is very effective after the blitz trap has been used a few times, because the natural tendency is for O1 to see X2, release his man, and attempt to dish the pass off quickly. If X1 is alert, he should be able to pick off that pass. Also, if the offensive team is beating your blitz trap by passing off before the rotation is complete, the blitz switch can be an effective way of controlling the tempo of the game, without leaving men open to be receivers.

Wootten 1.22

We advocate teaching the trapping and switching techniques through the use of four-man drills. The proper techniques in executing the trap and switch are essential in their success. Because of this, we feel that the coach should spend time examining these tactics only. After time has been spent working on the trap and switch alone, they can be used in the horseshoe drill or the five-on-five drill to examine the execution of the rotation.

SOURCE

Wootten, Morgan and Hank Galotta. (1971). *Blitz Defense*. Washington, D.C.: DeMatha High School.

LESSONS FROM THE LEGENDS trivia QUIZ

NAME THE NAISMITH HALL OF FAME COACH WHO...

1 Developed and popularized the Run-and-Jump defense?

Hint: He is the all-time winningest college coach in the history of the game.

2 Campaigned to adopt international basketball rules in 1969 and predicted that the United States would be beaten in future Olympic Games if they did not modify their rules?

Hint: He coached at Navy for 20 years and led the Midshipmen to five NCAA and two NIT appearances.

3 Had a job as a flagger for crop-dusting planes dispensing DDT?

Hint: His team won the 1997 NCAA championship and beat three number-one seeds in the process.

4 Received a Gold Medal in the 1952 Olympics and was so proud of his Olympic experience that he requested to be buried in his Olympic USA sweatshirt?

Hint: His innovative tactics and coaching prowess earned him the title "The Father of Basketball Coaching."

5 Dropped out of school to help his parents financially and became the first true "big man" in basketball with the "Original Celtics?"

Hint: He later coached St. John's to four NIT championships and coached the New York Knicks.

6 Became the first basketball coach at any level (high school, college, or professional) to reach 1,200 wins?

Hint: His 1965 team broke the 71-game winning streak of Lew Alcindor's (now Kareem Abdul-Jabbar) Power Memorial team.

7 Pioneered integrated basketball and heightened awareness of basketball at all-black colleges?

Hint: He led Tennessee A&I (now Tennessee State University) to three consecutive NAIA national championships.

8 Believed athleticism rather than size was crucial to a team's success and won two NCAA national championships (1980 and 1986) without a dominating center?

Hint: He served as an assistant under John Wooden when UCLA won three consecutive NCAA titles.

9
Compared the movements in basketball to those in ballet?

Hint: He led Portland to the 1977 NBA championship and is called, "Dr. Jack of Basketball."

10
Taught a man-to-man defense utilizing zone principles away from the ball that he called the "swinging gate?"

Hint: He was the first coach to win consecutive NCAA national championships.

11
Received 16 technicals while coaching a high school game?

Hint: He led his team past Kentucky to win the NCAA championship in 1966 in a game that is remembered as a watershed moment in sports history.

12
Conducted daily practice sessions during the early morning hours to help instill discipline in his players?

Hint: He earned a reputation as one of the top defensive coaches in the nation because of his match-up zone defense.

13
Graduated from West Point and played for future Hall of Fame coach Bob Knight?

Hint: He was selected NABC Coach of the Decade for the 1990s.

14
Designed and developed the one-three-one zone defense?

Hint: He is the author of more than 50 books on basketball including the popular Chip Hilton's Sport Stories for Young People series.

15
Led his teams to 10 NCAA national championships including seven in a row?

Hint: He earned the nickname "The Wizard of Westwood."

16
Won back-to-back NCAA national championships in 1955 and 1956 with future Hall of Fame players Bill Russell and K.C. Jones?

Hint: His San Francisco teams led the nation in defense on three occasions.

17
Introduced and developed the box-and-one defense?

Hint: He directed Temple to the Final Four in 1956 and 1958 and the NIT championship in 1969.

18
Was nicknamed the "Baron of the Bluegrass?"

Hint: He led Kentucky to four NCAA championships.

19
Popularized the defensive switch, which he called the "shifting man-for-man defense?"

Hint: He led Notre Dame to the Helms Foundation national championship in 1927 and 1936.

20
Played for future Hall of Fame coach Fred Taylor at Ohio State and was a member of the 1960 NCAA national championship team?

Hint: His Army teams led the nation in team defense for three consecutive years.

ANSWERS

1) Dean Smith 2) Ben Carnevale 3) Lute Olson 4) Forrest "Phog" Allen 5) Joe Lapchick 6) Morgan Wootten 7) John McLendon 8) Denny Crum 9) Jack Ramsay 10) Henry "Hank" Iba 11) Don Haskins 12) John Chaney 13) Mike Krzyzewski 14) Clair Bee 15) John Wooden 16) Phil Woolpert 17) Harry Litwack 18) Adolph Rupp 19) George Keogan 20) Bob Knight

ABOUT THE AUTHORS

JERRY KRAUSE

Jerry Krause has coached and taught basketball for over forty years and is widely recognized as a master teacher and clinician. The most prolific author in the history of basketball, he has written or edited 27 coaching books and has developed over 30 instructional videos. He is the chairman of the NABC Research Committee and former chairman of the NCAA Basketball Rules Committee.

In 1998, Krause received the prestigious NABC Cliff Wells Appreciation Award for lifetime contributions to basketball. In 2002, he was honored as NABC Guardian of the Game for Advocacy—developed a rim testing device to equate ball rebound in every gym and from rim to rim—a 20 year research project. He has been inducted into the NAIA Basketball Coaches Hall of Fame (2000) and the National Association for Sports and Physical Education Hall of Fame as a coach and physical educator (2000). Jerry Krause currently is the Director of Basketball Operations for Gonzaga University (The Zags).

RALPH L. PIM

Ralph Pim is an assistant professor in the Department of Physical Education at the United States Military Academy at West Point. He serves as the director of instructional administration and is a basketball sport educator.

Pim has coached and taught basketball at the secondary and collegiate levels for thirty years. As a collegiate head coach, Pim built Alma (MI) College and Limestone (SC) College into highly successful programs. His Alma teams were ranked nationally for points scored and three-point field goals, and the 1989 squad recorded the school's best overall record in forty-seven years. He also coached at Central Michigan, William and Mary, Northwestern Louisiana, and Barberton (OH) High School. Barberton won the 1976 Ohio State Championship and was selected the seventh best team in the country.

Pim spent ten years as the technical advisor for the Basketball Association of Wales. He implemented training programs to facilitate the development of basketball in the country of Wales and assisted with the training of their national teams.

Pim is the author of *Winning Basketball* and co-editor of *Coaching Basketball*. He has written numerous coaching articles and is a frequent contributor to the Naismith Basketball Hall of Fame Yearbook and Enshrinement Program.

Pim is a graduate of Springfield (MA) College. He earned his master's degree from Ohio State University and his doctorate from Northwestern Louisiana State University.